THE
WEALTH AND WELFARE
OF THE
PUNJAB

THE

WEALTH AND WELFARE

OF THE

PUNJAB

Being Some Studies in Punjab Rural Economics,

BY

H. CALVERT, B.Sc.,I.C.S.

REGISTRAR, CO-OPERATIVE SOCIETIES PUNJAB,
AUTHOR OF THE LAW AND PRINCIPLES OF CO-OPERATION.

KALPAZ

ISBN: 978-93-5128-457-4(HB)

First Published in 1922
Indian Reprint in 2017

Published by

Kalpaz Publications
C-30, Satyawati Nagar,
Delhi – 110052
E-mail: kalpaz@hotmail.com
Website: kalpazpublications.com
Ph.: +91-9212142040

CONTENTS.

PREFACE.

IT will be easy to criticise this book. There will be those who will say that it contains nothing new, that they knew it all before, and that they can see no adequate reason for its publication. To these I would reply in the words of Lord Morley : "We all know such a multitude of things of which it does us no harm to be reminded" ; also it may be admitted straightaway that the chief reason that has impelled me to write this book has been the lack of any other on the same subject. There will be other critics who will find the matter so new that they will freely contest its accuracy. To these I would plead that I have been at some trouble to give references wherever possible, and that, if they will look these up, they will probably become as impressed as I have been by the urgent need of a close study of the economics of the Punjab if this fine province is ever to reap the great harvest that the future holds for it.

Shortly after being appointed to the post of Registrar of Co-operative Societies, it became clear that the proper way to regard the subject was as a necessary branch of rural economics ; the position now occupied by co-operation in a modern State led me to study conditions in other countries dependent on agriculture, and the similarity of the problems with those that occupy, or should occupy, attention in this province suggested the idea that some good might result if the main considerations could be made available in terms of local conditions. To a large extent this book is a re-statement of well-known arguments in a form applicable to the Punjab. Now that a new system of government is being tried, it is of the greatest importance that those who are elected to look after the destinies of the province should have a sound practical knowledge of agricultural economics. For, argue as some will, it is not the interests of the educated that will have to be the first consideration, but the interests of that great mass of the population which derives its livelihood from the soil. Whether the rural population should themselves govern, or should allow the professional lawyer to govern them, the government must be one that they will tolerate. Now it is generally admitted that the towns, man, even the townsman of the first generation, neglects agriculture with a completeness that is almost inexplicable. (1) But it is the townsman who has the intelligence and wit to take advantage of such opportunities as come in his way ; and it is the townsman who will supply the province with its future councillors Any

(1) By " townsman " here it is not intended to pillory especially the townsman of the Punjab. It is almost a universal characteristic of residents in towns that they find little time to spare for the study of rural problems. Speaking of England, in an article in the *Contemporary Review* for July 1920 on " The Nation's Wheat Supply". Mr. A. Collett writes :—
" The ignorance of the urban majority in this country on agricultural matters is so colossal and so genuine as almost to deserve respect. "

attempt to arouse his interest in rural matters should not need any elaborate apology. So long as he has no means ready to his hand of studying rural economics, he has some excuse for his incomplete acquaintance with rural problems. If this book helps to arouse that interest, it will have served a useful purpose. If it induces someone, better qualified, to write a book of greater merit, it will have done all that I wish it to do.

It has been well said that Europe has for centuries been a vast social laboratory in which all sorts of experiments have been tried and some useful results, positive and negative, achieved. It is curious how persistent are the attempts to repeat the failures. It may be that these are so attractive in their untried form that they lure the would-be leader, in spite of all the teachings of history, or it may be that the would-be leader does not read history. Of real constructive effort there is everywhere a marked scarcity; of constructive genius the world is sadly in need. If genius consists in an infinite capacity for taking pains then it is to be hoped that someone will make an early start with the many problems that the Punjab, at this time, presents. This book does not aim at solving any problem, but at bringing to notice that there are problems, and that there is such a subject as Rural Economics. It is my belief that, if we could concentrate attention on the economics of the Punjab, much of the present discontent would disappear. When we find that this province has many features in common with other countries dependent on agriculture, such as Spain, Italy, Greece, Serbia, etc., all of which possess self-government, then it is obvious that these features cannot be due to the system of government in this province. They must be ascribed to some causes common to all. From such study of other rural countries as I have been able to make the impression arises that the Punjab, so far from being peculiar to itself, is very typical of countries dependent on agriculture. Even our educated townsmen exhibit very much the same characteristics as educated townsmen in other rural countries. In England the corresponding class is so heavily diluted by wealthy manufacturers and business men, who are seldom graduates of any university, that any attempt at self-assertion by them is out of the question. Even in this twentieth century a large number of business men do not believe in a college education.

The supremacy of the great British industries, shipbuilding and the mercantile marine, cotton, wool, coal and steel, owes very little to graduates from the universities. The chief pioneers of progress, as Professor Alfred Marshall points out, have been plain men, whose enthusiasm and ardent sympathy have been guided only by instinct and business judgment. Poverty and wealth seem to have been little affected in the past by the ordinary university education. The value of the latter in commerce and industry is only now being put to the test. To convert a poor country into a prosperous one there is needed that sound practical economic sense which the early English are supposed to have imbibed from their Norman conquerors. This inheritance seems to have taken an unduly long time to produce effect, as, so recently as 1825, the majority of the British people seems, as judged by modern standards, to have been desperately poor, ill-housed, ill-clad, ill-fed ; and, even now, the problems of poverty in the big English towns are probably more pressing than in the Punjab. In many ways, the Punjab is naturally a richer country than Britain. The soil is more fertile, and the climate permits of two harvests a year. As compared with Finland and the countries bordering the Mediterranean, Portugal, Spain, Italy, Greece and Serbia, this province must be counted wealthy. The fact seems to be that countries dependent on agriculture must be poor and remain poor until, with the progress of science, education and co-operation, the people learn to extract from the soil all the wealth it consistently and faithfully will give to those who know how to treat it properly. As an example, the instance of Belgium may be quoted. The soil of Flanders is said to be the worst in all Europe—sterile sand—and, although it has been fertilized by ten centuries of laborious husbandry, it does not yield a single crop without being manured once or twice. But the Belgian peasant-proprietor is an excellent cultivator and an extremely hard worker, and he has been aided in his struggle by an excellent transport system, a high standard of agricultural education and the development of the Co-operative movement. (1) Is there in this nothing for us to learn ?

In the pages that follow I have quoted freely from books on other rural countries, in the first place, because I wish to avoid the suggestion of constantly finding faults with the Punjab, and, in the second place, because I think that nothing but good would result from a wider study of the conditions that prevail in other States dependent upon agriculture. If we are to interpret local conditions correctly, we must make a broad comparative survey. Unfortunately, there is in the Punjab, as in other countries, a marked tendency for the educated to move to the towns. Our hope for a better state of things in the future rests upon those whose education has enabled them to undertstand the causes of poverty and the factors that make for prosperity. American writers comment bitterly upon the indifference of the townsman towards agricultural problems ; the villager is, of course, equally, if not more, indifferent to the problems of the towns ; but the towns possess the trained intelligence which the country lacks, and the whole burden of the numerous complaints of the country against the town is that

(1) Rowntree: Life and Labour : Lessons from Belgium, pp. 148, 155.

the former is in desperate need of the help and sympathy of the educated class, of which, at present, the latter possesses the monopoly. It has been represented by friendly critics that the sympathy of the educated townsman will be alienated, rather than attracted, by some of the arguments in this book. If this prove true, then its publication will render a grievous disservice to the cause I have at heart. The main argument of the chapters that follow is that the land is, and must continue to be, the main source of the new wealth of the province, including the raw material for those new industries which we all desire to see. If this be accepted, then a close study of rural problems is as essential to industries as to agriculture; and, if educated people can be induced to embark upon such a study, then the first stage in a grand progress will be within reach of attainment.

The material for this book has been collected over a series of years in the far too few intervals permitted to a busy official. Some has been used before. The chapters on the Land Alienation Act are founded on an article contributed to the *Bengal Economic Journal*, now defunct; that on the price of land is an expansion of an article published in the *Indian Journal of Economics*, to whose editor I am indebted for permission to use it again; some of the matter has appeared in lectures delivered in the past two years. The result is that there is a lack of continuity and some repetition. Lack of time prevents me from removing these defects. I should have preferred to postpone publication until a better book could be produced, but I found the subjects endless; further study brought further evidence in corroboration, rather than anything contradicting the main argument, so it seemed better to publish what was ready, which will probably take some digesting.

I am heavily indebted to the criticism of friends. In particular to Mr. H. W. Emerson, I.C.S., Settlement Officer of Multan, who made me rewrite whole passages; to Mr. A. C. C. Hervey, Professor of History at the Khalsa College; to Mr. W. Roberts, formerly Principal of the Punjab Agricultural College, and to others. If there be found any merit in the book, it will largely be due to them.

The book has no official authority whatever; I am solely responsible for the arguments and opinions contained in it. Where no reference is given in support of some statement of fact about the Punjab, it is probably extracted from an official document. In putting forward statements about other countries, I have tried to give a full reference to the book to which I am indebted for the information.

LAHORE:
1st January 1922.

H. CALVERT.

INTRODUCTION.

Every year, the Government of the Punjab publishes, in a paragraph of the Annual Report on its Administration, a note on the literary output of the province. For some unexplained reason, no one collates the information so supplied. If any one did, he would find that while religion, politics, poetry, and the adventures in love of popular heroes are dealt with in generous manner, there is an almost, if not absolutely, complete neglect of books dealing with the economic problems that beset the people of this great land of the Five Rivers. A good library will place at the disposal of the student information concerning all the various countries that compose the world in which we live ; it is not really a very large world ; but people in general know very little about it. In every country, agriculture is of paramount importance ; in every country there are widespread complaints that if only the knowledge available were utilised to the full, the land would produce much more wealth than it does. Countries differ in their stage of advance along the road of progress. All were sorely stricken with poverty in the past ; most are still in the same old rut ; a few have advanced somewhat along the lines indicated by scientific discoveries and have achieved a measure of prosperity, which, modest enough in the eyes of their inhabitants, arouses feelings of envy amongst those who might travel the same road, were local circumstances favourable to such a course. The basic fact is that a single man, trying to fight the battle of life unaided by capital, intelligent direction, enterprise and scientific knowledge, can with difficulty produce enough to maintain himself and, perhaps, a wife and children. It is this impossible puzzle with which the people of this province are struggling. After all, the producers of new wealth are the cultivators of the soil ; apart from them, there are few engaged upon what a modern economist would term productive employment. Man must eat. Man must have food. Food must be produced if man is to live. The production of food is the most important, the elemental, the absolutely essential need of life. Yet it is relegated to the ignorant, the despised, the people of comparatively low status. Educated men not only know nothing about the work, they regard it as beneath their dignity. The number of graduates in this province occupied in administering to this one absolutely necessary want of mankind could probably be counted on the fingers of one hand. The caste system obtrudes and holds its uneconomic sway over the land. Food production involves manual labour ; manual labour is distasteful to many amongst the educated, and so agriculture is not adopted by the educated as a means of livelihood. The same educated will write to the papers about the poverty of the people ; they will make or inspire speeches on the same subject ; but they will at the same time advocate measures calculated to keep the producers in poverty and bondage, and will steadfastly ignore the many opportunities of public service open to any with the spirit of real selfless devotion to the good of their fellows. They themselves conform to the very ordinary laws of human industry ; they will do what is advantageous; they will respond to the stimulus of gain, if the prize be large enough ; but they refuse to admit that the cultivator of the soil is a man of the same type as themselves, actuated by the same desires and ambitions, and subject to the same influences in the ordering of his daily life.

Poverty is, perhaps, the most universal feature in the whole world. Many peoples are still sunk deep in its mire ; a few are struggling successfully to escape from its strangling bonds ; some are well advanced along the road to freedom, but nowhere is there any country, or any people, so far advanced as to be free from the everhaunting fear of starvation in time of stress. Perhaps, on no single subject is there more misapprehension prevalent in India, than upon this one of poverty. There appears to be a widely-held belief that in England or elsewhere there is no poverty and there are no poor ; that every one has enough for his needs and that, accordingly, India is somehow unfortunately situated and an exception to the general rule of prevailing prosperity to be found outside its borders. Curiously enough, Japan, perhaps the most hopelessly povert<-striken country in the world, is regarded as the shining example of prosperity. Were Japan anywhere else but in Asia, it would be possible to bring some understanding of its special difficulties home to the educated men of the province. As it is, any attempt at comparison has to face the inevitable charge of partiality.

Of all the countries of the world, England possesses the most complete record in original documents of its history. The details available are a veritable treasure-house to the seeker after truth. Nowhere else is there the material at hand for the history of economic development in the same generous measure. England was not always rich. Its people were by no means always prosperous ; they, too, have had to face famines and pestilence, and have mourned the loss of large numbers of their fellows ; they have not always had wise guidance in their economic progress, just as they have been far from enjoying continuous wisdom from their political leaders. But there is one fact about England that gives its history a peculiar value to other countries ; and that element is this : England is by nature not a rich country, but its people, sprung from a mixture of races, have beyond doubt advanced far along the road that leads from poverty to wealth. The history of England provides guide-posts and warnings to all desiring to place their country on the sure road to prosperity. If it be assumed that there be a country, poor at this time, but actuated by a desire to step forward to better things, then there will be found in the economic history of England much material of value to those who happen to be at any time possessed of the power to decide upon measures designed to speed that country along the road to that better state which its people desire. Examine the steps which England trod, and from some among so many will be discovered those which lead to the goal. If there be a difficulty here for which a solution is sought, that same difficulty will be traceable in the history of England, and the method by which it was overcome will indicate the line that promises the best result in this country. This is due in part to the prolonged peace and security within the United Kingdom, and in part to the wealth of records available to the student and investigator. The former has permitted a steady unceasing advance towards better conditions ; while the latter has provided the material for sound criticism. Whereas, in other countries, invasions and revolutions have removed the shackles of feudalism, and broken the customs of centuries ; in England, the change has been slow but continuous. As no one can produce either invasion or revolution to order, the effects of these upheavals are less valuable as guides to deliberate progress than the long history of slow change.

In the sphere of agriculture, England has passed through stages which are still observable in other countries, and has got beyond many which those countries have yet to go through. When a particular custom is under discussion, it is of value to be able to point out the undeniable advantages which England has gained from its abandonment. For example, the vexed question as to whether tenancy or cultivating ownership is the better has to a large extent been settled by experience ; it has been found that what is required is not proprietary rights, nor even fixity of tenure, but security against irresponsible eviction. Security of tenure is the element of ownership which is necessary to good husbandry. Mere ownership alone may do more harm than good. In the Punjab, it is probable that the existing system of holding the land in millions of small parcels may retard progress when once the idea of competitive tenancy has taken firm root. Tenancy-at-will is generally regarded as an evil ; and, where it is coupled with a system of peasant proprietorship, it must always be a danger ; but when the time comes in which the more educated and more skilled will compete for larger farms against the unskilled and uneducated hereditary cultivator, then the system of small owners may prevent progressive agriculture by imposing an obstacle to the acquisition of enough land to supply the really first class farmer with full scope for his skill.

The fact is that agricultural problems are no more easy of solution than are political, industrial and social difficulties. They call for the best brains which the province possesses, but until the best brains are devoted to their solution, so long must the Punjab remain backward and poor. At present, for want of clear thinking and logical exposition, there are many who hold at one and the same time opinions quite contradictory to each other. Some complain of the high cost of living and advocate protection which will most certainly aggravate the evil ; others argue that there is not sufficient food produced within the country, and yet advocate measures which will restrict production ; at least one writer, while deploring the heavy pressure on the soil, urges the need for industrialising the country, as if a man taken away from agriculture to industries would affect that pressure or require less food ; one who urges the need for industries ignores the inevitable effect of a great increase of population and its consequence, an increased demand for food from the soil ; the same writer will deplore the present taxation and demand vast expenditure on projects which find favour in his eyes ; one will condemn the size of the bureaucracy and urge an immense increase in the sphere of governmental activities ; the elemental fact that the expenditure of Government must needs be influenced by its income is too often overlooked ; the policy of Japan is held up to praise by those who would never agree either to the heavy taxation by which alone that policy can be financed, or to the bureaucratic interference and control through which it is carried into execution. The simple fact is that in the sphere of economics there is too much talking and writing and too little study. It is not sufficiently realised that economic laws are not the dogmatic decisions of a few professors, but are the concentrated results of the world's experience. They cannot be ignored with impunity; experience is a hard taskmaster ; and he who prefers to trust to his own ideas and to his own narrow personal history will inevitably fail when pitted against those who learn the wider lessons which the world has to teach. The knowledge already collected is sufficient to guide a backward country along the right road to prosperity. America is learning from the close study of others ; Spain is stagnating because she refuses to benefit from that same study. In India and in South Europe, religious and constitutional questions absorb so much attention that the economic aspect is ignored. So much is this the case that it sometimes seems doubtful whether after all there is or is not a general desire to see the country progress along the road to material prosperity.

It has become a habit with some publicists in this country to confine their comparisons to England, with the natural result that India comes off second best; they ignore other States in which conditions more resemble those they know; for some reasons, England is not suitable as a standard; its land is for the most part cultivated by tenants under wealthy landlords; during the eighteenth century these landlords became the most zealous students of agriculture and the boldest experimentalists in the new methods of culture; with extraordinary zeal, activity and judgment, they made themselves acquainted with their own estates, and became the practical teachers to the small proprietors, the yeomanry and the tenant farmers. There is, says Thorold Rogers, hardly any service of a public kind which was greater than that which was done to English agriculture by many of the landowners of the eighteenth century. (1) There are big landowners in the Punjab, but there is not yet discernible anything approaching that same zeal or enthusiasm amongst them which brought such great advance in wealth to England. The Punjab is, however, a land of small holders; and it is apt to be misleading to compare it with a land of tenant farmers. The continent of Europe provides more parallel conditions: France, Germany, Belgium, Rumania, etc., are essentially countries of peasant proprietors; and the history of their agricultural development is rich in material for comments upon the present state of this province. Fragmentation of holdings, which is such a serious evil here, is still a considerable obstacle to progress in those countries, whose governments have not yet found a satisfactory method of eliminating it. French agriculture remained stagnant for five hundred years, a part of which period includes the years when the art in England was progressing by leaps and bounds. In Germany, it is common to date the agricultural reforms of the nineteenth century from the publication, in 1798, of Albrecht Thaer's "Introduction to the knowledge of English Agriculture." (2)

Besides the system of land tenure and the great services rendered by the English landowners, there is another factor in British history which makes the United Kingdom unsuitable as a basis for comparison with India, and that is the continuous struggle to practise thrift and to save. It is this which vitiates the popular ideas as to the average incomes of the peoples in the two countries; the average here is almost entirely based upon the bare earnings of the present

(1) History of Agriculture and Prices, Vol. V, Preface VII and XIII.

(2) Chapman.: Economic Development of France and Germany.

generation, unaided by any inheritance from their ancestors; the average in the United Kingdom is higher largely owing to the productive investments of former generations and the vast knowledge and experience they have handed down. Here, the common needs of the majority can be satisfied with the minimum of effort. On the great alluvial plains, a mere scratching of the fertile soil and a handful of seed will set the forces of nature to work at the production of a crop. Nature appears to be so bountiful that man need do little; the land is the gift of nature, and what nature provides, upon that man subsists. In England it is far otherwise; the land itself was never so fertile; as it exists at present it is almost entirely the work of man; the average value of agricultural land is very little if any more than the value of the improvements carried out by its successive owners. It has, for instance, been estimated that the roads, fences, gates, drains, etc., considered necessary for modern farming have cost £ 12 an acre, the buildings and farm-houses have cost another £ 9 making £ 21 out of the £ 25 which was the average value per acre before the war. Of the £ 4 left, most if not all is due to the fertility of the top nine inches which is practically the result of human labour. (1) Compare this with conditions as they exist in the Punjab, and it will be understood to what extent the present generation of Englishmen are indebted to their ancestors. It was prolonged grinding poverty, generations of hardships, recurring years of bad harvests and constant fear of starvation that forced them to adopt thrift as the one means of escaping death. Centuries of war against adverse climatic conditions have produced that dogged determination and endurance which form now their greatest asset. The present generation, both here and in England, is what its predecessors have made it; if there be discontent with present possessions or present wealth, it should be directed against those who have left so small an inheritance. A generation inherits what its forefathers have acquired for it; for nowhere, except in the most primæval society, is there any people dependent upon their own efforts, unaided by the accumulation of wealth or experience of those who have gone before. Where that accumulation is vast, that people is indeed fortunate; where it is small, that people find poverty their lot. In India, it would seem that economic advancement has seldom if ever been the ideal of the great leaders who have from time to time adorned the pages of its history. Hindu society is still based not upon economic lines but upon those of religion. Manual labour is still associated with loss of dignity, while agriculture is placed, in common estimation, below other callings as a genteel means of earning a living. In other countries, society is based on production; wealth is a power that enables its owner to force

(1) Curtler: The Enclosure and Redistribution of our Land, p. 167-8.

himself to the front, while poverty entails the loss of social position. Whether this is for the best is outside the scope of the present discussion ; what is important to remember is that concentration on the production of wealth leads to its accumulation, while neglect of production serves to retard this process. The Englishman is thus a product of economic forces, the Indian more one of religious thought. The past is responsible for the present, just as the harvest reflects the husbandman ; and the future will faithfully represent the struggle of the present generation to produce a better world for its children, just as it will yield a return to the capital about to be invested in new canal projects. If this province is to make progress, there must be more of the essentials to progress ; there must be a better understanding of what progress means, and what changes it entails ; there must be a greater readiness to accept those changes and to encourage those essentials. There must be more concentration upon the solid things of life, upon those permanent elements that tend to ultimate good, and upon those factors without which no country and no nation can progress far along the path to prosperity. Sentiment is apt to lead astray unless strictly controlled by a full appreciation of the basic facts of life. Guided into channels of productive utility, it will serve this province well. In what follows there will be found some attempt, admittedly imperfect, to indicate the sources of weakness and of strength from which are derived the wealth and welfare of the Punjab.

CHAPTER I.

SOME PRELIMINARY FACTORS.

Nothing, perhaps, blunts observation more than unchanging acquaintance with the thing to be observed. The visitor will be attracted by that which the resident passes by unnoticed. What is a matter of custom is apt to cease to be a matter of thought. Some stimulus, such as a marked discomfort, is required to attract attention. Cumulative causes of poverty may be present for years, perhaps for generations, without exciting remark, until a severe famine leads to enquiry ; popular misconceptions or beliefs may persist in the presence of easily accessible evidence in refutation, but, until the obvious truth is forced upon the consideration of the people, there may be little or no attempt to put these beliefs to the test. In the Punjab, situated as it is in a corner of India with deserts on three sides, there are special causes which account for the general omission to appreciate that there are such things as problems calling urgently for investigation and research. In a country with a sea coast and harbours, trade and commerce with other parts of the world, and easy access to distant ports, there is generally sufficient intercourse with foreigners to enable new ideas to permeate through old customs and old beliefs. England is blessed with a geographical situation that has put within reach of her sons unique opportunities for discovering what is going on in other parts of the world. Her debt to such rivals as Holland, France and the States that are now included in Northern Germany is incalculable. Not only did craftsmen and cultivators from the continent migrate to England, but Englishmen, from one cause or another, were constantly travelling abroad ; there was thus a prolonged interchange of ideas, and it is to the credit of the early English that they were not only receptive but were also enterprising enough to try to improve on the ideas they imbibed. In the Punjab, the successive invasions that have left such marked traces on the habits and customs of the people, and have further contributed even to their present composition, were not from the East or South where ancient civilisations existed, but from tracts to the West where developments in arts and science had not reached any helpful stage of progress. The successive invasions of England have all left results of immense value ; those that afflicted this province for so many centuries were less prolific in material advantage, while they exerted marked influence in retarding the growth of economic organisations. England is almost unique in the prolonged period of practically unbroken internal peace, which has lasted from the conquest of 1066 to the present day ; such disturbances as have occurred have not involved widespread destruction of institutions or of the records relating to them. The result is that England possesses continuous evidence of her history in original documents, as well as in survivals of ancient tradition. (1) This province possesses nothing of any considerable antiquity in the way of documentary evidence of past history ; it has yielded to the investigator coins, inscriptions, copper *sanads*, and traces of old buildings in quantity, but there is yet lacking that continuity of record which is essential

---

(1) Some other European countries possess wonderful records, but not in equal detail.

to perfect understanding, as well that detail which is necessary for comparison with other countries or present circumstances. There are no old libraries containing the original writings of the wise men of the past; in the special sphere of agriculture there do not appear to be any old books of fame or merit. Such information as is available suggests that this ancient art has made little progress for many centuries. The Old Testament contains descriptions that are applicable to conditions prevalent in the Punjab to-day. (1)

This absence of historical record may be responsible for the attitude generally held towards economic questions. Existing conditions are now much as they were in ages past. They have become customary. Poverty is customary. India is regarded as a poor country, so naturally the people are poor. If poverty attracts the attention of publicists, it is ascribed to whatever happens to be the popular butt of resentment at the moment. But poverty is an economic fact; it is due to economic causes; it calls for economic remedies. But it is a feature of almost all countries and all peoples that the responsibility of those people for their own condition is apt to be ignored, and the blame is apt to be placed on factors beyond their control. Over and over again, populations oppressed with misery and distress have turned to political remedies for the alleviation of conditions which are due to their own defects; disorder, strife, disturbances follow; the misery and distress are increased, and the one remedy open to the victims is not only neglected, it is too frequently prevented from exerting its fruitful influence. Political remedies will not cure economic ills. They can do a vast amount of harm; their record for economic good will with difficulty be traced in the history of positive achievement. It was not until the impotence of political agitation to improve their economic condition had become manifest to the working classes of England that they embarked upon that great campaign of self-help, now commonly known as the Co-operative Movement. The excessive importance attached to the political question in Ireland has, according to Irish writers, proved a serious factor in weakening the character of the Irish farmer as a producer of wealth. "The lack of application to the more material needs" it is said, "rendered the Irish mind receptive to more shadowy appeals; while the interest of the people in the single problem of self-government turned their minds away from more practical questions. Could but a portion of the loyalty and enthusiasm bestowed on this demand have been devoted to the practical problems of economic regeneration, the situation to-day would have been far different." (2)

The problem was one of poverty, the Irish question was, at bottom, an economic question, demanding primarily an economic remedy, and it has been the application of the great remedy for rural ills that has brought such prosperity to the island. Co-operation there was served by an intelligentsia, able not only faithfully to interpret the movement to its members, but also to ensure that its contribution to the national well-being was recognised and respected by the remainder of the population. (3) A discussion of the need

---

(1) As will be seen later, the same remark may be made about parts of Southern Europe.

(2) Rural Reconstruction in Ireland, pp. 16, 17.

(3) Better Business, Vol. V, p. 207.

for political change as an essential preliminary to economic development would be outside the scope of this book ; but where there seems to be some danger of repeating the same mistake ; where there is the same attempt being made to inculcate amongst the people a belief in the omnipotence of political change ; where the responsibility of the people to work for their own regeneration tends to be ignored, then it may be pointed out that, unless saner views find wider acceptance, there can only be the same result inevitable economic decay. Nothing here said should be twisted into an argument that political change should not take place. It is but natural that Indians, seeing poverty all round them, should press for power to attempt to solve the problems along lines that seem to them to promise good results. But unless those, in whose hands political power is now placed, study rural economics, unless the ministers make a close study of local conditions, and illuminate this study by a careful comparison with conditions in other rural countries, their attempts to devise measures, in consonance with local sentiment, to alleviate the ills from which the people suffer must prove barren of good, if not fruitful of immense harm. Political change alone will not bring economic benefit. It may prove to be a step along the road to material improvement, but for this it will be essential that mere political considerations do not overshadow the calculation of economic forces.

It needs to be emphasised that economic ills require for their cure economic remedies. The choice of remedies must obviously depend on the ills to be cured, and it is on these that attention must first be focussed. There must be such an examination of the existing economic situation in the Punjab as the material, available for the purpose, permits. If from that examination there emerge some of the causes of the prevailing low standard of living and low standard of production, and if for these causes some remedies can be found and applied in practical fashion, then some at least of the claims of the economist will be made good, and it will remain to the politician to press forward such legislative or administrative measures as may seem to be necessary.

The Punjab is essentially an agricultural province. But it is far from unique in this respect. It is, in fact, merely one of many states, similarly dependent upon agriculture; and from all (1) comes the same cry of poverty, and in nearly all there is now greater or less effort being made to examine the causes and to devise remedies. Rural England provides no exception. Everywhere the cultivators of the soil seem to have failed to increase their incomes to the extent demanded by modern requirements. Poverty is a relative matter. It does not seem to be true that the cultivators of this province are, on the average, less well off than cultivators of Japan or of the countries bordering on the Mediterranean ; it does, on the other hand, seem to be true that nowhere in the world is there to be found so large a body of cultivators, so prosperous in proportion to the requirements of their lives, as the colonists on the Lower Chenab Canal. It may be stated further, without fear of contradiction, that no other body of cultivators in any country can afford to spend the crores

(1) Except perhaps Denmark, the best co-operatively organised country in the world. But it was only when Denmark was on the verge of ruin and bankruptcy following on the disastrous Prussian War and the overwhelming of European agriculture with American wheat that it found a way to economic salvation in co-operation.

of rupees on litigation that the Punjabi cultivators spend. The Punjabi is far from being as poor as he is sometimes represented ; but as will be seen, he has before him a fair prospect of achieving greater prosperity than is open to his fellow in many other countries.

A brief survey of conditions in rural countries appears to disclose a considerable unanimity of opinion on three points. Agriculture has been neglected. Agriculture has been undergoing a slow change which is completely altering the position of the cultivator towards his calling: and, if it is to be restored to its proper position as the chief source of the wealth of the world, there is required a close study of the science and art of rural economics. Some further discussion of these three points is necessary to the argument.

The Neglect of Agriculture.

It is beyond all question that, in the Punjab, agriculture is the oldest and by far the largest and most important industry. It provides not only the food that is absolutely necessary for the lives of the people, but the raw produce by which alone imports are paid for, the commodities on which the commerce of the province is based, and the material for such industries as the province possesses.

The land constitutes not only practically the whole wealth of the province but it is almost the sole source of new wealth ; upon it, to greater or less extent, will depend the industrial future. And yet, with a few honourable exceptions, it receives little attention from the educated. The complaint is almost universal. (1) Amid all the rush of improvement in other callings, agriculture seems to advance but slowly. The farmer has been the forgotten man. The land has lacked the attention of the trained intelligence and the keen brain. It ever returns exactly what is put into it ; and because what has been put into it has, for generations, been what tradition has dictated and not what modern science would prescribe, it has yielded the same poor return. A very little consideration will illustrate this neglect. It is well-known that certain tribes have a greater reputation for good husbandry than others, that some succeed in extracting from the soil far more than their neighbours, that an Arain, for instance, is generally a better farmer than a Jat Sikh, a Jat Sikh generally better than a Mohammadan Rajput while even a Mohammadan Rajput can usually show his fields with pride to a Baluch or Pathan of the Indus Valley. If all the land in the Punjab were tilled with the same skill and care as that bestowed by the best cultivator, the additional annual increase to the wealth of the province would be immense. (2)

It is obviously unsatisfactory that the total production of the soil should be so considerably below what it would be if the output of all those engaged in agriculture came up to the level of the most skilful. It cannot be sound

(1) It is not confined to the educated class in the Punjab or in India but the charges levelled with good reason against the educated townsman in England, America and elsewhere. In England the paramount importance of agriculture was only brought home to the educated townsman when he found himself, at one period of the war, unable to get enough to eat. The possibility that such a result may follow on the neglect of agriculture was ignored and will, probably be ignored again.

(2) *Cf.* State Help for Agriculture, pp. 13, 14, 16, 28. Where the same complaint is made of agriculture in England.

policy for a country to have its most important industry in such a condition that it is doing less well and producing less wealth than may reasonably be expected; and yet in spite of these obvious truths, the people of education, while deploring poverty, are apt to overlook one of its basic causes, their own disinclination to do all that lies in their power to show the way to greater production. (1)

It is not only that too little interest is shown in improvements in technique or in the neglect of such methods as have been proved profitable, but other factors of importance in the progressive development of the province fail to attract the attention they deserve. The financing of agriculture is one and the interest charged by the financing agency is another. The point deserves close consideration, for if it is difficult to convince the general public of this country of the great importance of the rate of interest in regard to the development of industries, little surprise need be felt at the inadequate appreciation of the paramount influence of the rate of interest on agricultural progress. It is not so much that a low rate of interest allows of a larger margin of profit as that a low rate of interest permits of a profit being earned on many enterprises which otherwise would never be undertaken at all. The average of the net profits of all Indian railways is a little under 8 per cent. If this may be assumed to represent the normal expectation of the return from new lines, then the question whether these new lines shall be constructed or not, must depend on the rate of interest at which capital can be borrowed. Similarly there is a limit to the rate of interest which a farmer can afford to pay for borrowed money and derive a reasonable profit for its use. One writer puts this at 6 per cent. (2) But it is obviously impossible to fix any such numerical limit. Many improvements will yield a good profit even if 20 per cent. has to be paid on the capital borrowed to carry them out, while others will barely allow of 3 or 4 per cent. The rate of interest thus frequently decides whether a loan is "productive" or not; it may determine the question as to whether a farmer should hold up his crops for higher prices, as the higher price may be no more than the price at harvest time increased by interest for the period between harvest and sale; or it may decide the question as to whether it will pay to use artificial manures which improve the crops for, say, two years. It is perhaps unnecessary to point out the overwhelming importance of securing a profitable investment for all the capital available in the country in some productive employment. Agriculture is, before all else, the prime source of the wealth of this province; if, by wise employment of capital, the land can be made to produce an additional yield sufficient to cover interest charges and leave such a profit to the cultivator as will encourage him to further enterprise, then the owner of the money gains by the interest, the cultivator by his profit and the whole country by the additional wealth produced. In an industry

---

(1) A contributary cause to low production is bad seed; seed is usually sold by members of the same class as buy the grain and trade in it. The simplest regard for their own interests should be sufficient to induce these to sell only the best and most suitable seed, and to combine to punish any who hindered the expansion of trade by selling what was sterile or ill-adapted to the locality. Unfortunately such a long view is rare, but in Lyallpur and Montgomery there are over fifty shopkeepers acting as agents for the distribution of selected seed. A small beginning, perhaps, but, at least, a beginning.

(2) Saskatchewan Report, p. 19. Huebner, p. 331, says the average rate of interest on farm loans in the United States is about 7·75 per cent. ranging from an average of 5·8 per cent. in New Hampshire to 11·58 per cent. in Oklahoma. Herrick puts the average at 8·5 per cent.

subject to the law of increasing returns, a low rate of interest will facilitate the investment of so much capital as may be required to enable the manufacturer to reap the full benefit of large scale production while at the same time enabling him to reduce the price of his articles to the consumer. In such a case the gain is general. In agriculture, especially in a country of peasant proprietors, the interest factor is often ignored. So much so that the actual net earnings from some plots of land may easily be less than the fair interest realizable upon the sale price, so that the labour expended receives no remuneration. The average cultivator is not good at arithmetic, and interest is very much a matter of arithmetic. He wants money and gets it and complains that he gets into debt. He is not able to work out the profit and loss on the different undertakings that make up his year's work. (1)

Unfortunately the ordinary banking system has grown up among commercial men as a means for meeting commercial needs. It is not designed to meet the needs of agriculture and ordinary bankers are apt to look askance at the demands of agriculturists. Commercial banks deal chiefly in short-term loans, that is to say, loans for periods not exceeding three months. Such a large part of their funds consists of money on current deposit, that they dare not risk locking up any appreciable portion in loans for the longer terms required by farmers. The result is that farmers have generally to look elsewhere for the credit they require, to the money-lender, the shop-keeper or the implement dealer ; and they seldom appreciate the cost to themselves of this method of borrowing. Of this more will be said later, for the present the important point that it is desired to bring out is that, from whatever source the farmer derives the capital he requires for his industry, he has to pay for it a higher rate of interest than that at which a man in business in a town can usually borrow, and even when the nominal rate is the same, there are frequently incidental costs which result in the payment of exorbitant real interest charges, (2) or, perhaps it would be more accurate to say, result in the total cost of borrowing being very high. For instance, even when a farmer gets credit from a bank the bank is usually in a town far from his fields, and the farmer not only loses

---

(1) It is the demand for money by men unable to calculate what it is costing them that gives the money-lender his opportunity ; speaking of England in the early days, Marshall says : "When an able financier, whether Jew or Gentile, had once found a footing his resources were likely to grow by leaps and bounds, so long as he and his heirs maintained their ability and their liking for financial pursuits, unless, indeed, their careers were cut short by violence or powerful debtors repudiated some large debts. For the habitual rates of interest corresponded to the impatience and lack of arithmetical faculty of rich men and monarchs, who were not accustomed to be thwarted, and had no turn for accounts. The hasty and sanguine borrower often accepts a loan for a short period, say three months, at say 5 per cent. This would accumulate at compound interest to three times its original value in six years if no payment were made meanwhile ; and would be multiplied eighty fold in twenty-four years ; at 5 per cent. a month, a rate at which some people borrow now, a debt of one pound would become one hundred pounds if allowed to accumulate for eight years. Few people reflect on such arithmetical results ; but the professional lender has always known them." (Industry and Trade, p. 710).

The low return from agriculture is no new feature. In his chapter on Mediæval Agriculture (Vol. I, p. 21) Thorold Rogers wrote : it might be possible to give an estimate of the percentage of profit on agriculture during the period before us. It is certain that it fell far below the ordinary rate of interest on money......(p. 22). The rate of profit on agricultural operations, taken in the aggregate, and carried on under the management by a bailiff, was, I conclude, exceedingly low....(p. 34) such crops as were obtained, scanty as they were in amount, were not produced except at large relative expense.

(2) *Cf.* Huebner, p. 331.

the value of his days' work in going to and fro, but frequently has to pay the expenses of his sureties, including those for travelling and food. On a small loan, these add very considerably to the cost of borrowing. (1) The aggregate result must in the long run prove very serious. An American writer, discussing the situation in his own country puts the case strongly :—The great injustice has been that from lack of a proper system of agricultural credits, our farmers have been compelled to pay a higher rate of interest than has been paid by those engaged in other industries. This has, in effect, placed an annual tax of immense proportions upon agriculture, imposed upon our farming population unnecessary and unjust burdens and hardships, retarded the expansion of agriculture, our greatest industry, and thus held back the growth of our country, reduced its wealth and weakened the fabric of our national Government. (2)

There seems to be some malign fate which exposes this industry, the very foundation of civilization, to influences detrimental to its proper development. Wealth results from the productive employment of capital ; a farmer must employ wealth in the form of a large farm, of say 150 acres as in England, or capital sunk in highly intensive cultivation of a smaller area. The tendency of agriculture is to return, over a period of years, a steady income on the capital employed; and so, roughly speaking, the greater the capital that can be productively utilised by the average cultivator, the greater will be his profits. The patriotic economist must then desire to see the cultivators using more and more capital in improving the land or in crop production, or in stock, power, etc. (3)

Unfortunately, very little of the capital that flows towards the land is devoted to its improvement ; most goes to purchase from an existing owner, who, too often, sinks to the position of a tenant. (4) The investment of crores of rupees in land purchase does not of itself add an ear of corn to the wealth of the province. The reduction of proprietors to tenants increases the evils of tenancy. (5) On the other hand, there can be set off against this the fact that, in some tracts, good industrious tenants are acquiring land from thriftless owners. In the Hoshiarpur Tahsil, for instance, it is said that Sainis, Arains and Gujars, who compose the chief tenant classes, are becoming owners at the expense of the Rajputs who are less efficient cultivators and possess holdings larger than they can cultivate. In such a case, land purchase is a benefit to the province at large. Unfortunately, prior to the passing of the Land Alienation Act, the

---

(1) *Cf.* Irish Report on Rural Credit, p. 31 :—It is very frequently the custom for the small borrower to repay his obligation to a surety by giving his free services for a day or longer on the farm of the latter, or by furnishing the grazing of an animal, or the loan of a horse, or by conferring some similar benefit.

(2) Morgan : Land Credit, a plea for the American farmer, Introduction p. XII. In the Punjab it is not difficult to arrive at a rough approximation to the extent of the enormous drain on agriculture due to a very large number of unscrupulous usurers. The total for the last 20 years cannot be less than 50 crores.

(3) Shortage of capital in the hands of tenant farmers is said to be cause of backward farming in England. To attain the fullest efficiency a farmer should have at his command all the capital that his intelligence, energy and ability enable him to use with profit. *Cf.* Agriculture in Oxfordshire, p. 129. The sentence in the text must not be construed as a denial of the law of diminishing returns. The average cultivator need not be afraid of that law yet. In order to simplify the argument, the obvious qualifications regarding seasonal vicissitudes is not here dealt with.

(4) See ante The Price of Land and its effects. (5) See ante re Tenancy.

tendency was for land to pass into the hands of those who had no intention or inclination to cultivate it themselves or to develop it to its utmost productive capacity. Since 1901, there has arisen a danger that land will be purchased by money-lenders of agricultural tribes, who will rent it to tenants, who may be the former owners bereft of the chief incentive to industry. Here again the same objection arises, that land purchase absorbs capital that could better be devoted to improvement.

Besides capital, for the production of greater wealth from the land there will be required a higher technical and business training of the cultivators, and for this there will be necessary an almost complete revolution in the educational system. (1) All hope of progress must depend upon the proper growth of a sound public opinion, based on an appreciation of economic facts. Hitherto, the vast schemes that have added so much to the prosperity of the country have originated with Government. In the new order, more and more reliance will have to be placed on the opinion of those in whose hands political power will rest. From these there must emerge leaders, possessed of sound economic sense, or the decline of the one great national asset will be inevitable. (2) The present neglect of agriculture must give place to a real live interest in rural economics ; it is essential that this should be a well-informed interest, that the non-cultivating portion of the community should realise how the progress of agriculture reacts on their own prosperity, how this progress can be stimulated and how retarded, and to what extent and in what manner they can play a worthy part in the great task of rural reconstruction on sound economic lines. The interdependence of town and country is so complete, that the lack of practical appreciation of the logical consequences is difficult to understand. The difference between good and bad farming not only makes all the difference between growing or declining trade and commerce, but it affects the cost of living of the whole population. A sound agriculture ensures financial stability, and financial stability is the rock on which all lasting progress must be founded. The greater development of agriculture will not compete against other industries, but will rather assist them in providing the wealth, the raw material, the man-power and to some extent the market without which they cannot exist. (3)

In the foregoing pages, stress has been laid on the attitude towards agriculture adopted by the educated townspeople, because there is here, as in most countries a tendency for the educated and intelligent to collect in the towns ; it is the towns that will feel the benefit of the improvement of agriculture, and it is probable that from the towns will come the impetus to the serious study of the special problems of Punjab rural life. But if the apathy of the townspeople towards the biggest industry of the province is in any way remarkable; the general neglect of the big landowners is still more so ; while the fact that this neglect excites little or no comment illustrates, better perhaps than

(1) See Rural Education. (2) See Rural Leadership.

(3) For an interesting exposition of the argument see Sir H. Plunkett's Rural Life Problem of the United States. It is worth nothing that as far back as 1463 it was recognized in England that the land was the great fund of national wealth from which taxation was paid, and therefore whatever led to a rise of rents was a gain to the whole community, since the fund from which the revenue was drawn was increased. In the Punjab, it is all to the interest of the townsman that greater wealth should be produced from the land so as to give an increased revenue and so obviate the necessity of taxes on himself.

any other feature, the extent of the apathy towards rural problems. Although in the canal colonies, and occasionally elsewhere, well-to-do landlords, who live on their land have shown interest and adopted improved methods, and although several from amongst the non-agricultural class have been leaders in this respect, it remains true that in the province as a whole, it is not the rule but the exception for the big owners to take a prominent part in developing agriculture, and to set a good example in spending money on land improvement. Indeed, it is hardly incorrect to say that in the colonies, the peasant grantee is more enterprising in the care of his squares than the landed gentry. It is possible to quote instances where inundation canals have been constructed, embankments built and wells sunk, but these affect but a very small proportion of the whole cultivated land in the province. Of improved seed or implements or better methods of cultivation, little knowledge seems to be possessed or desired. An interesting sidelight is thrown on the general discussion by the Chakdars of Multan. Here the neglect of the proprietors, whether from apathy, lack of capital, or other causes, has afforded opportunity to the well-to-do members of the trading class to slip in between them and their tenants as Chakdars ; the Chakdar usually pays a rent in cash to the landlord, he sinks a well and sublets the land to a tenant paying rent in kind. The difference between the rent thus received and the expenses of the well, cash rent paid, etc., constitutes his nett profits. In 1859, the Settlement Officer wrote that "it is almost entirely owing to the existence of these Chakdars that this district owes its present state of comparative prosperity....They are almost invariably wealthy *Kirars*, who by the application of labour and capital have greatly improved the productive power of the soil....They never rest satisfied until they have realised for themselves a handsome profit of nett rent." In general the big owners take little trouble to develop the latent potentialities of their land and to insist on a higher standard of cultivation by their tenants ; and since half the cultivated land in the province is held by tenants who do not possess the capital, the intelligence or the initiative to venture on any improvement of methods, this fact is of great importance.

The pre-eminent position, once occupied by English agriculture, was in large measure due to the realization of the fact that the administration of the land was accepted as an important factor in the efficiency of production. The landlords were not, as too frequently in this province, merely rent receivers ; they equipped the farm with most of the permanent capital necessary for its working and wielded a considerable influence in deciding the system of farming. If a tenant contemplated any new enterprise or met with any considerable difficulty, he looked to his landlord for aid and support. On the other hand the landlord was prepared to invest more capital in the land where he could rely on his tenants to make an adequate use of it and to maintain the estate in a proper condition of efficiency. (1)

(1) It is interesting to note that English landlords were equally neglectful of farming, until about 1700 the lawyers and merchants from the towns began to buy land and invest money in it. Their example aroused the richer owners and some gentlemen of education and position took to agriculture, the result was great progress that continued until the gentry went off to the American and French Wars of 1775 to 1815.

Thorold Rogers found English agriculture stagnant for centuries, it was not until the eighteenth century that the art "progressed by leaps and bounds, and this was due to the fact that during the eighteenth century the great landlords were the most zealous students of agriculture, and the boldest experimentalists in new methods of culture." Vol. V, Preface).

It is frequently stated that agriculture needs more capital for its fuller development, and the English system whereby the landlord supplies most of the capital required has been found in practise to be the best that could be devised. (1) At any rate it is worth noting that amongst the English tenant farmers (*e.g.*, of Oxfordshire) it is said that there is not the slightest indication of any active desire to terminate their association with landlords or to assume the greater responsibilities of ownership. Where a large area of any country is cultivated by tenants, the fortunes of agriculture depend not only on the properties of the soil but on the nature of the relations which exist between the two partners. Landlords must support their tenants as far as may be consistent with sound economic management, and should exert their influence to secure from the tenants a high standard of farming. Where both parties are possessed of ability and understanding, there are many examples to show that agriculture compares well with many industries as a basis of investment. (2) More will be said later on the subject of tenancy; but from the above it will be clear that the success of any system of land tenure depends upon the spirit in which it is worked; unless the landlord rises to a full sense of his responsibilities, agriculture will remain stagnant, and the neglect of many big landowners in the province to aid, support and stimulate their tenants to improve their methods of production cannot but have serious consequences to the general prosperity.

It may be objected that this last statement ignores the possibility of Government regulation, illustrated by the example of the English Food Production Act, or by the more permanent example of Japan. In that country, "the farmer with his agricultural code is told exactly what he may and what he may not do—how his fields must be cultivated, what conditions are prohibited, and along what lines he is encouraged to go. The Government runs experimental stations and informs him as to the best lines to be pursued. Most of this advice he is more or less compelled to carry out.... Under Government auspices, farmers' guilds were established, which brought about mutual aid, the development of scientific agriculture, common purchase and credit. Eventually membership in these guilds was made compulsory on all farmers." (3) The present tendency in the Punjab is to decry official interference, so that for the progressive

In other countries, where peasant proprietorship prevailed, it needed the threat of ruin due to the invasion of American wheat to stimulate the cultivators on the European continent to adopt those measures which have now placed their industry on its present prosperous level. No one advocates that this province should await the threat of starvation before adequate steps are taken to produce from the soil all that modern science could extract, yet this policy of waiting holds the field outside the narrow circle in touch with the Departments of Agriculture and Co-operation.

(1) *Cf.* Professor Carver's view,—Principles of Rural Economics, p. 227. The best agriculture in the world is carried on under the tenancy system in England. It does not pay a farmer to buy his land as he can get a better return by investing the money in stock and equipment.

(2) *Cf.* J. Orr: Agriculture in Oxfordshire, Ch. VI. This and chapters VII and VIII deserve careful perusal.

(3) W. M. McGovern: Modern Japan, pp. 162, 235-6. The quotation is given for what it is worth. It is doubtful if India in its present mood is ready for so much Government interference and Government compulsion as exists in Japan. In that country, it has been readiness to subordinate personal feelings to the public good that has made phenomenal progress possible. As an example, it may be noted that while formerly for the consolidation of scattered holdings, the consent of two-thirds of the owners concerned was required, now the consent of a bare majority is enough. (*Cf.* Japan Year Book). It is doubtful whether in the Punjab any compulsion would be approved.

development of agriculture, reliance must be placed on the education of public opinion and on the imbuing of landowners with a proper appreciation of their responsibility. In this respect the outlook is very far from being hopeless. Many of the larger landowners are awakening to the possibilities of securing enhanced profits from the use of pure seed, new implements, and better methods of cultivation; but it is doubtful if any considerable number of tenants, in the West Punjab for instance, are being pressed to adopt these measures. The sale of new implements is as yet infinitesimally small, the number of harrows in use is minute, the use of pure seed is in most villages still a novelty, if not actually unheard of. There is in this no ground for pessimism. It took the English farmer a hundred years to adapt himself generally to the new husbandry advocated by the great writers of the eighteenth century, and all critics complain of his conservatism. The great truth which emerges from the foregoing discussion is that the soil represents wealth that is only potential; the extent to which this is converted into actual means for increasing human satisfactions depends upon him who tills it. He is the most important factor. He is apt to be slow and needs stimulating from outside. He must not be neglected. The relation of the farmer to the soil was well put by Thorold Rogers over forty years ago :—" The student of agricultural history.....will find that what economists call fertility, is not only that of the earth and the sun, but of that acuteness, skill, foresight, and diligence which constitutes the best qualities of a competent husbandman in our day. Fertility is and must be in the soil, but it is still more in the intelligence of the man who handles the soil. The former kind of fertility is, and may remain, a capacity only; the latter is an energy. (1)

If the Punjab is to enjoy all that its great potentialities offer, the human element must be aroused to a fuller sense of its responsibilities. The subject is important and will be treated at greater length in a later section. (2)

The Change in Agriculture.

The second feature regarding which, as has been pointed out, there is considerable unanimity of opinion, is that agriculture has been undergoing a slow change which is completely altering the position of the cultivator relative to his calling. This change is well illustrated by the fact that while about 1871—73 the Punjab exported only four lakhs of rupees worth of grain in a year, it now exports over fourteen crores worth, and there has been a similar expansion in the exports of cotton and oil-seeds. In other words, the cultivators of the province are growing proportionately less for their own needs and proportionately more for the world's markets. The great expansion in the area cultivated, which has been rendered possible by the construction of large canals, is responsible for this development. A considerable area of the land, newly broken up, has been devoted to crops for export,

---

(1) Thorold Rogers: History of Agriculture and Prices, Vol IV Ch. XXVI.

(2) The remark is true of the cultivating class of most countries, see for instance the following criticism of Ireland :—" The present tendency of the small holder is to go in for mixed farming, either because his father did, or because it seems to be the easiest thing to do, or because there is a generally accepted idea that the farm should be, as far as possible, self-supporting and self-contained......Every district must be specially adapted to some particular form of production, and it should be the object of instruction to make full use of that suitability." —*Better Business*, Nov. 1920, p. 43.

and the export trade has become a matter of close interest to the rural population. The world's demand for agricultural products is now beginning to affect the choice of the cultivator. The price of wheat in a Punjab *mandi* depends, not on local conditions, but on the price in Liverpool, which is the world's chief secondary market, and on the cost of transport between the two places. In former days, the cultivator grew for the needs of his household; even now it is customary for the same holding to contain a little plot of hemp for rope, a little plot of cotton for the womenfolk, and so on. But in the more progressive tracts, it is coming to be realised that it may be advantageous to grow a more profitable crop for sale and to buy the needs of the household from the proceeds. That is to say the cultivator is beginning to see that he must live, not on the products of his holding, but on the profits derived from it. For the present, the province seems to have arrived at the stage at which the tendency is to grow that which is most readily saleable. The cultivator has not yet reached the point when he will be able to choose that use for his land which will yield the highest net profit. He has not yet the knowledge required to enable him to tell for what crop his land is best suited. He grows wheat, not because wheat yields him the maximum net profit on his labour and land, but because everyone around him grows wheat, because wheat is readily saleable and because, with the water available, it is an easy crop to grow. He knows that potatoes and fruit bring in more money, but, apart from inherited prejudice, he knows that he may not be able to find so ready a market for these products. The cultivator, it will be seen, is beginning to be influenced by world prices and by problems of marketing. He is passing from what has been called the self-sufficing to the commercial stage; and markets and the fluctuations of market prices are for him matters of growing importance. (1) He is producing not what people want him to produce but what it will pay him best to produce. His crops, being in the main saleable crops, can now form the basis of credit; they are readily convertible into cash and so are available as security. If this credit can be wisely directed into productive channels, the next step will be for the cultivator to concentrate the greatest amount of capital on his land that his intelligence and technical knowledge and ability will enable him to use with profit. This steady change is curiously misunderstood. Mankind, outside a few scattered areas, has long since left behind the pastoral stage, when his wealth was counted not by his land but by his cattle. In the Sind Sagar Doab and other backward tracts, the people are still essentially keepers of flocks; and there is little difficulty in recognising, in other places, the different stages through which agriculture proper has passed. (2) Migratory agriculture still exists in parts of India. Surface tillage or stationery agriculture is found in the West Punjab; alternating agriculture requiring fallow, is by far the most common form; while convertible husbandry, in which the need for fallows is dispensed with, is becoming general around the larger towns. Those who deplore the scarcity of *ghi* and deprecate the breaking up of waste land, are in reality sighing for a reversion to the pastoral stage. Could they have their way, the whole prosperity of the province would disappear, trade and commerce would decline, and famine and starvation would reign over the land until the population had been so

(1) *Cf.* Carver : Principles of Rural Economics, p. 122.

(2) *Cf.* Saligman : Principles of Economics, p. 313.

reduced that the remainder could find sustenance on the small amount of food produced in a pastoral era. But in this book, the assumption is made that the progressive increase of wealth and prosperity is desirable, and accordingly all energy and effort should be directed towards pushing on the commercialization of agriculture, and not to pushing back the clock of civilization several hundred years.

To some it may appear that it is yet too early to speak of the commercialization of Punjab agriculture; and there is certainly a tendency in some quarters to deplore the movement in this direction. Some newspaper writers, for instance, appear to regret the export of large quantities of wheat when the internal price is high, and there are a number of people who are ill-fed. These seem to overlook the fact that the farmer, like every other worker, must seek the best return on his labour. If the surplus wheat could not be exported, it would not be grown. A farmer of any intelligence will not grow what he cannot sell. (1) Similarly no one in Lancashire or Bombay would dream of advocating any restriction on the export of cotton goods because many of the poor there were ill-clad. Objection is also raised to the efforts that are being made to grow a superior type of cotton that can be used in the Lancashire mills. This cotton cannot be easily used on the indigenous spinning wheel and is too good for the low counts of cloth usually made in India; but neither of these considerations should influence the farmer, if the new cotton yields him a higher net profit. These writers may ardently desire the welfare of the province, they are certainly not adopting the proper means to promote prosperity and reduce poverty. For these ends more wealth must be produced, and as there is a limit to the additional area from which this may be done, it is essential that increased wealth must be produced from the same area, that is to say that the same area must be made to produce crops yielding a higher net profit. As modern natural science yields up new and ever newer secrets of agricultural progress, the cultivator will not only be able to produce more wealth from the same land, but he will be in a position to invest capital in his undertaking with greater and greater confidence. The extent to which he will in practice do this will depend on the certainty he feels of securing for his product a price sufficient to repay him for his enterprise. Thus the very ancient art of agriculture passes from the old customary phase to an economic phase as science advances, (2) and it is neither sound sense nor sound sentiment to attempt to keep the cultivator poor just because some other people are poor.

---

(1) About 1857, the zamindars of Narowal tract (Amritsar) were called upon to pay two instalments of land revenue at once, and were obliged to borrow from the Sahukars. The latter converted their valuables into money and paid the proceeds into the tahsil on behalf of the zamindars. From these they received grain. But the price of grain fell. The market was glutted and a large portion could not find a sale and was in consequence injured. The Sahukars lost heavily. (Memorandum by Mr. Blyth on p. 98 of the printed report).

(2) *Cf.* Nourse, p. 18. In this connection the following extract from Cunningham's History of the Sikhs possesses some interest :—

"In India no one thinks of investing capital or of spending money on the improvement of the land, excepting, directly, a few patriarchal chiefs through love of their homes; and, indirectly, the wealthy speculators in opium, sugar, etc., through the love of gain. An ordinary village headman, or the still poorer ryot......has just so much of the produce left as will enable him to buy the necessary seed, his own inferior food, and the most simple requisites of tillage; and as he has thus no means, he cannot incur the expense or run the risk of introducing improvements." (First published in 1849).

Much misunderstanding on this point is traceable to the view that it is the duty of the cultivator to feed the towns; and, where Hindu feeling is strong, it is difficult to induce people to see that it is no more the duty of the countryman to feed the town than it is the duty of the townsman to buy from the neighbouring cultivator if imported foodstuffs are cheaper. If wheat from a neighbouring province or from Australia is cheaper than that grown locally, there is no discussion as to whether the townsman should sacrifice money in buying local wheat at the higher price. The cultivator must sell in the best market. He himself is indifferent as to the ultimate consumer of his produce. The middleman to whom he sells is equally absorbed in securing the highest margin of profit. A consumer in India is in no sense handicapped by an export trade; the market is open and he can buy with the rest. The actual export trade is not controlled by the producer, but for purposes of party feeling, this is sometimes conveniently ignored, and the blame for dear food is thrown on to the grower and not on to the actual exporter. The best hope for Punjab agriculture rests in the receipt by the cultivator of a full return for his labour; a man will not continue to work that others may gain, and he will be less inclined to improve his methods if he finds that the benefit accrues to someone else. If there is to be an adequate stimulus to better agriculture, it will be found in the higher reward resulting from the adoption of more scientific measures; and anything that serves to diminish that reward will to this extent diminish the stimulus to better agriculture. The commercialization of agriculture, then, is the best, as well as the necessary, means to that increase of yield which is essential to the growing prosperity of the country.

THE STUDY OF RURAL ECONOMICS.

Sufficient has now been said as to the neglect of agriculture and the change that is taking place towards the commercialization of the industry. Both point to the need for the close study of the science and art of rural economics, if the land is to be restored to its proper position as the chief source of new wealth in the provinc and almost the only source of the raw material of industries. As it has been assumed that there is a general desire for increasing wealth and prosperity, there should be little need for argument to show that the study of the means whereby this increasing wealth and prosperity can be attained is necessary to secure the end desired. The true scope of economics has been described as the study of the forces which contribute to the growth of the social income or public wealth and which regulate the shares of classes and individuals in this flow of wealth. (1) Rural Economics or agricultural Economics is primarily concerned with the study of all the factors which contribute to the production of wealth from the soil and to the better remuneration of him who works upon it. Jouzier defines it as the branch of agricultural science which teaches how to organize the various elements which constitute the resources of the cultivator, whether in relation to each other or with respect to persons, in order to assure the greatest prosperity to the enterprise. It aims at putting into the hands of cultivators the most complete intellectual equipment possible for the pursuit of their calling and placing at the service of administrators a knowledge of the best methods of conducting rural matters

(1) Saligman: Principles of Economics, p. 23.

in order best to advance business and make wealth. (1) Now that farming has become a business, the farmer must become a business man and must learn the methods of success in business. As he grows to sell, he must study not only the factors that make up the cost of producing his crops but also the factors that influence the price obtainable for his produce in the market.

The markets of the world and the methods of other farmers all over the world affect the daily life of every tiller of the soil, (2) for if any class of farmers can undersell him by using better methods, he must copy those methods or suffer. As agriculture provides the raw material for many industries, the farmer must study what those industries require and how far he can expand production with profit to himself. (3) He must not confine his activities to meeting the local demand if higher profit is to be gained by growing for a distant market, and so his view must extend beyond his own immediate neighbourhood. Ignorance of rural economics led to some strange results when, in the middle of last century, vast stretches of virgin soil in America were first opened up to cultivation. The immediate effect was a great abundance of cheap wheat which was transported in large quantities to the British Isles and the European continent. This great influx of wheat from America was a factor quite outside the control of European farmers, and its far-reaching consequences were ill understood at first. It was a new economic fact that upset the old routine, and the peoples affected dealt with the threatened ruin to their industry in ways reflecting the differences in national character. The Scotch, regarding home agriculture as definitely submerged, organised societies to encourage emigration to the lands where the new wealth was being produced. The English landlords, instead of insisting on better farming, reduced rents and converted the fields into pastures, while rural workers turned their attention to the growing industries of the towns. The Irish made of the invasion of American wheat a grievance against the English and followed the Scotch to America, not, however, like the Scotch as sturdy seekers after a share in the new wealth, but as exiles driven from their home land by what they liked to fancy was some act of English tyranny. In Belgium, Holland, Denmark, etc., there being no political grievance to bear the blame and no generous landlords to bear the loss, the people were driven to work out their own salvation by means of new forms of agriculture organised on co-operative lines. In Germany, co-operative credit was advocated by Raiffeison, and the new system soon gave opportunity for the introduction of modern methods of scientific farming. (4) The new factor, on the European continent, proved a great stimulus to agricultural improvement; more capital was employed in artificial manures, more profitable crops replaced wheat and the co-operative principle began to secure recognition as the one form of organis-

(1) *Cf.* Nourse: Introduction, also Gillette; Constructive Rural Sociology, p. 3.

(2) *Cf.* Rural Wealth and Welfare, p. 4.

(3) He must, for instance, become acquainted with the industrial utilization of by products such as cotton seed, if he is to secure full value for such products. Cotton seed in India is fed to cattle, but the seed can be made to yield several other articles of value and still leave a residue for cattle food.

(4) Scientific farming may be said to date from the publication in 1840 of Liebig's book, *Chemistry in its application to Agriculture and Physiology*. It traced the relations between the nutrition of plants and the composition of the soil and completely changed the attitude of contempt, founded on ignorance, which agriculturists generally had maintained towards chemistry. —Curtler: Short History of English Agriculture, p. 275.

ation not only suitable to agriculture but essential to it. The fact that the biggest and most important industry in Europe was threatened with ruin by the import of cheap wheat, naturally led to the study of the various factors involved in the rise and fall of agricultural prosperity. Up to this time economists had paid little attention to agriculture as distinct from land tenures and rent, etc. It may be that, as the industry is subject to the law of diminishing returns, the more enterprising may have preferred to invest their capital in those manufactures which yield an increasing profit, and economists naturally turned their attention to the problems of these new concerns ; or it may be that the inadequate appreciation of economic writers of the possibilities of what science could do towards improving crop production, led them to refrain from the discussion of a difficult subject. In England, sound commonsense has ever served the country well in the absence of scientific study. So far back as 1463 it was recognised that restrictions on the export of grain, which led to farmers and others selling their corn at low prices, caused detriment to the whole kingdom, as the prosperity of agriculture was considered indispensable to the welfare of the country, even if the consumer suffered. (1) In this country, the essential accuracy of this view still lacks recognition, and the town still cries for measures that may cause widespread loss in the attempt to secure a little cheaper food. Ignorance of rural economics may thus lead to unwise administrative measures that may aggravate the very evils they seek to cure. It is no part of the farmer's duty, it is no part of his business to provide food for the urban consumer if he can get a better price elsewhere ; just as it is no duty of the urban consumer to buy from the local farmer if he can get his goods cheaper elsewhere. The proper remedies for high prices are increased production, more economical production and the removal of unnecessary obstacles to, and avoidable charges in, marketing. (2) It may be urged that such an argument appears to support a clash of interest between town and country, and to encourage a selfish attitude on the part of the farmers. Such a view would be erroneous. As has already been pointed out, town and country are so interdependent that the country can never suffer without the town suffering too, or be prosperous without the town being prosperous too. Individual exceptions can be recalled, but speaking generally, in a province like the Punjab, the interests of the country are the interests of the community as a whole.

In pressing for a wider study of rural economics, it may be desirable to make it clear that this does not necessarily involve a neglect of other matters, usually reckoned as possessed of value in life. In the ultimate end, all life rests on a physical basis ; man must get his food, and therefore his living, from the soil. Though progress does not consist wholly of material advance, it does seem to be true that improvements in minds and morals are not found without it. The civilization with advanced methods of production is, in fact, found amongst the cultured, the politically progressive and the emancipated peoples. (3) No pure form of social and domestic life, no high type of morality,

(1) *Cf.* Curtler : History of English Agriculture, pp. 69-70.

(2) With, of course, increased production in other spheres so as to raise the purchasing capacity of the people, see *ante* the Price of wheat.

(3) Gillette : Constructive Rural Sociology, p. 25.

says an American writer, has ever been developed among any people except where it has been organised around some kind of productive work. (1)

Wealth and luxury based on the serfdom of others have never proved lasting. There is one other consideration: the forces of the material world, as has been pointed out by an eminent writer (2) are more powerful on their own plane than the forces of light, and are continually thrusting into a kind of powerless pre-eminence the religious, cultural and political ideals ostensibly ruling the minds of men (3). Where, as in the Punjab, there seems to be so little prospect of any common religious, cultural or political ideals, the unity of the people may yet be brought about by the recognition of an identity of economic interest. Every one can well work for the prosperity of all and leave each party its own special spiritual outlook.

The spheres of economics and ethics are not the same; but those who advocate the claims of religion or of a better social order are apt to trespass on the ground of the economist, and may, unless they are wary, find themselves preaching doctrines, the practice of which leads to the very opposite of what they desire. On the other hand, wider and wider recognition is being accorded to the consideration that morality has an economic value; sobriety and honesty make for the efficiency of labour; improvement in social welfare, education, the proper enjoyment of leisure, all contribute to economic progress, and much that was formerly regarded as altruism is now appreciated as profitable. In pressing, then for a wider study of rural economics, there should be no fear of opposition from those whose attention is more attracted by man's spiritual needs; while, were mankind less prone to prejudice, there should be prospects of more real unity of effort than seems capable of achievement along political, religious or other lines. It is almost impossible for a rational minded being, living in the Punjab, not to desire its improvement in prosperity; it ought to be impossible for such beings to withhold their aid and support from a campaign that promises to be so fruitful.

Under the new scheme of government, there will inevitably arise demands for interference in the economic sphere prompted by a natural desire for better conditions for some one or other section of the people. Where the constitution is no longer a matter for political controversy, and where foreign relations are debarred from discussion, as is the case in Provincial Legislatures, the activities of the Ministers will largely be concerned with the promotion of the economic interests of the population. As the Punjab is predominantly rural, there will be grave risk of mistakes being made, unless sound knowledge of rural economics can be spread abroad. History shows how easy it is to advocate the wrong thing, and how easy it is to adopt measures that promise good results to the short-sighted. Unless the factors that contribute to prosperity are well understood, it is difficult to see how they are to be encouraged. Unless the habits, customs and deficiencies that make for poverty and distress are well recognised, it is difficult to see how they are to be eradicated. There are

(1) Carver: Principles of Rural Economics, p. 24.
(2) Rural Reconstruction in Ireland: Preface by G. W. Russell, (A. E.)
(3) Marshall (p. 704) says the chief foundation of the place that England has won for herself in the world has been that deep-set firm resolve to concentrate energy on things which make for solid and enduring results.

people who appear to think that if the export of wheat were prohibited, it would still be produced and the price would fall; they would not apply the same argument to cloth manufactured in Bombay, for its fallacy is too apparent. There are people who think that the food supply of the country would be increased by a measure that would impose a heavy burden on production, not realising that already large areas are cultivated which do not yield a fair return for the labour expended. The close connection between diet and food supply is apt to be ignored; large quantities of cocoanut oil are exported from South India to England and there manufactured into an imitation of butter, called Margerine; the people of England cannot afford to use butter in the wasteful manner customary in this country, and the people of this country will not use the margerine which is available, but grumble at the scarcity of ghi.

Religious feeling prevents much good food from being consumed, and more good food from being produced. Where sentiment rules, the economist can only point out the truth and endeavour to save the people from making mistakes that may lead to poverty and distress. The political leader must know the economic view if he is to avoid leading his followers to destruction. Where there is lack of adequate knowledge of agriculture and of the conditions requisite for agricultural prosperity and progress, there is great danger that measures may be adopted whose result can only be economic decay. Good intention is no excuse for ignorance and will not serve to protect a man from the results of his own folly. Accurate knowledge must form the basis for any legislative measure that is directed at some economic end. It is the business of the Rural Economist to investigate the various elements that constitute sound agricultural progress; he is not an advocate of any policy, but the knowledge that he collects will not be ignored with impunity. It may, however, fall to him to expose the fallacy in a policy under contemplation, and to direct attention to an alternative that promises better results.

It would be easy to give from contemporary publications examples of fallacious reasoning on important subjects. Several resolutions have been proposed in the legislative assemblies that could never have been discussed amongst those with a knowledge of economics, and the increasing attention to public affairs is resulting in the proposal of remedies for admitted ills that could only serve to aggravate the evils complained of. The danger from the neglect of Rural Economics is considerable, and it can only be avoided by encouraging the study of this very intricate science. The most immediate danger is that the student will meet with rebuff from the ignorant when expounding the most obvious and simple truths. Where there are people who will not learn, there is risk of disaster. If there are any people who have made more experiments and more mistakes in parliamentary government than the English, their history is unwritten. But the English have learnt much from past errors; they have realised the difficulties in the way of finding short cuts to prosperity through legislative enactments; they are beginning to understand the value of knowledge gained by labourious investigators, and they are showing an increasing willingness to listen to those who have been able to devote more time to study special questions than is possible for the ordinary man. A somewhat similar attitude will be needed in this province in the future. Up and down the world there have been innumerable efforts at governmental interference with economic forces ; the experience gained cannot be ignored with impunity ; what is required is such a comparative study of conditions in the Punjab and other rural countries, and of the attempts at improving these conditions as will suffice to guide the new legislature safely along the path to progress. Needless to say most of the guidance will consist of warnings and admonitions ; positive directions will be rare. In the end it will be found that it is the human factor that will determine the rate of progress as well as its path ; legislatures can do little more than remove obstructions and provide opportunities.

CHAPTER II.

The Human Factor.

In dealing with the economics of agriculture, it seems almost impossible to exaggerate the importance of the human factor, and yet it is this human factor which is so often omitted from calculation in discussions on the subject. The cultivator has a reputation the world over for never being satisfied ; instead of searching for defects in his own methods he always seems to be grumbling at something else. The Government does not treat him as well as he thinks he ought to be treated, the soil is defective, the weather is capricious, the market is falling just as his crop is ripening, the bumper harvest will exhaust the field for next year, and so on. He seems disinclined to realise that other industries have their special calamities, and that the character of his land is very much what his own effort has made it or allowed it to become. (1) The difference between the worst land and the best, in old agricultural countries at any rate, reflects the difference between those who have handled it, and even in the Punjab the richest crops are found where capital and labour have been most freely expended. Where, as in India, knowledge of scientific agriculture is extremely limited, it is the absence of brain and intelligence that accounts for the low yields. It is not sufficient that the cultivator should be industrious ; he should possess the knowledge and ability to apply his labour in the right direction, and the capital requisite to employ is to the best advantage. Little progress can be made if the human element is unfitted for it. No difficulties seem able to deter where the people possess the character, the grit and the strength to fight through. Indeed the greatest skill is usually developed under the greatest difficulties. As Professor Carver says : "Communities and nations have remained poor in the midst of rich surroundings, or fallen into decay and poverty in spite of the fertility of their soil and the abundance of their natural resources, merely because the human factor was of poor quality or was allowed to deteriorate or run to waste". (2) It is the absence of well directed human effort that has allowed thousands of square miles of culturable land in Spain to lie barren or to remain so ill cultivated that the production of cereals is only about one-fourth of the average return per acre given by other European grain growing countries. (3) It has been well directed human effort that has converted the profitless waste of the Rechna Doab into one of the most prosperous agricultural tracts in the world. Natural resources are merely the material which the work of human beings converts into wealth. English soil was not naturally fertile but centuries of intelligent labour, perpetuated by an almost uncanny intuition of the value of the land as the great source of national strength, has so improved it, that the outturn of crops was for a long time unsurpassed. The rich appearance of an English country side is the result of from 400 to 600 years of manuring and improve-

---

(1) *Cf.* Agriculture in Oxfordshire, p. 130, Seligman : Principles of Economics, p. 45.
(2) Principles of Rural Economics, p. 174.
(3) Ward : The Truth about Spain, pp. 166, 167.

ment. The first great work on agriculture was written over 600 years ago, (1) and, with few set backs, progress has been steady and continuous to a degree that residents in this country find it difficult to realise. Neglect can turn the best land into the poorest, and the worst land can be converted into the most fruitful by human intelligence and energy. It is this fact which accounts for many of those differences which some people prefer to ascribe to political causes. As an Irish writer says: The wealth of a nation lies, not in the material resources at its command, but in the energy and initiative and moral fibre of its people; without these attributes no country can become permanently prosperous; with them, no unfavourable circumstances can long prove an insuperable obstacle. (2) Much the same truth was enunciated by an enlightened landowner of Spain: It is a vain belief that nations do not perish when they forget that the inexorable law of creation lays the foundation of national greatness in the cultivation of the soil, which gives men sustenance, and that the penalty for neglect is decay and destruction. Real riches is the work that creates. (3) Unfortunately, few people like to admit their own demerits; while the temptation to lay the blame for all defects on someone or something else appears to be irresistible. However, if the Punjab is ever to attain the height of prosperity which seems to be open to it, every factor delaying progress or perpetuating present poverty must be examined and displayed; and, in this task, it becomes necessary to point out that the absence of a prolonged effort at constructive progress must be held responsible for much of the present condition of the people. Those who deplore the poverty of their country should compare its history with that of the one they envy. Wealth and prosperity are the result of creative industry; poverty may be due to its absence or to the existence of a system whereby the profits of industry pass to others. The burden of maintaining, in comparative idleness, a parasitic class may be too great for an industry to bear. In by-gone days it was a crowd of courtiers and nobles, soldiers and serving slaves, who deprived the cultivator of the profits of his labour and left him a bare subsistence in good years and rather less in bad. With the disappearance of these classes of non-producers, there came gradually into being the class of unnecessary middlemen; and with the rapid increase of prosperity under British rule, the village usurer appeared and plied his devastating trade. The cultivator has never had a chance to show what progress he could make under adequate stimulus. As Mr. Keatinge points out, the small proprietor may be strong, industrious and intelligent; but if he is to do good work, he must be prompted by an adequate incentive and sustained by adequate food.....when a cultivator is so heavily indebted

---

(1) Walter of Henley wrote about 1250 a work which held the field as an agricultural text book until the sixteenth century; much of his advice is valuable to-day.

Cf. Curtler, Short History of English Agriculture, p. 31.

Mr. Curtler's work contains a wonderful record of trial and experiment, failure and success. It shows clearly the value of the human factor as compared with legislative remedies.

J. Orr in Agriculture in Oxfordshire says (p. 131). If the face of Oxfordshire to-day has a more attractive appearance than it had 700 years ago, if the fields give to the men who look to them for their living a greater assurance that they will be well-fed than they gave to their ancestors and predecessors, the difference is not due to the soil, or to the climate, but to the fact that twenty generations of Englishmen have built up by slow and patient work a better and better system of getting out of the soil and climate what they want.

(2) Rural Reconstruction in Ireland, p. 16.

(3) Quoted by Ward: The Truth about Spain, p. 170.

that all the produce of his land, excepting a bare subsistence, must inevitably go to the money-lender, his incentive to strenuous work naturally decreases. He sees little prospect of extracting himself from debt, and he is fairly confident that the *sahukar* will, in his own interest, see that he does get that bare subsistence,......the result is badly cultivated and undeveloped fields. (1) The condition bordering on economic serfdom, into which the cultivating classes have been plunged by past oppressions of former rulers and present oppressions of unscrupulous usurers must be held responsible for much of the lack of initiative that is so characteristic of them. But, in addition to this, there seems to be something in the nature of their calling, that leads farmers to belittle the influence of their own effort on the yields obtained from the land. Not only in India but in other countries also, the farmer is inclined to approach nature in a passive attitude, almost a fatalistic attitude, accepting what the fields give up and seldom seeking to coerce them into yielding more. (2) He is content just to go on farming. (3) The majority, even in England, are said to regard their occupation as providing a living rather than as a means of making money which can be extended and developed. (4) Where the old idea remains that a farmer has to live on the products of his farm and not on the profits, any difficulty in marketing, any obstacle to the receipt of the full return on his labour, seems sufficient to deter him from the extra exertion by which alone can be produced the extra outturn. Of Greece, for instance, it is said that it is not the ambition of the peasant farmer to get as much out of the land as he can. The difficulties of communication limit his market and he is usually content if he can satisfy the wants of his household, with perhaps a margin of profit. Tradition and the influence of climate combine to make these wants few and simple, and so to restrict the amount of energy employed. In Greece, as elsewhere, it is, in one sense, a misfortune that the peasantry are contented with so little. (5) Enough has been said to show that if the agriculture of a country is to be put into a state of progressive prosperity the cultivators must be encouraged by every legitimate means to develop their industry on economic lines ; and, as few men work for the mere pleasure of working, care must be taken to impress upon them the idea that good farming and the good farm are the result of the good farmer, and to ensure that the good farmer receives the full profit on his good farming. (6) Any thing that tends to deprive the cultivator of the profits of his labour militates against agricultural progress. There is ample evidence to show that a definite incentive is necessary to induce him to improve his methods. Everywhere he is apt to be conservative and individualistic, strongly influenced by custom and unreceptive of new ideas. As has already been pointed out, although the

(1) Keatinge : Rural Economy in the Bombay Deccan.

(2) *Cf.* Gillette : Constructive Rural Sociology, p. 162.
The Roumanian peasant is described as "unambitious and unthrifty, and generally content to live in a state of squalor". F. O. Handbook.

(3) Rural Reconstruction in Ireland, p. 256 The authors p. 52 express that opinion that as a result of the long cultivated belief in the omnipotence of political change, Irish farmers began to ignore their own responsibility towards their industry.

(4) Hall : Agriculture after the war. p. 26.

(5) R. C. Jebb : Modern Greece, pp. 104—108.

(6) An old farmer, on being asked where the best land in Oxfordshire was, answered : "The best land is where the best farmer is". This may be saying rather much, but it is undoubtedly true that the best farming is where the best farmer is, and not where there is the best land. J. Orr : Agriculture in Oxfordshire, p. 131.

cultivator is inclined to resent the advice of outsiders, great improvements in agricultural methods have frequently originated from men who were themselves not practical farmers ; and accordingly any tendency towards neglect of this industry by intelligent townsmen must be regarded as a serious hindrance to progress. In the Punjab, the tendency of cultivators, to ascribe good or bad crops to factors outside themselves, is accentuated by the fact that the amount and distribution of the rainfall exert such a great influence over the harvest. (1) But the extent of this influence is, in some part, due to defective tillage, and, within limits, it would seem that this dependence upon the seasons can be sensibly diminished by the adoption of scientific methods. Unfortunately, however, the tendency under discussion inclines the cultivator to underrate the value of education. When a man ascribes a good harvest, in large part, to natural forces outside his control and only in a minor degree to his own exertions, he is disinclined to listen to any advice to improve the efficiency of his labour. This attitude is somewhat strengthened by the unsuitable type of education offered. When, in almost every country, the farmer looks askance at the school, there would seem to be ample reason to believe that the school does not suit the farmer. The great economic importance of evolving a type of education that will appeal to the cultivator can hardly be exaggerated in a country so dependent upon agriculture as is the Punjab. On this very difficult question of agricultural education more will be said later. It is ultimately connected with the tendency of the more intelligent and educated people to migrate from the country to the towns, a tendency which must next be discussed. So far as the argument has gone, some attempt has been made to show that, in a province like the Punjab, the comparative neglect of agriculture is of grave economic importance. The change towards the commercialization of the industry renders desirable organisation on sound lines, the increased use of capital, and the improvement in the education of the cultivator so that he may learn to use this increased capital in the most profitable manner. Unfortunately, the cultivator, as a result of various causes is disinclined to make the extra effort required of him (2) ; he needs to be aroused to a proper appreciation of the prospects that await him if he will only bestir himself, and bring more intelligence, more industry and more capital to bear. This task of arousing the cultivator is not likely to be undertaken by the cultivators themselves. Hitherto, the town has battened on the wealth produced from the fields, and the townsman has been content to play the part of a middleman. So far from realising the truth that the abounding prosperity of the agriculturists would be the best guarantee of his own prosperity, he has striven to reduce them to a condition bordering on economic serfdom, and has, to a large extent, deprived them of the incentive to greater exertion. The prime source of wealth is production. A non-producing class may perform useful functions, but an unduly large non-producing class can only be a source of economic weakness.

---

(1) Mr. Keatinge writing of the Bombay Deccan says years of short rainfall have produced in the cultivator an exaggerated feeling that the outturn of his fields will bear little relation to his efforts.

(2) As agriculture is the oldest industry, it is necessary to take long views. One cause of this disinclination has been the extremely limited market for Punjab produce prior to, say, 1880. Whatever spirit and ability to improve his outturn the cultivator may have had must have been depressed by the uncertainty of his returns due to widely fluctuating prices.

Speaking generally, the wealth of a country varies in some measure, with the proportion between producers and non-producers. The presence of an unduly large number of persons engaged in trade or commercial pursuits was remarked as a feature of Ireland in the days of poverty, before co-operation came to facilitate direct trading and eliminate wasteful competition. (1) A similar feature may be observed in the Punjab where whole castes avoid productive labour and derive a living from callings that add little or nothing to the wealth of the community. Where there is a useful function to be performed, as, for instance, the distribution of goods, there are too many people doing it. Of small shopkeepers and traders in foodstuffs, there is one to every 21 of the population; of bankers, and money-lenders, there is one to every 100. Figures like these must be considered in the light of the economic truth that the fewer there are in any nation who get their living at the expense of others, and the more there are who get their living by productive, serviceable practices, the better it is for that nation and the more it will prosper. (2)

This discussion on the human factor in agriculture cannot be closed without a reference to a peculiarity of the rural mind that appears to be general. Cultivators live much with themselves, they are apt to resent advice from outside, and they are inclined to distrust the efforts of others to improve the conditions under which they live. This distrust extends to public bodies and they are usually found to be possessed of little enthusiasm for administrative councils entrusted with public improvements. Of the American farmer it is said that he still clings to the traditional convention that it is unwise to expend money for the common good through governmental agencies. The tax for the support of government is one of the sore spots in country life. Cities have gone ahead developing many things on a community basis, such as streets, sewers, water supply and so on, paying for them largely out of public funds secured through taxation. The farmer does not care to spend money in this way and still looks upon public office as a means for supporting a host of unproductive parasites on the public purse. The farmer still looks upon government as a necessary evil to be limited in every way possible to the minimum of activity. (3)

A somewhat similar feeling prevails in England. There it is said that although agriculture suffers from lack of facilities which ought to be provided by public authorities, the farmers adopt an almost hostile attitude towards the activities of administrative bodies. The prospect of an increase in rates, no matter in respect of what service it shows itself, seems to shock the farmer as if it were only the prelude of some vague but fearful catastrophe. He seems to see farming crushed out of existence by their weight. He forgets what local bodies have done for farmers. To some extent this may be due to the compulsory form in which new charges are imposed on rate-payers, but it is also largely due to the inadequate interest taken in the work of local authori-

---

(1) *Cf.* Rural Reconstruction in Ireland, p. 227.

(2) Carver: Principles of Rural Economics, p. 2. For a striking example of poverty and decay following the absorption of too large a proportion of the people in non-productive pursuits, Spain is worth study.. About one quarter of the population is engaged in agriculture, while only seventy-five in the thousand are employed in other forms of productive industry. Bad administration and obstinate adherence to a faulty economic policy have helped the impoverishment of the country (Foreign Office Pamphlets).

(3) Vogt: Introduction to Rural Sociology, pp. 191, 192.

ties. (1) The same may be said of the cultivating classes in the Punjab. They forget that the management of the whole district is as important as the management of a single holding, and that there must be many works of development that would prove profitable to themselves and to their industry. The local rate is limited to a small fraction of the revenue but any proposal to raise it meets with opposition, even though the need for new roads, new dispensaries, etc., is admitted. If marketing conditions are to be improved, if the present waste of wealth due to bad roads, preventible sickness, cattle disease, etc., is to be diminished and the rural areas thoroughly developed, this disinclination to pay more local rate must be overcome. To achieve this, it would seem to be absolutely necessary to spread abroad a sound knowledge of the economics of rural life and for this some system of adult education appears to be required.

A study of rural conditions in different countries of the world leads to the conclusion that far more depends upon the human factor that is commonly supposed. Defects in character can and will nullify the richest gifts of nature ; while what may appear to be insuperable difficulties are apt to disappear before the sustained application of human energy, human intelligence and human knowledge. Denmark is the classical example of a naturally poor country being converted into one of the most prosperous by well-conceived and well-directed effort. Throughout the world the cultivation of the land seems to lead to the appearance of similar characteristics amongst those so engaged. The cultivator is cautious and slow. He has found Nature's rules so rigid that he sees little room for divergent opinions about other matters ; he suspects the politician with his short cuts to wealth ; he suspects the townsman with his book knowledge ; he is inclined to underrate the share of the harvest due to his own skill, energy and effort, and to see in his crops the bounty of nature or the goodness of God. Much in the way of calamity that foresight might have prevented he ascribes to the Divine Will. On the other hand, he looks askance at public bodies that prepare to tax him to avoid a danger or secure some common good. Almost everywhere he is apt to underestimate the possibilities of his calling. He farms for a living ; and so long as a living is forthcoming, he hesitates to put forth the effort that would bring him more. Yet, more than any other man, he knows that the fields of one do not yield the same as the fields of another ; that it is the good farmer, rather than the good land, that will produce the best crops. Where he fails is in a peculiarly inadequate realization of his own personal responsibility for his own position. In examining rural conditions in such countries as Holland, Denmark and Belgium, the feature that stands out most is the effect of the character of the people rather than of their natural resources. It is not only the capacity for hard sustained work, and the willingness to put this capacity to the fullest strain, but there is a sense of the value of discipline, appreciation of the need for self-restraint in favour of the common good, of the need of the long-sighted view, and of subordination of the present to the postponed advantage, that occupy so large a portion of the picture. On the other hand, the effect of the actual Constitu-

(1) Orr: Agriculture in Oxfordshire, pp. 93-4-5. It is interesting to find that in Oxfordshire, as well as the Punjab, "the money spent on education appears to most farmers to be badly invested, and it would require a long argument to prove that it is a sound financial scheme".

tion of the State is hardly discernible. The State may interfere, success seldom follows. The State may prohibit, but it is the farmer who decides. The State may assist, but there must be farmers willing to reap advantage from the opportunity. The State can do much to enforce measures which the farmers know to be good. It cannot induce them to do what they believe to be inimical to their interests. The land reflects the cultivator; the cultivator is convinced that he knows best what his land can do; he may be wrong; prolonged conflict with practical difficulties has given him a distrust of anyone who has not this same experience. The personality of the cultivator is the most important factor in agricultural prosperity. If progress is to be gained, the cultivator must be trained to be progressive. If, in the past, the land has not received the treatment that it required, that neglect must be made good. No laws, no political changes can dispense with the need. Just as it is useless to press forward measures which the cultivator will not accept, so it is useless to propose measures without taking into consideration the peculiar characteristics of this class. If change is desired, a beginning must be made with the education and training of the man on the soil. The State possesses an almost unlimited capacity for causing damage; Spain affords an obvious example, Turkey another. It may, as in the Punjab, utilise its resources to stimulate agriculture and to bring to the land the water or other essential element that it needs. Such State enterprise will not of itself prevent decay, though it may postpone it. The fruits of such activities are only garnered when the cultivator responds in the manner required. (1) In the end it is the character of the cultivator that counts.

The Urban Movement.

The tendency for the towns to grow at the expense of the country is a feature of nearly all civilized countries which has excited wide discussion. (2) Its importance varies with the nature of the urban immigrants and the motives that incite them to migrate. Emigration from Ireland to the towns of America was a sign of agricultural decay, but a similar movement from country to town in England was largely due to rapidly increasing industrial activity. It is not a new feature. It disturbed King Richard II who about 1389 tried to stop it by an Act forbidding those who had served in agriculture until 12 years of age to be apprenticed in the towns and directing them to abide in husbandry. (3) This Act was renewed a few years later because many agricultural labourers were becoming weavers; and, in later times, London was regarded as a source of great evil to the country by attracting the young and energetic thither. (4) One result, so far as England is concerned, was vividly shown by the medical examination of men in the great war; but another, that is apt to be forgotten, has been the amalgamation of agricultural holdings into farms of such considerable size that a good tenant is able to earn an adequate income and maintain a reasonably high standard of living. This process of amalgamation was largely a result of the industrial revolution, which attracted labour to the

(1) The Mazhbi Sikh in the colonies affords an example of this.

(2) *Cf.* Gillette: Constructive Rural Sociology, p. 97 Amongst the most advanced nations the city trend is universal. Our modern populations are caught in the whirl of a civilization which rests on scientific and technological principles.

(3) Curtler: Short History of English Agriculture, p. 64.

(4) Ibid, p. 209.

growing towns and in consequence created a steady and increasing market for food. (1) Thus the actual loss of population in itself may not be an affliction to the country. It may lead to enlarged farms and a widening of the scope of agriculture for those who remain. (2) But the result may be baneful; there may be a decline in national physique or, if the necessary labour supply departs, even a decrease in the cultivated area. (3) The most serious result, however, is the steady drain on the rural intelligence and more especially of potential rural leaders. Where the more educated, and the more enterprising of the country population are year by year drawn by the attractions of the town, and the less vigorous, less capable and less enterprising youths are left in the country, the quality of the rural population must inevitably deteriorate. The new science of agriculture demands high intelligence and a high standard of education; the whole future of the industry is bound up with the increasing application of scientific knowledge to old problems, so that for the prosperity of an agricultural country it is absolutely essential that the cultivators should be either themselves trained in scientific methods or should be closely guided by those possessed of the necessary qualifications. No industry can continue to prosper unless it is continually recruited by intelligence, and the interests of the whole State as well as of the cultivating class require that the new standard of knowledge and technical skill shall be freely forthcoming. (4) The urban movement may be good if it withdraws to productive work in the towns the surplus unskilled labour or the struggling cultivator of an uneconomic holding; but it threatens the whole foundations of national prosperity when it results in the most important industry being left at the mercy of the least intelligent and the uneducated. The omission on the part of the educated to show any effective practical interest in agriculture or to take a prominent part in securing for this vital industry the attention which its paramount importance demands, is all the more remarkable as so many of them are country stock. (5) According to the last census reports the proportion of the big towns who were foreign born was follows :—

	1911	1921		1911	1921
Delhi	.. 36	48 per cent.	Lahore	.. 43	54 per cent.
Amritsar	.. 20	22 per cent.	Multan	.. 26	20 per cent.
Ambala	.. 43	45 per cent.	Jullundur	.. 18	39 per cent.
Sialkot	.. 20	35 per cent.	Ferozepore	.. 49	52 per cent.

(1) *Cf.* Curtler, p. 162.

(2) *Cf.* Gillette : Constructive Rural Sociology, p. 95.

(3) *Cf.* Carver Principles of Rural Economics, p. 254 :—In so far as the movement from the country to the city has the result of maintaining medium scale farming rather than small scale farmiing as the function of an agricultural proletariat, it is a wholly commendable movement—this is the only way by which a higher standard of rural living can be maintained.

(4) *Cf.* Carver : Principles of Rural Economics, p. 200.
Hall : Agriculture after the War, p. 49, *cf.* also Orwin: Place of Agriculture in Industry, and Mr. Freemantle's excellent pamphlet.

Mr. Rountree considers that the reason why the Belgian cultivator can pay a higher rent than the English is that in England the more intelligent type of agricultural labourer is drawn to the towns, leaving the farmer with only the labour of second rate qnality, while in Belgium the labour on the farm is done by the peasant himself who reaps the benefit of his exertions and so works with a greater will and with more intelligence. Land and Labour : Lessons from Belgium, p. 150.

(5) In stating a fact, it must not be inferred that blame is being imputed. The edncated townsman can advance good reasons for his neglect—lack of opportunities, lack of any

These are high figures and illustrate clearly the extent of the modern urban movement. Were it not for this, the population of the big towns would steadily decline. For while, in the period 1901—1911, the average birth-rate was 4·04, the average death-rate was 4·69. On a total urban population of approximately 2,117,000 this difference should be sufficient to cause a decline of over 13,000 a year, so that were these rates a permanent feature, a migration from country to town would be necessary to this extent to maintain the town population at its existing level, and any increase of the towns would be due to further migration.

This migration is recruited mainly from three classes, unskilled labour, sons of traders and educated youths. It is probable that very few of the peasant proprietor class are included so that there is as yet no indication of an increase in the size of peasants' holdings being due to this cause.

The chief evil, as has already been indicated, is the steady persistent withdrawal from agriculture of the more intelligent and enterprising youths. These seem to be firmly imbued with the idea that the cultivation of the land offers no sufficient scope for their newly acquired education, that farm labour is unworthy of them and that a better career is to be found in some clerkship in a town and yet only a very small minority come to prominence in the new sphere. It is, of course, very largely true that agriculture as at present practised in the Punjab offers little scope for education and intelligence ; but that is just because education and intelligence have not been applied to the task of evolving a more scientific type that would not only afford full opportunity for the highest qualities of the cultivator but would return ample profit on his enterprise. To keep the educated young man in this industry, it must be shown that it is as profitable as other industries and that it offers as great opportunities for the individual of merit as does a town life. (1) It will, also, probably be necessary to make country life more interesting and more diversified and to put new vigour into old community institutions or even to introduce new ones. As Mr. Keatinge has pointed out, in a country where such a large proportion of the population depends directly on agriculture a large part of the legislative and executive action of government must of necessity be connected with the welfare of the cultivators. There can hardly be such a thing as a farming interest or a landed interest apart from the general interest of the community, since most people have some connection with the land and with agriculture. (2) Under the new Reforms Scheme the ultimate political power will rest with the rural voter and those who desire his suffrage will have to satisfy him of their worth. For the ordinary political shibboleth agriculturists generally care very little, but they are usually shrewd enough on any question that has a practical bearing on their work. The new system of government

---

organization or of leaders, preoccupation with his own troubles, the absence of facilities for the study of rural problems and so on. But the fact remains that the trained intelligence of the towns must be attracted to agricultural questions.

(1) *Cf.* Carver : Principles of Rural Economics, p. 340.

Lee Coulter : Co-operation among Farmers, pp. 10-11

(2) Rural Economy in the Bombay Deccan, p. 181.

may thus serve to stimulate amongst the educated a more living interest in problems of rural economics, and may even brighten the evening discussions with topics of immediate practical importance. The spread of the Co-operative Movement is another, and, perhaps, a still greater, factor in invigorating village life; it is setting up new village institutions under democratic control, it aims at inducing the actual producers to take under their own management every stage in the work of production from the purchase of necessary material to the sale of the final product; it seeks to arouse their interest in the business side of their industry and to ensure them the fullest returns from any new enterprise. By reducing the rate of interest it makes improvements profitable; by cheapening necessaries it makes a higher standard of living possible on the old expenditure; by selling in the dearest market it affords the worker a vista of progress. Above all, it should, and to some extent does now, bring to the front those endowed with the capacity for leadership. Hitherto, the results have not attracted the attention they deserve, but the introduction into village life of well-educated and zealous young men, preaching a new doctrine of economic emancipation and economic progress, and bringing to the cultivators the knowledge derived from a wide study of other rural countries, cannot but have a widespread and far-reaching effect that, in time, even the most apathetic person will not be able to ignore. As has already been stated, the urban movement as far as it affects surplus rural labour may bring good to the province, though it entails an increase of crime, immorality and ill-health which seem to be inseparable from town life. The flow of the intelligent and the educated must be turned the other way, so that the vast potential wealth of the province may be exploited to the full. (1)

Rural Education.

It has already been pointed out that the great source of present and future wealth in this province must be the land. Under proper treatment land can continue to produce wealth without exhaustion; under scientific treatment it can be made to yield an outturn that steadily increases. But the area of culturable land in the province is limited, and accordingly, if more wealth is to be produced, this must be effected through the intelligent progressive utilization of more and more capital. The productive utilization of capital calls for high skill and enterprise and it would thus seem that the development of the skill and enterprise of the agriculturist class is of prime economic importance to the province. (2) Thus far there is probably wide unanimity, but in the devising of means to achieve this end, there appears to be room for considerable

(1) In the article on "Recent Economic Developments in the Punjab" read before the Royal Economic Society in 1900, Sir James Wilson wrote :—"Unlike western countries, there is no marked tendency for the population to drift from the villages into the towns, for the proportion of rural to total population at the last three censuses has been 87·1, 88·4 and again 88·4; the fact being that agriculture has been so prosperous that there is little temptation for the rural population to forsake it for a town life"; as has been shown above, the tendency exists and is especially marked amongst those who have acquired some education.

(2) Not, of course, to this province only but to every country in the world. Lack of research and lack of education in agriculture as a science among the rank and file of agriculturists are included in the causes militating against the proper development of agriculture in Great Britain (*cf.* evidence given before the Royal Commission on Agriculture, 1919).

divergence of opinion. The one thing that would seem to be almost universally recognized is that the cultivators, the world over, show little appreciation of the type of education offered to them ; a second point, that would seem to be recognized by all except the educationalists themselves, is that this type is unsuitable. A third point, of great practical importance, would seem to be that no really suitable type of education for agriculturists has yet been evolved, or perhaps it would be less controversial to say, has yet received general recognition. Of criticism there is plenty, for the necessity of awakening the cultivators to an adequate recognition of the possibilities opening before them as a result of the rapid progress in scientific agriculture, is appreciated by thinking men in all countries. Take for instance the following quotation : "If we wish to apply scientific knowledge, such as has been obtained to-day, and to draw from our soil the greatest possible return it is necessary to change entirely our methods of cultivation. But what is, above all things, necessary to our agriculture is well-organized education, which is able to aid in the improvement of the technical side of production. Although almost the entire population is occupied with field work, we do not possess, frankly, any agricultural education worthy of the name. The creation of a certain number of practical schools in the agricultural areas has been discussed, but these schools do not as yet exist. The whole system of education with us is exclusive and incomplete ; and it is sterile, considered from the economic point of view. Our schools prepare the young people exclusively for public service, and for the liberal professions, instead of giving them useful knowledge, and preparing them for independent professions and for some sort of a practical life. The systematic organization of technical education fit to give to the younger generation an adequate agricultural and industrial preparation is an absolute necessity in our country. But unfortunately our authorities do not seem to realize this as much as they should". This quotation does not refer to the Punjab, to which it applies with startling accuracy, but to Serbia, (1) a country from which the Punjab may learn some useful lessons. It would not be difficult to give other quotations of similar tenour relating to other countries. The almost universal complaint against the present system of education is that it is town-made ; it seems almost as if it were designed to drive country children into the towns ; it bears no relation to the life they are to lead ; it is so divorced from life as it should be lived in the country that most rural children lose interest in it, while the more intelligent, finding that what they have learned is useless to them on the land, seek an outlet for their new knowledge in town life. The village schoolmaster himself fails to encourage his smarter boys to remain in the fields, but pushes him on to the High Schools, which, usually situated in larger centres of population, have a strong tendency

(1) Serbia by the Serbians · edited by A. Stead, p. 245. Of Japan, W. M. McGovern in Modern Japan, pp. 225-6 writes :—The government has a horror of seeing its young men full of general and scrappy information, which can be of no real use to them or to the country—of education such as we find it in India, which prepares a man for being only a doctor, a lawyer or a journalist, with the result that most become political agitators. Even in the Japanese primary schools we find evidences of specialization. In towns the elements of commerce and book-keeping are given ; in manufacturing districts ideas of industry, and the ends and means of engineering : in agricultural districts they are taught how to cultivate the soil most efficiently while on the sea coast scientific methods of catching fish are shown. Girls are everywhere instructed in sewing and cooking, and in many cases the elements of sericulture.

This quotation is given for what it is worth. It will, of course, not meet with general agreement, and, indeed, can hardly be regarded as representing an impartial view.

to divorce them from the country and to raise their ambitions towards professions which all call for less patient labour. (1) It is not only in the Punjab that the College boy acquires a distaste for the plough, and it is not only in the Punjab that the charge is laid against the schools that the whole atmosphere is opposed to the true spirit of rural life. They seem to reflect a spirit of veiled contempt or at best of passive indifference towards agriculture. They fail to instil into the youthful mind any sense of the dignity and importance of the greatest of all productive industries, and any ambition to devote their lives and their energies to the development of the districts in which they live. They seem to miss their great opportunities to implant in their pupils a proper sense of agricultural progress, of agriculture as a vocation second to none in its unlimited scope for improvement, and in its unique responsiveness to human effort. The attitude of the teachers and of the superior staff must be held largely responsible for the general lack of interest in the one big industry of the province. Agriculture is just taken for granted ; and where agriculture is backward, education must be backward too. Once the importance of securing scientific progress in agriculture is fully realized the problems of rural education will be within easy reach of solution. Education in England was largely evolved in the interest of the leisured classes, it grew up as a training for cultured leisure and, in spite of the increasing stress and competition of modern life, it is still regarded by many as a mental polish designed to enable a man to mix well with his fellows. The English Public School and old type University are probably unequalled as training grounds for those who are to make their living out of other people or by guiding and controlling other people, but they were singularly ill adapted for those who have to earn a living by guiding and controlling the forces of nature. Among those whose success depends primarily upon power over men, Professor Carver enumerates the politician (the example par excellence), the lawyer, the actor, the preacher, the teacher and the salesman, everyone in fact whose active work consists mainly in talking or whose success depends mainly upon being judges of human nature. (2) Everyone else must, in greater or less degree, depend for his success upon his knowledge of physical forms and the properties of things and upon his skill in applying that knowledge.

To no one, perhaps, is such knowledge and skill more important than to the agriculturist. It must be remembered, that the assumption has already been made that the raising of the people of the province to a higher plane of material prosperity is the economic ideal. To this end the problem of the employment of leisure may well be left to those who are likely to enjoy it. Experience amply proves how easy it is to turn out a certain standard of lawyer, teacher and clerk, but the competent farmer is as difficult to produce as the ideal teacher. In this province it must always be borne in mind that

(1) *Cf.* Sir H. Plunkett : Rural Life Problems of the United States, p. 132. American Evidence : F. E. Green : The Awakening of England. *Cf.* also W. H. Wilson : The Evolution of the Country Community, p. 96. The French Philosopher Desmoulin has said that Anglo-Saxon supremacy is due to the Anglo-Saxon love of the land and of education. The American represents these two passions, and of the two love of education is, at present, the stronger. The community which is weak in its schools will not hold its people.

(2) Principles of Rural Economics, p. 12. The passage is quoted not as an attack on a system but to illustrate the argument that while the study of mankind may be the highest study of man it is not the best equipment for a cultivator.

griculture is and will remain the greatest amd most important industry, and that the land is and will remain the greatest, and most important and inexhaustible source of new wealth. A proper system of education must not only take count of this, it must be based upon it. The closer the relation to agriculture the studies can be made to bear, the more active is the interest of the agriculturist's son likely to be, and so long as these studies are sufficiently liberal, the better they are likely help in the economic problem. It is, perhaps, worth noting that knowledge of men and the power of managing them, while of great value to the large landowner or employer, are of minor importance to the peasant proprietor. It has been said that even a tramp can live on the fat of the land, and so he can if he knows mankind well enough. But the problems of a province of peasant proprietors belong to a different category. There will always be need for the councillor and the lawyer, but the system of education must not be that specially designed to produce them. What this system should be, is not easy to prescribe; but some general principles may be stated with confidence. It must awaken the youth to an appreciation of man's power over nature, to a realization that progress largely consists in increasing power to harness natural forces to serve human ends. Where comparative poverty is the general condition, it must implant into the growing mind the idea of progress from a worse to a better state of things; it must avoid that backward look, that dwelling on the past, whether it be a past of grievances or glories, that has done such infinite harm in poor countries; it must implant a firm hope in a better future attainable by human effort; it must concentrate attention on the practical opportunities lying just outside the schoolroom door; and on the need of community action to seize and develop them. It must of itself provide an incentive to learn; whether education is to remain voluntary or to become compulsory, it must appeal to the rural parent. State compulsion is a concomitant of civilization; effective compulsion is only possible in highly civilized countries; and the Punjab has not yet reached the stage where compulsory education can be effectively enforced without the active support of parents. The Khatri sends his son to school because he realizes that it pays him to do so; the education he receives will qualify him for employment, even if only as a clerk. Whatever the idealists may say, education has only spread where it has provided qualifications for the adult life. The zamindar's son has gone to school when the school education was necessary for his future position in government service, but not because he thought it was necessary for his future career as a good zamindar. There is an amazing amount of cant talked and written about the narrowing effects of vocational training, chiefly by people who give their sons the education they consider will fit them to mix with those amidst whom their future lives will be spent. What is required is a similar education that will fit agriculturists' sons to mix well with agriculturists. Experience has shown the almost insuperable difficulties of bringing the cultivators' sons to the school; the school must be brought to the cultivators' sons. If these will not imbibe what is provided for them, they must be furnished with what is more to their taste. The cultivating class cannot be ignored, it cannot be left in an unprogressive rut. (1)

(1) The following evidence was given before the Royal Commission on Agriculture (1919): The agricultural industry has got to look to education on a very wide scale being introduced in the near future. It will cost a good deal of money. Many young men leave our districts for the towns to seek industrial employment so that the education rate tends to be high because we are educating the people for other places;

The enormous potential wealth in the soil of the Punjab will be converted to actual wealth as fast as the cultivator can be taught to extract it and no faster. He is the custodian, the only possible custodian, of the millions of acres upon the produce of which everyone else is dependent. It would hardly be an exaggeration to say that, whatever principles and ideals of the educationalists may have to be sacrificed, the cultivator's son must be sent back to the land a better and more enlightened cultivator and a more intelligent and valuable citizen. The fascination of agriculture to the mind whose interest in its possibilities have once been thoroughly aroused should remove many difficulties. Given a good teacher, one thoroughly conversant with his subject, and fully alive to the opportunities it affords for stimulating the intelligence of the growing child there is very little that man requires to know that cannot be imparted through the medium of nature study. It is his intimate knowledge of nature, and the play of natural forces that makes the cultivator such a pillar of political stability. He learns what he can mould and what he cannot thwart. A cabbage seed may be induced to produce a good or a bad cabbage, not all the political ideals ever conceived nor all the political speeches ever delivered will make it grow into a cauliflower. The cultivator has usually a sound political sense because he realizes that nature has inexorable laws that man can neither avoid nor neglect. He needs to be educated to realize the immense power of the human brain to extract the rewards which nature freely offers to those who study her laws. He must be impressed with the truth that what the Punjab expects from him is not so much improvement on the old agriculture as a new agriculture based on modern scientific knowledge. He must, as Sir Horace Plunkett has pointed out, regard his industry not only as the basis of rural existence but as a science, a business and a life. (1)

When it is asked in what practical fashion all these general principles are to be given effect to, it has to be admitted that the time has not yet come when a cut and dried curriculum can be offered as embodying the perfect solution. But there are two points on which stress may suitably be laid. The most satisfaction amongst agriculturists with the system of education seems to exist where the control has rested in the hands of the agriculturists themselves. The evidence collected by the American Commission only found a really optimistic view held in North Dakota, where the university, agricultural college, experiment stations, farmers' institutes and country schools were all reported to be adequate and progressive and practically in the hands of the farmers. In Europe the most suitable system seems to be found in Denmark where again the actual farmers have organized themselves to set up what they consider to be best adapted to their needs.

The second point is that in the discovery of a lasting solution for this province the co-operative movement seems destined to play a leading part. Mention has already been made of the desirability of teaching children the need of community action to seize the opportunities that lie open to them; they should be taught to work together for the common good, and should be brought to a larger sense of loyalty to their own neighbours and to the class from which

(1) Rural Life Problems of the United States, p. 89.

they spring. (1) If success is to be obtained, the human factor must be studied. The Irish small holder, it has been remarked, on account of his inferior education was often content to remain where he was ; he had neither the initiative nor the self-confidence to demand instruction on his own account. Only in a society, in combination with his fellows, did he acquire the confidence which is essential for any step towards a better technical knowledge. Nowhere did farmers carry on their farming on a business basis. For them it was an occupation which in goo dyears brought a good living and in lean years made it hard to get along. (2) Much the same may be said of the Punjab. It has to be remembered that while other big industries can call to their aid the best ability available, the individual farmer has had to rely entirely on himself, on his own brains and his own resources. In the Punjab he is usually a small man who, even if he possessed initiative, would be unable to give it scope. (3) It is here that the co-operative movement steps in. It introduces the cultivators to the business aspect of their industry and develops whatever latent business capacity they may possess. It makes education effective inasmuch as it ensures to the more intelligent the increased return that their intelligence earns. It supplies a practical education in economics and encourages the growth of the very community feeling upon which it is based. In other countries co-operative societies have been found to be veritable commercial schools for the villages. They show the practical value of education and create the demand for more. They go even beyond this, they convert the people into a willingness to pay for what they appreciate. The co-operative movement everywhere stimulates the desire for education. In Denmark it has led the farmers to form joint stock companies to run both People's High Schools and Agricultural Schools. In the Punjab it is already giving a lead in starting night schools for adults, and has contributed towards the opening of middle schools. (4) Another valuable feature of the movement is that it makes for continuity : individual cultivators die, but their society possesses unlimited life with the extra advantage of being able to change the manager. The outlook is thus widened and a longer view becomes possible. It has been pointed out that the great advantage of the joint stock company system over the individual owner in business is that, while a great business may be created by a single owner of exceptional capacity, it may happen that his son and successor may lack even the capacity to carry on what he inherits ; while, under the joint stock form of organization, it is open to those concerned to secure as manager a succession of the best men available. In a province of peasant proprietors the same advantage accrues to the co-operative society, the individual cultivator can invest more money in improvements with the confidence that the advice and experience of the society coupled with the aid of the scientific experts with whom it is in touch will help the son through difficulties, and they can start schools knowing that, under the co-operative form of organization, the best manager will probably be put in to manage it.

In one other direction co-operation should help the cause of rural education.

(1) *Cf.* Vogt: Introduction to Rural Sociology, p. 270.
(2) Rural Reconstruction in Ireland, p. 238
(3) *Cf.* State Help for Agriculture, pp. 16, 23.
(4) Adult education in the villages is very difficult to secure owing to the dearth of men of education to serve as teachers. The drain of the literate to the towns retards the spread of literacy in the villages.

It is essentially a business organization and observes business principles; amongst these are recognized the necessity of adequate record and accounts, and for these someone of education is required. Unless there be in a village one or more people possessed of the necessary educational qualifications, it is difficult for the people to enjoy to the full the benefits of co-operation.

Co-operation thus not only finds work for the educated in the village, it creates a demand for educated people. As soon as a society is well under weigh members desire to understand its working and in order to do this they feel the need of becoming educated themselves.

Minds immersed in ignorance or clouded in superstition will not be able to give the Punjab the extra produce it must have if there is to be any improvement in the general standard of prosperity. (1) What is wanted is a progressive attitude of mind, a genuine desire to be always improving, and for this there is required such an educational system as will serve to enlighten the people sufficiently to throw off hindrances to progress and to get rid of all that prevents them from enjoying the full benefit of their own new technical skill. (2)

In the above pages attention has been more particularly directed to the schools. It should, however, be unnecessary to point out that the education of the farmer should not stop there. Beyond the school stage the opposition to specialiszation begins to disappear. Beyond the age of 15 years a youth may, by general consent, be given a more strictly vocational training. What form this should take is still a matter of experiment. Let it be understood clearly that what the Punjab requires is a body of cultivators, of such assured skill in the productive employment of capital, that this alone will go a long way towards securing for them all the capital they require. To call such an intelligent progressive body into being agricultural colleges alone will not suffice, though a number of these are necessary for future progress. The province wants more than a few hundred trained graduates, it wants two million trained agriculturists. It is not only the progressive farmer in the Chenab Colony who requires to be taught, it is the lakhs of unprogressive cultivators in every district of the province. (3) As an American writer puts it :—

We must have some active means of reaching the last man on the last farm. The State owes it as a duty to its citizens to provide those persons in difficult positions with the best possible means of making their property thoroughly serviceable. It is fairly incumbent on the State organization to provide effective means of increasing the satisfaction and profit of farming in the less fortunate areas as well as in the favourable ones, both as an agency of developing citizenship and as a means of increasing the wealth of the State. (4)

---

(1) *Cf.* Gillette : Constructive Rural Sociology, p. 327.

(2) *Cf.* Carver : Principles of Rural Economics, p. 202, 248.

(3) That is to say, apart from the special colleges, there is required widespread education in the elements of agriculture in something of the nature of vocational Middle and High Schools. The two million agriculturists do not need college training but they do need training in practical agriculture on modern lines.

(4) Bailey : The State and the Farmer, p. 50.

Fortunately for the province, recent years have witnessed the commencement of an effort to give to the people a system of education more suited to their needs. But a long period must elapse before a really good type can be thoroughly established; (1) every year that passes before the agriculturists are fully trained in both the technical and the business side of their industry means the loss of the annual increase of wealth that may reasonably be expected to be gained by them when fully trained. For rapid progress in this direction educated public opinion is necessary. It is of little use government embarking on a progressive policy if public opinion remains unprogressive. What is wanted is not the blind advocacy of proposals to reduce the demands upon the cultivator, but such progressive agricultural improvement as will enable the cultivator to pay these demands with increasing ease. The best means to this end, as has already been stated, are still to be discovered. Demonstration farms have their uses, but these uses are curiously misunderstood. So far back as 1876 the annual Land Administration Report contained the remark that "the experimental farm at Amritsar does not pay, and it is unlikely that it ever will be a financial success". An experimental farm is not intended to pay, nor is a demonstration farm. A farm that is intended to demonstrate methods of tillage, or new crops, or new seeds, serves its purpose if it demonstrates these things. A farm to demonstrate the financial side would be run on entirely different lines. Such a farm is advocated by Professor A. D. Hall, F.R.S., who writes: "There would seem to be room for the introduction of a new type of instruction in business methods by the setting up of demonstration farms run solely for profit, but which keep a strict set of accounts and make public the costs and results of every part of their work. (2) It is very doubtful if the Punjab is ripe for such a farm yet, as so little progress has hitherto been made in the study of Punjab Rural Economics that it would not be possible to determine either the size of the farm or the crops to be grown. For the present it would seem that the best method of arousing the interest of the cultivators would be to induce one or two of the most intelligent in each tehsil, zail or village to run his holding as a model farm, or at any rate to cultivate some fields on model lines. The Co-operative department is trying to popularize this.

Before leaving the subject of education, something must be said of the need for the development of those other faculties, beside mental alertness, that count for efficiency. It is unnecessary to dwell here on the great economic value of good health and physical fitness; and present knowledge does not, perhaps, enable a reliable estimate to be given of the extent to which the disinclination to prolonged hard work is to be ascribed to the prevalence of disease. But it is of little use imparting to cultivators the knowledge how to improve their economic position if they are unwilling or unable to put forth the extra exertion required in the use of it. Apart from these considerations, however, there are two others that strike the European observer. One is the low standard of manual dexterity shown by the ordinary cultivator and the other is his limited control over the animals he uses. The first may

(1) The selection and training of teachers alone will require several years.

(2) Agriculture after the War, p. 69. The Development Commission in England has recently agreed to advance £40,000 for demonstrations of the commercial success of dairy farming on purely arable land.

be in some measure due to the existence of village artisans paid by a customary share of the produce. In such circumstances the cultivator saves nothing but time by doing his own repairs and so has not developed much skill in the use of his fingers. The result is seen when any new implement is put into his hands and explains in some degree his disinclination to use these. If solid progress is to be made, considerable improvement must be effected in manual dexterity and in the cultivator's knowledge of the animals he uses and of his control over them.

Rural Leadership.

In the foregoing pages some attempt has been made to discuss that element in the production of wealth that is commonly referred to as enterprise. The province possesses ample land, labour and capital but, beyond these, there is required something else to bring them together in the right proportions and to make such use of them as will result in the highest possible production of wealth. It has been shown that the cultivator is inclined to regard his holding as a source from which his own household needs may be met and the revenue paid. He seldom sets himself to extract from it the maximum yield which every hour of labour and every rupee of capital he can put in would give. This attitude is, in some measure, accounted for by the drain to the town of the more intelligent and educated, and in further measure by the belief that the present system of education is of no value to him in his avocation. It has also been pointed out that for any considerable improvement in material prosperity there must somehow be inculcated into the cultivator's mind the idea of progress and the firm belief that progress to a better life is possible through his own exertions. The retrospective habit must be curbed ; history is eminently useful to show how to profit by past mistakes, and how to advance to new successes, but tales of past glories or past grievances, real or mythical, are not only of no economic value, they do positive economic harm when they absorb time, intellect and energy that could be devoted to constructive work. It is the future that has to be faced and not the past ; it is the future that attracts the self-reliant, the strong and the vigorous ; the past exercises a strange fascination over the weak, the lazy and the decadent.

Assuming, however, that all these principles acquire general acceptance, there will still remain one important faet without which most human beings are but as a flock of sheep. This factor is leadership. In a rural community the conditions of life militate against the development of this peculiarly valuable faculty. The most serious effect of the shift of the intelligent, enterprising and educated from country to town is the loss of leadership sustained by the countryside (1) and the decline of agriculture in Great Britain has been ascribed in part to the loss of young men with trained intelligence. (2) In many European countries the clergyman, the schoolmaster or the doctor have done what lay in their powers to stimulate the agriculturists to improve their position, and the clergy in particular have ardently supported the movement towards agricultural co-operation on account of its moral value. (3) In India this element has not been available, and beyond all doubt much of the present-

(1) *Cf.* Gillette : Constructive Rural Sociology.
(2) Hall : Agriculture after the War, p. 49.
(3) *Cf.* Plunkett : Rural Life Problems of the United States, p. 163.

day poverty, and much of the backwardness of the people are due to the lack of good leaders, men capable of taking hold of the commonest problems, of working them out to a practical solution and of convincing the people by actual demonstration that they were worthy of trust. To some extent, perhaps to a very large extent, present conditions may in turn be due to the absence of historical records. It is hardly possible that past generations have not contained men of unusual discernment or of a high constructive instinct, who grasped the pressing difficulties of the day and saw through them to a more advanced stage. But the conditions of life, the absence of any system of facile record, and the succession of invasions and political struggles prevented their wisdom from being accumulated, and passed on to the profit of others. "During the greater part of the life of the world", writes Professor Marshall, "most of the people have spent nearly the whole of their time in the fields: compact centres of life and thought were rare, and, before the days of printing, a scattered population had little opportunity for the stimulus and suggestion, which one man can derive from the thoughts and experiences of another. Tradition ruled; and particular experiences seldom developed into successive steps of cumulative progress. These facts go far to account for the slow progress of technique until recent times. It may be true that the native brain power of the individual has not greatly increased with the ages; and it is certainly true that emergency and opportunity have frequently proved agricultural populations to be strong in resource as well as in resolution. But yet the conditions of agricultural life have not been such as to bring to the front those men who had the faculty requisite for making great occasions for themselves; one reason for this being that the ownership of land has come by inheritance in a somewhat greater degree than the ownership of considerable industrial resources. Further, every agricultural problem has peculiarities of its own; and some sides of it can be mastered by shrewd, experienced, alert, instinctive judgment, better than by systematic reasoning based on ordered knowledge. Therefore the agriculturist has never been apt to search for the general in the particular, and the particular in the general. His instinct and insight have for the greater part died with him. The progress of his art remained for the greater part empirical until men trained in industry, or commerce, or in scientific schools, came to his aid." (1) In the history of English agriculture which is unusually rich in original detail very few names stand out as leaders in, say, the last 600 years. Of America it is said that the leadership of the rural regions is undeveloped or is largely lacking as compared with what could be expected of such a populous and wealthy portion of the nation;(2) and in general it has been found that the leaders of rural movements have not themselves been agriculturists. In industry it was a valuable faculty in the good employer that he could recognize among his workers those who possesssed the judgment and resource that would enable them to bear greater responsibilities with credit. In agriculture there is ordinarily no one amidst the small individual workers to select him who possesses the faculty of leadership and to set him in a place of authority. And yet the country requires leaders of constructive ability, it requires them to organize rural communities on business lines, it requires

(1) Industry and Trade, pp. 199, 200. The reference, of course, is to agriculture in general and not to India in particular.

(2) Gillette: Constructive Rural Sociology, p. 106.

them to show a way out of present difficulties and to construct for them the stairway to a higher plane of prosperity. The leader must be possessed of a solid foundation of agricultural knowledge ; the big landowners will never become leaders of their tenants and be able to develop their estates except by hard work and unremitting industry. The fairest and most perfect plan will fail unless leaders of the right type are forthcoming. Were the Punjab townsmen less preoccupied with other matters than agriculture and more soundly educated in rural affairs, their sharper intelligence and more developed capacities would incline to gain for them the vacant post, but until there is what may be called an educated laity in rural economics the leaders must be searched for amidst the villagers who understand rural conditions and rural communities. In this, again, the best hope rests in the Co-operative movement, which everywhere, as Sir Horace Plunkett testifies, brings to the front a new type of local leader, not the best talker, but the man whose knowledge enables him to make some solid contribution to the welfare of the community. (1) The scope is immense, but it will require time for the man of unusual discernment and capacity to discover himself and to be discovered by others. Already there are several enjoying the confidence of their fellows over a wide area who can take the lead in the simpler matters of organization, but there is as yet no indication of anyone coming forth fully equipped with the requisite technical knowledge as well as with the supreme gift ; and until the province can produce such men progress must largely depend on the activities of the trained official.

There is not, in this, any ground for pessimism. The tendency to concentrate thought on matters of a religious or spiritual nature may serve to explain the fact that India has produced few leaders in the economic sphere ; her people have only recently devoted themselves to the accumulation of wealth, and few have yet grown into giants of productive enterprise. Scientific agriculture was introduced into this province only a few years ago, and already it has several achievements of considerable value to its credit. A new generation is springing up to whom modern methods will appear less strange. Undoubtedly education is gaining in popularity, and may soon come to be recognized as a thing worth spending money on. From the interaction of Science, Education and Co-operation there may reasonably be expected to emerge leaders fully equipped with all the necessary qualifications. The present dependence upon official action and stimulus may rightly be regarded as a phase of progress. There are indications that the new leaders may achieve poor results from a tendency to too much diffusion of energy. Concentration is essential to economic progress. But concentration is hostile to evanescent popularity. What the province requires are men who will work at their own doors ; men who will strengthen their arguments by the demonstration of accomplished fact ; and who will therefore concentrate on the accomplishment before they embark on the argument. Success breeds imitation. The real leader must know in what success consists if he is to lead along the difficult road of constructive economic progress.

---

(1) Rural Life Problems of the United States, p. 123. History shows that rural leaders need not be drawn from expert cultivators. Arthur Young was not a successful farmer; Raiffeisen was not a farmer at all. True, some of the biggest names in English agricultural history are those of landowners, but the exceptions should encourage men of original genius, even if they possess no land.

CHAPTER III.

WHY DOES THE CULTIVATOR CULTIVATE ?

A Study in Elementary Rural Economics. What is the Land for ? What should the Cultivator do with his Land, and with his Capital ? Wants and their Satisfaction. The divergence of interest. The Market determines production.

The question "why does the cultivator cultivate ?" may appear at first hearing one of those flippant riddles with a catch in the answer or with no answer at all beyond a further puzzle. It is, however, put seriously. It is, and it is intended to be, a reference to one of the most important problems which every country has to decide. For agriculture is still the largest and most important single industry, not only in the world, but in nearly every country in the world. Even in England, Scotland and Wales, industries are confined to well-defined areas. There are large tracts given up almost wholly to this calling. Three-fourths of Ireland are for the most part dependent upon this one source of wealth. France possesses industries in the North-West, where the Germans made their onslaught ; elsewhere she is dependent upon her soil for her annual income. South-West of Paris there are to be found only such industries as are themselves dependent upon the produce of the well-tilled fields. In Germany there are industries where there are to be found iron, coal, or some other special local advantage. Throughout the greater part of that empire agriculture is the chief means of livelihood. It would be easy to continue the recital in connection with other countries ; all have the same tale to tell ; America has one State, New York, with large scale industries ; for the rest it may be said that there is no State whose industrial output exceeds that of one single big town Japan looms large these days in the minds of Indians ; the chief industry of that miserably impoverished country is agriculture ; next in order is sericulture ; the factory industries supply, or attempt to supply, foreign demand for cheap goods, they do not rêly on the home market. It is one of the peculiar results of the modern system of education that it encourages the concentration of attention upon manufacturing industries and ignores the chief, the oldest and the most vital industry of all. It may be freely admitted that economists are guilty of participating in this offence, for nearly all accentuate the problems of the commercial and factory system, and neglect those that await solution from the silent tiller of the soil. Although the land is everywhere and by everybody acknowledged to be the chief source of national wealth, there is an almost universal disposition to neglect the simplest questions that its use gives rise to. Take one. "What is the land for ?" What should be done with the land in this country ? What is its part in the life of the nation ? The question sounds simple enough ; but the answer is difficult to discover. If current literature be studied, there will be detected a number of theories never quite openly expressed but always present in the minds of the writers, that somehow do not clear up the real problems.

An opinion, commonly held here and elsewhere, is that the land exists to provide food for the towns, that it is the duty of the cultivator to supply ghi, milk, and wheat, all at cheap rates, to those who form the urban population. (1) There is not recognised any reciprocal liability on the part of the townsman to buy from the cultivator, if, say, wheat from Australia is cheaper. This idea is leading now, as it led in England some centuries ago, to a demand for restrictions on the export of wheat from the province, so that, even though the cultivator suffers, the townsman will gain. There was something similar in England during the war, when farmers were told to grow wheat instead of cows. In that case, there was a crisis to be met and a war to be won ; but here the idea that the land exists to feed the towns existed prior to the war and exists still to-day. Another idea is that the land is put there to produce the material for trade and commerce, and, accordingly, if any of this material can be used for industries, it should be sold at a cheap rate to factory owners. Those who hope to start mills for making cloth are agitating for an export duty on cotton, so that it will become cheaper even although the cultivator suffers ; they are also urging the imposition of a protective duty on imported cloth, so that they will be able to sell their cloth at a dear rate. The cultivator will suffer a second time when he buys cloth ; but that is what he is there for. Sometimes, the idea is put forward that the land exists to afford allotments to agricultural labourers, so that their wages can be kept low, sometimes it is suggested than the land should be used to provide employment for those who are unable to earn a living in the towns ; at present this idea is being pressed in order to find work for those who have been demobilised. In Italy, the land is regarded as a means of affording relief for those who cannot get enough work all the year round. This idea that the land exists to supply employment appears in several forms in different countries ; and it is very popular with some writers, who seem to think that all that is required is to put a man on to a few acres and leave him there to do what he can without capital, training or experience.

Then, there is the idea present in books, if not anywhere else, that the land is a breeding ground for a fine race of men, who are to go and do whatever fighting may be necessary ; while the weaker townsman can stay at home and make large profits from his business. Some such idea dominated Germany's agrarian policy for many years. There is a sound basis for this idea. Somewhere or other, there must be a supply of men of good physique who can be drawn upon in time of need, and work on the soil tends to produce such men. A government for this reason must keep a watchful eye on the progress of agriculture and must always be prepared to undertake measures to secure a happy and prosperous body of cultivators. If there be any danger of such a decline as would lead many to abandon the land for the towns, agriculture cannot be left entirely to the play of economic forces. Connected with this is the idea that the land must be well peopled in order than there may be a sufficient supply of men and women to maintain the towns. The town born population tends to decline. The birth rate is lower and the death rate higher than in the country ; so that if there were no migration from village to city the latter would run a risk of becoming depopulated. Those who are pressing for the encouragement of industries regard the villages as the source of labour. (2)

(1) *Cf.* a witness before the Fiscal Commission said the people had a *right* to wheat at 16 sers to the rupee.

(2) It has been said that industrial employment devours its children in, on the average, three generations. *Cf.* also the exploitation of girl labour in Japan.

The land must produce children, feed them bring them up, pay for their education and then make a free gift of them to the factories. To a considerable extent this actually happens in some countries. In the British Isles the farmers complain against the education rate because they say they pay for the education of those who drift to the towns, so that the towns get their labour educated at the expense of the country. Thus, there are a variety of purposes to which some one or other thinks the land ought to be put ; and if they are examined it will be seen that they all hinge on the idea that the land exists for the good of the towns ; it must supply labour when the towns require it and absorb labour when the towns cannot employ it ; it must produce fighting men when the country is in danger and take back the cripples when the danger is past ; it must produce food when imported food is dear, and must accept loss when imported food is cheap. It must supply the commodities required in commerce and the raw material needed in manufactures,but if imported raw material is found to be cheaper than the home grown variety, then the land must not demand protection against the rival article. In short, the land has many duties to the State, but no right to consideration when the townsman prefers to neglect it.

From these various ideas, it becomes clear that there are many interests which to some extent conflict. The manufacturer wants his raw material cheap, the cultivator wants the highest price he can secure for his produce ; the trader and merchant want the biggest volume of trade and commerce, and therefore the highest outturn ; the cultivator must look less to outturn than to profits ; the townspeople want food sufficient for their needs ; the cultivator may find that food crops pay him less than some other crops, such as oilseeds or cotton. The industrialist naturally enough desires the mass of the people to purchase and use the articles he manufactures, the mass of the people want the best value for their money. It is this conflict of interest which is referred to in the cry of town *versus* country ; it is as old as towns are. As soon as a portion of the population in any country took to trade, to distribution, to marketing, or to manufacture, and collected in towns, there very soon arose this conflict of interests. This is easy to understand. But what is not so easy to understand is why the townsman expects the cultivator to be influenced by considerations different from those that guide the activities of other workers. In this country, for some unknown reason, agriculture is not even regarded as an industry. There is a cry for industries, but when it is pointed out that there already exists the oldest, the most important and the largest industry in the world, there is almost a sneer at the thought that agriculture can be regarded as quite a respectable calling. In the towns, it is almost universally considered that no intelligence is required for the cultivation of the land ; that it offers no scope for the educated ; that it is good enough for the illiterate and for the unskilled labourer but is quite impossible for the young man from college. This idea is not found in this province only, but is to be found in almost every country where there are educated me n to hold it. American writers in particular are insistent in calling attention to it ; British authors deplore it ; and elsewhere, those who have given thought to the immense possibilities opened out to the highly trained scientific man by modern discoveries unite in denouncing this view of agriculture as something good enough for serfs and clodhoppers, but quite out of the question as a career for young men with a good education. Now when it is remembered that agriculture is, and must remain the main source of new wealth in this province, that there is even now more scope for increasing wealth in this line than in any industry that has ever been suggested, this attitude of the educated becomes important, and it is necessary to probe the matter with a view to arrive at a better understanding of the real facts.

There are several reasons for this attitude : the cultivator himself does not yet bring to his task much brain, intelligence, or education ; he, too, thinks that the educated son should go to the town as there is no scope for his education in the tilling of the soil ; and the most important questions relating to agriculture are neglected by the people who would benefit most from a proper understanding of them. A manufacturer of cloth, or ships, or of railway material, or of almost any other article, makes his goods in accordance with the orders he receives. A man does not make a ship in the hope that a purchaser will come along and buy it. A man does not make railway engines in the hope that someone or other will want them, and even in the manufacturing of cloth orders in advance determine the purchase of cotton, and the enlistment of labour. The cultivator, however, works to a time table fixed by nature. It is no use to him that a demand arises for wheat after the time for sowing has passed away. He cannot put his fields on half time ; he cannot wait to sow until a purchaser is found. He must adapt himself to a general demand for this or for that crop, and try to grow what he knows he can sell. (1) It seems to be this difference between the manufacturer and the cultivator that leads the townsman to entertain the belief that the cultivator will go on growing wheat or cotton, whether the price of these is artificially brought low or not. He does not know why the cultivator cultivates ; he assumes that he will just go on cultivating no matter what is done against his interests in the way of interference with his right to sell his produce to the highest bidder. The townsman does not understand Rural Economics.

But the townsman is not altogether to blame for his omission to make himself acquainted with the proper answer to the question " Why does the cultivator cultivate ?" the cultivator himself is not quite certain ; he would find difficulty in explaining the reasons for his own actions. The fact is that agriculture in this province has not yet been placed upon a proper economic basis ; and there is not at present any opportunity afforded either to practical cultivators or to students to learn how to put it on to this basis. To explain what is meant, the question " Why does the cultivator cultivate ?" may be put in another way ; let it be assumed that there is a young man starting life with capital for which he seeks some suitable investment ; he may prefer something in the industrial line, but finds that there are at present not the knowledge, the skill, and the organisation which are necessary if risk of loss is to be avoided. He next considers the prospects of agriculture, and finds that he is confronted with some difficult questions. Should he invest his capital in the purchase of land, and try to cultivate as best he can without any further expenditure ? Or should he invest only a portion in purchase and keep

---

(1) *Cf.* the efforts of the cotton planters of America to stabilise their profits from cotton by limiting the outturn to regular trade demands ; similarly with rubber, and some other special products.

some for current needs ? If so, then how much should he invest in the one and how much keep for the other ?(1) Or should he take a lease of land and utilise all his capital on agricultural operations ? Should he buy a small plot and put all his remaining capital into the intensive cultivation of it ? Or should he buy as much as he can and try his luck with extensive cultivation? Should he search for the most fertile plot he can find, in the hope of extracting therefrom an easy livelihood ? Or should he bear in mind Thorold Rogers' dictum that "The real fertility of the land is the progressive skill of the husbandman. The richest soil may be exhausted by overcropping......the poorest, if it be capable of improvement, may be made a garden by judicious treatment." (2) If he adopts this, he may decide to buy land capable of improvement and to devote every ounce of energy, every anna of capital and every bit of brain and intelligence he possesses to its exploitation. If this young man, anxious to embark upon a career, elects to look around him before coming to a final decision, he will find many things that need explanation. Here is a man with 25 acres, why does he cultivate only half and let the remainder on rent ? Does he get more from the rent than he would by cultivating it himself ? On the portion he cultivates, he expends little capital, why does he not concentrate upon a small portion and cultivate a few fields well and let the rest on rent ? Instead of ploughing two fields eight times each, why does he not plough one sixteen times ? If this imaginary young man is given much to thought he will soon find so many questions that demand some sort of answer that his life could be spent in investigating them. In short, a young man with capital, about to embark upon a career in agriculture, must know something of rural economics or he will pay for his ignorance.

But throughout the Punjab the problem generally assumes a different shape. A young man finds that he has inherited a little land and some potential capital in the form of jewels ; and the question arises : should he cultivate that land or should he let it on rent and seek a livelihood in the town ? Should he sell those jewels and spend the money on the land or bury it for safety. If he decides to stay on his ancestral holding, he is confronted with still more problems. His father cultivated wheat. Should he cultivate wheat ? Why did his father grow wheat ? Should he resolutely plod along the same way or try to strike out a new line ? He sees one neighbour with fifteen acres growing wheat ; he is told that as the land depends upon the rainfall, wheat is the best crop to grow as it has deep roots and so resists drought well. A short distance away, another man with only four acres and a well is also growing wheat. He explains that as he has a well, wheat is the best crop to grow. In another direction is a canal, and there also the cultivators are growing wheat ; they explain that, as the land is canal-irrigated, wheat is the best crop to grow. Should he grow wheat also or try some other crop ? Can the same crop be best for *barani*, *chahi*, *nahri* lands ? What is meant by the *best* crop? The biggest yielder, the most profitable, the best seller, or the easiest to produce ? Some writers assert that wheat does not afford much scope for

(1) In England, in the fourteenth century, the stock of a well-cultivated estate was on an average three times the value of the soil (Thorold Rogers, Vol. 1.) It is possible that in the Punjab under Sikh rule the stock was more valuable than the land. In some parts of the western districts this is still the case.

(2) History of Agriculture and Prices, Vol. V, p. 99.

the scientific farmer, that it does not respond so well to scientific treatment as other crops, so that while it is good enough for the lazy and the ignorant, it should be avoided by men of education, skill and capital. There are some who would like to see wheat disappear from canal-irrigated lands, and be replaced by crops which would pay a higher water-rate. There are some who believe that to grow wheat on land irrigated by wells under the control of the cultivator ought to be regarded as a crime against the spirit of progress. Why does the cultivator grow wheat?

These are not idle questions ; they are absolutely vital to the progress of this province. It is not sufficient that a cultivator should possess a thorough knowledge of technical and scientific matters relating to his land and his crops ; production is not the end but the means ; it is only a part, a very important part, but still only a part, of what a cultivator ought to know. The answer to the question "Why does the cultivator cultivate ?" is not "to produce crops", but "to make a living" and as he wants to go on living he cannot afford to eat up his capital, and so must live on the profits of his labour, his land and his capital. (1) The cultivator cultivates to make profits, and the sensible cultivator cultivates in order to get the highest profits he can. He is not a philanthropist who loves to work that the town may be fed ; nor is he a slave who is compelled to work in order that the town may be fed. In fact, the feeding of the town is not the object of his labours at all ; the town is the market for his produce, it is the market from which he seeks to derive his profits.

Cultivators, then, cultivate in order to satisfy their wants. Man is continually wanting something, and so is continually seeking satisfaction for his wants. The wants vary with the man, and with the conditions under which he lives. It is his wants and his circumstances which determine his work. It is a very important characteristic of man that he is disinclined to work any more than is necessary to satisfy his wants. If his wants are few, and are easily satisfied, he does little work ; as his wants increase, he has to work harder. In other words the standard of living at which he aims determines the amount of work he is prepared to do.

This general statement requires some modification in this province. Almost all the cultivators have inherited the land which they cultivate ; they did not deliberately choose agriculture as the way to earn their living. The result is that many cultivate because they do not know any other way of getting a living ; they are forced by circumstances to work on the land. In other words, to some extent, agriculture is a sweated industry ; it yields a bare livelihood to many, who only continue on the land because they do not know what else to do. They get food, and some clothing and practically nothing else ; they seem unable to improve their condition.

Apart from these, there are a large number of others who seek a little more than food and clothing ; and a careful examination of their activities will show how wants determine the amount of work they are prepared to do. One who owns 50 acres of irrigated land could secure quite a good living from

(1) It is a mistake to say that the cultivator lives on the produce of his land ; he lives on the surplus after costs of production have been met.

it, but he rents half of it to someone else. Why does he do that ? Why does he not cultivate the lot ? Because although he may want more things than he has got, he does not want them quite so much as he wants leisure. His aversion from too much work is greater than the want he feels for something else. Indeed, if he inherited 50 more acres, he would probably let the whole out on rent and do no work at all. He would prefer to limit his satisfactions rather than increase his income by working; the cultivator ceases to cultivate when his wants can be satisfied without his cultivating.

Take another case; there is up and down the province lots of land remaining uncultivated; if it be asked why this is so, the answer will be that there are not enough tenants. There are tenants in the neighbourhood, but they do not want to cultivate more than they already have. They are probably poor, they could increase their income, but they would rather limit their wants than put forth extra exertion. (1)

One more example may be given. A celebrated English writer, Arthur Young, once visited France (1787-89), and was much impressed with the excellent cultivation he saw there; he described how wretched sand had been converted into garden land by incessant industry, and remarked that "the magic of property turns sand into gold." He was accustomed to the large farms in England cultivated by tenants, and thought that the great improvements effected in this sandy soil was due to the fact that those who worked on it were the proprietors, and that it was this ownership that was responsible for the great labour expended. The real explanation is more probably this: in England the farmer had a large holding, so that the profits required to satisfy the wants of himself and his family were derived from a larger area, and therefore the average profit per acre might be small, but the total would be large. In France, the holdings were tiny, the same wants for husband, wife and family had to be satisfied from a much smaller area, so that the average profit per acre had to be large. The French cultivator did not work hard because he liked doing it or merely from the desire to improve his land; he had to work hard or starve; he had to improve his land because unless it were improved it would not yield him enough for his needs. There is no magic about property at all; (2) it was not the property but the small size of it and its natural infertility that made the owner work hard and turn the sand into gold. If those owners whom Arthur Young saw had possessed large estates they would probably have let their property on rent and lived in idleness on the proceeds.

From what has gone before, it should now be clear that the cultivator cultivates to satisfy his wants. The means he employs are the production of crops and the keeping of cattle. To produce crops and to keep cattle involves expenditure, and this expenditure must be recouped from the sale of the crops or of the milk and *ghi* before the cultivator can afford to take anything for himself: that is to say, the cultivator satisfies his wants,

(1) In 1868 it was noted that each agriculturist on the average cultivated only $2\frac{1}{6}$ acres out of 4 acres available. But as profits became more assured the average area cultivated by each increased considerably.

(2) It is security of tenure that the cultivator requires rather than property.

not from his cattle or from his crops, but from the surplus left over after meeting all the expenses of producing those crops and feeding those cattle. The cultivator lives on the profits of his industry ; he cultivates for profit, and it is the expectation of profit that stimulates him to labour. Reduce that profit and the stimulus to labour is reduced also ; take away that profit and the incentive to work disappears.

This may sound elementary, but it is important, and unfortunately it is apt to be forgotten. Restrictions on the free trade in wheat are advocated in order that the price may fall ; the cultivator would lose a part of the price which free competition would give him and the townsman would gain cheaper wheat ; but the loss to the cultivator would come from his profits, and would diminish the incentive to grow wheat ; unless the price of other articles was decreased at the same time, the effect might be to render wheat production unprofitable. Similarly the suggestion that the export of cotton from India should be prohibited in order that Indian manufacturers might get cheap cotton for their mills, would reduce the profits on cotton growing and would tend to remove the incentive to produce it. It must be remembered that the cultivator will not cultivate if his wants can be satisfied without labour, or with less labour ; that there is land lying idle now because the people can satisfy their wants without it ; that many would rather reduce their satisfactions than increase their exertions, and it becomes clear that anything that tends to diminish the incentive to labour tends also to diminish the production of crops.

In this country it is particularly noticeable that people will accept a low standard of living with small exertions rather than strive after a higher standard by greater exertions.

It has been pointed out above that the cultivator regards the town as the market for his surplus produce. If he were sufficiently expert in the technical aspects of his calling, he would devote himself more to that use of his land which would yield the greatest profit, and rely upon the town markets for his food. So far from it being his duty to feed the towns, he should not grow food-grains at all if other crops paid better ; provided always that food was easily obtainable from others. The point which it is here desired to emphasise is that the cultivator is as much an industrialist as is the manufacturer ; he is no more bound to grow what his neighbours want to eat, than is a manufacturer bound to make what his neighbours want to use, and he should have and exercise the same free choice as to the disposal of his produce.

If it be clearly understood that the cultivator cultivates for the highest profit, then many ideas concerning the land become untenable. Germany employs more men on the soil per hundred acres than does England, and, in consequence of the use of more labour, obtains a higher yield per acre, but the English farmer secures the higher profit per man. The yield of wheat per acre is far higher in England than in the United States, but the yield per man is greater in America. The common measure of yield in maunds per acre is a test of production per acre ; it gives little clue to the real state of agriculture, it does not indicate profits per acre or profits per man employed. (1).

The essential points may be illustrated as follows :—

Gross outturn per acre, less costs of production per acre, equals nett profit per acre.

Gross outturn per holding, less costs of production per holding, equals nett profit per holding.

Gross outturn per man, less costs of production per man, equals nett profit per man.

For trade and commerce, it is usually desirable that the gross outturn should be as large as possible, as this provides the maximum amount of commodities to be dealt in ; an owner who takes rent in kind (*batai*) wants the maximum yield per acre ; the cultivator is only concerned with maximum profits. If he works by himself, it is maximum nett profit on his holding that he seeks ; if he employs hired labour, it is highest nett profit per man that he should aim at. A Government which claims a share in the nett profit per acre looks to this aspect and not to the profit per holding ; whereas, were profits from land subject to Income Tax, it would be the profit per holding that would interest the Collector. In actual practice, the highest yields per acre generally afford the highest profits per acre, as the cultivator seldom, if ever, reaches a stage where the diminishing returns cause loss ; but these do not always give the highest yields per man or the highest profits per man, which more nearly concern the cultivator. It is this difference in the test which accounts for the divergence of view apparent amongst writers. They see different aspects and forget why the cultivator cultivates. Where there is no export trade, an increase of produce per acre may lead to a diminution of the area sown, as the local demand may be thus met. Thus the problems involved in the question as to what the cultivator should do to get the highest profits are many and intricate. They require for their solution accurate knowledge of so many subjects that the science of Agricultural Economics or Rural Economics becomes a special study ; or, ought to, for it is much neglected. Every locality possesses some special facilities for the production of some crop ; and that locality will become the wealthiest which can devote itself to the production of this crop. It is not always a matter of technical skill alone ; this will enable the farmer to grow a crop which will win a prize at a show, but if he could not find a market for it he would soon come to grief in spite of his technical skill. The crop for which the locality is best suited is not always the one which can be grown, for there are several other considerations that determine the decision of the cultivator as to what he should grow. Where communications are defective, as in such a place as Kulu, it is necessary to limit the production of fruit to so much as can be readily sold, and, instead, to grow food-grains, often of inferior type. In England, with well-organised communications with every other country, it is possible to import wheat and other foods, and to concentrate on what will pay better, such as milk production, or the small garden fruits. In the Punjab some fruits will grow well, but this province is so far removed from the sea that it will always have to produce the larger portion of the food required for the

(1) The history of cotton cultivation shows that production may increase without any total increase in value ; increase of yield per acre does not necessarily cause either an increase in value of the crop per acre, or an increase in profits per acre.

people, while it would be difficult to find a market for all the fruit it could produce. It is this consideration which makes wheat such an important crop ; it is not the one which is most profitable for any single cultivator, but for the mass it ranks high as a paying crop, because there is always a market for it. Thus the original question as to "Why does the cultivator cultivate ?" leads to the study of the problems of marketing ; the market determines production.

In California, where food can be brought in from outside, it is possible for the farmers to concentrate upon the production of fruit, and to find a market for all they can grow by highly specialised organisation, which in turn is made possible by good communications. In Denmark it is possible for the land to be devoted to cattle and cattle products, because this country has good sea communications and has also a large market for its special products in the British Isles. Similarly, in Holland, parts of France and the Channel Islands, the land is devoted to growing fruit, flowers and other specialities for the English market. Thus the market determines what shall be grown. The production of wool in Australia and New Zealand illustrates the influence of distant markets ; wool is very valuable for its bulk, and accordingly, when pressed in bales, it can be transported long distances at a comparatively small cost in proportion to its price. Australian land could produce more wheat, but this if carried to England would have to compete with wheat from Canada, whereas Canada does not produce wool, and the Australian produce accordingly fetches a good price. There are of course, other factors involved, but these do not detract from the essential truth of the dictum that the market determines production. (1).

The chief thing essential for everyone is food. Where the whole world can be drawn upon for the supply, the local farmers can trust to being able to buy their food, and grow what will yield the higher profit. But for the country as a whole there must be adequate assurance that sufficient food will be available for the whole population. The farmer may not find food production as profitable as other crops, because the effect of competition with food-grains imported from other countries may bring down the price so low as to leave him little or no profit. As man must have food, he will pay almost whatever price is demanded rather than do without it ; if food from abroad is subjected to a protective duty, it may become more profitable to grow it at home. That is to say the cultivator may be persuaded into growing what ordinarily would not yield much profit by measures designed to increase those profits. Government might, as it did recently in England, guarantee such a price for wheat as will ensure a good profit from its production. The point to bear in mind is that as the cultivator cultivates for profits, his profits must be increased if he is to be induced to cultivate more than he does at present. Restrictions on export will lead to decreased production ; if the towns wish to be certain of an adequate supply of food at all times, they should press for those measures which will increase the profits of the cultivator. But they are not likely to do this until they thoroughly understand the correct answer to the question "Why does the cultivator cultivate ?"

(1) The demand for fodder from a big town like Lahore results in several villages almost confining themselves to the growing of these crops. All big towns exert a dominating influence on the use to which the surrounding land is devoted.

CHAPTER IV.

The Economic Position of the Punjab.

Geographical Position : Roads, Railways and Canals : Increase in Trade.

No discussion of the economics of a country can proceed very far without a clear understanding of its geographical position. No person produces all he requires, he is dependent upon someone else for one article or service or other ; no country produces all the goods its people require in the exact proportion in which they require them. There is always a surplus or a deficiency, and the disposal of this surplus and the supply of this deficiency constitute the foreign trade, appearing respectively as the exports and the imports. There is a widely held belief in some quarters that exports produce weakness, while imports indicate existing weakness. It seems to be thought that what is exported should be retained in the country to benefit its inhabitants, and to lower prices; while what is imported should be produced within its own borders. In a normal year the Punjab produces more wheat than its people require for their own consumption, (1) and the amount in excess of current needs is exported. It is of little importance to the producer or to the merchant whether this surplus is sold to England or to Bengal ; it is sold to the highest bidder, and that is good for both. In discussing the Punjab, it is not necessary to enter into the question whether India as a whole produces less than her people require for the full maintenance of health and efficiency. The people of this province are for the most part wheat-eaters, and the fact that large quantities of wheat are exported may be accepted as proof that an actual surplus exists. Whatever may be true of the rest of India, there can be no doubt in this province at any rate the production of food is increasing faster than the population. Were there no outlet, no purchaser, for this surplus, it would not be produced. The cultivation of land requires the expenditure of energy and capital, and if there were no return for part of this expenditure, the agriculturist would not put forth that amount of energy or waste that portion of capital.

In the opinion of some people this surplus wheat should not be exported. If the reply be made that in that case it would not be grown, it is argued that the labour and time thus saved should be devoted to the production of those things that are now imported. This argument based upon a strangely complete misunderstanding of the whole requirements of a country's prosperity, ignores the importance of geographical position and all that is bound up with it. If any country is to become prosperous, its people must concentrate upon the production of those things which all its circumstances combine to enable it

(1) For a discussion of the subject see Prof. Kale's Indian Economics, 3rd Edition. p. 160 ff. By ignoring some very obvious facts, it is possible to paint quite a dismal picture. Sir James Wilson, in 1910, estimated the annual surplus of the Punjab at 1½ million tons of food-grains.

to produce to the greatest advantage, or at least to the greatest profit. It is not a question as to whether it is technically possible to produce in the Punjab this or that article that is now imported from some other province or country ; but whether the substitution of this or that article for something now produced in excess of local requirements would yield the greater profit. Most countries have characteristics that render the production of some things easy and of others difficult. Climate, natural resources, geographical situation determine to a considerable extent the ends to which the energies of the people are directed. Until transport and communications attained something approaching their present efficiency, there were many places where people continued to produce things for the production of which local conditions were not well adapted ; with the steady improvement in communications and the cheapening of transport, competition has tended to drive out local industries from places whose special conditions did not favour their continuance and to concentrate them where there are unusually valuable facilities. It thus becomes of great importance that a close study should be made of the special local conditions of the Punjab enforced by its geographical position. The latter cannot be changed, although it is possible to imagine measures which would enhance the advantages or mitigate the disadvantages. If progress is to be stimulated, all the conditions precedent to such an effort must be clearly understood and their influence defined. In promoting industries, for instance, the technical problems may be the easiest to solve ; the cost of production is an important factor but not necessarily the most important. For success, the commodity must be transported to the consumer and must by its quality, price, etc., prove not less attractive to him than competing commodities open to purchase at the same time and place. The Punjab could grow other things in place of wheat, oranges for instance, that would yield a higher nett profit per acre and of considerably greater gross value ; but it is far from certain that a satisfactory market could be found for all that could be produced. It is this problem of markets that will exercise a determining influence on the future development of agriculture and industries. If the province is to compete successfully with rival areas it must have in its favour some advantage that the other areas do not possess in the same degree. That is to say, the province will have to devote its attention, not to articles which people would prefer to make, but to articles for the manufacture of which its local conditions are in some special measure adapted. Sentiment may influence sales in the home market, more material considerations will affect trade in foreign cities. It is the consumer who will determine whether the Punjab shall manufacture cloth for export, and it is the consumer who will have the last word in the development of industries whose outturn exceeds the local demand. The access to possible markets is thus a matter for serious study. Japan consists of islands with a large number of good harbours, giving free passage to the continents of Asia and America ; its State-stimulated industries depend for their existence on the export trade, there being comparatively little consumption of the manufactured articles at home ; the effect is to place Japanese industries at the mercy of the foreign consumer, and, when the foreign consumer rejected the shoddy stuff that was submitted, an acute industrial crisis resulted. China is situated within easy distance of Japanese harbours and the profits of transport are earned by the

Japanese ; but, unfortunately for the people of this province, the markets for its produce are distant, and the profits to be derived from transporting them thither are likely to go into the pockets of other than Punjabis.

The province is completely landlocked, it possesses no rivers, navigable for even medium size craft, giving it access to the sea ; (1) and it suffers from the further disadvantage of being bounded on three sides by countries that offer no markets for its products. The province, in fact, represents a densely populated peninsula thrust north-westward into a very sparsely populated area. On the north lie Kashmir, Ladakh and Tibet and beyond these again the deserts of Turkestan. On the west are Afghanistan and Baluchistan and beyond these Persia. On the south lie Bikaner and Rajputana, comparatively sparsely populated and undeveloped. In all these countries there is not the number of consumers required to make them valuable markets for Punjab produce. With them there will not, for many years, be any great volume of trade.

On the East, the United Provinces present a rich market but the two areas are so similar in soil, climate and people, that they produce similar commodities, and so compete with each other for customers.

The geographical position of the Punjab has had, and must continue to have, very far-reaching consequences. Its corner position, amidst comparative deserts, prevents it from having any considerable through trade and deprives its people of the opportunity, so important in England, of acquiring wealth as middle men and carriers of trade across its frontiers. (2) Prior to the advent of the railway, such trade as existed was almost confined to Afghanistan and Central Asia, but it was never of great value or of great volume, and has shown little, if any, capacity for expansion. There was practically no trade of importance with Bombay and very little with Karachi. The rulers of the province who preceded the British were not great road builders ; stone metalling was practically unknown ; the great rivers were unbridged ; organised transport facilities did not exist. In time of plenty grain was cheap to an extent as almost to be unsaleable, for there was no market for the surplus ; in time of scarcity grain could not be imported from distant places and starvation resulted. Even now, the rivers impose serious obstacles to commerce where bridges do not exist. The Jumna from Delhi to Ambala can only be crossed by ferry, and no considerable traffic adopts this method. On the West, the Indus imposes a still more difficult barrier. For several months in a normal year, when the five internal rivers are in flood, there is very little trade across them except by rail or bridge.

In the absence of organised facilities for transport, the need for an adequate network of communications assumes supreme importance (an importance now recognised by the constitution of a permanent Board of Communications); in the absence of a modern transport system, highly specialised agriculture

(1) That is to say no rivers so suitable for light traffic as are the rivers of Europe. There is a great deal of misunderstanding in India due to the different connotations of the same word when used by Europeans and Indians.

(2) Holland supplies a contrast: up till recently it had no mineral resources, few manufactures, no highly organised agriculture and yet grew prosperous as carrier and middleman. Its geographical position was its chief asset.

is impossible far from the big towns. For many agricultural products nearness to market is essential. Good communications foster good cultivation; the market determines production; a weak market retards and a strong market stimulates progress. Until there were constructed railways and metalled roads, there was no possibility of attaining highly intensive agriculture away from the immediate neighbourhood of the towns. The first railway line was put under construction in 1856, and opened for traffic in 1861. (1) Wood had to be used as fuel. The line from Lahore to Multan, which at that time was connected with Karachi by the boats of the old Indus Flotilla, was opened in 1865. Coal was introduced in 1872, in which year one goods train left Lahore daily for Ghaziabad. Through communication with Calcutta and Bombay was established in 1883. Thereafter progress was steady, if not rapid, as the following details show (2) :—

Main Line.—

South to Lahore	231	miles, opened in	1870
Lahore to West	418	ditto	1878
Lahore to North	242	ditto	1880

Branches.—

Golra-Basal	47	miles, opened in	1881
Amritsar-Pathankot	67	ditto	1884
Rajpura-Bhatinda	107	ditto	1889
Sind-Sagar	342	ditto	1890
Sialkot (1884) Jammu	36	ditto	1890
Raewind-Ferozepur	33	ditto	1892
Southern Punjab, main line	400	ditto	1897
Narwana-Kaithal	23	ditto	1899
Kundian-Campbellpur	120	ditto	1899
Ferozepur-Bhatinda	55	ditto	1899
Wazirabad-Khanewal	201	ditto	1900
Ludhiana-Jakhal	79	ditto	1901
Kalka-Simla	59	ditto	1903
Ludhiana-Macleod ganj	152	ditto	1906
Jech-Doab	149	ditto	1906
Shahdara-Sangla	55	ditto	1907
Khanewal-Lodhran	56	ditto	1909
Amritsar-Patti (1906) Kasur	54	ditto	1910
Kasur-Lodhran	208	ditto	1910
Khanpur-Chachran	22	ditto	1911
Chichoki-Shorkot Road	136	ditto	1911

The effect of cheap transport is to make it profitable to grow more than the local demand absorbs. As markets must be reached before sales can be effected, internal development depends upon the existence of markets within reach or upon the bringing of distant markets within the area of profitable

---

(1) Another account says the line from Amritsar to Lahore began working on April 10th, 1862.

(2) From the Report on the Administration of the Punjab and its Dependencies for 1911-12. In that year there were 4,043 miles of railway in operation in the Punjab, of which 307 miles were double track.

trade. Until railways were provided to carry surplus produce to distant markets, it would have been of small advantage to press forward measures calculated to increase production; it is obvious that if the additional food-grains grown could not find a market, there would result no profit from the growing of it and it would not be grown. (1) There was thus no advantage in pushing on the construction of canals ahead of the provision of railway facilities; while at the same time, until there was the mass of commercial commodities to move, the building of railways would hardly prove profitable. The two works were mutually inter-dependent, and their construction year by year rendered possible the rapid development of the province which is such a conspicuous feature of the history of the last fifty years.

The Bari Doab Canal was opened in 1859, (2) and the Sirhind Canal in 1870. Thereafter progress was rapid as the following figures show :—

DEVELOPMENT OF THE PUNJAB. (3)

Year.		Railway mileage.	Canal mileage.	Miles of metalled roads.	Cultivated area million acres.	Land revenue rupees.
1872-3	..	410	2,744	1,036	18·8	201 lakhs.
1882-3	..	600	4,583	1,467	23·4	206 do.
1892-3	..	1,725	12,368	2,142	26·7	223 do.
1902-3	..	..	16,893	..	26·8	230 do.
1912-13	..	4,000	16,935	2,614	29	360 do.
1919-20	..	4,441	19,664	2,938	30	400 do.

The railways, with unimportant exceptions, enter and leave the province at the four corners; the lateral boundaries are practically uncrossed. Almost all the lines now constitute one system, the North-Western Railway, the largest under single management in the world. The province is served by about 660 stations, or approximately one to every 50 villages and towns. It is not easy to state the cost of the lines within the province,

---

(1) The truth of this simple argument is sufficiently obvious, but as it is apt to conflict with what some people would prefer to believe it is frequently ignored. The fact is that no surplus was grown. The area cultivated per cultivator was very small, but as soon as communications with markets which could absorb the surplus were established, this average area began to increase. The facts are on record and are not open to serious dispute.

(2) *i. e.*, water was admitted; regular irrigation does not appear to have commenced before 1860.

(3) In an article contributed to the Royal Economic Society in 1910, under the title of "Recent Economic Developments in the Punjab", Sir James Wilson gave the following figures and comments :—

		1886-7.	1908-9.
Average area under cultivation (millions of acres) ..	..	22	28
Average area irrigated (millions of acres) ..	..	6	11
Average area sown (millions of acres) ..	..	20·5	28
Total population (millions)	..	18·5	20
Average area sown per head of population (acres) ..	..	1·1	1·4

In the last 22 years (writing in 1910) the average area sown has increased by 27 per cent. It is necessary to allow for the great increase in the average yield due to the extension of irrigation; for an irrigated acre produces on the average about double the produce per acre given by unirrigated land........We find that the increase in the total produce must be nearly 50 per cent.; and the average produce per head of population must have increased by 36 per cent.

but the capital expenditure on the system and nett earnings have been as follows :—

1917-18, 5,226 miles open to traffic, Rs. 9,671 lakhs outlay, and nett earnings 7·9 per cent. on this capital.

1918-19, 5,341 miles open to traffic, Rs. 10,016 lakhs outlay, and nett earnings 6·64 per cent.

There is still scope for the profitable investment of many more lakhs in extending communications and transport facilities, and the economic progress of the province will largely depend upon such extension.

The major irrigation works of the province supply water to several Native States so that care must be taken to avoid confusion ; further they are still being improved and developed, so that the figures vary from year to year. The capital expenditure up to 1920-21 was Rs. 24 crores, of which Rs. 155 lakhs were contributed by the States and Rs. 2,252 lakhs by the British Government. The length of channels in operation in March 1921 was 4,392 miles of main and branch canals, and 15,240 miles of distributaries, or 19,632 miles in all. The gross receipts were Rs. 468 lakhs, working expenses amounted to Rs. 141·6 lakhs, leaving a nett revenue of Rs. 326·8 lakhs. This represents 14·51 per cent. on the capital outlay, or 11·25 per cent, after deducting interest charges.

The minor canals have cost Rs. 6 lakhs ; they have about 110 miles of main canals and 106 miles of distributaries. Their nett return is about 10 per cent.

The two together irrigated in 1919-20, 10·46 million acres out of a total cropped area of 25·36 million acres ; and in 1920-21, 10·25 million acres out of a total cropped area of 17·18 million acres. These last figures deserve special consideration, because the decrease in total cropped area compared with the previous year was due to a monsoon 43 per cent. below normal, and to winter rains which in 16 districts were 80 per cent. below normal. The result was a fall in cropped area of over 8 million acres, and the province was only saved from famine by the extensive canal system.

The nett revenue on capital outlay for the various works is as follows (interest charges not deducted) :—

Western Jumna.	opened in	1871	11·27	per cent.
Sirhind,	do.	1883	12·63	do.
Lower Jhelum,	do.	1901	19·16	do.
Upper Jhelum (1)	do.	1915	0·25	do.
Upper Bari Doab,	do.	1860-1	17·31	do.
Lower Bari Doab,	do.	1913	15·68	do.
Lower Chenab,	do.	1892	44·35	do.
Upper Chenab,	do.	1912	8·64	do.
Upper Sutlej Inundation			15·64	do.
Indus Inundation			3·09	do.
Sidhnai			17·65	do.

(The above figures refer to the year 1920-21.)

(1) The Upper Jhelum is largely a canal for carrying water to other canals in the triple system ; it irrigates a small area on the way. It is worth recording that the Western Jumna Canal is a result of repeated remodelling. Firoz Shah III constructed a portion about 1356 ; and Ali Mardan Khan, about 1626, effected considerable improvements. It was this Ali Mardan Khan who constructed the Hasli Canal about 1633 ; this was the forerunner of the Upper Bari Doab Canal.

It is sometimes said that the canals have had the effect of reducing the fodder supply of the province and so diminishing the production of ghi, etc. But much of the land through which they now flow was formerly desert, unpeopled or sparsely occupied by a few wandering tribes ; as a source of wealth it was practically worthless, and it can hardly be seriously argued that an acre of barren dry desert yielded more fodder than an acre of irrigated crops.

The fact that an appreciable nett profit has accrued to the State from the construction of these great works has exercised considerable influence on the speed with which they have been designed and carried to completion ; but this consideration has not been the main argument. For several years the canals did not pay expenses but the overpowering need for some means of preventing famines weighed heavily with a government acutely alive to its responsibilities. In the case of metalled roads, the stimulus of direct profit has been absent, while their value in helping to protect the population from the rigours of recurring periods of scarcity was overshadowed by the demand for railways. The enormous saving to the agriculture of a country from good communications is hardly to be disputed ; but until it could clearly be foreseen where the railway lines of the future would be laid, it was not possible to design roads which would continue to retain their value after new railways had been opened. The result is that the Punjab is inadequately provided with metalled roads ; it possesses less than five miles to every railway station, or about one mile to ten villages. In considering these figures it must be borne in mind that it was not until after 1897 that the province definitely surmounted the elementary financial difficulties of making ordinary ends meet ; up to that time, the revenues of the Indian Empire were far from secure ; the recurring surpluses of later years could not be foreseen, and it was not deemed practicable to borrow more than was already being done for other works. The result is that such roads as there are have been constructed out of current revenue, and have been limited by the sums available. It would, perhaps, be unfair to argue that this deficiency illustrates the neglect to appreciate the value of good roads ; these lie at the basis of all rural institutions and largely determine the type of agriculture in vogue. For the profitable production of many commodities, especially those of a perishable nature, such as fruit, etc., easy access to markets is essential. "Youth," says Professor Marshall, "is the chief merit of egg ;" and its youth at the time of consumption depends upon accessibility to the consumer. The same can be said about many kinds of fruits, and vegetables ; at present, highly intensive cultivation is confined to the immediate neighbourhood of the big towns, where land values and rents are accordingly very high. Good roads would remove the handicap under which the rural cultivator suffers, by facilitating transport of manure to his fields and of the produce from them, and would enable him to include in his husbandry crops that at present are confined to urban areas. They would tend to level up the more out of the way tracts to an equality with those better circumstanced and would increase their value as sources of wealth. (1) It is probable that had Government adopted and per-

(1) *Cf.* Seligman : Principles of Economics, p. 311. The most fertile land may be so far removed from the market that, notwithstanding the great potential supply of the produce, the land will be valueless because there is no effective demand for its products. The mutations in value due to changes in situation are in modern times far greater than those due to changes in fertility.

sisted in the policy of charging tolls so that the users of the roads would contribute towards their upkeep, the present meagre mileage would have been considerably extended. Certainly, in England, the income from tolls on roads and bridges (some of these latter were constructed and owned as private ventures) afforded an incentive to enterprise, although in the end disadvantages were found to outweigh the advantages. (1)

From what has been said above it will now be clear that the Punjab could not have advanced far along the road to intensive economic development prior to annexation. Even if the early canal builders had designed such great works as we are now familiar with, there would have remained the difficulties due to lack of capital and labour, and, in the absence of railways and roads, the surplus produce could not have been transported to market. It was not until the early nineteenth century that railways and metalled (macadamised) roads made their appearance in Great Britain and there was no time for the new idea to reach India before the death of Maharaja Ranjit Singh. Although only a small part of the total area of England is far removed from water that will carry a boat or small barge, yet that small part remained thinly populated, and England remained backward, owing to the lack of good roads, till the beginning of the nineteenth century.

Situated geographically as it is, the Punjab could have made little advance until it had been linked by railways to the great ports and so to the markets of the world. Once communication had been established, trade and commerce expanded rapidly. The following figures relate to rail-borne trade :—

	Imports.		Exports.	
	Weight.	Value.	Weight.	Value.
		Rs.		Rs.
1882-3 ..	63 lakhs mds.	710 lakhs.	103 lakhs mds.	373 lakhs.
1892-3 ..	122 ,, ,,	920 ,,	160 ,, ,,	694 ,,
1902-3 ..	251 ,, ,,	1,546 ,,	249 ,, ,,	1,150 ,,
1911-12 ..	551 ,, ,,	2,984 ,,	566 ,, ,,	2,688 ,,
1919-20 ..	655 ,, ,,	5,287 ,,	413 ,, ,,	4,405 ,,

(The figures given for export in 1892-3 represents the three years, average, as that year was abnormal.)

The figures for value are those recorded in the Punjab ; thus the value of imports presumably includes the cost of transport to the market, while the value of exports is exclusive of this item.

It is interesting to note that the United States department of agriculture conducts investigation and experiments in road building.

(1) It would seem that according to the Japanese Road Law issued in 1919, those who derive benefit from any works on the roads must bear part of the expenses, while those who, in pursuit of their business, cause damage to the roads, are to pay part of repair expenses (The Japan Year Book, 1919-20). It is said of Spain that 45 per cent. of its area is exposed to economic loss through difficulties of communications.

The table affords an example of the truism that without railways it was impossible for great wheat-growing tracts to come into existence. Similarly cotton would have been too bulky for pack transport. The great jute industry of Bengal could not spring up until transport to European markets became available. Without railways concentration of production is not possible. (1)

The mere fact that foreign trade has expanded in such large measure is not by itself proof of an increase of prosperity to the same degree. But, as Professor Marshall points out, on the whole it is reasonable to suppose that an ascertained increase in a country's foreign trade reflects an increase in her general prosperity. (2) Fortunately, in this discussion, as will appear, there is ample evidence to corroborate the view that there has been a marked advance in general prosperity in the last fifty years.

The influence of geographical position on prices in the Punjab may be illustrated by the instances given below. The pre-war figures are given first and the later figures on the right. (3)

One Case containing 100 pairs India pattern Men's Shoes.

Pre-war.	£.	s.	d.	1920.	£.	s.	d.
At works unpacked 4s. per pair	20	0	0	12s. 6d. per pair ..	62	10	0
100 cardboard boxes @ 1½d. each ..	0	12	6	4d. each ..	1	13	4
Zinc lined case	0	18	0	Paper lined case ..	1	10	0
Carriage to port	0	2	6	..	0	6	0
Dock dues and cartage	0	2	3	..	0	5	6
Bill of lading, stamp, postage, etc. ..	0	5	3	..	0	10	6
Steamer freight to Karachi	1	11	6	..	6	0	0
Insurance on £ 28 and stamp	0	2	10	Insurance on £ 90	0	13	6
Seller's profit at 5 per cent.	1	3	9	..	3	13	5
Total ..	24	18	7	Total ..	77	2	3
	Rs.	a.	p.		Rs.	a.	p.
Exchange at 1s. 4d. per rupee	373	15	0	At 2s. per rupee ..	771	2	0
Customs duty (4)	28	3	0	..	49	9	0
Clearing, landing, cartage to goods-shed ..	2	8	0	..	3	8	0
Railway freight at Rawalpindi	12	8	0	..	12	8	0
Total ..	417	2	0	Total ..	836	11	0

(1) But a valuable article like indigo could be carried great distances. See Moreland: India at the Death of Akbar, pp. 105, 119. Our knowledge of the conditions essential to industrial success precludes the placing of too great reliance on old tales of past glory.

(2). Industry and Trade, p. 16. "We may not measure her prosperity by her foreign trade."

(3) For these figures I am indebted to Mr. W. H. Levy.

(4) Customs duties fall outside the scope of this book, but it may be noted that general import duties were abolished in 1882, re-imposed in 1894 at 5 per cent. *ad valorem*, increased to 7½ per cent. in 1916, and to 11 per cent. in 1921. The duties given here should be raised to bring them up to date, but they have been retained at the 1920 rate, because the other figures relate to that year.

Ten bales (each 15 pieces) unbleached long-cloth (grey shirting), each piece 30 inches × 40 yards.

Pre-war.	£.	s.	d.	1920.	£.	s.	d.
8s. per 40 yards delivered at the mill ..	60	0	0	24s. per 40 yards	180	0	0
Making up, folding, heading, stamping 4d, per piece.	2	10	0	10d. per piece ..	6	5	0
Packing and hooping, 2s. 6d. per bale ..	1	10	0	8s. per bale ..	4	0	0
Conveyance to port	0	10	0	..	1	5	0
Dock dues and cartage	0	10	0	..	1	0	0
Bill of lading, stamp, etc.	0	3	6	..	0	10	0
Steamer freight to Karachi	2	5	0	..	10	0	0
Insurance on £ 80	0	9	0	Insurance on £ 225..	1	13	9
Seller's profit at 5 per cent.	3	7	10	..	10	4	8
Total ..	71	5	4	Total ..	214	18	5
	Rs.	a.	p.		Rs.	a.	p.
Exchange at 1s. 4d. per rupee	1,068	4	0	At 2s. per rupee ..	2,149	3	0
Customs duty	38	0	0	..	64	15	6
Clearing, landing, cartage to goods-shed ..	12	8	0	..	15	0	0
Railway freight to Lahore	40	0	0	..	40	0	0
Total ..	1,158	12	0	Total ..	2,269	2	6

Three cases saddles and harness.

	£.	s.	d.		£.	s.	d.
Cost at works	75	12	0	..	187	10	0
Tin lined cases	2	5	0	..	6	0	0
Carriage to port	0	6	6	..	0	15	0
Dock dues and cartage	0	4	3	..	0	10	0
Bill of lading, stamp, etc.	0	5	3	..	0	12	0
Steamer freight	2	5	6	..	8	0	0
Insurance on £ 90	0	10	0	Insurance on £ 240 ..	1	16	0
Seller's, profit at 5 per cent.	4	1	5	..	10	5	2
Total ..	85	9	11	Total ..	215	8	2
	Rs.	a.	p.		Rs.	a.	p.
Exchange at 1s. 4d. per rupee	1,282	7	0	..	2,054	1	0
Customs duty	96	3	0	..	138	7	6
Clearing, landing, cartage to goods-shed ..	6	12	0	..	10	0	0
Railway freight to Lahore	20	0	0	..	20	0	0
Total ..	1,405	6	0	Total ..	2,222	8	6

These figures bring out clearly some of the effects of the peculiar position occupied by the Punjab. The cost of carrying the ten bales of cloth from Liverpool to Karachi was less than the cost of carriage from Karachi to Lahore : in the case of saddlery the charges are about the same. The distance by rail from Lahore to Karachi is about 750 miles and from Lahore to Bombay

1,250 miles. Thus 5,000 miles of sea may be a less impediment to trade than 750 miles of land ; and the landlocked position of the Punjab must tend to diminish its profits from foreign trade both by increasing against it the price of imported goods and by decreasing the price received for its exports.

Another point worth noting is that, in so far as the customs duty has any protective effect, this is enhanced by the cost of carriage from port to the Punjab. The freightage from Liverpool to Lahore should serve as a very effective protection to local industries.

A further point is that as the customs duties are on an *ad valorem* basis, the great increase of prices in Europe has automatically increased the duties on the articles.

The railway freight from port to the Punjab represents an advantage which local industries would have in competing in the provincial market against goods manufactured in Bombay or Karachi. On the other hand, it would handicap Punjab goods in competition with Bombay goods in the Bombay market. (1)

Thus goods, manufactured in the Punjab, would be protected from goods manufactured in Europe, by sea freight, customs duties and rail freight, and from goods, manufactured in Bombay, by rail freight. There is thus apparently a favourable prospect for industries supplying local needs. The same factors, however, would handicap Punjab industries in developing an export trade. These considerations lose weight if the articles dealt with combine great value in relation to bulk. Thus the charges on saddles and harness bear a less proportion to the total cost than they do in the case of more bulky cloth.

If the Punjab is ever to develop a big export trade in manufactured goods, it must do so by concentrating on articles that comprise a large value in a small bulk, such as silk, or on those of which it possesses a partial monopoly, such as turpentine. In discussing these questions, it must be borne in mind that the same considerations do not apply with equal force to raw materials of which the world is in constant need. The Punjab's supply of wheat, oil seeds, etc., is needed in the worlds' markets but a future supply of Punjab manufactured cloth may not be needed. The areas in which particular plants will grow freely is limited by climatic and other conditions, which do not apply, or apply with less stringency, to manufactures. Those who lament that the Punjab produces only raw materials and has few factories, are apt to lose sight of the consideration that this may be because the province is well-fitted by its natural advantages to produce raw materials, and ill-fitted by natural deficiencies to manufacture goods. These natural deficiencies include lack of coal, distance from the sea, etc. If we compare the conditions in Lancashire and the Punjab, we find that the former place has become possessed of a very large and very highly organised cotton industry. Capital is

---

(1) It will be noted that railway rates in India, alone of all the charges, have not gone up, and the local manufacturer thus loses advantage. If a serious effort were made to supply the local market by local manufacture, there might arise a conflict of opinion on railway rates, the manufacturers desiring heavier inward rates and lower outward rates, while the body of consumers would press for lower inward rates.

plentiful, interest charges are low, and accordingly the manufacture of cloth on a large scale has been facilitated with the result that full advantage has been secured of the increasing returns that accompany large scale production. The county borders the sea. Liverpool is the centre of the world's shipping and so has free access at relatively cheap rates to all the ports of the world, north, south, east and west. In the Punjab capital is shy: interest charges are high ; there is no direct access to the sea ; north, west and south there are no markets within easy access, and accordingly it is not possible for the province to establish the manufacture of cloth on such a large scale as to secure the full advantage of increasing returns.

From the above it will be clear that the fact that cloth can be manufactured in the Punjab is, by itself, not a conclusive reason for this manufacture to be undertaken ; the same capital, labour and enterprise may earn a larger profit by being devoted to some other industry, in which the province has some natural advantage (*e. g.*, resin and turpentine), or to one whose product is so valuable in proportion to its bulk that the natural disadvantages from which the province suffers would not prevent the establishment of a large export trade. The production and manufacture of silk may be an example of the latter. The argument tends to show that in so far as the Punjab has a natural advantage in the production of raw materials for which there is a constant demand in the world's markets, attention may, with profit, first be directed to working up these raw materials a stage nearer to that in which they are finally consumed. For instance, tropical countries seem to be peculiarly rich in plants yielding vegetable oils for which there is a great demand. The Punjab at present exports oil seeds, whereas the oil has to be extracted from the seed before it can be used and the oil cake is consumed separately.

Whatever may be the industrial future of the province, it seems certain that geographical position will be a dominating factor, and it would be well if this could receive greater recognition. It will be useless encouraging industries that will require large export trade before they can be organised on the most economical lines. It is doubtful if the province can succeed in establishing what may be called imitative industries ; as new factories will not be able to compete with the economies of mass production. This will be discussed later. At present it is only intended to draw attention to the influence of geographical position on economic development, and to lay stress upon the necessity for concentrating efforts on those things for the production of which the province possesses special facilities.

The importance of the geographical factor has been enhanced lately by the rise in the cost of freights between Karachi and England, and will be further enhanced when the goods rates on the North-Western Railway are increased to meet the great rise in running expenses. Wheat, for instance, is only exported when the price in the Punjab is less than the price in Liverpool by a sum sufficient to cover the cost of carriage, insurance, etc., and allow of a margin for profit. This sum must now be larger than before, so that the export will only yield a profit when either the Liverpool price is unusually high or the Indian price unusually low. The result will tend to be a decline in the amount of wheat exported and a consequent fall in local prices. This tendency may be counteracted by a low exchange or a continuance of high prices in England.

The same influences will tend to afford greater protection to local industries against imported manufactured goods. The margin of efficiency need not be so small as before, and less highly organised industries in the Punjab may be better able to survive in competition with articles produced in the mass in the industrial centres of Europe.

On the other hand the difficulties of selling Punjab manufactured articles in foreign markets will be enhanced in proportionate degree. So that the factors tending to insulate this province from the rest of the world will exercise a greater influence than before so long as the costs of transport and distribution remain high.

CHAPTER V.

THE SOIL.

Decrease in Economic Pressure and its Result : Improved Standard of Living as a Stimulus : The Influence of the Revenue Demand.

Second only in importance to the geographical position in its effect upon the economic potentialities of the Punjab is the fact that the major portion of the province contains a deep alluvial soil. It would be difficult to say whether, hitherto, this has proved an advantage or a disadvantage. An alluvial soil possesses great natural fertility ; it yields good crops with very little cultivation ; it is less dependent on manures than other soils and does not require the same elaborate rotation (1). The soil varies from a rich to a light sandy loam, containing very little clay ; it requires very little artificial drainage, unless its natural condition has been altered by excessive irrigation and it requires the expenditure of very little capital to bring it under cultivation and to maintain its crop bearing capacity. In these respects, the people of the Punjab are far more fortunate than agriculturists in other countries. In England the land is not naturally fertile, in early days a large part of the country was swamp, heath and jungle. For six hundred years there has been controversy as to whether it paid to produce wheat, and a continuous series of measures have been resorted to in order to encourage the corn grower (2).

Although adding lime to the soil was practised so far back as the fourteenth century, harrows were used in 1600, the drill was invented in 1701 and from about the same time leases contained a clause insisting on the straw being returned to the land as manure ; it has taken all these centuries of careful tillage and manuring to bring the land to its present state of fertility ; but no farmer even now would think of sowing without previous manuring. There are still large tracts in the British Isles whereon no crops can be grown, and generally speaking the soil returns only what is put into it. It does not seem to be sufficiently realised in India that the British farmer, and indeed the farmer of all north Europe, works strictly to the rule of putting back into the land as manure as much as he takes out of it in crops and foodstuffs. During the war it was not possible to get sufficient artificial manures, basic slag or even cake for cattle food, and there was not available the labour required to keep the land cleaned and drained. It was stated, in evidence before the recent Royal Commission on Agriculture, that, owing to these causes, fertility had decreased, and it might take as much as five pounds sterling per acre to restore it to its pre-war state.

In Denmark neither the soil nor the climate are favourable to the farmer ; the soil is, or rather was, largely loose sand, swept by the sea winds, but the Danish farmers have used all the forces of science, organis-

---

(1) *Cf.* Seligman : Principles of Economics, p. 313.
(2) *Cf.* Curtler for details.

ation and human effort to produce the present fertility. In Belgium there is said to be the worst soil in Europe, so sterile that, after centuries of laborious husbandry, it will not yield a single crop without being manured. (1) No region is naturally fertile, and the system of land tenure tends to reduce efficiency ; yet the history of Belgian agriculture is a record of the triumph of knowledge and industry over natural conditions. Science and skill have brought prosperity. More manure per acre is put on to the land than in any other country. The success achieved, it is said, (2) is largely due to the provision of facilities for education and training in agricultural methods, and to the institution of a co-operative system, which neutralises some of the defects of the conditions of land tenure. The high standard of agricultural education has produced great skill in the selection of seeds and in the use of artificial manures.

Of Spain it is estimated that 10 per cent. is bare rock ; 35 per cent. is naturally unproductive soil, lying at a great height or destitute of water ; 45 per cent. is fairly good land, lying where the communications are difficult, and ill-watered because it has to rely on the rainfall, which is very erratic throughout the interior. The remaining 10 per cent. is good soil advantageously situated. The true sources of the country's wealth are agriculture and pasture, which are those most neglected. The cultivation of the land is left to men who are too poor, as well as too ignorant, to do it justice. The system of tenure is most injurious. The standard of agriculture is bad. (3) Of Greece a large portion is waste, being rocky or marshy ; only about 24 per cent. of Old Greece is culturable. The methods and implements of agriculture are very primitive, there is little use of manure or scientific rotation of crops. In Thessaly the wooden ploughs used differ little from those of more than 2,000 years ago. (4)

Large portions of Japan are absolutely unfitted for anything else than forests, and only one-sixth of the total area is under cultivation ; in Italy, too, the area open to cultivation is but a fraction of the whole, while in Russia vast tracts are infertile. (5)

Of Old Serbia one-third was cultivated ; but of the new territories acquired in the Balkan Wars not more than 8 per cent. was cultivated. In Bulgaria the cultivated area amounts to 42 per cent. ; in Roumania it is 60 per cent. (6)

When attention is turned to the Punjab, it is seen that in its soil the province is undoubtedly fortunate ; one-half the total area is already returned as cultivated, and more will be available as the new canal projects are carried to fruition. As soon as the people can be taught to make the best possible use of this almost inexhaustible source of wealth, the prosperity of the country should reach a very high standard. Hitherto the

---

(1) Rowntree : Land and Labour : Lessons from Belgium, p. 148.
(2) Foreign Office Handbook on Belgium, pp. 112, 113.
(3) Do. do. do. Spain, pp. 42, 43.
(4) Do. do. do. Greece, p. 90 ff. Also Jebb : Modern Greece.
(5) Rowntree states that the proportion of land under cultivation in Belgium is 64 per cent., in Germany 63, in France 65, in England and Wales 73 and in Scotland 25 per cent.
(6) See Foreign Office Handbooks.

soil has yielded freely without the expenditure of any considerable amount of capital on manures or improvements so that a larger proportion of the produce can be reckoned as profits of cultivation. Unfortunately, however, it is a weakness of human nature that the easy acquisition of wealth restrains the growth of the spirit of enterprise ; there seem to be grounds for believing that the natural fertility of the soil, which readily yields a crop to the minimum of labour, is responsible in some measure for the backward state of agriculture. Difficulties bring forth industrious men. The greatest skill seems to develop under the greatest hardships. The average human being exerts himself to secure satisfaction of his wants and to the extent required for this satisfaction.

Until the soil of the province shows signs of exhaustion, there will be no full appreciation of that feature of agriculture in old settled countries which consists in putting into the land what is relatively cheap in order to get out from it what is relatively dear. So long as the cultivator can reap a crop without much exertion and without the exercise of much intelligence, he will tend to be satisfied with what nature yields. When nature inclines to refuse her favours until some material in the way of manures and some energy in the way of physical aeration are supplied, the cultivator will begin to look around for fertilisers that will repay their use, and for methods that will yield him profit. The exertion put forth by the cultivator tends to vary inversely with the unaided generosity of nature. Almost everywhere the cultivator tends to look to his land just for a living and not as affording an opportunity for accumulating wealth, and so an easily won income serves to retard progress ; while wherever conditions are hardest, naturally or otherwise, there is to be found the most painstaking cultivation in the province. The carefully tended plots around the wells in the Sind Sagar Doab or the terraced fields in the hills may be quoted as examples. The Ahir, struggling with the capricious rainfall and sandy soil of Rewari, is far more industrious than the ordinary agriculturist in rich Lyallpur. Where rents are high, as in the immediate neighbourhood of big towns, or where holdings are small, the standard of cultivation is found to be better. (1),

Experience shows that an improvement in cultural methods or a change towards more intensive agriculture seldom comes except as a result of economic pressure. Farmers do not usually expend more capital and more labour on a given area until they are driven to it. The highly intensive system of cultivation in Japan, which is the most characteristic feature of its agriculture, is not due to the natural industry of the Japanese, but to the absence, until within recent years, of any outlet for its rapidly growing population. It was the only alternative to starvation. In America, where land has hitherto

(1) The Settlement Reports of the province contain ample evidence, *e. g.* " cultivation is very good in many charkhari villages where the owners are hardworking and the holdings small " (Gujranwala Tehsil). It is not intended to argue that an all-round increase of rents would lead to an all-round increase of production. High rents form a factor tending towards more intensive methods. They result from the existence of men who are willing and able to adopt these methods and they serve to keep these men working up to a high standard when a reduction might lead to a decline in method.

been plentiful, farmers have preferred to secure a small outturn per acre from a large area to striving after a higher yield from a smaller area. The object of the farmer is always the same, to secure a good income for himself; and, in accordance with the Law of Diminishing Returns, it is easier to secure the same income from a large area extensively cultivated than from a small area intensively cultivated. Where the large area is not available, intensive cultivation is forced upon him. A well-known saying of Arthur Young, (1) that the magic of property turns sand into gold, was based on a comparison of the methods of the British tenant farmer with the peasant proprietor in Europe. But while the former had probably 150 acres wherefrom to extract his living, the latter had from 25 to 30, and his laborious industry that so appealed to Arthur Young, was forced upon him by the extreme difficulty of his task. It is this painstaking, laborious industry that turns sand into gold. The effect of proprietorship is to secure to the cultivator the full return on his labour; the element that counts is fixity of tenure; ownership is not essential to good cultivation. (2).

If, as it is here urged, economic pressure be necessary to stimulate the cultivators to improve their methods, it must be expected that the relief from economic pressure will tend to remove this stimulus and so will to some extent militate against progress. It has been pointed out in another connection that one of the obstacles to improvement is the difficulty of bringing home to the cultivator a proper realisation of the extent to which the outturn of his fields is a reflection of his own methods and his own exertions. Where, then, the cultivator finds himself in a vastly improved position, in possession of a valuable property, yielding a greatly increased income, without any extra effort on his part, his sense of responsibility for his crops must be weakened. In the Punjab these conditions have been fulfilled. The effect of the British administration has been to place great wealth in the hands of the cultivating classes. At annexation there seems to have been no recognised sale value for land. In 1862-3 the average price paid by Government was about Rs. 8 per acre. In the five years from 1862-63 to 1866-67 the compensation paid for land acquired for public purposes was, on the average, Rs. 13-4-0 per acre. The average for the next five years was Rs. 50-2-0. It continued to rise steadily until 1895-96. Then came the opening of the great Chenab Canal. Wealth came to the province from the new colony and from emigrants abroad and an era of almost unbroken prosperity set in. The price of cultivated land rose from Rs. 59 in 1895-96 to Rs. 252 in 1917-19.

At the same time, the demand of the State for revenue was being reduced; the owner's position was being strengthened and markets were being opened up. Until communication with the great seaports was established by railways, prices of produce fluctuated widely. The price of wheat on 1st June 1868 was 19½ seers; a year later it was 13 seers; on 1st June 1871 it was 20 14/16 seers. It fell to 27 5/16 seers in 1877 and two years later it was 14 seers. In remote places like the present Mianwali District, wheat after a good harvest might

(1) This greatest of British writers on agriculture was born in 1741 and died in 1820.
(2) *Cf.* the history of agriculture in England.

fall to 40 seers a rupee, that is to say, it was practically unsaleable. Under these circumstances, agriculture was a gamble in prices as well as in rain. But with the opening up of railways, prices became steadier and the average level rose higher than before. The cultivator's income from the sale of his produce was thus raised by influences outside his own control.

Two other factors came into play, further enhancing the average income. The new canals, irrigating millions of acres, caused a great increase in the total yield ; while, in so far as they brought water to tracts previously uncultivated, they led to a great expansion in the area under crops. The great increase in the cultivated area that has taken place in the Punjab in the last fifty years has been almost wholly covered by irrigation. The figures for cultivated area in acres (1) are as follows :—

	Irrigated by canals.	Irrigated from wells, etc.	Unirrigated.	Total cultivated area.
1868-69	1,373,000	4,612,000	14,187,000	20,172,000
1918-19	9,000,000	3,500,000	16,500,000	29,000,000

The value of the crops produced by canal irrigation was in 1919 estimated at 55 crores of rupees. The effect of the railways and canals combined is shown in the great increase (it might almost be said in the birth and development) of the export trade. Prior to annexation there was no export of agricultural produce worth mentioning. In 1871-73 the wheat exported was valued at 4 lakhs of rupees, forty years later it was valued at 1,448 lakhs.

The area sown with wheat in the former period was 5·5 million acres, in the latter it was about 9·5 million acres. It is now nearly 10 million. Thus there has been a great increase in the cultivated area, a much greater increase in the irrigated area, and consequently a marked rise in the average outturn per cultivated acre, and, in addition, a very considerable enhancement in the prices of agricultural produce. (2) The population that shares this wealth, however, has not increased in the same proportion.

The total population for the same area in the present boundaries of the province has been as follows in the years referred to :—(3)

Year.	Population.	Average annual rate of increase.
1868	16,250,000	·47
1881	17,270,000	+·47
1891	19,000,000	+·96
1901	20,330,000	+·67
1911	19,975,000	—·18
1921	20,685,024	

(1) Figures from 1868-69 refer to the old province as then constituted and so the increase is really much greater than would appear. The figures for 1918-19 are rounded. Economists are apt to assume that extension of cultivation involves a decrease in average yield, as the best lands are cultivated first and extensions bring worse land under crops. In the Punjab the new canals have opened up rich virgin-soil and accordingly extension of cultivation has increased the average yield. *Cf.* Moreland, India at the Death of Akbar, pp. 115—118.

(2) It may be estimated that the crops grown on irrigated land are worth not less than 17 crores of rupees a year more than crops grown on the same area of unirrigated land ; but this does not give full value to the benefits accruing from the canals, as a large proportion of the area now under irrigated crops would probably have remained barren waste if these canals had not been constructed.

(3) Census Report, 1911.

As the figures given for 1868 are probably an underestimate, it may be said that the population has increased about 20 per cent. while cultivation has increased 50 per cent., and the gross value of the produce has risen from roughly 35 crores of rupees a year to not less than 100 crores. (1) To put this in a different form, the pressure on the soil has declined, the total population per 100 cultivated acres has decreased from 83 in 1868 to 76·4 in 1911; while the number of agriculturists per 100 cultivated acres has declined from 46 to 43. (In the Census Report of 1868 it is mentioned that between 1855 and 1868 the population increased 11·5 per cent. while cultivation increased 31·6 per cent.) The average value of gross produce per head of population has thus arisen from rather less than Rs. 22 to not less than Rs. 60, and it is certainly safe to say that the gross earnings of an agricultural family have trebled.

This great increase of income has, in the main, resulted from the acts of the British administration. It is very doubtful if any very appreciable part is due to the cultivator's own exertions although undoubtedly improvements are now being affected. There appears to be little evidence that he has increased the intensity of his cultivation to a degree that would affect the general prosperity. Not only has the number of workers on the same area of land declined but there seems to have been a decrease of bullocks per 100 acres cultivated. Some Assessment Reports actually mention a decrease in the efficiency of cultivation, (2) and if the argument as to the effects of economic pressure is correct, this is to be expected. The cultivators find their income mounting up without extra exertion on their part; a few began to find that it was not necessary to work at all, for the area given to tenants increased and owners began to mortgage their property for larger and larger sums and thus to exploit the rising value of their land.

The Punjab thus presents certain economic features of great interest. The administration has introduced improvements of great magnitude, resulting in a marked and rapid increase of wealth to the people, who, to this extent, have been relieved of the pressure of their former poverty. These measures have given a value to land which has soared to unprecedented heights. This rise, as will be seen presently, is in part due to the increase in the cash value of the net rental obtainable, and in part to the great amount of new wealth, resulting from the measures referred to, seeking investment and being sunk in land in consequence of the backward industrial and commercial state of the province. The progressive rise in the value of land has attracted the usurer and, indeed, anyone possessed of fluid capital; for it afforded the proprietor a basis for credit, and the new facility for borrowing, offered to a class to whom credit had hitherto been barred, proved too insidious a temptation to resist. As has happened with peasant proprietors in other countries, the rising value of land has led directly to a steady increase

(1) In the Annual Land Revenue Report, 1918, the gross value of produce was estimated at Rs. 25 per acre or over 72 crores in all. This was probably carrying official caution to excess. At present prices any estimate less than 150 crores would be liable to challenge.

(2) *Cf.* for instance that on the Gujranwala Tehsil, p. 17. Here the number of bulls and bullocks declined from 153 per 1,000 cultivated acres in 1892 to 106 in 1909. It is, of course, true that there has been some improvement in certain tracts but the argument is that the gross result is, beyond all dispute, in largest measure due to the action of Government in constructing the great canals and railways.

in the total mortgage debt. Credit is a powerful agency for good in the hands of those who know how to use it, but it is a danger to those who do not understand it; and, in the Punjab as elsewhere, the number of the latter far exceeds that of the former. The rise in the price of land and its effects, including the abuse of rural credit, will be dealt with at length later. To complete the present discussion, it seems necessary to look ahead and to try to foresee what the play of economic forces will result in.

Hitherto, the natural expansion of the population has been more than amply provided for by the effect of the great canals in throwing vast stretches of barren waste open to cultivation. The projected Sind Sagar Doab Canal is expected to serve two million acres, most of which is, at present, not cultivated; another great scheme, the Sutlej Valley Canal project, will provide water for two and a half million acres (including, however, large tracts in Bahawalpur and Bikaner States); while yet a third scheme, the Bhakra Dam, will increase considerably the area irrigated by existing canals. It is thus unlikely that the increase of population alone will impel agriculturists to resort to improved methods of cultivation. There is, however, another factor which may serve as a stimulus to further effort and this is the growing desire for a higher standard of living. There is no doubt whatever that in the last twenty years a great change in this respect has come over the province. The returns for imports of Lancashire cloth merely corroborate, what is obvious to every observer, that the people are far better clothed than formerly. In food, wheat is replacing inferior grains such as millet (bajra); the buffalo, once a sign of a prosperous household, is almost ousting the cow in favour, and more meat is being consumed. Morally, the progress is less easily determined, but there is a steady increase in the number of pupils attending schools and more reading matter of every description is being produced. It is probable that in a considerable number of cases the desire for a higher standard of living has been met not altogether by the increase in the holding nor wholly by the increase in the outturn nor yet by the higher price obtained for produce but in some measure by the fatal facilities for borrowing. Many crores of rupees have changed hands through sales and mortgages of land and a proportion of this has been used to meet a higher, or a more extravagant, standard of living than the income permitted. The landowners are to this extent living on their capital and to secure a more healthy condition of affairs it is necessary that this abuse should be stopped. (1).

If expenditure can be confined to income or to what is productive, the desire for better living should serve as a stimulus to economic development. There are five factors, so closely interdependent, that any change in one must result in a change in another. These are the population, the cultivated area, the production on this area, the standard of living and migration. If an increase in population is not compensated for by a corresponding increase in the cultivated area, then the people must either produce more from that area, by improving their methods of cultivation; or they must reduce their standard of living; or they must send their surplus numbers to indus-

---

(1) Mr. Darling's enquiries showed that out of 43,000 proprietors, who were members of co-operative societies, only 17 per cent. were free from debt. The tendency to make a wasteful use of the enhanced credit deserves close attention, for unless checked it will gather strength and once more involve serious dangers.

tries or other callings or to other countries. The present low standard of living in India is almost certainly in part due to population outstripping production; the people did not know how to increase the yield from the soil, and conditions did not permit of an extension of cultivation or of migration. (1) The modern alternative of borrowing was not then open to them. If this be correct, then it indicates that economic pressure does not, as in some other countries, lead to any display of originality in discovery or invention. The people give way under stress of hard times instead of rising against it. In England native originality was deliberately supplemented by attracting artisans from abroad. To quote Professor Alfred Marshall:—"England's first great undertaking, that of drainage on a large scale, was carried out for her by Dutchmen; the first English iron cannons had been cast in Sussex by a Frenchman; and lessons from French and Italians, Dutch and Flemings, Germans and Swedes had been required to equip Englishmen as workers in cloth and silk, pottery and paper, as miners and metallurgists". (2) The early Kings, to increase their revenue and to educate their people, favoured the settlement of foreign artisans among them and this educative policy was truly constructive. It was by their aid that England began to be able to sell manufactured stuffs abroad; and it was these and others who later sought refuge from persecution, coming from many parts of Europe, who introduced that astonishing variety of manufacturing processes which became characteristic of the country. The English improved on their teachers, and, later on, developed a conspicuous talent for invention.

The economic pressure on the land in England was never so severe as it is in Japan, but the latter country preserved her strict isolation until compelled by armed force to admit foreign trade; and it was still later that her Government adopted the policy of bureaucratic stimulation of industries, and began to invite foreign experts to teach Western methods, and to send agents abroad to learn whatever could be adapted to Japanese conditions.

Up to the present, the Japanese have shown a considerably greater faculty for imitation than for invention; they have copied old, rather than discovered new, processes; and it would seem that India may show the same characteristics. The conclusion to be drawn would seem to be that, if economic pressure is to lead to progressive development of agriculture or industries, it must be supplemented by extraneous teaching and example. There should be no hesitation in calling in experts from outside, and a too sensitive patriotism that would place race and birth before other qualities required for ensuring a steady enhancement of the general welfare is to be deprecated. The position at present is peculiar. Most people desire a widespread increase of prosperity. Hitherto, such an increase has been directly due to the efforts of the British administration, and not to any

---

(1) Without an organised system of transport and communications there is a tendency to produce only what is required for the needs of the present. A surplus would find no outlet and so would bring little recompense. Thus cultivators would restrict the area under crop to an amount sufficient to meet the current demands for local consumption. When unfavourable seasonal conditions appeared, there would be no elasticity in supply. Under present conditions the Punjab can meet an enforced restriction of cultivation without danger of starvation.

(2) **Industry and Trade, p. 40-41.**

conspicuous change in the exertion made by the people. The success of these efforts has resulted in mitigating the pressure of poverty, and so removing a stimulus to the improvement of methods of production ; and this success is likely to be repeated and continued by various large projects under consideration. The effect of administrative measures in diminishing the stimulus to exertion may be offset by a desire for a higher standard of living ; but there are reasons for believing that this desire has, in the past, failed to maintain itself in times of stress, and that, in the present, it may seek satisfaction in living on capital and so mortgaging the future. This last-named tendency has been only partially checked by the Land Alienation Act ; and the Usurious Loans Act appears to be insufficient to fill the gap. Much good is being done by the Co-operative movement but this must be supplemented by more rigorous laws against persons lending money for unproductive purposes, by a comprehensive scheme of agricultural research and education that will show the people how their natural desire for a better life can be met by the application of more intelligence, skill and capital to their own fields ; and by the encouragement of small industries, subsidiary to agriculture, without which small holders are not likely to become prosperous. As, moreover, wealth only increases by a people consuming less than they produce, all sources of extravagance and waste must be discouraged.

A few observations may be offered on possible criticisms. It may be objected that the above sketch contemplates an increase of officials and of official control and that there is already enough of both in the province. In reply it may be pointed out that, according to the return of occupations in the last Census, public servants (including apparently the army) and their dependents formed 1·73 per cent. of the population, while the proportion for beggars was 2·42 per cent. The province is thus far more beggar-ridden than official-ridden. Further, it may be pointed out that the rapid progress of Japan in recent years has been achieved as a direct result of official stimulus, official interference and even of official compulsion. At the same time, however, it is pertinent to remark that those who are called in to help in the regeneration of the province need not be officials. The State need only employ where private enterprise fails to do so. If privately organised bodies of men arise with sufficient foresight to engage skilled workers from other countries to train local labour, then there will be the less occasion for the State to interfere. The important point is that the prosperity of the people must be increased either through the working of private agencies, or, where these fail, through further Government action. In so far as the future of agriculture is concerned, it is doubtful if any private agency, adequate to the task, will come into being. The number of agriculturists is so great and their average income so small, that it is unlikely that sufficient funds would be forthcoming from voluntary contributors, and it will probably be found necessary to fall back on State expenditure and such measure of control as State expenditure involves.

This discussion of the need of some form of economic pressure as a stimulus to progress cannot be closed without reference to the effect of revenue rates on the standard of agriculture. In former days the State demanded one-third of the gross produce, and sometimes more, and it is obvious that a cultivator striving to secure at least sufficient for a bare subsistence would have to produce more than if the demand were considerably less. Where there is practically no alternative to agriculture, it is possible to make heavy demands on the agriculturists without driving them to abandon their industry. In other chapters, it is pointed out that the decrease in the revenue demand under British administration has facilitated the introduction of the evils of facile credit and consequent debt, and of high land prices and resultant speculation by non-agriculturists; that is to say, the decrease in revenue demand, which was intended to benefit the cultivators, has actually involved them in temptations which they have been unable to resist and in troubles which were new. Experience shows that the people prosper more under a full but moderate assessment than under a very low one. It does not necessarily follow that a large enhancement of the revenue demand would lead to a marked increase in prosperity, but it does seem to be true that the reduction in the demand has tended to remove a stimulus to improvement. From a sum estimated at one-third of the gross produce, the demand has been decreased to one which, according to the returns from the Court of Wards, is, on the average, less than 5 per cent. of the gross produce. (1) As has already been pointed out, the cultivator is apt to confine his exertions to what is necessary to gain a bare living, and, in so far as this is true of any considerable number, the reduction of the demand must have removed the need for some of the exertion. That this conclusion is not far-fetched evidence is forthcoming from other countries. When the rapid opening up of the great American prairies to wheat cultivation produced a marked decrease in prices of agricultural produce in Europe, the resulting fall in the farmer's income acted as a great spur to increased efficiency of production; the introduction of scientific agriculture was expedited and better methods and better business organisation were adopted. On the Continent of Europe most of the cultivators were owners of their fields; in France 77 per cent., in Germany 88 per cent., in Denmark over 80 per cent. are owners and accordingly these had no one but themselves to look to for help against the consequences of low prices. In Ireland, however, the depression was met largely through a decrease in rents and there was little effort at improved methods of production. (2) Later, when the land purchase scheme replaced rents by annual instalments of the purchase money which were frequently less in amount, there was some danger of a drop in productivity which was only averted by the introduction of co-operation and the institution of a Department of Agriculture. (3) Somewhat similarly in England, it is said that the failure to develop new methods has been fostered by the willingness of the landlords to reduce rents instead of insisting on better and more energetic measures being tried. The distress which stimulated continental farmers to revolutionise their methods was met in England by a reduction of rents, amounting to about 30 per cent. of the whole. The landowner's very kindness, his easiness towards unprogressive tenants in difficulties, has thus injured, rather than helped, the industry as a whole. (4)

---

(1) Writing in 1910, Sir James Wilson estimated that "the land revenue equals about 6 per cent. of the average value of the gross agricultural produce, without taking into account the very large income from live stock".

(2) Rural Reconstruction in Ireland, p. 24.

(3) Ibid, p. 34.

(4) State Help for Agriculture, p. 41.

Curtler: Short History of English Agriculture, p. 310, Hall: Agriculture after the War, p. 64. a Dutch critic of British agriculture, in a letter to "The Times" in January 1922, ascribes its relative backwardness to the low rents charged by landlords (among other causes).

In the Punjab it is not easy to define, with anything approaching precision, the influence of revenue on production ; but the high rents obtainable for lands in the immediate neighbourhood of towns illustrate the general tendency. The men who become tenants of these lands are willing to pay these rents because they know that by resort to highly intensive farming they will be able to make a living. If a tenant were unable to pay the rent he would be ejected and replaced by another. In the province generally, the tenant class has hardly begun to compete for fields by offering higher rents, but as soon as this element of competition is introduced, as it is beginning to be to some extent in the canal colonies, the resultant rise in rents will be accompanied by an improvement in methods of production. If a time arrives when intelligent young men, trained in agriculture, take to farming they will be able to outbid the unprogressive cultivators and to secure holdings large enough to afford them full scope for their enterprise and to ensure them a decent livelihood. The old type of tenant will then have to alter his methods or go under. The existing revenue system is not sufficiently elastic to play the same part that a shrewd landlord can do, but it would be possible to adjust the water-rates so as to bring pressure on the cultivators to abandon a poor paying crop like wheat for one more valuable. (1)

---

(1) The great increase in the profits from cultivation may account in some measure for the increase in cultivation by tenants. Owners find they can derive quite a good income from rents without the exertion of labouring themselves on their holdings.

CHAPTER VI.

THE PUNJAB HOLDING.

In previous chapters some attempt has been made to discuss the effects on the economic state of the Punjab of its geographical position and its alluvial soil. The third very important factor is the small size of the majority of the holdings. The total cultivated area of the province is between 29 and 30 million acres, and this is divided into over ten million holdings; but the same owner has frequently a share in more than one holding, many of the colonists in Lyallpur, Shahpur and elsewhere, for instance, have land in their home districts, and many others own land in two or more villages in the same district. What the exact number of separate owners is cannot be discovered from the official reports. The Census Report suggests that there are over four million proprietors amongst the population, but this number does not agree with another official statement (1) that the total number of persons paying land revenue is 3½ millions. The average revenue paid is Rs. 10 to 12, the average area being between 7 and 8 acres. At a rough estimate 7,200, including crown tenants, pay Rs. 250 or more, the average holding of these being somewhat less than 150 acres; 100,000 pay Rs. 50 or more, their average holding being about 35 acres; 300,000 pay Rs. 25 or more, their average holding being about 18 acres; while somewhere about 3 million pay less than Rs. 25 so that their holding is less than 18 acres. But this last figure includes small plots of land attached to houses, temples, etc., or given to menials to keep them in the village, or given to Brahmins on the death of a former owner. If all plots which are not the chief means of livelihood could be excluded from calculation it is probable that the average holding of the last three million owners, who rely upon their land for a living would be about ten to twelve acres. Sir James Wilson (2) estimated that the average area owned per owner was 15 acres; the average area cultivated by owners was, per owner, 7 acres; the average area cultivated by tenants was 5 acres per tenant. This average for the province does not represent the actual facts fairly. In the congested tracts, Jullundur, Gurdaspur, Hoshiarpur, where irrigation from wells is common, the average holding is four acres. In the south-east, where there is no irrigation, holdings are much larger, and similarly in the west.

To compare the Punjab holding with that in other countries, the following figures may be quoted :—(3)

	Including holdings of less than one acre.	*Excluding these.*
	Acres.	Acres.
Belgium	5·7	14·5
France	15·05	24
Germany	19·25	33·5
Denmark	35·59	49
England	26·95	70
Scotland	56·31	57
Wales	38·05	62

(1) Prepared in connection with the electorate for the Reforms Scheme.
(2) Recent Economic Developments in the Punjab, 1910.
(3) Rowntree: Land and Labour; Lessons from Belgium, p. 106.
The figures relate to pre-war conditions.
The Statistical Report of the Amritsar Division (1861) gives the average area of each holding and average revenue as follows :—
Amritsar 13 acres and 13 rupees, Gurdaspur 15 acres and 20 rupees, Sialkot 17 acre and 16 rupees.

Such figures are apt to be misleading unless they are grouped so as to show more exactly the conditions under which agriculture is carried on. In America the average size of the farms has been declining for the last 60 or 70 years. It is now about 130 acres; but by a farm an American understands an area of 150 to 250 acres. In England a farm means something about 150 acres; about 70 per cent. of the land is held in farms of over 100 acres, but the majority of holdings are "small holdings" of under 50 acres. The number of these small holdings, in spite of their advocacy by several publicists, is decreasing; while there is a tendency for farms of 50 to 300 acres to increase. (1) A holding of under 5 acres is termed an allotment.

In Belgium, of 700,000 proprietors of land, about 520,000 are owners of less than 5 acres each. There are only about 35,000 who own more than 25 acres each, while over 400,000 own less than 2½ acres each. There is a steady and continuous movement towards a still further reduction in the average size of the holdings, for Belgian law, like Punjab custom, requires a man to divide the greater part of his property equally amongst his children. The large holdings in England, on the other hand, are due to the land being permanently settled on the eldest son or heir. Turning to other countries, it may be noted that in Bulgaria the average holding is about 11 acres. In Roumania the land is largely in the hands of big proprietors and the tenants are little more than serfs. In Serbia 95 per cent. of the proprietors own less than 50 acres each, while over half own under 8 acres each. In Japan the average holding is between 2½ and 3 acres. From the above it will be seen that the Punjab is not singular in the small size of its holdings. Where it seems to be peculiar is that the owners prefer to cultivate smaller parcels of land than they need. It is probably correct to say that every owner of more than 25 acres lets part of it to a tenant. There is no effort to achieve large scale farming, even by those who can do it on their own land. Similarly tenants seldom attempt to cultivate more than 25 acres, although more may be available. If anyone obtains a lease for a greater area he sublets a portion.

Apart from this peculiarity, it will be seen that there are many countries with which it should be possible to make a comparison with advantage. Japan affords an interesting example of the state a country can drift into when it ignores modern knowledge, especially modern scientific agriculture and modern methods of organization. As a matter of deliberate policy, the country was kept secluded from intercourse with the nations of the West until 1853; and it was not until 1872 that the feudal system of government was replaced by the present Imperial regime. In the last fifty years remarkable changes have been effected, but the people are still miserably poor. Cultivation is still done by human labour with rude implements. Only occasionally is the farmer assisted by a horse or an ox, but seldom by a team of animals. Most of the work of transport is performed by human labour, either carrying packs or hauling primitive carts with heavy loads over bad roads and absurd bridges built like an arch to obviate grading. (2)

---

(1) Arthur Young calculated as early as 1768 that the average size of farms over the greater part of England was slightly under 300 acres, *e. g.*, Curtler: Short History of English Agriculture, p. 202.

(2) *Cf.* Commercial No. 1 of 1920. Report on Japanese Labour.

The tiller of the soil is unable to extract even the most frugal living from his tiny holding in spite of the great labour he expends on intensive cultivation and the free use of night soil; this fact accounts for the subsidiary occupations, for, without sericulture, the Japanese farmers would hardly be able to maintain themselves. About 15 to 17 per cent. of the total yield goes in taxes, as compared with less than 5 per cent. in the Punjab. The annual land tax is fixed at 3 per cent. of the total value of the land, and the local tax at 1 per cent. In the Punjab the land revenue is about one-half of 1 per cent. of the land value. Thus the Japanese farmer has practically no oxen to do the heavy work for him, he is heavily taxed, he has a minute holding and his poverty is so great that he is forced to have recourse to some additional means of livelihood, such as sericulture, manufacturing articles from rice, straw, etc. In everything he is assisted by the labour of his wife and children. The Punjab peasant may well congratulate himself that he is far better off than his fellow in Japan. (1)

It should be unnecessary to point out that where holdings are small only the most unremitting industry will serve to provide a livelihood. The system of cultivation must be highly intensive and the income from the land must be eked out by income from some subsidiary occupation. In Japan even these combined are hardly sufficient to ensure a decent living. In Belgium Science and Co-operation have shown the industrious small holder how to employ capital with profit. The result is interesting and should be convincing. It is that, if a large amount of capital is to be employed in scientific agriculture on a small area, human food crops must give way to crops for feeding live stock; vegetable products, such as wheat, must be replaced by animal products. In Japan religious sentiment prohibited the use of animal food (except fish), the few cattle that existed were beasts of burden and milk and butter were little known. The Japanese were thus barred from using the land to the best advantage and have remained poor in consequence. In Belgium only 9 per cent. of the cultivated area is devoted to wheat (2); the land is utilised chiefly for such valuable industrial crops as sugar beet, tobacco and flax and to raising food for cattle. More manure is used per acre and more cattle are carried per acre than in any other country. The great importance of the human factor in agriculture may be exemplified by comparing what is said above about Belgium and the description of the Russian peasant who, putting nothing into the soil, took out all it could be made to yield; abhorring intensive culture, he thus plundered the land, exhausted its fertility and then clamoured for more. The average amount of land possessed by the peasant ought to have sufficed had it been tilled as in Prussia or Belgium. (3)

The main lessons that the Punjab may derive from Belgium are that the

---

(1) *Cf.* Japan Year Book, Modern Japan, Japan by the Japanese, etc., Silk reeling and weaving are the most important cottage industries; others are hosiery and match-making, buttons, brushes, lacemaking, plaiting of hemp and straw braids, beads and imitation pearls. The wife often has to go out to work, otherwise she remains at home doing cottage work. The children when not at school are similarly employed. Even when playing in the streets they plait straw as they run around. *Cf.* Official Report on Japanese Labour.

(2) Mr. Rowntree (p. 177) gives the following further percentages:—France 21, Germany 5, Great Britain 5, Denmark 1.

(3) E. J. Dillon: The Eclipse of Russia, p. 57.

smallness of the holdings is not necessarily a bar to prosperity (1) ; that enterprise, science, co-operation, capital and painstaking labour will yield a decent living from a small area ; but the land must be devoted to those uses which will give the highest returns to human intelligence and skill. In short, if the Punjab peasant is to become really prosperous, he must revolutionize his methods.

As a contrast to Belgium, Serbia may be referred to. Holdings, as has already been stated, are small and manifest a tendency to still further subdivision. But cultivations, as in the Punjab, is still extensive. Education in matters of rural importance is backward, capital is lacking. The people prefer agriculture to industries, villages to towns. Railway communications are sadly undeveloped. The geographical position provides no access to the sea, and so places the country in a state of economic dependence on powerful, and not always friendly, neighbours. Of the total exports 90 per cent. formerly went to Austria either to be consumed there or on their way to more distant markets. The agriculturists retain primitive methods of cultivation ; they use little manure to improve the soil and in consequence obtain but a poor yield ; the use of artificial manure is unknown. Of the total area only 32 per cent is cultivated. Maize is the most important cereal, and forms the almost exclusive cereal food of the peasants. The wheat that is produced is exported or consumed in the towns. Cattle raising, however, is the most important branch of production ; cattle and products of cattle are the chief exports, pigs being foremost and horned cattle coming next in order. All the agriculturists raise pigs and make much profit therefrom. A further important branch of production is fruit growing, especially plums, which are dried and exported. Each district is obliged by law to possess a nursery of fruit trees covering at least 12 acres. Serbia is a poor and backward country, but its leaders are beginning work on the rural problems before them. It has already realized the truth that the small holder cannot live by food crops alone. (2)

It may, perhaps, be misleading to refer to Denmark in this connection as the holdings are considerably larger than in the Punjab, but it is relevant to the argument to note that, although this wonderfully organized country produces chiefly cattle foods, putting very little land under wheat, etc., it imports feeding stuffs, corn, flour and meal, and exports cattle, cattle produce (butter, cheese, meat, etc.) and other animal products (bacon, ham, eggs, etc.) (3)

When, after this brief survey of other countries, attention is brought back to the Punjab, several noteworthy features emerge. The cultivators persist in extensive cultivation and in the use of primitive implements. They put hardly any animal manure back on to the land and no artificial manure. They devote a large area (nearly one-third) to wheat and very little to cattle food. They grow practically no fruit in any quantity and have no export trade worth mentioning in cattle and animal products, except raw hides.

(1) There are over two million holdings of less than $2\frac{1}{2}$ acres in France and nearly as many in Germany

(2) Servia by the Servians, Chapters XV, XVI.

(3) Mr. Roberts points out that Denmark and Belgium are favoured in having a large industrial country like England as a market. But the Punjab is prepared to consume a larger amount of ghi, etc., than is at present produced or imported ; and if industries grow up there should be little difficulty over a market. Mr. Roberts further points out that if the Punjab cultivator is to go in for intensive methods he will require more water than the canals at present allow.

Religious sentiment serves to prevent horned cattle being produced with profit. In other countries the most prolific sources of food are potatoes and pigs. The one is not yet a staple article of diet, the other is barred. The actual cultivators have no subsidiary occupations, except perhaps hiring their bullock carts for transport. Where handiwork is to be done, special castes or tribes exist to perform it. The efforts to popularize sericulture have met with little success. Bee keeping is rare. The profitable work of rearing geese, turkeys, ducks, pigeon and poultry for sale is almost entirely neglected. (1) The growing of vegetables is looked upon as degrading to a real agriculturist, and *malis* (market gardeners) are actually giving up vegetable growing for wheat in order to raise their social status. The Punjab small holder, in short, is trying to make a living out of his few acres without the aid of animal husbandry or domestic industries, a task which nowhere in the world seems to have been accomplished with any profit. He is able to persist in this hopeless task partly because his wants are small and partly because of the great productive works carried out by Government. (2) Thanks to these, he is better off than the cultivator in Japan and, in proportion to his needs, is probably no worse than the cultivator in Portugal, Spain, Italy, Roumania, Bulgaria, Greece and Serbia. If any considerable improvement is to be effected a very searching enquiry will be necessary to solve the problems as to what the crops can be grown in the Punjab with most profit, or rather as to what is the most profitable use to which the land can be put, consistent with the religious sentiments of the people. The qualification is necessary because the production of cattle for milk alone is no more profitable than the keeping of poultry for eggs alone or the production of sheep for wool alone. The great sheep breeding industry of Australia and New Zealand would not pay those engaged in it unless a market could be found for the meat and the hides. These latter are by-products of the wool producing industry. (3)

Of the crops, which such an enquiry would show to be most profitable, it is unlikely that wheat would be one. Wheat is a crop for extensive cultivation where land is abundant and cheap. It requires comparatively little work to get a moderately good yield, but it does not respond so vigorously as other crops to human effort to increase the outturn. It is a poor crop for intensive cultivation. It is a bulky crop to transport five or six thousand

(1) Poultry keeping was wellnigh universal in England so long as 600 years ago, and Fitzberbert, writing in 1523, describes the farmer's wife as going to market to sell butter, cheese, milk, eggs, chickens, hens and geese. Curtler, pp. 41, 85. Thorold Rogers, Vol. IV, Ch. II.

(2) The Japanese Ambassador to the United States told an American audience : "Our people are not in want because their requirements are limited to the barest necessities of life. We have a very small area of food-producing country from which to draw, and by necessity every bit of it is most intensely cultivated. Our credit has been created by a frugality of living and a sacrifice of the individual to the State, in order that the State, the Nation and the Individual may survive".

Fitzherbert, who wrote on Husbandry about 1523, remarked that stock-raising is as necessary to a farmer as corn cropping. Without both, he will be a buyer, a borrower or a beggar. (Thorold Rogers, Vol. IV, Ch. II.)

(3) Pigs are to some extent a by-product of dairying. That cattle production for milk alone does not pay is conclusively proved by the fact that no Hindu capitalist attempts it. The gradual replacement of the cow by the she-buffalo is probably due the absence of any restraining religious sentiment as to the disposal of the she-buffalo. A European cow will give more milk than an Indian buffalo.

miles to market. As agriculture advances, wheat retreats. It continues to a small extent in England as it happens to fit in well with the system of crop rotation; but, although the great campaign to increase food production during the war led to a rise in the area sown, this has not been maintained. In the United States the area under wheat has for some years past been declining in favour of other crops and, as has been already shown, it finds little place in the small holdings of Northern Europe. Wherever scientific methods are introduced, wheat loses favour. It declines in area as farms grow smaller, as cultivation become more intensive and as more capital is employed. (1)

Where, however, there is little capital available and the more intensively cultivated crops are not grown, wheat persists; (2) and it may continue to form a popular crop in the Punjab if its outturn can be increased nearer to European standards. One objection raised to putting nearly one-third of the total cultivated area under wheat is that vegetable growth is much more active in the Kharif (hot weather) season than in the Rabi (cold weather) season; and so a given area under wheat will produce less vegetable growth than the same area under a Kharif crop. (3)

Against all these considerations there must, however, be set others that tell in favour of wheat. It stands transport without much loss or deterioration; it commands a ready market, and, owing to the constant demand, the producer can nearly always rely on getting a full price. It is, of course, an excellent crop for the ignorant agriculturist possessed of neither the capital nor the intelligence to produce something more valuable.

As an alternative to wheat, cotton has much in its favour. It responds better to intensive cultivation, it seems more capable of improvement under scientific treatment, and it grows well in the hot season. The demand seems to be fairly constant and unlimited. The pressed fibre comprises high value for small bulk, it is easily handled, is always saleable and stands transport over long distances. In the Punjab it possesses one great advantage over wheat inasmuch as water in the canals is generally plentiful during the cotton growing season but is apt to become scarce while wheat occupies the ground.

If, however, the province is to see changes that have accompanied the development of small holdings in other countries it is probable that more valuable crops than either cotton or wheat will gain popularity as the practice of intensive cultivation is acquired. Already around the big towns intensive cultivation is freely resorted to, and with an improvement of communications, resulting in cheaper and quicker transport, the further spread of

(1) In Australia it is said that the least area on which a satisfactory living at wheat growing can be made in Victoria is six hundred acres. This was a dry area.

(2) *Cf.* Ashly: Allotments of small holdings in Oxfordshire, p. 64. Wheat remains the most profitable cereal crop for an allotment. For the general argument *cf.* Carver, Principles of Rural Economics, pp. 113, 167; Gillette, Constructive Rural Sociology, p. 39 ff.; Rural Wealth and Welfare, p. 77: Vogt; Introduction to Rural Sociology, p. 70; Rowntree: Land and Labour: Lessons from Belgium, pp. 173-7.

(3) This, I understand, is the argument of Mr. W. Roberts, late Principal, Agricultural College, Lyallpur. It may be noted that if the Punjab agriculturist adopted a four year rotation as in England the area under wheat would be thereby reduced considerably. In the selection of crops the amount of water available is a determining factor. Sir James Wilson estimated that the average outturn per acre sown was 32 bushels in Great Britain, 22 in Canada, 16 in the United States of America and 13 in the Punjab.

these methods may be anticipated. The chief obstacle to speedy change seems to be the difficulty in obtaining markets to absorb all that could be produced. (1) The present extensive system of cultivation is characterized by absence of manuring, long fallows, routine methods, lack of intelligence and originality, and limiting of sowing to seasonal crops. It is the system which attracts those who possess no security of tenure : it, in practice, involves great waste of both land and labour. The change to intensive cultivation may be brought about by making a fuller use of the existing plentiful labour, by investing more capital in manure, improvements, implements, etc., and by using more scientific methods of cultivation. It is claimed by American writers that extensive cultivation on a large area gives a higher return per farmer or per person employed than intensive cultivation on a small area, and this seems to be true. In comparing systems of agriculture it is important to distinguish between production per acre and production per man ; for instance, the production of food per acre is much greater in Germany than in England, but the production per man is fully 20 per cent. higher in England than in Germany. The reason is that, while in England less than 16 per cent. of the land (2) consists of holdings under 50 acres, in Germany nearly half the land is so held. In the Punjab the area available per man is not large and no one advocates, what actually here exists, the cultivation of a small holding by extensive methods. With small holdings the production per man must be small. The capacity of the average human being to earn an income from production is very limited. Labour alone produces very little wealth per unit employed. The Punjab peasant must learn to use more than his labour. He must use every particle of intelligence he has or that can be instilled into him and he must learn to employ more capital. (3) From the point of view of the province as a whole there can be no question that the change to intensive methods is highly desirable. As land is the chief source of present and future wealth, the more wealth it can be made to produce the better for the general prosperity. The rural areas are suffering from a glut of labour ; the average cultivator has too much spare time, too much leisure and in consequence earns too small an income. It is not the case that a large number of people are out of work all the time, but there is a very large number out of work a considerable number of hours in the year. If from the cultivator's income there were deducted the interest on the sale-price of his land

---

(1) Transport may almost be described as the vital factor in securing markets and problems of transport are much neglected. Mr. and Mrs. Howard have rendered invaluable service in demonstrating how some problems can be solved. Quetta fruit suitably packed can be sold in distant places and Quetta vegetables suitably dried can be sent almost wherever a purchaser is to be found. Science, originality and enterprise can achieve wonders. Mr. Emerson would add, as a further obstacle to speedy change, the difficulty in getting manures that yield a profit. But there is no very keen competition for town refuse.

(2) But this 16 per cent. of the land comprises 66½ per cent. of the farms.

(3) For the general discussion of extensive versus intensive methods see Seligman, pp. 45, 315, 341 ; Gide, pp. 177-179 ; Carver, pp. 166-169, 239-247. Carver (p. 156) says : It is sometimes assumed that a large product per acre is a desirable thing in itself. Such is not the case ; what is really to be desired is a large product per man. It is only where the product per man is large that there is a high standard of living and a high standard of well-being for the average man. Where the land is abundant a large product per man is most easily secured by extensive farming. A large product per acre is desirable as a *means* of getting a large product per man and is not desirable in any other sense whatsoever. A large product per acre with a very small product per man is always accompanied by squalor and misery and we find this to be the actual situation in those countries which can point to the largest produce per acre.

and the wages of his labour there would in the great majority of cases be no profits left. (1) And yet it is said that there are few better paying industries than farming. (2) The apparent paradox is due to the fact that, under a hereditary system of land tenure, a large number of people remain cultivating ancestral lands who would never earn a living by the same exertion at any other occupation. Were Punjab agriculture organized on a sound economic basis, and the land put to the most profitable use, were the labour available steadily and regularly employed throughout the year, and were present waste eliminated, the cultivators would soon begin to show a profit on their intelligence and enterprise.

It may be argued that as the holdings are not economic holdings the agriculturists can never be prosperous. An economic holding, says Mr. Keatinge (3), is a holding which allows a man a chance of producing sufficient to support himself and his family in reasonable comfort after paying his necessary expenses. But it is of course impossible to fix accurately the size of such a holding for it is impossible to fix accurately what should be regarded as a reasonable standard of comfort. Situation with regard to markets, fertility and the uses to which the cultivator can put it are determining factors It may be true that a very large number of holdings in the Punjab are uneconomic now when extensively cultivated that would come well within the economic margin, if the system of cultivation were changed, communications with markets improved, and expenses decreased and income increased by means of Co-operation. It is not area but net product that determines what is an economic holding.

A certain area may constitute an economic holding, if situated close to a large market and intensively cultivated with the help of much manure, which would prove well below the economic limit if situated, say, in the Salt Range or the middle of the Sind Sagar Doab. Proximity to market may be as important as fertility and even more important if facilities for transport are not susceptible of improvement. Fertility is nowadays largely a matter of intelligence, industry and the correct application of capital. Similarly a given area may provide a decent living if irrigated from a well under the cultivator's control, while it might prove inadequate if irrigated from a canal working on a rotation. For it is not only the amount of water available, but also at its availability at the time best suited to the requirements of the particular plant, that determine the use to which the land can most profitably be put.

Again, a holding of five acres in a compact block, irrigated from a well, in a district like Jullundur, may be ample for the support of a cultivator of skill and enterprise, but may be completely uneconomic if scattered in ten or twelve different places, irrigated from several wells in each of which the cultivator owns only a fractional share or right. In most districts of the province, and more especially in the central districts, holdings have been subdivided into numerous fields, not contiguous, but scattered throughout

(1) Carver: Principles of Rural Economics, p. 315, says: The *profits of farming* are what is left of the farmer's annual income after allowing himself wages for his own labour, rent for his own land and interest for his own capital. It is doubtful whether half the farmers of this or any other country make any profits at all, while it is certain the poorest of them do not.
(2) Orwin: Place of Agriculture in Industry.
(3) Rural Economy in Bombay Deccan, p. 52.

the village area. Numerous instances could be given of villages consisting of a thousand or more fields of which the average area does not exceed one-quarter of an acre (2 kanals); in several villages the average area of the fields is not more than one-eighth of an acre (1 kanal). Of these fields some are too small to be cultivated, others are so narrow that it is not easy to plough crossways. In such tracts it is clear that many holdings, at present uneconomic, would have their value greatly enhanced by such a regrouping of the fields as would allot to each owner a solid block of land; the work is not free from difficulties, but is being attempted with some success through the agency of special Co-operative Consolidation of Holdings Societies. From what has been written above it will be realized that the term "uneconomic holding" refers to more than the mere area cultivated by each occupier, and that pressure on the soil can be relieved by other measures than migration.

Under most systems of cultivation known to European farmers an area of about 25 acres is necessary to provide for a family. (1) It may be that the standard of living of that family is higher than the average in the Punjab, but it is not so much higher as some people think. On the other hand, the labour put into the farm is very much greater. The majority of the farmers in Great Britain are small holders (*i. e.*, they have less than 50 acres) and nearly all are tenants. The evidence given before the Royal Commission on Agriculture in 1919 was to the effect that the small holders' life is rather a dog's life, they are always at work and never done. They work hard for long hours assisted, when that is possible, by their families—wives, sons and daughters. For many years in Wales the farmers earned less money than their paid labourers, if reasonable interest on their capital be deducted. No class of man on the land has to work harder; with a farm not exceeding 50 acres, it is usual for the farmer to work it himself together with his sons and pay no wages to any outside labour; if he has no sons he may employ a man wholly or for part of the time. The only man who improves his position is the man who has worked hard and for long hours and applied himself to his industry in every possible way, and saved every penny that could be saved. The paid labourer has preferred his own position to that of his employer and has refused to change it for that of a small holder when land was offered to him. (2)

From the above it will be seen that nothing is to be gained from a discussion as to whether holdings in the Punjab are economic holdings or not. This term has to be used in relation to the standards of cultivation, industry, frugality, etc., prevailing in the locality. In this province it is noteworthy that anyone owning 50 acres or more is apt to regard himself as a big landlord, to give up cultivating with his own hands and to rent his land and live on the proceeds.

In a discussion of the position of small holders in different countries it is necessary to point out that there is not in the Punjab anything approaching to the rich pastures of England. Writers sometimes deplore the decrease in the area of pasture land in the province, and ascribe to this

(1) A market gardener, of course, can thrive on much less.
(2) Answers 14990-2, 15506, 15818, 15888-9, 15964.

cause the decline in the number of cows and the high price of milk and *ghi*. The fact is that what is called pasture land or grazing ground here results from the neglect of agriculture, while the rich pastures of England are the result of the expenditure of much capital, labour and skill. Neglect of a natural resource is not the way to acquire wealth, and there can be no shadow of doubt that 100 acres under irrigated crop produce more food for both man and beast than did the same area lying waste before the canal came. (1) The effect of extensions of cultivation is to produce more fodder than before, but this fodder is required for the bullocks needed to cultivate the land, whereas in the old pastoral days the herdsman had little use for bullocks and turned his available fodder into milk or *ghi*.

From the above discussion it would appear that what is wrong in this province is that the system of cultivation is not the one best adapted to the local conditions. The Punjab cultivator must not be confused with the farmer of England, America or even Denmark. He is hardly a farmer at all in the usual significance of that word. He is a small holder, a very considerable number are mere allotment holders; yet nearly all follow methods of cultivation that could only pay with a holding of several hundred acres. His position is not worse, it is in many ways better, than that of the cultivators in Southern Europe ; it need not remain unsatisfactory ; but it will so remain unless he wakes up to a realization of what is essential to his prosperity. He is at present attempting the impossible task of making a living out of a small holding or an allotment by methods adapted to extensive areas. He ignores all the elements of success. Stock-keeping is almost unknown. At the most a few cattle or goats constitute his live belongings. Animal husbandry is restricted by religiou ssentiment, by ignorance and by prejudice ; and without animal husbandry only intensive cultivation can make a small holding pay. As there seems no immediate prospect of increasing the size of holdings, there must be a change in the use to which the land is put. The great Punjab problem is : What is the best and most profitable method of utilizing a holding of from five to fifteen acres ? The cultivation of wheat is most certainly not that method, although it will probably always pay to have a proportion of the land under this crop. The Board of Agriculture in England has recently announced that information, made available by research and experiment, was sufficient to show that the number of cows which could be maintained on the produce of a given area of land is from two to three times greater when that land is under the plough than when it is under grass, and that it is possible for a small holding of from 17 to 25 acres to be made an economic undertaking. To show that dairy farming on purely arable land is sound from the commercial point of view, the Development Commission has agreed to advance £40,000 for ten demonstrations. (2)

The Punjab problem is not insoluble. But, if a solution is to be found, there must be a generous provision for research and experiment, and there must be highly skilled investigators to make the best use of this financial

(1) Even of England Sir A. D. Hall says that a given area of land will produce when under the plough, in addition to its usual yield of wheat and barley, just as much cattle food as the same area of land under grass ; Agriculture after the War, p. 24, also p. 32 :—We may conclude that the crops from land under the plough, when used for feeding cattle, will produce of either meat or milk more than twice as much as the same land will yield when under grass.

(1) Report of the Development Commissioners, 1919.

provision. The experience gained elsewhere, though valuable as indicating what should be done towards the solving of the problem, will not go far towards the actual solution. For in this province the dominating factor is water. Rich pasture is probably impossible to secure with our present knowledge. Highly intensive cultivation over a large area is seemingly prohibited by the amount of moisture available. Fruit growing is only to be considered if there be ample water at the time when the expanding fruit needs it; for it is not only the quantity of water available that will determine the ultimate future of Punjab agriculture, but the time when this quantity can be supplied. Canals and artificial reservoirs will do much, but there must be the capital to construct them, and the security to support the credit necessary to attract that capital. To these must be added the development of a vastly greater interest in agricultural improvements, the discovery of a suitable system of agricultural education, the organization of the cultivators to make the best use of this new knowledge and their protection from factors tending to depress their enterprise. Amongst these latter may be included that widespread ignorance of agricultural economics that would allow the advocacy of measures designed to please a section, but certain to end in the destruction of all hope for the future prosperity of the people at large. No race, no nation can ignore economic laws with impunity. There is apt to be a section favouring the adoption of measures designed to meet its own needs, such, for instance, as the restriction of the export of wheat in the apparent interest of the town dwellers. It is not sufficiently realized that anything that tends to reduce the price of agricultural produce tends in like measure to discourage agriculture. Cheap wheat from America in the first half of the last century nearly ruined agriculture in Europe, led to political disturbances and social upheavals and finally caused a revolution in methods. Ultimately, it may be, good resulted, but much suffering had first to be endured.

There may be met with advocates of low prices who argue that high prices benefit no one, as if every producer did not seek the highest return for his industry and enterprise. (1) Such writers ignore the big problem of the Punjab. The cultivator has to make a living out of the land he has in his possession, whether it be as owner or as tenant; that land is limited in area, and accordingly methods which might be open to large holders are not suitable; what system he should adopt is the question that dominates all others. He must grow what he can sell or consume, and accordingly what he can sell is a paramount consideration. The profit to be gained is the deciding factor, and not the selfish interest of other sections of the community. Utopian thinkers dream of a social system wherein everyone thinks of someone else, and subordinates his activities to their ends. Experience dictates that the interests of all are best secured by everyone looking after his own, subject to such restraints and restrictions as are enforced in civilized countries for the public good. An owner of five acres has no margin for philanthropic adventures in favour of the rest of society, his choice of what he shall sow and what he shall breed are too limited by the overwhelming necessity to

(1) *Cf.* Thorold Rogers: Vol. IV, Ch. XXVI. "A rise in the price of agricultural produce, unless it be the result of moderately bad seasons, is always advantageous to those who are tilling land, whether it comes from a change in the value of money, or from an increased demand or from a greatly deficient supply."

earn a living out of a holding that is barely sufficient for the purpose. As it happens, however, it is, in the long run, to the advantage of the towns people that the cultivator should extract the highest profit out of his fields; agricultural prosperity means prosperity for all. When agriculture is unprogressive, wealth can be accumulated but slowly; and, in consequence, the supply of capital for industries and other productive ends is apt to fall short of the requirements of the time. Progressive agriculture, on the other hand, brings wealth to many, if not most, of the community. Big industrial populations must be fed so that, until there is produced food in excess of local requirements, there can be no surplus to satisfy manufacturing centres, and these last cannot come into being. Progressive agriculture stimulates foreign trade by producing the wherewithal to exchange for commodities not obtainable at home. It renders possible the maintenance of a greater population in a given country that could be supported when the industry is stagnant. (1) From the point of view of the nation at large, agriculture must be progressive if the country is to enjoy the modern amenities of life and take its place in the world. The conditions to that end are several. Undoubtedly one is that the advantages and limitations of existing factors should be well investigated and understood. Among the limitations the size of the Punjab holding is one of the most important. The average is not much below that to be found in several countries in Europe, but local conditions, including religious feelings, preclude the land from being devoted to purposes that elsewhere have made prosperity possible. The Punjab must solve its own problem.

---

(1) *Cf.* Thorold Rogers: Vol. IV, Ch. XXVI.

CHAPTER VII.

THE EXTENT AND EFFECTS OF TENANCY.

No discussion of the major economic factors of the Punjab would be complete without an examination of the extent and influence of tenancy. (1) Tenancy is increasing and its influence on economic development will increase rapidly as the commercial view of agriculture becomes more widespread.

It is difficult to compile a connected account of the important changes that are taking place as the bases of official statistics have been altered from time to time; but there will be little difficulty in demonstrating the existence of these changes.

The first is that the number of tenants is increasing. The following figures make this clear :—(2)

		Tenants-at-will	*Occupancy tenants.*	*Total.*
1872-73	..	650,000	379,000	1,100,000
1882-83	..	1,096,000	512,000	1,608,000
1892-93	..	2,874,000	758,000	3,632,000
1902-03	..	3,077,000	940,000	4,017,000

These figures do not accurately represent the change as—

(*a*) more and more of those shown as tenants-at-will seem to be proprietors who have rented a small plot from a neighbour, and

(*b*) the colonization of new canal irrigated areas has led to a large increase in the number of crown tenants. However, there can be no doubt that the number of tenants is increasing. In the Census Report of 1911 it is noted that 58 per cent. of the total population lived on agriculture or means subservient thereto, made up as follows :—

31·4 per	cent. of the total	population	are rent payers.
19	ditto	ditto	cultivating proprietors.
2·6	ditto	ditto	rent receivers (not cultivating proprietors).
5	ditto	ditto	are classified as miscellaneous.

(1) The Conference of the Agricultural Commission of the American Bankers' Association in 1919 recorded that :—"Farm tenancy is a constantly increasing menace to a permanent, prosperous and safe agriculture, and a contented country life. It has resulted in the loss of the priceless fertility of the soil—the creation of an unsettled farm population—illiteracy —an inefficient country school system—a drift from farm to city—and unprofitable methods of agriculture". In America, however, the tenant stays on the average about four years only on one farm; In England tenancy is regarded as having reached perfection, owing largely to the excellent efforts of the owners to promote agriculture. *Cf.* Boyle: Agricultural Economics, pp. 62, 81.

(2) Extracted from Annual Report on the Land Revenue Administration. The total number of tenants of all kinds in 1872-3 was 1,100,000 and of cultivating proprietors 2,000,000 but the details given in the report do not agree with the total given in it.

The second change to be noted is that the area cultivated by tenants is increasing and the third is that the proportion of the area cultivated by tenants to total cultivated area is also increasing.

In 1875-76 44 per cent. of the cultivated area of the province was held by tenants (of whom 30 per cent. had occupancy rights). In 1918-19 the proportion was over 51 per cent.

The area cultivated by tenants-at-will alone increased as follows :—

1892-93	..	9,026,000	acres out of	22,500,000 or 40 per cent
1902-03	..	14,133,000	do.	25,780,000 or 43 do.
1916-17	..	12,450,000		

In 1918-19, out of a total cultivated area of 29,140,212 acres, the area cultivated by tenants (all kinds) paying rent was 14,832,884 (=51 %). (1)

The area cultivated by occupancy tenants and the average area cultivated by each are declining.

The fourth change is that cash rents are decreasing in proportion to kind rents.

In 1875-76 52 per cent. of the tenants-at-will were paying cash rents. By 1902-03 this proportion had fallen considerably, and, owing largely to the high prices obtainable for agricultural produce, landowners are tending more and more to secure rents in kind. (2) This change, however, must not be exaggerated. In theearly days, up to 1882-83, rents in cash consisted, to a very large extent, in the payment by the tenants of land revenue and cesses only.

One important factor influencing the figures for tenancies is the increase in the number of mortgages. 3,116,000 cultivated acres or about 10·9 per cent. of the whole cultivated area are at present under mortgage. The number of mortgages is 1,400,000. As the mortgagor is, in the great majority of cases, entered in the records as tenant cultivating under the mortgagee, the number of tenants tends to increase with the number of mortgages. (3)

---

(1) Sir James Wilson in his "Recent Economic Developments in the Punjab" wrote :—" Between 1889 and 1907 the area cultivated by owners themselves decreased from 14¼ to less than 13 million acres, the area cultivated by tenants increased from 7½ to 11½ million acres.' The change has continued since 1907. Sir J. Wilson suggests that, as the increase in cultivation in the last 50 years has been almost entirely in the area under irrigation, the average profits per acre (as well as the average outturn) has increased. Thus the owner can secure the same outturn and the same profits from a smaller area. At the same time, the increase in profits stimulates would-be tenants to offer good rents which tempt the owner to part with possession.

(2) *Cf.* Lahore Settlement Report :—" The popularity of kind rents has considerably increased since last settlement". Also Gujrat :—" The area under cash rent is almost negligible....Rent in kind is lenient for the tenant in bad years and profitable for the landlord on the whole." Amritsar :—" The tendency of late years has been for the landlord to insist on receiving a share of the produce on the better irrigated lands ; as a rule he will accept a cash rent only on unirrigated fields, where the crops are always uncertain." Gurdaspur :—"The landlord's tendency is decidedly towards a rent in the form of a share of the produce."

(3) Figures are taken from the Land Revenue Administration Report for 1920. The average mortgage, it will be observed, is fo rabout 2¼ acres, paying Rs. 3 land revenue. It thus appears that the land under mortgage is about (but not quite) average quality, also that not more than 35 per cent. of the owners can have a mortgage.

For information as to the increase in mortgages see the discussion on the Abuse of Rural Credit.

The outstanding fact in the above is that half the cultivated area of the province is held by tenants-at-will with only conditional freedom to carry out improvements, no fixity of tenure and imperfect protection against enhancement of rent or eviction if they increase the productivity of their fields by sinking capital in them. (1) The proportion of tenants to owners varies with the community. In 1872-73 it was noted that amongst Sikhs, who had a short time before been the ma sters of the province, there were 100 proprietors to 23 tenants; amongst Mohammadans, owing to the large owners in the western districts, there were 100 proprietors to 61 tenants. The Hindus come in between with 100 proprietors to 53 tenants. More recent figures do not seem to be available. But, comparing the four districts on the east (Hissar, Rohtak, Karnal and Ambala), where 74·3 per cent. of the population are Hindus and only 25·3 per cent. Mohammadans, with the four districts on the west (Rawalpindi, Attock, Mianwali and Muzaffargarh), where 12·3 per cent. are Hindus and 87·2 per cent. Mohammadans, it is found that the cultivated area is held as follows :—

	Owners.	*Occupancy tenants.*	*Other tenants.*
East ..	53 per cent.	11 per cent.	36 per cent.
West ..	48 per cent.	11 per cent.	41 per cent.

Of the cultivated area in the more central districts, the proportion cultivated by the actual owners is 48 per cent. in Amritsar, 44 per cent. in Lahore, while in the Mohammadan district of Gujrat the proportion rises to 56 in Gujrat Tehsil, 61 in Kharian and 60 in Phalia. The large proportion of tenants among Mohammadans is thus due not to religion, but to the number of large estates in the Mohammadan districts along the Indus.

The proportion of the land cultivated by the owners is said to be 35 per cent. in Belgium, 86 per cent. in Germany, 88 per cent. in Denmark, 47½ per cent. in France and 12 per cent. in Great Britain. (2) In Japan the proportion appears to be about 53 per cent. There seems to be a distinct tendency for tenancy to increase in other countries than the Punjab. It has certainly increased in England with the disappearance of the yeoman farmer, (3) it is increasing in Belgium, and in the United States, where its economic and social effects are described as the central phase of the American land situation. The chief cause is the increase in land values which serve to prevent tenants from saving enough to purchase their holdings. With the exception of England, where the relationship between them and their landlords is, perhaps, the best in the world, the desire to acquire rights of ownership seems to be general. Of the effects of tenancy in the Punjab it is more difficult to write. What follows is based on replies received to a series of questions issued to Inspectors of Co-operative Societies, with the same instructions

(1) The Tenancy Act allows a tenant-at-will to make an improvement with the assent of his landlord; if he can prove this assent he cannot be ejected and his rent cannot be enhanced until he has received compensation for his improvement. But local conditions make it very difficult to prove assent.

(2) Rowntree : Land and Labour : Lessons from Belgium, pp. 113, 114. The figures are not recent ones. But, in another way, in France 77 per cent. of the farmers, in Germany 83 per cent. own all or a part of their farms. In the United States 38 per cent. of farmers are tenants. *Cf.* Gillette : Constructive Rural Sociology, p. 220.

(3) But, the extensive sales of land since the war seem to be leading to an increase of cultivating ownership again; the old tenants are making great, and not always wise, efforts to purchase.

as were issued in the case of the enquiry into the effects of the rise in the price of land. The Inspectors were directed to compare in as much detail as possible several holdings cultivated by their owners with several holdings cultivated entirely by tenants who are not relations of the owner.

The first question put was : "Is there any difference in the methods of cultivation, number of ploughings, manuring, etc.?" So far as the occupancy tenant is concerned he has practically the same security of tenure as the owner and works on the same lines. His case need not be discussed.

The replies nearly all distinguished between tenants-at-will and lessees, and between tenants when paying *batai* (kind) rents and when paying cash rents. Lessees are said to devote more time and energy than owners and secure higher yields. There seems to be agreement that a tenant paying a cast rent works harder, ploughs more frequently and puts more manure on to his land than one paying in kind. If he pays a kind rent on certain crops such as wheat and a cash rent on fields under other crops such as sugar-cane, he concentrates on the latter and may even plough it more often and manure it better than the owner. A careful enquiry made in Gurdaspur showed that on the average the tenants gave 19·4 ploughings to sugar-cane while the owners gave 15·7.

All replies agree that a tenant paying a kind rent ploughs the land less often than an owner, manures it less and gets a smaller yield. The former has fewer implements and renews them less frequently. Where new ploughs are being introduced and pure seed is being used, it is the owners, and not the tenants, who take the lead in adopting them. Some investigators say that the tenant obtains 25 per cent. less outturn than do the owners. It is worth noting, however, that even the tenant-at-will cultivates better than the paid labourer of the big landlord. Thus it would seem that the system of paying rent in kind and tenancy-at-will both serve to bring about a low standard of cultivation, while tenancy coupled with a cash rent is less inimical to good husbandry. (1)

The second question put to the investigators was whether there was any difference in the cropping by tenants and owners. Where a tenant is also an owner, he tends to cultivate the best crops, such as sugar-cane, cotton, etc., on his own land and the less paying crops on fields on which he pays rent in kind. On the other hand, an owner, who cultivates a portion of his holding and rents the rest, is inclined to keep under his own cultivation those

---

(1) *Cf* Carver : Principles of Rural Economics, p. 231 :—"Generally speaking, the seasons are overwhelmingly in favour of cash rents ; under the share system the tenant is less assiduous in cultivating the soil ; cash tenancy leads to more thorough farming, but endangers the future fertility of the soil. The cash tenant gets all the advantage of his own superior cultivation, whereas the share tenant gets only a share of that advantage. Under the principle of diminishing returns the cash tenant can afford to increase the intensity of his cultivation up to a higher point. In favour of the *batai* (rent in kind) system Mr. Emerson urges that it secures (*a*) automatic adjustment of rents to prices, conducing to better relations between landlord and tenant ; (*b*) automatic adjustment of rents to seasonal conditions; (*c*) mutual interest between landlord and tenant in good cultivation. But, where the landlord is purely a rent receiver, as is too frequently the case in the Punjab, it is not easy to see why a landlord should gain from rising prices of produce ; he may gain from rising profits if the rise leads to more competition for his land,

fields which are most suitable for the better paying crops. These tendencies lead to a difference in cropping. The area put under fodder by a tenant depends to some extent on the custom governing the share which the landlord takes. Where the rent is a fixed proportion of the crop, this proportion is based not on the whole yield, but on the remainder, after menials, etc., have received their dues. It is said that tenants are more willing to pay a higher share to labourers as this does not all come out of their portion of the produce, also that in harvesting the crop the tenant is apt to be careless as anything left behind in the fields can be picked up by his womenfolk. The general tendency is for a tenant, holding on a kind rent, to grow more wheat than an owner and less of any crop involving expenditure of capital. A cash rent is more favourable to the production of valuable crops such as sugar-cane or cotton; a *batai* rent results in less valuable crops being grown. On the whole a tenant grows less valuable crops than an owner.

The third question was: "Is there any difference in perennials such as trees, etc., on the holdings?"

Tenants practically never plant trees nor take any care of those already planted. In the colonies it is reported that there are fewer trees in squares cultivated by tenants than in those cultivated by owners; in safedposh chaks there are many trees where the safedposh settled on the land originally and few where they gave out the squares to tenants.

A careful count in Gurdaspur over a considerable number of holdings cultivated by owners and tenants showed a very much higher proportion of trees (actually 10 times higher for the same area) in the former than in the latter. Tenants regard trees as inimical to crops and, accordingly, there is a tendency for owners to keep fields with trees on them.

Fruit trees, gardens, etc., are planted by owners, and practically never by tenants.

Apart from the hills, there are practically no perennials (tea, coffee, fibres, small fruits, etc.) planted as crops.

The tenants' antipathy to trees is commented on by all.

The fourth question was: "Is there any difference in efforts at improving the land?"

"He who stays for a night at an inn does not go on to the roof to stop a leak; he shifts his bed." There is general agreement that the tenant makes no efforts at improvement; he cares less for careful rotation, though, being frequently more industrious than an owner, he may extort a higher yield. The owner will root out weeds, level the soil, erect small embankments round his fields to retain the rainwater and allow more fallow. He is more particular in putting manure on to his fields, while a tenant more frequently sells his cow-dung. Wells, of course, are sunk by owners, and not by tenants, and the *kuhls* and other irrigation channels in the hills are made and kept in repair by the owners. The replies are emphatic on the point that the tenant does nothing to improve the land, while the owners are doing what they can. (1)

(1) "The rapacity which has deterred the tenant from making improvements lest he should have to pay on his own outlay has done more to hinder the growth of agriculture as opposed to stock breeding than any other cause." Thorold Rogers, Vol. IV, Ch. II.

The fifth question was : "Is there any difference in the cattle, etc., kept ?"

The general opinion is that, although owners may keep more expensive bullocks and, perhaps, more ponies, tenants keep more cows and she-buffaloes and look after their cattle better. This result does not quite correspond with what was to be expected on theoretical grounds. But in former days a cultivator's bullocks were worth much more than his land and he looked after them accordingly ; nowadays his land is worth more than his bullocks and he is more inclined to improve his land. The tenant, however, has in his cattle his only property of value and looks after them accordingly. He looks to his cows or his she-buffaloes to add to his scanty income by the sale of milk and *ghi*, he looks to his oxen to gain him a few rupees in transporting goods. It is also said that, as a tenant may get the worse land, he has to keep stronger oxen. Some reports say there is no difference discernible, while one or two say the owners keep more, as well as better, oxen and more she-buffaloes. Where the landlord takes little or none of the fodder grown, there is a tendency for tenants to grow more fodder crops and keep more milch cattle.

Opinion seems to be unanimous in reply to the sixth question as to buildings, that those of owners are more spacious and better constructed ; the wood used is frequently of better quality, deodar or chil, while tenants use local wood.

In the colonies the difference is more marked than in old settled villages. Briefly, it may be said that the owner has a residence; while the tenant has a shelter. One or two reports mention that there is a tendency to improvements in tenants' dwellings, partly as a result of the high prices obtained for produce and partly owing to the income earned from sources other than agriculture.

The seventh question was : "Is there any difference in the education of the children ?"

The bigger owners are much more inclined to have their children educated than tenants ; but there is less difference between these latter and small owners. Beyond the primary stage the tenant's son hardly appears at all. The bigger owner is frequently able to pay for services which, in the case of the tenant, must be performed by the children. Only one report mentions any tendency of owners to withhold education because the boy will have ample means of livelihood from the land. In no case is there any mention of any tendency for tenants to get their sons educated so as to relieve the pressure on the holding or so as to help the family with his earnings. As primary education for agriculturists is free, the cost is not a factor ; the neglect of tenants to send their children to school is to some extent due to apathy and ignorance resulting from a narrow outlook, but to a larger extent to the need for the child's labour in looking after cattle, etc.

In the eighth question the Inspectors were asked to report whether they could discover any difference in the careers of the children (*i.e.*, working as agriculturists, engaging in other business, migrating to towns, taking service, etc.). The replies received reveal nothing definite. Both classes cling to the land. The educated son of a bigger owner seeks service, the tenant's son is more free to migrate to the colonies. The owner is tied to his fields, the tenant may be compelled to seek labour in the town. The disinclination to abandon agriculture is equally strong, except only in the case of the educated youth. A much more detailed statistical enquiry will be needed before any very definite conclusion can be drawn. As to whether there is any difference in the standard of living or in indebtedness, it is pointed out that the owner has to incur a higher level of expenditure, in accord with his social position, and he is also more liable to be involved in litigation. As he possesses greater credit he can borrow more freely for his luxuries. In food and clothing he lives better than the tenant ; the latter; for instance, has to sell his milk or *ghi*, while the owner consumes it. (1) The difference is very marked in some tribes and less amongst others such as the Gujars and Arains. The fact that the tenant has little credit forces thrift upon him so that he wastes less on litigation or luxuries, works harder and is generally more careful over his expenditure. The average debt of owners is almost everywhere much higher than that of tenants, owing to their better credit. Tenants living near towns are improving their position by doing miscellaneous work in their spare hours and, in some cases, seem to be becoming better off than the small owners whose dignity forbids them to engage in non-agricultural occupations.

The tenth and last question was whether tenants joined co-operative societies as freely as owners. The bigger owners do not join these societies freely. The medium owners do, though the unlimited liability is sometimes a stumbling block. The tenants stand to lose very little, but they have grown so accustomed to receiving no credit from the moneylender that they have learned to pull along without it.

In some cases owners are disinclined to admit tenants on an equality or to lend them money after admission ; in others it is found that the outlook on life of the tenant is so narrow that he cannot appreciate the objects and benefits of co-operation. He is not a co-sharer in the common land of the village and sometimes find difficulty in grasping the idea of an equal co-partnership with owners in a society.

Where, as in the colonies, tenants are not permanently settled in a village, this serves to keep them from joining. In the old settled districts, especially where the co-operative movement has acquired a firm hold, tenants join freely, but not, apparently, in the same proportion to their numbers as owners. On the whole there seems to be reason to believe that tenants are joining societies more freely as the principles of the movement are being more widely understood.

To sum up the argument thus far, it may be said that over half the cultivated area of the province is tilled by tenants, and that this area tends to increase steadily. These tenants generally take less care in preparing the land for crops, plough it less often, manure it less and use fewer implements upon it than owners. They grow less valuable crops, especially avoiding those

(1) Mr. Emerson points out that, with the rapid increase in prosperity, tenants are less inclined to sell their *ghi* and this is a considerable factor in the shortage of that article.

requiring the sinking of capital in the land; they make little or no effort at improving their fields; they keep a lower type of cattle; they avoid perennials and bestow no care on trees. They show a stronger disinclination than even small owners do to have their children educated, and have not yet grasped the importance of organizing themselves for the more profitable conduct of their industry. The system of paying a proportion of the crop as rent (*batai*) accentuates most of these tendencies and militates against a proper rotation of crops; this system is steadily supplanting cash rents. (1)

The evil is increased by the high price of land, which is rising faster than rentals, and so making it not only impossible, but unprofitable, for tenants to become owners; while mortgages and sales are steadily adding to the number of fields cultivated under tenancy conditions.

It is not possible to give any accurate idea of the extent of the evil as a considerable number of tenants are owners of adjoining plots who have exchanged cultivating possession with other owners, and others are cultivating their own lands under mortgagees. Moreover it is not known to what extent tenants migrate from plot to plot or from village to village, or to what extent they till the same fields semi-permanently (2). Tenancy itself is not necessarily an evil; most of the farms in England are given on short (yearly) leases to tenants, who do not seem to desire longer ones. In Scotland leases run from 7 to 19 years, many being for 14 years. (3). In Wales, again, yearly agreements are general. The arguments for and against occupying ownership, long leases and yearly tenancies are interesting and deserve careful

---

(1) The *batai* system favours extensive cultivation, *i.e.*, the highest gross return for labour. It discourages intensive cultivation owing to the law of diminishing returns.

(2) The following abstract of an account of tenancy in the United States of America, taken from the International Review of Agricultural Economics for April, 1917, affords an interesting comparison:—

In the United States of America a tenant stays on a given farm hardly three years. The share tenants move a little oftener than do those paying cash....farms operated by owners are held by a given owner probably about 16 years.

American farm land has been rising rapidly in value. It has been, in consequence, for sale. As a result many a farm changes occupants because of a change in ownership, and the owner, so long as he holds the farm for sale, is bound to lease it for short periods of time. Another important cause of short tenures is the fact that the tenants are themselves developing into farm owners. The great majority of those who stay in the farming business a lifetime manage by some means to become landowners......the short period of occupancy of farms by tenants is in no small measure due to the constant rise of tenants to ownership on their own account.

Tenancy follows as a natural outcome of conditions, chiefly of the character of the agriculture in practice....he owns little livestock, he plants few perennials or trennials, he invests little money in fertilizers or sub-soil ploughs—he wants a chance to sow, harvest and sell all within a year. Tenancy is most prevalent in the cotton, corn and wheat districts..He produces more grain than the landowning farmer, and less of the crops used for feeding young stock..he does not go in for dairying or fruit growing, but does for tobacco and vegetables as these require little equipment and but few months. The tenant is an exploiter of the soil.

Rentals do not rise as readily as the selling value of land and therefore, other things being equal, it is cheaper to rent land than to buy it. The labour income of the tenant is larger than that of the landowning farmer.

In America neither landlord nor tenant takes a great deal of interest in permanent agriculture. The landlord expects to sell the land, the tenant expects to leave it....tenants raise as much grain per acre as is raised by the owners. It is a rare thing for the tenants to wish to make improvements. Tenants as a class are seldom found in organizations They are poor community members.

(3) A Scotch witness before the Royal Commission on Agriculture, 1919, said: "You cannot expect men with brains and capital to put their whole endeavour into agriculture unless you give them some assurance of a return for a period of years". Q. 12, 772.

consideration in this province where it may be thought that the simple remedy for the evils of tenancy described above is a Land Purchase Bill similar to that which converted Irish tenants into proprietors. The problem of tenancy in Ireland, however, was complicated by alien landlords who had never recognized the obligations of their position and by a peasantry who had preserved a feeling of ownership in the land which they had so long occupied and from the rights in which they regarded themselves as having been unjustly expropriated. The remedies for the evils of tenancy asked for and granted were fair rent, fixity of tenure and free sale of tenant right. The British farmers desire not fixity of tenure, but security of tenure. American farmers have always assumed, as a matter of course, that it is better to own the land upon which they work, because, in the first place, the rise in the value of land is considered as part of the profits of farming, and, in the second place, no intelligent system of leasing land has been put before them. "We have not", writes Professor Carver, "worked out the problem of a system of tenancy which is attractive to a progressive and far-sighted farmer. Our system of short leases is about as well calculated to stifle initiative and enterprise as anything could well be. The interests of the landlord are so poorly safeguarded as to make it hazardous for him to let his land on a long lease. And yet the best agriculture in the world is carried on under the tenancy system" (in England). (1) If the land should decline in value the disadvantages of ownership are obvious. The British farmers are fully alive to this danger. At present, land in the United Kingdom is being sold on an extensive scale and tenants are being tempted to buy their holdings to secure possession of their farms. They do not want ownership, but security of tenure, and acquire the former to preserve the latter. The result is that many are crippling themselves in the carrying on of their industry by investing all their capital in the land, and not in the stock and farming requirements. Where, as in England, the rent is so small in proportion to the price as to represent a low rate of interest, it is better for a capable farmer to pay rent and to invest his available capital in livestock, machinery, etc., which will yield him a higher return. (2) Perhaps, in the Punjab, where so little is done towards expending money on improved agriculture, it may be difficult to realize that a British farmer is estimated to employ on the average from £15 to £25 (Rs. 150 to Rs. 250) per acre, apart from the permanent equipment, in buildings, drains, fences, etc., which is usually found by the landlord.

The argument against farmers owning their own lands in England is that it fixes the size of the farm. Under a tenancy system a farmer may begin on a comparatively small scale with, say, 100 acres, and, if he prospers on that, he can expand his holding to 200 acres. Assuming that he is saving money as a result of his energy and skill, he would naturally desire to invest these savings in his own business, and as time went on he would desire to take up more land for this purpose. The tenancy system thus provides a "ladder" by which the enterprising and energetic small farmer can rise to be a large farmer.

(1) Principles of Rural Economics, p. 226.

(1) *Cf.* Carver, p. 230. The evidence given before the Royal Commission on Agriculture, 1919-20, on security of tenure, leases and sales is briefly summarized in the following pages.

The arguments in favour of long and short leases depend on the security of tenure promised or guaranteed. The Scotch long leases are said to lead to a higher type of farming than is found under the short lease system of England, but there is a tendency during the last three years or so to exhaust the soil of its surplus fertility. This tendency is largely counteracted by the excellent relations between landlord and tenant, and especially by the landlord's willingness to renew the lease to a good tenant. For the English system it is claimed that it is more elastic, that it does not bind a farmer to go on paying a high rent during periods of low prices, while a good farmer can always rely on lenient and just treatment from his landlord. English farmers urge that a long lease induces the tenant to spend more upon improvements, for which he may not get adequate compensation.

In both cases, the sense of responsibility shown by the landlords of the old type plays a large part, and it is admitted that if the new type, that is now buying up land, acts in a purely commercial spirit, it will be necessary to give the tenant better protection. The successive Agricultural Holdings Acts have been framed to give security of tenure, but not fixity of tenure, nor even fixity of rent. The landlord's right to possession of his land is not disputed but the law now ensures to the tenant compensation for his unexhausted improvements and also for unreasonable disturbance due to a landlord's refusal to renew his occupancy. The farmers' representatives would estimate the compensation at from one to four years' rent. As to rent, reasonable farmers admit that it must to some extent follow prices. As they desire a reduction when prices fall, they admit the justice of an increase when prices rise. In the foregoing the problem has been discussed from the point of view of the actual cultivator. The landlord's view differs but little. But it is important to note that one eminent authority disagrees with the view that mere security of tenure to the sitting tenant will ensure a progressive improvement of agriculture. In his opinion, if there is no competition for land, rents will be low and tenants will make a sufficient income by cheap methods. Competition for farms will force up rents and so stimulate enterprise and a high type of farming. (1) From the above it will be clear that it would be incorrect to regard the abolition of tenancy as the remedy for its ill effects. Even a yearly tenancy is quite compatible with a high standard of farming, provided either that the landlord recognizes his responsibilities to his land and its cultivators or the law protects the tenant from the idiosyncrasies of one who does not. A proper partnership between the two is essential, and it is appreciation of this fact that leads an American writer to say that experience indicates that a good tenant system cannot be made by law,(2) and he may be fortified in his opinion by the frequency with which the Act relating to Agricultural Holdings has been amended.

Applying the arguments of the above discussion to the tenancy system in the Punjab, it would appear that the best remedy for the present situation lies in stimulating amongst the tenants the spirit of competitive enterprise. They require to be firmly imbued with the idea that a proper holding for a tenant is not 8 acres or 12, but 50 or 100, and that command of the larger

---

(1) Sir A. D. Hall : Agriculture after the War, p. 64.

(2) Gillette : Constructive Rural Sociology, p. 223.

area may be acquired by outbidding others for its hire. To pay the higher rent they must bring to bear more energy, better skill and trained intelligence. The best service the graduates of the Agricultural College could render their country would be to pioneer this movement, and, by this means, to oust from the land those who are least fitted to cultivate it. The plea that distress would thereby be caused requires little consideration. Many now occupying the land derive but a miserable subsistence from it. They could probably do better for themselves by supplanting those foreigners who at present fill the market for unskilled labour, or by recruiting themselves in the new industrial movement. Such a movement, of course, assumes that there is in the province, or can be produced, a body of men prepared to put forth the exertion required to cultivate the larger area. At present, as has already been noticed, the tendency is to reduce the area cultivated if the same profits can be obtained from a smaller area. The growing demand for a higher standard of living should operate to counteract this, but it will be some time before the real competition for land between cultivators of varying capacities will serve to stimulate the less efficient to improve their methods.

One defect of the present system is that the cropping followed almost everywhere leads to alternating periods of hard work for long hours with other periods of light labour for many days. If progress is to be achieved, it is not only a revolution in the use to which the land is put that will be required, but a big change in popular opinion as to what constitutes a fair year's work. The Indian cultivator seems to be unique in his avoidance of alternative means of adding to his income when his land does not fully occupy his time.

CHAPTER VIII.

The Price of Land.

One of the most conspicuous features in the economic history of the Punjab has been the rapid and continuous rise in the price paid for agricultural land. This rise has had a marked effect on the development of the province; it has attracted the lawyer and middleman class in general, as well as the cultivator, to invest their money in purchase, rather than improvement; it has tended to encourage gambling in a future rise, which has appeared more important than increased production; it has led to the enactment of special legislation, which, in turn, has been used as a political grievance suffered by a class who conspicuously abstained from acquiring property when it was cheap; it has supplied the basis for a facile credit which has brought immense harm to a population insufficiently educated to understand its dangers; it has served to encourage tenancy and to hinder the tenant from rising to the position of proprietor. To it can be traced not a little responsibility for the economic backwardness of the province, for it has drawn into land investment many crores of rupees that, but for the hope of further rise, might have been forced into industrial enterprise or put to productive use. It has made the land too attractive as a source of investment, but it has yielded little advantage to the cause of agriculture as a whole.

The subject is possessed of such great importance, and it is beset with so much misapprehension, that it seems desirable to discuss it in detail.

In the Punjab it is quite a modern feature. Prior to the advent of the British, rights in land, which now are recognised as proprietary or quasi-proprietary, were found under earlier rulers in one or other of two typical forms—the right to collect the revenue due to the State; and the right to hold certain land on condition of payment of the revenue due upon it, either to the State direct, or to a farmer who enjoyed the first form of right. (1)

Of the holders of the first form, some were recognised by the early British Government as superior proprietors (*e. g.*, the Talukdars of Oudh), in which case the actual cultivators have become inferior proprietors; others were recognised as full proprietors (*e. g.*, the great landowners of Bengal), in which case the actual cultivators have been given the status of tenants. The first form of right was not really a right in the soil, but a right in the revenue derived from it, the Kardar or the revenue farmer collecting more than he paid to the State. (2)

(1) Professor Kale in his interesting "Indian Economics", Ch. XV, admits that, in the turbulent times preceding the advent of the British, the conquerors of the day dispossessed those who had cleared and reclaimed the land, reduced them to the status of tenants or gave their lands to favourites; but contests the natural deduction that these rulers must have regarded themselves as empowered to do what he admits they did. He seems to hold the view that those who cultivated had rights of proprietorship maintainable against their rulers. Under Sikh rule the more powerful Kardars freely took land away from one party and gave it to another who promised a larger revenue. They acknowledged no right as against the State. A proprietary right is of little, if any, use if it cannot be enforced. When a ruler made his own laws, if he asserted a right and could enforce that right, he is correctly regarded as possessing the right which he claims.

(2) The jagirdar of the present day has a right to the revenue assessed by the State, and to no more; he has no proprietary right in the land from which he derives his jagir unless this happens to be his own quite independently of the jagir.

The second form of right was clearly of no value to anyone except to the actual cultivator. The State or the revenue farmer, to whom he paid the revenue, had to leave to him at least so much of the produce of his labour as was necessary to keep him on the land ; but it was no object of the State or the farmer to leave him any more than this ; the demand of the State or the greed of the farmer resulted in the taking of the whole profit of cultivation. The cultivator in such circumstances could pay no rent separate from the revenue, there was no room between him and the revenue receiver for anyone living on rent alone. The person who paid the revenue had perforce to be the actual cultivator. As the cultivator was left with nothing beyond a bare subsistence, whatever right he possesed in the land was of little value ; if anyone wanted land to cultivate he could break up the waste and so would not be likely to offer any price for a right that was of so little worth. In the Punjab where the revenue demand fell on a village community, and not on the individual, it was not at all uncommon for this community to persuade others to come from outside to cultivate the waste and lighten their burden by sharing it. Abandonments of whole villages, owing to the revenue demands being excessive or to political changes, were not infrequent. Sometimes a man of enterprise would obtain, on payment, a grant from the State to cultivate a certain area of land, in which case he might, on the strength of his grant, claim superior rights to the existing cultivators, or he might introduce his own. These in turn might later on oust him and become proprietors. There was little fixity of tenure and little of any value to attract a purchaser, had any such been forthcoming. It is unnecessary to discuss here to what extent, if at all, Hindu law ever prevailed in the Punjab. The whole spirit of that law is opposed to the idea of an individual controlling ancestral property and it is very doubtful if it included the idea of its sale. The Mohammedan invaders were not agriculturists but pastoralists ; they lived on their flocks and counted their wealth by these movable possessions. In so far as they have now any customary rights in land, they have imbibed these from the Hindus amongst whom they settled or from whom they are descended. There is ample reason to believe that, prior to the British entry into the Punjab, sale of land was very rare. (1) Instances may be quoted of transfers close to large towns, or of the sale of an improvement like a well, but the whole history of the province for five hundred years previous to annexation militates against the ideas of permanent tenure, (2) of rights of any value and of the sale of those rights. In those disturbed days it is doubtful if many people possessed any savings or would acknowledge their possession by purchasing land.

---

(1) The information available goes to show that it had no sale value.

(2) For an interesting account of land tenures in an early period See Moreland : India at the Death of Akbar, pp. 96-100 and 129-130. That the ordinary peasant was in constant danger of having his holding taken from him is illustrated by Jahangir's order that officials and jagirdars should not forcibly take the ryots' lands and cultivate them on their own account.

In opposition to the view here expressed, it is interesting to record that Sir Edward Maclagan, while Settlement Officer of Multan, collected information as to several cases of sale of land prior to annexation. It is not clear how a good title could be secured or how the purchaser could be protected from disputes. In Rumania, until very recently, owing to ignorance of the peasants and the absence of any system of registration of title, it was practically impossible to obtain a good title to land. There were always numerous persons claiming an interest in each piece of land. (*Vide* F. O. Pamphlet.) It is not easy to conceive of free sale without some form of registration of title, however primitive.

Under the Sikh régime, when "the cultivator ploughed with a sword by his side and the Collector came for the revenue at the head of a regiment", land, except in the immediate neighbourhood of big towns, was practically unsaleable. (1) Prior to the mutiny transfers were almost unknown, and in some parts of the province sales do not appear to have occurred before 1868. The province, it will be remembered, was annexed in 1849. It was looked upon as a country of deserts and barren wastes and its addition to the Empire was regarded as merely another burden upon the already depleted finances of the Government of India. With the introduction, however, of settled law and order, fixed moderate assessments and security of right and tenure, the Punjab embarked upon a remarkable career of prosperity which has continued, practically without interruption, down to the present day, and to which, with improved communications, expanding irrigation and rising prices for its agricultural produce, no end is at present visible.

As already remarked, prior to 1857 sales of land were comparatively rare ; but, shortly after, they began to attract notice, and by 1872 the increasing volume began to cause disquiet to Government. It is of special interest to note that in the districts with more regular rainfall the moneylenders preferred a mortgage to a sale ; ownership to them at that time would have been an encumbrance. (2) In Gurdaspur, in 1871-72, 66·5 per cent. of mortgages were in favour of moneylenders, while 63 per cent. of the sales were to agriculturists. In the districts of precarious rainfall the moneylender could not become an economic factor till much later, and mortages were rare, and sales represented the common form of transfer ; but most of these sales were to other owners.

The Punjab is essentially a province of petty peasant proprietors. The typical owner possesses some eight acres and probably cultivates four acres more as a tenant. The agricultural tribes are generally distinct, easily defined bodies, possessing valuable martial qualities which endow them with considerable political importance. To secure their contentment and prosperity has for nearly seventy years been the main object of the administration. Their expropriation by tribes of non-cultivating capitalists would obviously have proved a grave source of embarrassment and the Annual Land Administration Reports testify to the solicitous care with which the Punjab Government watched the rapid increase in sales of land by the ancient owners to moneylenders and shopkeepers. The prolonged official anxiety finally led to the passing of the Land Alienation Act in 1901. Throughout this period, however, the continued rise in the price of land has been regarded as a matter for pride and congratulation, and no doubts seem to have arisen as to whether this process had not continued past the limits at which it could be viewed with complacency. It is this question which forms the subject of this chapter.

---

(1) In England in 1086 the normal annual value of land was about twopence an acre ; land, apart from the stock upon it, was worth very little, perhaps not more than a shilling an acre. Curtler : Short History of English Agriculture, p. 19.

(2) Where the summary assessment pressed too severely, the zemindars are described as suffering privations ; they sold their cattle to the Sahukar, and they *deserted* their lands for neighbouring districts where the Government demand was lighter. They did not *sell* their lands ; but where there was a well they might sell that.

Undoubtedly the efforts of the British administration to confer on the agriculturists all the requisites of a prosperous peasantry were the initial cause of the rise in price. Reduction of the revenue assessment, preparation of an accurate record of rights and the legal protection accorded to these rights, affording security of title and freedom from disputes, together with a system of cheap transfer, all gave land a market value.

Where the right in land was the first of those described above, namely, a right to collect revenue, on payment of a fixed sum to the State, the new administration accepted the revenue farmers as superior proprietors, and increased the value of their right by limiting the State demand for revenue and even reducing it. At the same time no restriction was imposed on the amount demanded from the actual cultivators. The major portion of the province, however, was in the possession of the communities holding the second form of right, namely, a right to cultivate subject to the payment of revenue. Almost everywhere the early settlement officers reduced the revenue, with the result that, instead of the State taking the whole of the profits of cultivation, it takes, in theory a half, and in practice a very much smaller proportion. (1) Thus for the first time the cultivator began to find himself left with a margin of profit over and above what was previously left for his subsistence. This margin of profit obviously possessed value and could be an object of sale. In Bengal the Permanent Settlement Regulations of 1793 and 1795 conferred upon the great zamindars the full and unfettered power of alienating their lands without the sanction of Government. The idea gradually spread through Northern India, and, though transfer was discouraged in the Punjab, the right gradually established itself. Thus there were two factors at work. The State demanded less than the cultivator had been accustomed to pay and so left in his hands a surplus ; it was open to a middleman to step in, buy up the proprietary rights, take from the cultivator what he had previously paid and keep the surplus for himself. This surplus would then be what is commonly known as rent. Along with this change there spread in the Punjab the idea that land could be sold. But, as already noticed, it was the surplus (or rent) that first attracted the moneylenders who sought to secure it by taking land on mortgage.

These two factors alone would not have been sufficient to account for what next occurred. Before land can be sold there must be buyers and these buyers must be possessed of capital and this capital must have been accumulated. Prior to annexation, the number of people with any savings must have been very limited ; there was very little trade ; the State, the various governors and minor officials limited their exactions only to what they

---

(1) See Sir James Wilson's Paper on Recent Economic Developments in the Punjab (written in 1910) :—

" All land in India has from time immemorial been liable to pay a share of its produce to the ruler for the time being . . . When the Punjab came under British rule this share must on the average have absorbed at least one-third of the gross produce of the agricultural land of the province . . . At first, the general standard of assessment was, roughly, one-sixth of the gross produce, or about half the share taken by the Sikh Government . . the actual assessment has not in recent years kept pace with the rise in prices . . . . . . In 1889 the average assessment was just under one rupee per cultivated acre ; it took 40 lbs. wheat to pay the land revenue of an average acre ; on the average of the last nine years it took only 29 lbs. to pay the present average land revenue per acre . . . . . . It now only takes 4 per cent. of the gross produce of the average acre to pay the land reveue on the land".

thought they could squeeze out; such men as possessed wealth lived in the bigger towns under the protection of the local chiefs and certainly never went about buying rights in land throughout the countryside.

But with the advent of the British there was established all the paraphernalia of a civilised administration. Regular cantonments were constructed and garrisoned by troops receiving regular pay; public works were put in hand and the labour was paid for in cash. There arose markets for produce and opportunities for traders to earn money by supplying the needs of those in public employment. The cultivator was not the only person who, under the new régime, found himself in a position to save.

In 1869-70 the average price paid for over a hundred thousand acres was Rs. 10 per acre, equivalent to 18 times the annual land revenue. By 1875-76 it has risen to Rs. 20 per acre, or 31 times the land revenue. This rise was probably connected with the heavy export of grain to famine stricken Madras. In the next few years the province experienced short rainfall, and bad crops, the area sold increased and the price fell to Rs. 17 an acre. The effect of the reduction of the assessments was to bring the price in 1882 to what was then regarded as the "unprecedented multiple" of 36 times the land revenue. (1)

The extent of this reduction of assessment may be illustrated by the following figures showing the Government share of the proprietary produce in India as a whole :—(2)

1812	..	91	per cent.	
1822	..	83	,,	
1833	..	70—75	,,	
1844	..	67	,,	of the average anticipated net assets.
1855	..	50	,,	
1875	..	50	,,	of the existing net assets.

The early assessments seem incredibly heavy; they were inherited from the predecessors of the British. They obviously left no such surplus as would be sufficient to give a right of transfer any value.

Other factors which, at this time, exerted a marked influence on land prices were railways and canals. The first railway in the province was commenced in 1858 and was opened for traffic in 1861. The line from Lahore, the capital, to Multan, which then had a connection by steamer with Karachi,

(1) Or 18 years' purchase, a stage reached in England about 1600-1688. Curtler, p. 117.

(2) The Court of Wards Report for the year ending September 1919 shows that land revenue and cesses amounted to less than 15 per cent. of the income derived from rents and sale of grain. In some cases it was less than 5 per cent.

The percentages that follow are taken from official reports.

Sir P. Fagan has stated that in the Punjab the following is the proportion of estimated net assets taken in recent assessments :—

Hoshiarpur	..	26 per cent.	Jullundhur	..	21 per cent.
Ferozepore	..	20 ,,	Ludhiana	..	27 ,,
Lahore	..	22 ,,	Shahpur	..	28 ,,
Amritsar	..	25 ,,	Ambala	..	28 ,,
Gujrat	..	22 ,,	Multan	..	29 ,,

(Mr. Fagan in Council, August 1st, '21.)

was opened in 1865 and the province was linked up with Bombay and Calcutta in 1883 by which time there were about 1,100 miles open for traffic. (1)

Inundation canals existed before annexation and were speedly extended afterwards. Big irrigation schemes were rapidly put in hand. The Bari Doab Canal was opened in 1859 and the Sirhind Canal in 1870. (2) The vigorous extension of canals and construction of railways created a great demand for labour which was further intensified by the Afghan War of 1879-80. Prices rose considerably and, in spite of the severe famine of 1868-69 and the scarcity of 1877-78, the cultivating classes increased in prosperity. The railway enabled large amounts of grain to be exported to Bengal in 1873, and to Madras in 1876 on the occasions of famine conditions in those two presidencies, and shortly afterwards the European market was brought into touch with the province.

This had the effect of steadying prices ; there was now an outlet for any surplus ; the appreciation of gold stimulated export ; the producer became assured of the profits on his cultivation and so was stimulated to greater activity, knowing that in a good year he would not be left with unsaleable grain on his hands. The cultivated area increased 31·6 per cent. between 1855 and 1868 and continued rapidly to expand. Between 1855 and 1881 the population was estimated to have increased from 11,500,000 to 17,270,000 or just over 50 per cent. (3) Instead of a revenue paying community seeking for tenants to come and share their burden, there were tenants seeking for land to cultivate.

The result was a rapid increase in the number and value of transactions in land. The gross sum paid for land was 10 lakhs in 1869-70 ; five years later it had risen to 15 lakhs, and in 1879-80 it was 30 lakhs of rupees. That these sales were due to surplus money seeking investment, rather than to straitened economic conditions, is indicated by the fact that they were most frequent in the most prosperous districts. The moneylending buyer (bania) was, at this time, not always allowed to take possession of his purchase in peace, but, as the power of the courts increased, his policy of steady aggrandisement at the expense of the old landowning class was made more safe and more profitable. About 1876-77 the tendency fo agriculturists to embark on money-lending attracted notice. Nearly half the land sold was transferred to members of agricultural tribes, and the eager readiness with which the farming class bought up plots in their immediate neighbourhood undoubtedly contributed to the upward movement of prices.

In the quinquennium ending with 1877-78 the average area annually sold was 93,000 acres; in the quinquennium ending with 1882-83 it was 160,000 acres ; in the next it was 310,000 acres and in the following one ending with 1892-93 it was 338,000 acres. In spite of this remarkable increase in the area sold (which includes mortgages converted into sales) there was a still more remarkable rise in the price paid. In the early days land in Sirsa sold for 6 annas an acre ; about 1869 the average for the province was 10 rupees.

(1) Prior to the construction of railways, instances occur of the local market being glutted, grain becoming unsaleable and, in consequence, damaged. If the produce of land is apt to become unsaleable, the value of that land will not rise high.

(2) Remodelled in 1884 with the present weir.

(3) This is probably an exaggeration due to an underestimate of the population in 1855.

Thereafter the upward movement may be illustrated by the following figures for the province :—

			Rs.	
1875-76	..	Average price per acre	20 or 31 ×	land revenue
1880-81	..	,, ,,	18 or 32 ×	,, ,,
1885-86	..	,, ,,	16 or 36 ×	,, ,,
1809-91	..	,, ,,	30 or 50 ×	,, ,,

The official figures now give the average rate per cultivated acre as follows :—

				Rs.	
1885-86	..	..	..	30	
1890-91	..	..	..	61	
1895-96	..	..	..	59 or 56 ×	land revenue.
1900-01	..	..	..	77 or 89 ×	,,
1905-06	..	..	..	85 or 105 ×	,,
1910-11	..	..	..	124 or 127 ×	,,
1916-17	..	..	..	227 or 157 ×	,,

In the Land Revenue Report for 1919 it is noted that the average price of cultivated land has fallen from Rs. 252 per acre in 1917-18 to Rs. 184 (or 127 × land revenue). In the following year it rose again to Rs. 275. (1) A considerable amount of Government land was sold during the year to crown tenants in the Sohag Para and Sidhnai Colonies at merely nominal rates, which depressed the provincial average sale price. The majority of the districts reported a rise in the value of land owing to the continued high prices of agricultural produce.

In the 21 years from 1896-97 to 1916-17 about 967,000 plots of land, totalling some three million acres of cultivated land (nearly 10 per cent. of the whole), have been sold for 33 crores of rupees.

Looking at the figures, it may be said that from 1868 to 1891 the rise in price was not more rapid than might be expected to result from lenient assessments, improved communications, wider markets and other accompaniments of settled government. The continuance of the rise is more difficult to explain. It is not due to increasing density of population, for this in 1881 amounted to 514 of the total population per square mile of cultivated area, and in 1911 it had fallen to 499, due to the opening of the great canal colonies (2).

It is not due to better cultural methods or to improvements in the soil. The number of agriculturists per hundred cultivated acres has declined from 46 in 1868 to 43 in 1911, and it is believed that there has been a similar

(1) Or 199 × land revenue. In Lahore, excluding urban lands, the average was Rs. 360, in Jullundhur Rs. 668, Hoshiarpur Rs. 537 and Amritsar Rs. 452.

(2) The principal cause which acts on the value of land is the growth of population, but the mere agglomeration of population does not involve such an increase of value if it is accompanied by a lessening of business prosperity and therefore a diminution of income of the consumer and tenant. Seligman : Principles of Economics, p. 312.

decrease in bullock power. The question of improvement due to manuring or the introduction of clovers or root crops does not arise. In part the upward movement is due to the increase of irrigation from canals, wells, etc., from nearly 6 million acres in 1868 to over 12 million acres in 1917. The cost of the well is usually included in the price of the land. And in any case the expenditure of several (probably at least 5) crores of rupees on wells and of over 23 crores on canals constitutes a productive improvement that has greatly increased the value of the land. This increase is all the greater owing to the comparatively low price charged for water. (1) It is important to observe, however, that the general rise in price is also marked in districts without canal irrigation and in tracts without wells.

In part the increase is due to the price of agricultural products, but the influence of this factor is difficult to estimate. (2) In 1869 wheat was selling at 13 seers per rupee; it fell steadily from 1871 (20 seers) to 1877 (27 seers) and then rose sharply to 13½ seers in 1879. The continuous steady high price in recent years due to better communications with good markets may account for part of the increased value of land in exporting districts, but it cannot have had as much effect in districts which consume their own produce. The expenses of cultivation have risen considerably. Bullocks were Rs. 35 each in 1870, now the average price cannot be less than Rs. 80; and other items have similarly gone up in price. It must always be remembered that any increase in cost of production affects the whole produce, while a rise in the price of the produce only affects the portion sold.

In this connection, however, it is important to remember that fully half the cultivated area of the province is in possession of tenants, the great majority of whom pay rent in kind. The increased expenses of cultivation fall on the tenant, while the landlord receives the full benefit of the rise in value of his share of the produce. The Government demand in terms of produce is steadily declining; thus the return to the landlord is increasing from these two causes and he is induced to purchase more and more land at a higher and higher price. The marked leniency in assessment of the Government demand is undoubtedly an important factor. In 1868-69 the demand averaged Re. 1-1-3 per cultivated acre, equivalent to about 22 to 28 seers of wheat at the average price of those years. At present it is Re. 1-8-6, equivalent to about 15 seers of wheat. This latter average demand is higher in money than the earlier one, almost solely because the area assessed includes a much greater proportion that is irrigated. The increase in the Government demand on the same class of soil is actually less than the increase in prices of produce so that the real burden has been lightened. (3)

---

(1) The average water-rate per acre is Rs. 5-1-0 (1920), while the average value of crops raised per irrigated acre is estimated at Rs. 62.

(2) For instance, in Denmark it is estimated that although, as a result of very intensive cultivation, the annual value of the harvest has increased since 1870 by over 100 per cent., the price of land has only increased by 5·38 per cent. The price of produce is a factor in profits, but it is far from being the only one.

(3) It seems doubtful, however, whether the influence of the leniency of the land revenue demand is not sometimes overestimated. In a recent annual report the demand is given as Re. 1-8-0 per acre, the price over 150 times this and the average produce as Rs. 25. If the rent is half the produce, or Rs. 12-8-0, then the return is 4·9 per cent.: total remission of the demand would increase this to 5·5 per cent. and doubling it would reduce it to 4·2. Such small differences can hardly account for present high prices. The land revenue, in short, is so lenient that a further reduction can have little effect.

One factor that might be considered as tending to restrain the upward trend of prices is the fragmentation of holdings; each holding consists of several fields and these fields by successive partitions of ancestral property have become scattered all over the village area. The result is a diminution in the efficiency of the cultivators' labour as much of his time is wasted going with his bullocks from plot to plot and further time is wasted in the frequent turnings in ploughing a small plot; there is also a loss of area in the large number of boundary ridges. A further objection is that the fields are frequently too small to permit of a well being sunk with advantage. In Japan, where much attention has been paid to the matter, the official calculation is that readjustment of scattered fields will increase the yield by 15 per cent., while the unproductive areas (ridges, etc.) now utilised are expected to amount to 3 per cent. of the area adjusted. (1) If the attempt at Co-operative Consolidation of Holdings in the Punjab meets with any considerable success, the result may be a rise in land values; but experience in Belgium suggests that fragmentation facilitates sale and tends to enhance prices because the small fields are within the means of more prospective purchasers.

Experience seems to show that low industrial wages tend to raise land prices. Where, as in the Punjab, half the land is cultivated by tenants, there must be a large number of these tenants who would be attracted to the towns if conditions there were sufficiently favourable. (2)

High industrial wages and decent conditions of living might reduce the number of tenants seeking land and so reduce rents and, with them, land prices. High wages in towns tend to keep down land values in England, low wages in Belgium keep the people on the land. At the same time the affection of the people for the land may counteract this tendency. It is possible that high wages might attract workers who would save all they could with the ambition of purchasing a plot in their native village.

It has been stated that there are only two causes capable of checking or recovering this upward movement. The first is the competition of new land following on great colonising enterprises and improvements in the means of transport; and the second consists in some great and sudden improvement in the art of farming. (3) The classic instance of the first cause is, of course, the opening up of the great American prairie lands to wheat cultivation. Between 1860 and 1880 the production of wheat in the United States trebled. Vast stretches of virgin soil were opened up with the most astonishing rapidity by railroads. The cost of transport fell greatly, and Europe was flooded with foreign corn and meat. (4) The value of land in Western Europe fell about 30 per cent.; in some parts of England the drop was as much as 50 per cent., and prices had not recovered up to the outbreak of the Great War. Even in America itself the opening up of land in the western states and in

---

(1) Japan Year Book, 1919-20. pp. 541-2. The smallness of a field may serve to reduce its value, but where the field is not too small for economical cultivation, its small size brings its price within the reach of a larger number of purchasers and so tends to increase the competition for it.

(2) The modern industrial tendency of Japan and the migration of rural population toward cities are making it more and more difficult for the landlords to find tenants.—Japan Year Book, p. 537.

(3) Seligman : Principles of Economics, p. 513.

(4) Curtler : Short History of English Agriculture, p. 293.

Canada led to a general steady decrease in the value of farm property in New York State, and a similar shrinkage of land values is shown by Ohio. (1)

The great expansion of cultivation due to the construction of canals in the Punjab and the irrigation of what were formerly largely barren tracts does not seem to have exercised any effect in checking the rise in land value. Within the last 28 years the area under cultivation has increased 40 per cent. ; the area under canal irrigation has advanced from three million to ten million acres ; in the same period the population has increased by only 5 per cent. so that the pressure on the soil has been considerably lightened. The gross produce has probably been doubled but, so far from this resulting in lowering prices, these have practically doubled also. (2) The migration of colonists to the new irrigated areas has not resulted in any decline in the price of land in the older districts. It seems clear that in a province of small holders, like the Punjab, no expansion of cultivation that can be contemplated is likely to check the upward rise.

The second cause, mentioned above, is some great and sudden improvement in the art of farming. One factor affecting this province is the great improvement in railway facilities and communications that bring the Punjab into regular intimate touch with the great markets. The land, prior to the considerable expansion of cultivation just referred to, was sufficient for the production of the people's food supply in normal years. As the cultivated area has been increased, the production of wheat has increased, and there has been a large surplus for export. This export is, of course, due to a demand for wheat in the European markets, and its continuance depends upon a continuance of the demand from those markets. It is improbable that any scientific discovery in regard to, say, the part played by soil bacteria, or nitrogen fixation, will enable European importing countries to grow all the wheat they require and so lead to a decline in their demand for foreign grown produce. Such an event is not impossible ; moreover it is not beyond all possibility that a discovery should be made that would enable a far heavier outturn than at present to be secured from Punjab fields. A sudden increase in outturn, if it caused the supply to exceed the demand (3) for a few years in succession, would tend to throw much wheat land out of cultivation as well as to reduce the price, and as a result land values might decline. These, however, are speculations. It is possible to imagine similar results from causes that are already familiar. Anything that interrupted the export of wheat to Europe would tend to have the same effect as a decline in demand. A paralysis of the railway to the ports due to political causes, of a prolonged interference with the free export of wheat in the interests of the urban con-

(1) In Belgium prices almost exactly doubled in 50 years, 1830-1880, but the severe crisis brought about by the reduction in the price of corn, owing to the opening up of the American corn fields, led to a marked decline in the price of arable land by no less than 33 per cent. between 1880 and 1895. The price of pasture land depreciated somewhat less by 23 per cent. Rowntree : Land and Labour : Lessons from Belgium, p. 146.

(2) See *ante.* The great canal schemes brought great wealth into the province, and it is this new wealth which is the chief cause in the rise in the price of land.

(3) Or even to exceed the capacity of existing transport facilities to remove it. The outturn on most canal lands would be largely increased by the use of better ploughs, harrows, etc.

sumer, would tend to reduce prices in the local markets and so to remove the incentive to grow wheat. The cultivator grows wheat primarily in order to secure the wages of his labour and some profit on his enterprise. As has been mentioned in the discussion of the Human Factor, the farmer seems disinclined to expand his enterprise or improve his methods ; and a clear and strong incentive is required to stimulate him to further effort. Remove the incentive of profit and his production will decline and land values fall in sympathy. In a province where half the land is cultivated by tenants it is clear that land values must be largely dependent on rents. As will be shown later, cash rents have not risen so rapidly as the price of land, and as the price of land has risen more rapidly than prices of agricultural produce, it would seem that already land values have soared to a height that is not supported by the rents, whether in cash or kind, on which they are in the long run dependent. Anything that leads to a reduction in rents threatens a collapse in land prices. To illustrate the argument it may be permissible to call to mind what happened in England last century. Towards the close of the Napoleonic wars wheat rose in price, and, as year followed after year and high prices were maintained, both landlords and tenants jumped to the conclusion that they would be permanent. Rents increased rapidly, and speculation in land became general. Many people outside the old landlord and farmer class put all they possessed or could borrow into agricultural lands. Unlike the practice in the Punjab the boom caused large sums to be sunk in improvements ; manure was procured from the most remote quarters ; rapid and extensive progress was made ; tillage was improved and much bog and waste land reclaimed. But prices began to fall. The Corn Laws were repealed and a period of depression set in. Even after the abolition of the Corn Laws, however, many competent judges held the opinion that the land would continue to rise in value. It was argued that as the area could not increase and the population was steadily increasing land must become dearer. Men failed to foresee the opening of millions of acres of virgin soil in other parts of the world and the coming improvements in transport. When the American wheat flooded the English market prices collapsed. Rents had to be reduced ; the total decrease being estimated at 23 per cent. in fourteen years ; the profits of the occupiers fell on the average 40 per cent. ; and between 1875 and 1894 the capital value of land decreased over 49 per cent. (1)

This brief reminder will serve to show that land is not necessarily bound to go on rising in price ; two possible causes that may lead to a decline have been mentioned. Two others suggest themselves as within the bounds of probability. The price of land, as has already been pointed out, depends on the long run on rents or profits of ownership. These may be reduced in two ways. The village labourer may, with the spread of industries or other developments competing for his labour, insist on receiving a higher wage for work in the fields, and owing to this and similar causes, the costs of cultivation may be so increased that the landlord may be forced to remain satisfied with a smaller proportion of the produce as his rent. A similar result will

(1) Curtler : Short History of English Agriculture, pp. 243—310.

follow if the tenant secure for himself a larger share of the produce as wages of his labour. (1)

The other probable cause is an increase of taxation. India has for long enjoyed what is probably the cheapest form of administration of any civilised country. With the change to democratic institutions it is to be anticipated that there will come the great increase in public expenditure that seems almost inevitably to accompany such a change everywhere. The demand, for instance, for universal free compulsory education, can only be satisfied by a very large expenditure of public funds that must be raised by taxation. Some objects of public expenditure as, for instance, improved roads, medical attendance or veterinary aid against cattle disease, yield advantages within a comparatively small period of time ; but expenditure on education requires a long interval before anything approaching a financial return can be shown. During this interval the owners or tenants or both will be called upon to pay taxes assessed on the land, and to this extent the advantages of ownership will be diminished. It is not improbable that some such factor will come into play and will restrain the present upward trend of prices.(2)

This, however, concerns the future rather than the present. The most recent reports are of special interest. In the Lower Bari Doab Colony there was an increase in the price realised at Government auctions from Rs. 229 per acre in 1917 to Rs. 331 in 1918. This was probably due to the discovery that the land was suitable for American cotton. (3)

In the following year these high prices were exceeded, an area of nearly 8,868 acres being sold at an average price of Rs. 493 per acre. The highest price realised was Rs. 1,018 per acre for a lot of 25 acres in a village one mile from Khanewal Railway Station. That these high prices are largely due to the plethora of money seeking investment is illustrated by the fact that the sale for sites for new town shops in Montgomery yielded a price of Rs. 5,82,212 per acre. (4)

The continued rise in price appears to be the result of the local conditions in each village. The owners are hereditary cultivators born and brought

(1) In England about 1348 A. D. the Black Death caused a heavy decrease in the supply of labour; the result was that the cost of cultivation rose and landlords' profits were seriously diminished, the area cultivated by the owner with the aid of paid labour declined and, more was let out on lease to tenants.

Thorold Rogers estimated the profits of farming under the old Bailiff system, before the Great Plague, as 18 per cent. in a year of average or rather more than average, fertility. After the pestilence had subsided the profit sank to a miserable rate, less than 4 per cent. on the capital invested in the estate. "Property had become, at first sight, utterly valueless. There was a great depression in the value of the most important article of farm produce-wool, and a prodigious exaltation of all products of manual labour." (Vol. I., Ch. XXVIII).

(2) Compulsory education will also tend to withdraw from field labour the children of the cultivators, and the work these now do will either have to be left undone or to be done by paid labour, thus adding to the costs of cultivation.

(3) The introduction of a highly profitable crop may send land values up, as the introduction of hops into England did to an almost incredible extent. *Cf.* Curtler, p. 149. Any new economy in production or improvement in the art of agriculture would tend to enhance rents, and therefore the price of land.

(4) The official report states "as with agricultural land, so with these town sites, the extra ordinary high prices are due in some measure to the existence in the country of large amounts of money for which there is no available investment carrying public confidence". The situation is one singularly favourable for industrial development if this confidence could be enlisted by the pioneers of industry.

up in the same village, which they have no intention of leaving unless they can secure land in a colony. In this village there is practically no open market for land; a newcomer could not rely upon being able to buy if he chose to leave his own home and migrate to this one. There is hardly any such thing as "land for sale". Progressive sub-division of holdings, consequent on the custom of inheritance whereby each son has a right to succeed to a share, has led to the land being cut up into small parcels that, in the vast majority of cases, are less than the owner could cultivate with his existing resources. These holdings can only be increased by snapping up any plots that happen to be for sale. So that the majority of owners are prospective purchasers of any field that may be offered. The small holdings, and the fact that each is scattered over the village area in ten or a dozen places, facilitates sale. A farm in England that consists of 150 acres could only be sold as a farm; it would not be cut up into parcels and sold in fragments. The provision of buildings, etc., would not permit of the farm being broken up into separate plots. Thus prospective purchasers are reduced to those who can afford to buy the whole, and these are apt to be fewer in number than those who could raise money to buy a field. Here, the small fields, and the fact that already fields cultivated by the same person are not contiguous, render sale easy. The average area sold in one transaction is very small, and accordingly the price is not beyond the means or the credit of many in the village, nearly all of whom, as has been remarked, are anxious to add to their own possessions. The average area sold per transaction was, in the

quinquennium	ending	1901,	5·9 acres total,	and	3·3	acres cultivated.		
,,	,,	1906,	5·7	,,	,,	3·4	,,	,,
,,	,,	1911,	5	,,	,,	2·8	,,	,
,,	,,	1916,	4·5	,,	,,	2·68	,,	
year		1919-20	4·06	,,	,,	2·6	,,	,,

Thus the plots are not only small, but are steadily becoming smaller. A parallel may be found in Belgium, the greater part of which is covered with small holdings. "Whenever a little plot of land becomes available, the possible buyers or tenants are on the spot; whereas in England, even if a large farm were divided up, there would seldom be a sufficiently large number of people anxious to buy or rent in the immediate neighbourhood to cause so active a demand as in Belgium. Thus it may be said that the tendency of sub-division to raise the price of land is cumulative. In both countries the demand for small farms is greater than the demand for large ones, as comparatively few persons are possessed of sufficient capital either to rent or buy the latter; and so there is but little competition to acquire them when they come into the market. But this is not the case with small ones."(1)

Much the same considerations apply to the Punjab. The fact that the average holding is smaller than could be cultivated by its owner without further help, serves to create a constant demand for land to be added. The small size of the fields brings the price within the reach of most of the neighbours; while the mere fact that a field purchased is not contiguous to others owned by the purchaser is not considered a drawback.

---

(1) *Cf.* Rowntree: Land and Labour: Lessons from Belgium, p. 151.

To these influences there is to be added one of great importance. The opportunities for adding to the holding are very rare indeed. In the province there are roughly 2½ million families, who may be regarded as directly supported by agriculture in the 33,400 villages. In 21 years, as recorded above, the number of recorded transactions was 962,000 or about 46,000 a year, or 29 per village in the course of 21 years. Thus each family has, on the average, only one chance of buying a plot in 54 years; or, if we assume that vendors and vendees are equal in numbers and quite separate people, then the chance of buying two or three acres of cultivated land comes but once in 27 years. This fact undoubtedly is responsible for the large prices now paid. Competition is very keen. (1) Land is endowed with a scarcity value; and it is this scarcity value that accounts for the high prices paid in such remote tracts as Kulu. In this Himalayan canton the average price for the period 1871-91 was Rs. 27 per acre; for the period 1891-1912 it was Rs. 85 per acre. The writer of the *Gazetteer* remarks that the price of the land bears no relation to the profit to be made out of it. Across the Central Himalayan Chain the price is Rs. 157 in Lahul and Rs. 133 in Spiti. These high prices are almost entirely due to the intense scarcity of land suitable for cultivation, while the scattered nature of the habitations adds a high site value to the land. (2) The people make a little money by trading and labour and have no other possible investment for it than land or stock. It is, in these lonely spots, no good to a man with money in one village to know that land is for sale two villages off.

It is becoming increasingly clear that the factors referred to have raised the price well above the economic limit. (3) A recent Report on the Court of Wards in the Punjab deals with a cultivated area of over 200,000 acres; the estimated value is only Rs. 94 per acre. The gross income accruing from this large area works out at under 7 per cent. of the value; after paying land revenue, the rate is reduced to 5 per cent. and, when the cost of management and ordinary repairs is deducted, the resulting profit is 4½ per cent. If the land was valued at 157 times the land revenue (the multiple for 1916-17) the net profit would be 3 per cent. The Report published in 1920 gives a similar result. It is difficult to form an accurate estimate of the profits of farming anywhere at any time, and in the Punjab there is nothing very reliable of this nature on record. The figures quoted have the merit of being

---

(1) Where there is land freely open to purchase, the price responds to temporary factors such as the price of grain, wages of labour, etc; but where the demand exceeds the supply these exert little influence.

(2) These figures are interesting as the areas to which they relate are not affected by the factors usually mentioned as the causes of the high prices of land. The population is not increasing with any rapidity; there are no new markets; no railways; no industries; no urban population; the roads are as they have been for ages, with one exception; there is no export trade in agricultural produce that could account for the rise. Peace and security under British rule, a low revenue demand, profits from trade with Tibet and Central Asia facilitated by special measures, are responsible for the rise. Land there, as elsewhere, is no longer a burden and an excuse for an exorbitant State demand, but is a means of livelihood that can be enjoyed in security.

(3) *Cf.* Rowntree : Land and Labour : Lessons from Belgium. Other than merely commercial reasons influence buyers of land in Belgium for gilt-edged securities are considerably more profitable (p. 148). So great is the competition for small plots that prices much in excess of their real worth are frequently paid. This means that the yield from the land is not sufficient to give reasonable interest upon the price paid (pp. 152-3). In the Punjab it is difficult to discover what is the actual price paid owing to the insertion of exaggerated figures to defeat the pre-emption law.

actual accounts relating to a large area scattered over the province, and illustrate the point that the present price is higher than would be justifiable in the case of a man buying land solely for the value of the yield he was expecting to attract from it. The general prosperity of the province already referred to, coupled with a large income from service in the army, etc., and an appreciable sum from the earnings of emigrants to Australia, America and other places, (1) have brought into the possession of the people large sums of money for which they can think of no investment except the land and jewels. In former times the latter was a popular form of keeping surplus money, but there is always a loss on realisation. In the case of land, the rise in price is a prime factor in the continued rise of price; that is, the common experience is that an investment in land will yield a profit on realisation. If the land is not, at the time of purchase, quite worth the price demanded, it will probably become so in a few years. There is thus a tendency to forestall the increase in price. Another factor is the wealth accruing to professional men for which they are unable to find a safe and suitable investment. Industries are unimportant and joint stock enterprise is moribund. In 1868 there were 40 pleaders in an area which now finds work for about 1,300, and these and other professional men evince a natural desire to become owners of property which will not decline in value. In these cases the direct return is of minor importance.

It will be seen from what has been said above that the continued rise in prices, so far from being a subject of congratulation, is really a matter for serious concern. (2) Speculation in land has seldom proved of much help to agriculture, whereas it has frequently, as in Ireland and the United States, caused considerable harm. (3) As has been pointed out, a great factor in causing the rise is the rise itself. If land were to decline in value, it would rapidly fall out of favour as a source of investment, and the capital thus set free would be available for development in other directions. It is an obvious evil that the new capital is invested in the land, and not in improvements to the land. Of the several companies owning railways in the province, none has attracted much of its capital from within it, yet the official report shows that nearly 2½ crores of rupees were spent on buying land in 1917-18. (4) This money neither adds to the area under cultivation nor increases the produce from the present area. It is remarkable that the rapid rise in price, the demand for purchase and the wealth seeking investment have not resulted in any marked movement towards reclaiming waste areas, draining swamps, recovering land damaged by torrents, etc. A very large area of the province is at present not culturable, but a goodly portion of this could be made so by the judicious expenditure of capital. The almost complete dearth of enterprise in this

---

(1) The net result of foreign money orders first gave the Punjab a surplus about 1895-6. The excess of sums received over sums despatched was Rs. 25 lakhs in 1900-01, Rs. 43 lakhs in 1910-11 and over 58 lakhs in 1917-18.

(2) It is of course a matter of congratulation as conclusive evidence of the abounding wealth of the province and lightness of the revenue.

(3) A Danish Minister is quoted in Better Business, Vol. IV, No. 20, p. 109, as saying that the value of land has become an object of speculation in Denmark instead of a common source of national labour and self-support. This state of things is detrimental to the best interest of the nation and a hindrance of its welfare.

(4) This figure is probably an exaggeration, resulting from the custom of entering larger sums in sale deeds than are actually paid in order to defeat would-be pre-emptors. In 1919-20 the sum was 392 lakhs.

respect deserves more notice than it at present receives. Another serious drawback in the existing situation is that inflated land values render it practically impossible for the small owner or a tenant with a little capital to obtain land. There is no means of arriving at the number of owners who have been expropriated in recent years. But of the 960,000 sale transactions in the last 21 years a certain proportion must represent reductions of holdings below the limit of economic livelihood, and a further proportion must represent the fall of ancient owners to the position of tenants. It is no answer to say that there have been corresponding additions to other holdings. It is of little moment whether the well-to-do adds a few acres to an estate already large enough for his support in comfort. It is of considerable importance that tenants and owners of uneconomic holdings should be able to look forward to acquiring lands (1) as a reward of thrift. Nearly half the land of the province is cultivated by tenants-at-will, many are themselves owners in the same or a neighbouring village; but a considerable number are not owners, and it would strengthen the economic position in the province if they could become so. In other countries it is practicable to buy land on borrowed money and to repay this in instalments; in the Punjab the yield would in many cases not suffice to meet interest charges,

The rise in the sale price has been accompanied by a corresponding rise in the average sum obtainable on a mortgage, but here again the enhanced credit has been productive of evil rather than of good. It has not yet been used to raise funds for productive purposes, and the volume of unproductive debt tends to rise steadily with the increase in credit. To one who desires to sell his land the present high prices may be welcome, but to the cultivator intending to spend his life on his holding these merely bring temptation to borrow. It has been said that countries under a poor system of agriculture with inefficient labour cannot maintain a high value of land, and it is not improbable that the existing uneconomic rates in the Punjab will give way if other avenues for the investment of money are opened up under conditions calculated to inspire confidence. One effect of the war has been to raise the interest receivable from Government securities until it differs little from the return from land leased on a cash rent. Another effect may be to induce British holders of shares in local railway companies to sell at rates which would prove attractive to local capitalists. Any such tendency would probably bring benefit to the province, as it seems clear that its rapidly increasing wealth is, for want of opportunities for productive employment other than land investment, giving rise to a distinctly unsatisfactory situation. (2)

---

(1) Or such rights in land as ensure security of tenure. Apart from the sentiment, there is no special virtue in proprietorship. If security of tenure (*i.e.*, security against capricious ejectment) can be ensured, it is better that the culti ator should devote his available capital to stock, implements, manures, etc., rather than to purchase. The former should yield to him a much higher return.

(2) The following extract from the Land Revenue Administration Report for 1919-20 is interesting in connection with the above discussion :—"How far the increase of mortgage debt is a direct result of the increase in the value of land and how far it is a result of an increase in the expenditure of the agricultural population, whether on necessities or luxuries, are questions to which it is very difficult to give very definite answers under the changing economic and social conditions of the present time. All the factors are inter-related and operate on each other mutually. It may, however, be said with some confidence that the enhanced value of agricultural lands has enlarged the credit of the landowner and cultivator and made it easier for them to raise funds to meet an expenditure enhanced by the higher prices of necessaries as well as of luxuries".

Whether a cycle of industrial development would serve to diminish land values or retard the rise is by no means certain. The greater portion of the population is Mohammadan, and a very large number of these will not buy any securities bearing interest or even profits. They hesitate to acquire shares in railways or mills. Many even avoid trade. For them the rate of profit accruing from the acquisition of land is of little importance beside the fact that land purchase is permitted to them and affords a secure investment. There is thus an additional force driving Mohammadans into the purchase of land. The possession of large areas already does not deter them from desiring more. Agriculture is an industry that appeals to Mohammadans as being free from any religious impediments. What is the extent of the influence of this feeling on prices is not open to estimation.

CHAPTER IX.

Effects of the Rise in the Price of Land.

It is a moderately easy task to work out the tendency of economic forces under circumstances which permit of these forces producing their full effect. But it is more difficult to discover what in actual life these effects are when the tendencies are influenced by custom, prejudice or ignorance. The Punjab is very far indeed from being organized on economic lines, but there is a distinct, if slow, movement towards that state. In order to throw some light on the economic effects of the rise in the price of land a list of eleven questions was sent to those Inspectors of Co-operative Societies who were graduates (nearly all in economics). They were instructed to try to find out actual facts, and to keep these separate from their own opinions. Their opinions were to be given on each point after the facts they had ascertained had been related. They were to make enquiries in the ordinary course of their inspections.

The questions and a general summary of the answers received constitute this chapter.

The first question called for such information as might be readily available relating to the rise in the price paid for land. It was not easy to unearth many cases of resale of the same plot after a period of years, so that it is difficult to say more than that land has risen in price throughout the province. The rise, however, is uneven. It is greater near the larger towns and in the case of land bearing two crops a year and in the case of irrigated land. The Inspectors generally ascribe the rise to the high price of produce, the great prosperity of the cultivators resulting in their becoming possessed of large sums of money and the absence of any alternative for investment. In the Lyallpur Colony squares of land (about 27 acres) sold for Rs. 4,000 each in 1914, Rs. 6,000 in 1915, Rs. 8,000 in 1917, Rs. 10,000 in 1918, Rs. 16,000 in 1919, and Rs. 22,000 in 1920. These are not averages but actual instances and illustrate the extent to which money is available and the determination of those possessing it to obtain land at any cost. Some actual instances of resale of the same plots collected in Gurdaspur are as follows :—

Area.	Price on first sale.	Price on second sale.	Period between sales.
	Rs.	Rs.	
2½ acres ..	1,000	1,400	12 years.
3 ,, ..	240	350	5 ,,
7 ,, ..	900	1,340	5 ,,
3½ ,, ..	1,000	1,575	5 ,,
2 ,, ..	100	250	6 ,,

One Inspector illustrates the view of land in Sikh times as a burden by the tale current in his own village of a man who was sentenced by a *punchayat* to be given 50 acres of land to cultivate and to pay the revenue on it as a punishment for singing in the streets so loud that the women in *purdah* could hear him.

It is worthy of note that in no case is there any suggestion put forward that the price has gone too high or that the yield does not give a good return on the investment.

The second question concerned the reasons given by the people for this rise.

According to the replies received, the people themselves ascribe the rise in the price of land to one or more of the following causes :—

(*a*) Rise in the price of produce ;

(*b*) increase of wealth ;

(*c*) improvement in communications ;

(*d*) development of canal irrigation, and the prospects ot further development ;

(*e*) increase of population ;

(*f*) the cultivators are stimulated by the high prices to work at their calling with greater exertion than formerly and so secure higher yields ;

(*g*) the people are more ready to spend money than in former times, they seek to invest it in land instead of hoarding it, or spending it on jewels ;

(*h*) as the Land Alienation Act restricts the opportunities open to money-lenders to acquire land, they pay a higher price for such land as is available for purchase by them ;

(*i*) the remittance of money from Punjabis in Australia, America and other foreign countries ; this is invested in land almost regardless of the price ;

(*j*) the land has been improved and rendered more fertile ;

(*k*) the continued sub-division of land amongst members of the family, as a result of the custom of inheritance, has increased the demand and so the price ;

(*l*) the decline in the value of money, and especially the paper rupee.

The general view is that the rise is due to the increasing price obtainable for produce, the widespread increase of wealth and the fact that land is the only investment recognised by the cultivators. It will be admitted that on the whole the reasons given are sound, though those numbered (*f*) and (*j*) are rather surprising.

No mention was made of the influence of the objections of Musalmans against taking interest. It is possible to criticise a purchase on the ground that the income will not be equal to a fair interest on the price ; but where interest cannot be taken, any return is better than nothing.

The third question was—Has this rise in price had any effect (encouragement or discouragement) on land improvement ?

In areas irrigated by canals or wells it would appear that the high price of land has not had much effect in encouraging improvements, the general idea being that so much depends on the supply of water. There is, however, a tendency to use more manure. The high price of produce, rather than the high price of land, is stimulating the cultivators to improve the yield. In areas dependent on rainfall the opinion is practically unanimous that considerable efforts are being made to improve the land ; fields are being levelled, the use of manure is becoming somewhat more general, waste land is being put under the plough and new wells are being sunk. In eleven villages in Gurdaspur, in which enquiry was made, it was found that the number of wells had risen from 23 to 40 in five years, and this in spite of the fact that the cost of a well has increased considerably within this period.

It seems clear that the cultivators are becoming more interested in land improvement, and, where a man has paid a high price for a plot, he tries to secure profit from his investment. They are also beginning to take a more commercial view of their industry. It would seem, however, that this is largely due to the high price of produce and only in a minor degree to the rising price of land. The efforts of the Co-operative organization are also resulting in an increasing demand for better seed and improved implements. The enquiries were naturally made chiefly from co-operators, and concerning these, it can, apparently, be stated with some confidence that greater attention is being paid to problems of land improvement and of extracting a bigger yield, but that lack of knowledge of what would prove profitable is an obstacle to progress.

Theoretically, as Mr. Emerson has pointed out, it might be expected that the increased credit would facilitate improvements by owners possessed of sufficient enterprise, but this effect does not appear to be much in evidence.

The fourth question was as to whether the rise in the price of land had any effect on rents . Rents have undoubtedly been rising rapidly in value. Where the rent is paid in kind as a proportion of the crop (*batai*), the proportion has not varied ; where the rent is paid in cash the rate has increased rapidly in the last five years.

In Gurdaspur cash rents for *barani* lands have risen from Rs. 2 to Rs. 8 per acre ; for *barani* and *chahi* lands, the rent has risen from Rs. 8 to Rs. 16 per acre.

In Toba Tek Singh Circle, the rent for a square is reported to have risen from Rs. 200 in 1914 to Rs. 800 in 1920. In some cases as much as Rs. 1,200 per square is being paid. In Sangla Circle, the rise is reported to be from Rs. 300 to Rs. 800. In Lahore it is reported that rents in cash have risen four or five-fold in recent years. In Jullundur cash rents are said to have doubled in ten years.

This marked rise in cash rents, however, is partly due to the direct influence of high prices of produce and partly to the indirect influence in stimulating competition among tenants desiring to cultivate more land. Where there is any difficulty in finding tenants, cash rents do not seem to have risen. There does not seem to be any evidence that the rise in rents is due to the rise in the price of the land, apart from the rise in the price of the crops.

It is not clear that cash rents have risen as fast as the price of land. On the other hand the evidence from recent Settlement reports tends to show that rents are lagging behind. (1) For instance, concerning Amritsar the following information is extracted concerning the changes that have taken place in the period of 20 years between the last two settlements :—

Tahsil.	Rise per cent. in *Price of land.*	Rise per cent. in *Cash rents.*
Tarn Taran	114 per cent.	66 per cent.
Amritsar	73 do.	39 do.
Ajnala	7 do.	25 do.

Within this period the population first rose steadily and then declined, owing to plague. From 1881 to 1891 it increased 11 per cent., from 1891 to 1901, it increased a further 3 per cent. from 1901 to 1911, it declined 14 per cent. The cultivated area contracted slightly, owing to the spread of saline efflorescene by 2 per cent. in Tarn Taran, and 1 per cent. in Amritsar. The Lahore Settlement Reports give the following :—

Tahsil.	Rise per cent. in *Price of land.*	Rise per cent. in *Cash rents.*
Lahore	Nearly doubled	131 per cent.
Chunian	Do. trebled	53 do.
Kasur	More than trebled	34 do.

In the Government review of the Jullundur Settlement Report it is stated that during the period between settlements prices of produce rose 50 per cent., the selling value of land rose 400 per cent. and cash rents 200 per cent.

In the Gujranwala Tehsil, information is forthcoming regarding each assessment circle for the changes that have taken place in the period 1892 to 1911.

Circle.	Price of land.	Rise in cash rents.	Rise in Chakota rents.
Charkari	From Rs. 17 to Rs. 58	53 per cent. on *chahi.* 72 do. on *barani.*	32 per cent. on *chahi.* 66 do. on *barani.*
Bangar	From Rs. 13 to Rs. 29	31 per cent. on *chahi.* 74 do. on *barani.*	22 per cent. on *chahi.* 142 do. on *barani.*
Bar	From Rs. 11 to Rs. 28	6 per cent. on *chahi.* 79 do. on *barani.*	100 per cent. on *chahi.* 60 do. on *barani.*

(1) The information that follows was not obtained from the enquiry ; it conforms to what is known to be the general rule elsewhere.

(The above figures indicate a considerable decrease in the return by way of rent on the value of the land).

Other examples could be given but these will be sufficient to show that cash rents have not kept pace with the rise in price of cultivated land. The result is that landlords are pressing for the extension of rent in kind (*batai*) while tenants show an increasing preference for cash rents. Owing to the weakness of the tenants, cash rents are become less frequent.

The fifth question was—Has the rise in the price of land had any effect on tenancy (apart from rents) ? Has it led to increase of tenancy ? With one exception all the replies agree that tenancy is increasing, the chief change being that village *kamins* are now cultivating land as tenants. This increase is due chiefly to the high price of produce which is making agriculture more profitable. The result is some competition for land and this enables land-owners to exact better terms (*e. g.*, in labour or service) from tenants. In the Lyallpur Colony, however, it is said that owners are being tempted by the high profits to resume the land formerly given to tenants and to cultivate themselves. The only effect of the high price of land is to prevent tenants from becoming owners. [In the discussion on tenancy it will be seen that while sales and mortgages tend to increase tenancy, the high price of land prevents this tendency from being counteracted by purchases of holdings by tenants.] The great rise in the profits from cultivation has led to a demand for more land by tenants and a willingness of owners to let on rent.

The sixth question was—Has the rise in the price of land had any effect on cropping ? The replies agree that more attention is being paid to the selection of crops that will prove most profitable and also that methods of cultivation are being improved, but this is ascribed to the high price of produce rather than to the high price of land. It seems to be clear that the high price of land has not yet had any effect towards replacing annuals by perennials such as fruit, etc.

The seventh question was whether the rise in the price of land has discouraged the sowing of fodder crops ? Fodder crops tend to decline in area to the absolute minimum required to feed the cattle ; but owing to the high price of fodder and the high price of cattle, great care is taken to see that there is sufficient fodder sown. There is no sufficeint reason to believe that the high price of land has any influence on the area.

There seems to be a tendency for tenants to grow more fodder than do owners ; specially where under the system of rent in kind the owner takes a smaller share of such crops.

The eighth question was—Have sales during the last ten years been made to old residents in the villages or to outsiders ?

In the great majority of cases sales have been made to old residents of the village. This is almost universally the case with small plots. Outsiders may purchase if a large plot is being sold.

The remaining three questions were :—

(1) Can you compare the rise in the price of land with the rise in the cost of production ?
(2) or with prices obtained for the produce ?
(3) or with wages paid to village labourers ?

The general result of the enquiry is that the rise in the price of land is greater than the rise in the cost of cultivation and the rise in the price of produce and that of labourers' wages. But the details vary very considerably. In Jullundur while the price of land has trebled, the cost of bullocks, male buffaloes and bullock carts has rather more than trebled, the price of produce has about doubled, and the wages of labour have increased six-fold.

In Ludhiana the cost of bullocks, buckets (*charsa*), manure, plough shares and bullock carts has increased about three-fold in 20 years ; the price of produce has increased 2½ times, and of labour four-fold. But land has increased six to eight-fold.

Hissar reports somewhat similar figures.

A very careful report from Gurdaspur agrees with the above but puts the rise in the price of land much lower. It had not doubled in the periods taken.

From Rawalpindi comes a similar reply ; the price of land has doubled, while costs of cultivation have much more than doubled and the price of produce in the hill tract has increased nearly four-fold (chiefly potatoes).

Taking however the reports as a whole the various increases come in the following order :—

(1) Price of land.
(2) Wages of labour.
(3) Price of produce.
(4) Cost of cultivation.

If this is correct it means that the small owner, cultivating by himself, or a tenant, is gaining a higher income than before and so also is the labourer. The large owner cultivating through tenants paying *batai* is also more prosperous. On the whole, in spite of the increasing cost of labour and of other expenses of cultivation, agriculture seems to be more profitable than before.

In conclusion it would appear that the dominating factor at present is not the high price of land but the high price obtainable for its produce. The latter is acting as a stimulus to greater exertion and greater interest. The high price of land brings no benefit to agriculture, while on the other hand the increase in the expenses of cultivation and the greater wages of labour have not yet served to prevent the price of land from mounting still higher. These last two conclusions are of very great importance.

It should be noted that a high price for land is apt to put in the way of improvident owners a great temptation to sell while it enables the more careful to redeem a larger portion of their holdings by sale of a smaller one. Both these tendencies are at work in this province ; but the object of the inquiry was to ascertain the effects, if any, of the rise in price on the system of agriculture.

CHAPTER X.

The Abuse of Rural Credit and the Land Alienation Act.

I.—The Abuse of Rural Credit.

A glance at the history of the Punjab for three or four centuries preceding 1848 discloses an almost unending series of invasions, wars, rebellions and famines. Sometimes the invader attempted to establish something approaching settled government, sometimes he was the leader of a mere plundering expedition; whatever his intentions the result was several centuries of unsettled conditions during which economic progress was practically impossible. Under circumstances such as these, industries could not flourish, capital could not be invested in a form that might attract the cupidity of the invader, the possession of moveable wealth could not be disclosed. Those around the court might make a display that would attract the attention of the traveller but the mass of the people were concerned in hiding from prying eyes such surplus wealth as they might have secured. The governments, such as they were, were despotic and whimsical. Rights of the people against the State were not recognised. Private property in land, such as is now known, was non-existent. Even in Sikh times, when some sort of settled administration was devised by Maharaja Ranjit Singh, the great Kardars would evict from the land those who offered too little revenue in favour of those who offered more. A new favourite would receive a grant of land irrespective of whether it was already occupied or not. If it were under cultivation by others, the grantee had the choice of leaving these as tenants paying rent to him, or of evicting them in favour of his own retainers. Whether there was such a thing recognised as proprietary right which could be enforced against the governing power is not, for the present discussion, of any great importance. Professor Kale writes that "Lands really belonged to those who or whose ancestors had cleared and reclaimed them. But in the vicissitudes of fortune, in times of foreign invasion and civil wars, these proprietors were dispossessed and were reduced to the position of tenants. These conquerors were themselves later on made to give up their ownership when another wave of invaders or immigrants came, and they became tenants of a superior kind. Old princes and chiefs who were thus brought under subjection, were often, as a matter of policy, continued in possession of their lands on condition that they collected and paid into the public treasury the tax levied upon their tenants, deducting and reserving a certain share thereof for themselves. Farmers of revenue and revenue officers of government often made the lands, whose revenue they collected, their private property. Leaders of turbulent and restless tribes took advantage of the confusion of the times and also became proprietors." (1) From this and similar conclusions arrived at by other writers, it is clear that there was no such thing as clear undisputed title of any value; and it would appear to be beyond doubt that land in general (without reference to special localities) could not be a foundation for credit. It is not difficult to find instances where

(1) Indian Economics (3rd edition), p. 456 clearly, in the conditions described, it is difficult and dangerous to talk of rights in land, or of land belonging to anybody but the state.

the possession of land was an encumbrance rather than a privilege ; where the revenue demand was so great that the fields were deserted, and the cultivators went to other parts of the province. They did not sell their land to the shopkeeper or other capitalist, but just left it and went away. The persons who were responsible for the revenue did not regard themselves as owning a valuable and transferable commodity, but as possessing a right to cultivate on condition of meeting the State demand.

Whatever may have been the conditions prior to the successive invasions from the West, there is no doubt that for centuries land could not have been a basis of credit in the Punjab.

The same unsettled conditions militated strongly against the accumulation of wealth ; for thrift and saving there must be peace and security. The postponement of a pleasure or satisfaction is not likely to be popular or general if the subsequent enjoyment be uncertain. At all times unprogressive agriculture leaves little scope for the accumulation of capital. There is seldom a surplus from which savings can be effected, and accordingly there is little chance of repaying a loan if one were obtainable.

Thus there would be little capital with the predecessors of the present usurers, and little chance of recovering any advance made. Credit, as now known, could hardly have existed. That there was usury, as well as credit, is clear from ancient Hindu law relating to its control, but it could never have been that facile operation which is now known under the name. Widespread debt was impossible because (*a*) there was little accumulation of capital to lend; (*b*) there was little surplus from which a loan could be repaid (1) ; (*c*) there was practically no security to offer ; and (*d*) there was no sure means of enforcing recovery against a recalcitrant borrower.

With the advent of the British came the introduction and maintenance of law and order, the levy of an equitable system of taxation in accordance with easily ascertainable principles, the recognition of private rights in property even against the State, the systematic recording of those rights, with cheap facilities for transfer within the custom of the locality or race, and above all the sustained endeavour to encourage all efforts to improve the economic position of the people. All the essentials of sound credit that it was possible for a Government to confer were soon present. Unfortunately, the change in the administration was not accompanied by the development of the economic sense amongst the people. A succession of fleeting empires and short-lived principalities has served to inculcate habits and customs the reverse of those required for material progress ; and the experience of the last seventy years has been insufficient to lead to as radical a change as the new circumstances made desirable. The rise of the Sikh power under the great Maharaja Ranjit Singh was a military event ; it was not accompanied by any considerable effort to improve economic conditions. The civil administration of the time has been described by Sir Lepel Griffin as "the simple process of extracting out of the

(1) The net exports from the Punjab prior to the advent of the British could not have been more than a few lakhs of rupees worth of commodities ; in 1918-19 the value of exports was 52 crores, a sum not much less than the estimated total rural debt. It is obvious that, while the province was formerly producing little, if any, more than it needed, it now produces a great surplus.

unhappy peasant every rupee that he could be made to disgorge; the limit of oppression being only marked by the fear of his revolt or the abandonment of his land through discouragement and despair. The Sikh farmer of revenue did not wish to kill the goose that laid the golden eggs, but he plucked its feathers as closely as he dared" The State frequently took as much as one-half the gross produce besides a multitude of cesses, and any accumulation of arrears was apt to be met by the despatch of a regiment to collect it. In the Punjab land was, and still in theory is, held by village communities paying jointly the demand of the State. There was ample land but there were not always enough cultivators to join in meeting the common burden. The State, or the revenue farmer beneath it, took all there was to be taken and the cultivator was left with no surplus. Thus there was no room for an idle landlord between the cultivator and the State; such a landlord would not have been able to exact more than the State already did and so would have been unable to secure any owner's profits. In these circumstances land had little value; transfers were practically unknown. There was nothing to be gained from taking it in payment of debt. It yielded more responsibilities than profits and offered no security for credit.

Between the death of Ranjit Singh in 1839 and the annexation of the province ten years later, the civil administration practically disappeared amidst the internal dissensions and rebellions that ended with the second Sikh war. A period of great administrative activity then ensued but progress was interrupted by the mutiny of 1857-58, and in the next decade the province passed through a cycle of bad seasons commencing with the famine of 1869. The officers for the new province were largely drawn from Agra and Oudh and brought with them ideas of a revenue demand which were soon found to be ill adapted to a tract with a rainfall far more precarious than that of the country from which they originated. The summary settlements almost everywhere reduced the demand of the Sikhs, but it would seem that cash payment and rigidity of collection largely set off the advantage to the cultivator. Previously the proprietary body was the body responsible for the revenue. If hey could persuade others to share in this responsibility, the advantage gained was a wider distribution of the burden; the tenants helped to pay the revenue, they did not pay any rent to the owners in addition. The immediate effects of annexation were the maintenance of law and order, security of tenure, a moderate fixed demand, and the encouragement of trade. The province advanced rapidly in prosperity and the agriculturist class found themselves in possession of a valuable property such as they had never known before. The land now yielded a profit in excess of the cultivator's immediate requirements and this margin of produce could obviously form the basis of credit. It was possible to find a tenant who would pay a rent higher than the Government revenue. A difference between rent and revenue began to appear and owners' profits emerged. (1) The land revenue

(1) *Cf.* S. C. Ray: The Permanent Settlement of Bengal. "The shares of the zemindars and of the Government in the rental were in the ratio of 1 : 9 at the time of the Permanent Settlement. As the Government revenue in 1793 was nearly 360 lakhs, this represented nine-tenths of the total rental, which was therefore 400 lakhs. Now the present rental is about 1,500 lakhs, which is four times the rental at the time of the Permanent Settlement. The Government revenue being now fixed at, say, 400 lakhs, a sum of 1,200 lakhs is shared between the ryots, the tenure-holders, the zemindars, etc." Obviously a body of men whose rental was

being fixed for a period of years, expansion of cultivation was encouraged so that, for instance in the five years between 1868-69 and 1873-74, the cultivated area increased from 202 lakhs of acres to 226 lakhs and the average revenue on this declined from Re. 1-1-3 to 15 annas 7 pies. At the same time, as the cultivator was beginning to save a profit out of which he could repay the debt, the newly established regular courts not only aided the lender in recovering his dues but introduced the novel principle that, whether the land was specifically pledged as security or not, it could be seized in satisfaction of a decree. This power was assumed by the civil courts without legislative authority. In many provinces, Chota Nagpur, Oudh, Central Provinces, Berar, Coorg and Ajmer, there have for long existed restrictions on the alienation of ancestral property. In 1852 the Board of Administration for the Punjab issued a circular requiring a landowner, who wished to sell his share, to offer it, in the first instance, to the whole community, or to some individual co-parcener, at a reasonable rate to be fixed by agreement, failing which the revenue officer and three assessors were to determine the fair value. Later (1858) the sale of agricultural land in execution of decrees was subject to the sanction of the Commissioner. In 1859 the sanction of the Judicial Commissioner was required when the property was ancestral. Later, proposals for sale had to be submitted to the Financial Commissioner. Since 1866 no interest in land could be sold in satisfaction of money debts without such sanction. (1) The first Civil Procedure Code (1859) confirmed the power of the civil courts to attach agricultural land in execution of decrees, but this code was not extended to the Punjab until 1866, and the sections relating to attachment and sale of agricultural land were subject to special modifications in certain provinces, including the Punjab.

Prior to annexation, the system of joint ownership was a powerful factor preventing transfer to outsiders, and the alienation of ancestral property was so opposed to the feelings of the people that it may safely be said that such alienations, though not unknown, were outside the ordinary current of life. So much is this the case that it is difficult to trace examples of transfers ; Sir Edward Maclagan, when Settlement Officer of Multan, was able to collect several such examples, but it is not clear what it was which was transferred, as it is well known that the great Sikh Kardars, or farmers of revenue, would not hesitate to replace one cultivator by another who undertook to pay more. It does not appear that there was any transferable right that could be enforced against the Government of the time.

The forced sale of hereditary land for debt was, it would seem, not recognised under Indian rule. The whole spirit of Hindu law is opposed to the control of the individual over ancestral property, and the Punjab Mohammadans generally follow a tribal law derived from their Hindu ancestors. The sale of land in execution of decrees was almost unknown in the Punjab as recently as 1873-74, and it has never attained very serious proportions owing to the restrictions imposed by law and custom.

The advent of the British into the Punjab was followed by a series of novel

---

40 lakhs in 1793, could not borrow as much as their successors with a rental of 1,200 lakhs. Debt depends not upon poverty, but upon prosperity, as Mr. Darling has pointed out in the *Economic Journal of India*.

(1) *Cf.* Land Administration Manual, paras. 17, 51.

features : the land, from being a burden entailing the satisfaction of a crushing State demand, became a valuable property ; improved communications opened up markets for the sale of surplus produce ; a bumper crop, instead of being almost a calamity from its effect of rendering surplus produce unsaleable, became a source of enhanced wealth ; property of all kinds rose rapidly in value. Further, the introduction of fixed laws and the general security following on the enforcement of order, rendered the land available as the ultimate security for loans. Another factor of great importance was the growth of a money economy and the increase of wealth as trade developed. In the early days, the moneylender did not advance large sums for several reasons : he had not the money to advance : he had not the means to enforce repayment : he did not see with the cultivator any surplus from which repayment could be made. Grain itself was of little use without a certainty of being able to sell it, and until roads, and, later, railways, brought distant markets within his reach, this certainty did not exist. In 1858 the grain dealers of Amritsar were nearly ruined. Owing to the disturbances of the time, there had been delay in securing payment of the revenue, and two instalments became due together ; the *banias* advanced the money and took the produce ; but the harvest was a bumper one ; there was no demand for the stored wheat which became unsaleable and rotted in the godowns. Another disturbing factor obstructing credit was the variation in prices owing to the dependence on local harvests and the absence of the balancing effect of distant markets ; it would be impossible a few months ahead to estimate whether the price of wheat would be 30 seers a rupee or 12. The writings of Munro, Elphinstone and others make it clear that there was much debt in India before the British became a power in the land, but, for the reasons stated, it could not have been as great, measured in rupees, as it soon became.

In 1874-75 regular civil courts were established which took over from District Officers and their staffs the settlement of suits for debts against agriculturists. These courts were, for the most part, presided over by Munsiffs recruited from the towns and so ill-versed in rural affairs and customary rights in land. The complaint that the unsuitability of the civil courts and the civil law are in part responsible for the increase of debt is heard from most parts of India, as well as from other agricultural countries, such as France. The peasants, according to Mr. Thorburn, soon came to regard them as agents and debt collectors for the moneylenders. (1)

The latter, however, conspired not for the land. but for the produce. They were intelligent enough to realise that the commercial value of the land was derived from what it yielded and as soon as peace and security brought good markets within easy reach they set themselves to get possession of the grain at the lowest possible price. The simplest method was to get control over the cultivator and shortly after the mutiny a new class of village usurer sprang up, the members of which began to use their superior intelligence and every advantage which the new laws and new courts placed at their disposal to entangle

(1) Report on Peasant Indebtedness, 1896. The bitter feelings of agriculturists against the lawyers led Thorold Rogers into making some strong remarks ; *e. g.*, perhaps the greatest enemies of public and private liberties which the seventeenth century had were the lawyers who could not ultimately be tied to common honesty, except by giving them freeholds in their offices. Vol. V., p. 5.

the Punjab peasants in a mesh from which the newly passed Evidence Act would permit of no escape. It is customary to blame the cultivator for improvidence but it is not explained why this characteristic developed after 1849 and has been practically confined to owners, especially to owners of the best lands. The charge of extravagance on marriage expenses was reduced to relatively unimportant limits by the Deccan Ryots Commission, and Mr. Thorburn, Mr. Keatinge and Mr. Datta have corroborated their finding. The old landowners' power of borrowing had been limited not only by the limited nature of the security which he had been able to offer, but also by the uncertainty which attended the recovery of debt in the absence of any law more certain than the pleasure of the ruler. Imprudent borrowing, prior to annexation, had been impossible. Even after annexation it was abundantly clear that a moneylender could not rely upon obtaining peaceable possession. Public opinion, in the forcible shape of an indignant crowd, too frequently expressed resentment in a form that could not be misunderstood.

A good many years passed before a written bond or a legal decree supplied anything approaching an assurance of respect for the right transferred. As a matter of fact, the moneylender did not want the land. but the crop. The land would have been of no use to him without a cultivator, and so long as land was plentiful and tenants were scarce, the proprietary right by itself was of little value. Two facts illustrate this. In the early years the land sold was nearly all cultivated land ; there was little or no attempt to buy up the waste in view of future development. Further, the moneylenders showed no inclination to become owners or purchasers of occupancy holdings, as the proprietary right yielded little profit. This latter fact is of great importance in the proper understanding of rural credit. The occupancy tenant is debarred from alienating his rights and yet he not only enjoys all the credit he needs but it is a matter of common observation that he is frequently more prosperous and less involved than the small proprietors among whom he lives and whose right of transfer is less unfettered. (1)

If thus becomes clear that the active factor in peasant indebtedness has been the desire of the village usurer to get hold of the produce. Prior to 1849 there was little or no surplus produce to get hold of ; but the British administrators reduced the revenue from the whole of the surplus to a theoretical half and practically about a quarter, and so left the cultivator with a margin which he could dispose of. The existence of this margin gave his land a saleable value. In many Native States the demand still absorbs the greater part of that margin and transfer of land is, in the majority of cases, almost unknown. A landowner's right to sell would there be useless. Prior to 1849 a mortgage could have been of little value as such a charge requires a settled tenure. With the advent of British rule, the Bengal form of mortgage appeared ; by 1874 there were 13 lakhs acres encumbered, of which 10 lakhs had come under mortgage within the previous six years, so that there could have been a very small area so encumbered on annexation. (It must be remembered that the Cis-Sutlej territory was already British before the annexation of the Trans-Sutlej Punjab

(1) The indisputable fact that in earlier days the moneylender would take the cultivator's cattle, but *not his land*, is carefully ignored by those who, in these days, elect to regard the land Aleination Act as a class measure and a grievance.

in 1849, and the Delhi territory was transferred to the Punjab from the United Provinces after the mutiny.) (1)

Enquiry in 1871 (2) showed that in Gurdaspur 66·5 per cent. of the mortgages were made to moneylenders, but only 37 per cent. of the sales. As the area sold was generally less than half of that mortgaged, there is further evidence that the moneylenders were anxious to secure the produce of the land without assuming the responsibilities of ownership. As was pointed out in 1882, as purchaser of the land he got only the land, but as mortgagee he got the land and a hardworking submissive owner-tenant as well. Further, it is repeatedly a matter of comment that the mortgages were mostly taking place in districts known to be prosperous and were in favour of moneylenders and that the lands so encumbered were the most fertile ; while the sales were in precarious districts and were mostly in favour of other agriculturists. The writers of the early reports found consolation in the comment that the agriculturists only sold their cheaper lands and were able to retain a lien on the better fields ; but it was officially admitted that " once in possession, the mortgagee adds loan to loan and interest to interest until the mortgagor, or his descendant, becomes involved beyond the power of extrication by ordinary means and the creditor becomes *de facto*, if not in name, proprietor of the estate". The fact was that the Punjab peasant was being confronted with a new form of credit, and, like his fellow in other countries, he was in danger of being ruined by it. Official enquiries showed that 94 per cent. of the money raised was for unproductive expenditure ; " the people", the Report of 1871 says, " do not as yet understand the advantage of constructing reproductive works with borrowed money. They mortgage their land in most cases merely to raise money for immediate necessities or to stave off importunate demands", and in the Report of 1874 we read, "the facility of raising loans on mortgage is increasing". At this time it was considered that legislative interference to prevent reckless alienations would be opposed to economic principles, but no authority was given for the suggestion that economists viewed with unconcern the expropriation of peasant proprietors in favour of capitalist landlords cultivating through tenants. Credit is notoriously double-edged and the story of the Punjab fully corroborates Professor Gide's comments: (3) " It has often been said that credit holds up the landowner as the rope holds up the hanged man...It is only to usurers that the loan on mortgage is a profitable business...In those countries where it is practised on an ignorant and improvident population..in Algeria, the countries of the Danube, and in Russia..it does incalculable harm"; and we may agree with him that, if a calculation could be made of the number of landowners ruined as compared with the number enriched by it, its abolition would be called for ; and further (4) that " the more easy mortgage credit is made the more dangerous will it become and the more surely will the small landowner be delivered into the hands of the usurers". Unfortunately the

(1) Although there is evidence that some sort of encumbrance on rights in land existed prior to the advent of the British, it is abundantly clear that what is now called a mortgage was very rare indeed.

(2) It is not easy to secure earlier evidence. Until a phenomenon excites remark, their are no comments upon it. But about 1858 certainly the *sahukar* was still sharing the vicissitudes of the cultivator and not exploiting them.

(3) Political Economy, p. 394.

(4) P. 397.

Punjab cultivators had not then fully realised the truth of the warning of Schulze-Delitzsch to have nothing to do with the man who would offer the deadly gift of easy credit. Mr. Keatinge tells practically the same tale of the Deccan cultivator (1): " the cultivator fell a victim to the insidious ease with which he could raise money on the security of his land and failed to foresee the inevitable day of settlement". Similarly Mr. Datta in his Report on the Rise of Prices (2): says "with increased wealth in the country there are now more persons with money to lend than before, and they compete with one another in offering loans to the cultivators at lower rates of interest...Land has considerably risen in value,..and now forms ample security for a much larger loan,..and this increased credit the ryot is fart oo prone to utilise for foolish and improvident purposes. The temptation is too strong for him to resist borrowing, the dangers of which are unrealised...This applies specially to the case of cultivators with small holdings." The Deccan Ryots Commission in 1875 reported that the much talked of improvidence of the ryots " consists rather in the shortsighted imprudence of an ignorant class ready to relieve present necessity by discounting future income on any terms and unable to realise the consequences of obligations foolishly contracted than in an extravagant expenditure or misapplication of income. The facilities for the recovery of debt offered by our civil courts had called into existence an inferior class of moneylenders dealing at exorbitant rates of interest with the lower strata of the agricultural poor";.." another cause of the increase of indebtedness is the facility with which the moneylending class can command the assistance of the law in the recovery of debt, and, consequent upon that facility, an expansion of the ryots' credit, inducing numbers of small capitalists to compete for investments in loans". The Famine Commission Report of 1880 mentions that the classes which have the best security to offer are the most eligible customers of the moneylenders, and further that " a rigid, elaborate legal system has too often proved an additional cause of ruin to the impoverished agriculturists". The Famine Commission of 1901 similarly reported of Bombay that " the unrestricted right of the cultivators to transfer their holdings was an accentuating cause of indebtedness and further that it invariably happens that, when an ignorant and improvident peasantry can dispose, without restriction, of valuable rights in land, the cultivators sink deeper into debt and their property begins to pass out of their hands". The initial cause of indebtedness was thus the action of the British Government on annexation in conferring clear titles to land and in so reducing the revenue demand as to leave a considerable margin of profit to the cultivators. As Mr. Thorburn says: (3) " the agriculturists naturally made use of their expanding credit". The rise in the value of land of agricultural produce attracted the attention of the regular moneylenders, and the high remuneration from their business led to the petty shopkeepers following suit with money borrowed from the big *sahukars*. Whatever the needs of the people might be there was no lack of lenders to accommodate them. The growing wealth of the province only increased the amount of available capital and in the absence of industrial enterprise the land was almost the only safe investment. The word " investment " is used advisedly. It seems abund antly clear that mere moneylending alone would not have accounted for the

(1) Rural Economy in the Bombay Deccan, p. 84.
(2) P. 160.
(3) Report on Peasant Indebtedness, 1896, p. 73.

heavy sum of indebtedness. The fact was that the lenders did not want their money back so much as they desired to retain a permanent lien on the produce. As already remarked, it was the crop and not the principal sum which they wished to see paid into their coffers. The usurer invested his money in the hope of a recurring annual return and seldom pressed for redemption of the mortgage. From the above it is clear that the advent of British rule served to provide a profitable field for the village usurer ; prior to this event, the usurer could not have had much opportunity to ply his trade ; he could not have had the liquid capital to lend or invest, and he could not have had any security for repayment. To this extent he may be said to be the creation of British rule. (1) In Ireland, when absentee landlords regarded their property solely as a source of rent and tenants were impoverished by uncertain tenure, recurring potato blight and competition for cheap American wheat, there was little room for the usurer. But when the tenant secured first fixity of tenure, fair rent and a free right of transfer, and later, under the various Land Purchase Acts, became proprietor of his holding, he came into possession of rights which could be used as security for credit. It was possible to exploit him and the usurers flocked to the country. In 1881, before the introduction of the Land Act, that conferred on the Irish tenant farmers rights which are, in the Punjab, akin to occupancy rights, but which were popularly styled the three F.'s (fair rents, fixity of tenure and the right of free sale of their tenancies), the number of Jews in the Island was 472. By 1911, after the Land Purchase Acts had come into force, the number had risen to 5,148. The number of moneylenders registered increased threefold in twelve years.

Turning to the Punjab there is unimpeachable evidence that the prosperity of the agricultural classes has attracted a large number of the trading classes to moneylending. The number of bankers and moneylenders (including dependents) returned at the Census of 1868 was 53,263 ; at the Census of 1911 this figure had been increased to 193,890. Between the two years, it must be remembered, there had also come into being a large number of agriculturists who added to their income by lending money to their neighbours, (2) but who would not be classed as moneylenders.

Some idea of the rapid increase in moneylending in recent years is to be obtained from the Income-tax Returns. The annual reports give the number

(1) The following extract from the "Imperial Gazetteer of India" Vol. III, p. 90, sums up the situation for the country generally :— "Generally speaking, the agriculture of India is in the hands of small men, and the capital required for the cultivation of the soil is supplied in small sums by small capitalists to men of small commercial intelligence. The peasant in India, as in most other agricultural countries, works on borrowed capital ; and the question whether he is more or less indebted than his compeer in other countries is open to discussion, but there can be no doubt that in certain parts of India at least the indebtedness of the peasant is economically excessive. This feature of the agricultural situation is largely the product of the last half-century. On the one-hand, the land, which is the peasant's ultimate security, has risen immensely in value under British rule, and the peasant has been tempted by the enhancement of his security to plunge into unnecessary debt. On the other hand, the increase in the value of the security has had little or no effect on the price of the capital supplied, and the moneylender has utilized the commercial helplessness of the uneducated peasants and their increasing competition for loans to maintain rates of interest which tend to make the business of agriculture impossible. On the one hand, there is excessively wide credit ; on the other, excessively dear money ; and the agriculture of India has suffered equally from the one and the other". (Published 1907.)

(2) The figures given are the best available ; many moneylenders have other sources of income ; on the other hand, many persons returned as traders engage in moneylending.

of persons assessed and the tax assessed. As the incidence of the tax is known, it is a simple calculation to work out the estimated income subject to the tax. To arrive at the capital employed to yield this income is more difficult. The rate of interest varies from 18 to 36 per cent., but while interest is not the only benefit that accrues to the lender it must be remembered that the interest charged is not always paid and that part of what is collected is expended in litigation and a further portion must be set off against losses. It will probably not be unfair to assume that the net profit (*i. e.*, the taxed income) represents about 12½ per cent. of the capital on loan.

In the following table incomes below Rs. 1,000 a year are omitted :—

Money-lenders in the Punjab.

Year.	Number assessed to tax.	Tax.	Income subject to tax.	Money on Loan.
		Rs. Lakhs.	Rs. Lakhs.	Rs. Lakhs.
1897-98 ..	..	3·8 ,,	150 ,,	12,00 ,,
1902-03 ..	8,400	4 ,,	165 ,,	13,00 ,,
1907-08 ..	10,300	4·38 ,,	188 ,,	15,00 ,,
1912-13 ..	12,500	5·13 ,,	213 ,,	17,00 ,,
1917-18 ..	15,035	7·42 ,,	350 ,,	28,00 ,,

As, up to a few years ago, incomes between Rs. 500 and Rs. 1,000 per annum were also subject to tax, it is a simple matter to estimate now the number of money-lenders earning between Rs. 500 and Rs. 1,000 per annum (1) and to these must be added the few money-lenders earning less than Rs. 500 a year. The result gives a figure somewhere about 40,000 as the number of money-lenders in the province and, as the average family consists of about 4·7 persons, this agrees with the number (193,890) of money-lenders and their dependents returned at the last census. The above figures indicate, amply enough, the rapid increase in money-lending and in the capital employed. In order to arrive at some idea of the relative importance of this calling in the province, the income-tax returns may again be consulted. These show that out of 40,690 assessees in 1917-18 no less than 15,000 were bankers and money-lenders, leaving only some 25,000 for all other professions, callings and industries. The tax assessed on money-lenders was 7·4 lakhs out of a total of 30·7 lakhs, and their income taxed was 350 lakhs out of a total of 750 lakhs. As the number of persons dependent on money-lending is only 1 per cent. of the population, as compared with 5·5 per cent. in other trades, 1·73 public servants, 2·49 professions, etc., and 20·32 industries, it is clear that the *average* income of money-lenders is above that of any other calling.

The actual total net income is, of course, not ascertainable, but a rough estimate may be framed from the information available. Before the limit

(1) *i. e.*, in 1897-98, out of 44,594 assessees under all heads, about 28,000 were earning under Rs. 1,000 per annum and 16,000 more than this.

of income subject to income-tax was raised from Rs. 500 per annum to Rs. 1,000 per annum, the proportion borne by the total of all incomes of money-lenders between Rs. 500 and Rs. 1,000 to the total of all incomes of money-lenders over Rs. 1,000 was about 15 : 38.

The total net income of all money-lenders earning over Rs. 500 is thus about 500 lakhs of rupees and, if allowance is made for income from money-lending not subject to tax, the total must be well over this sum. The net earnings of the North-Western Railway in 1917-18 amounted to 764 lakhs ; the net revenue of the major irrigation works in the Punjab for the same year was 267 lakhs. These figures will afford some idea of the relative importance of money-lending in the province compared with the great constructive works of development. There are more tax-payers amongst the money-lenders than are found amongst all others engaged in commerce and trade. All manufactures, other than companies (which are almost negligible), yielded only 575 assessees, paying Rs. 43,000. Barristers, pleaders, etc., to the number of 1,073 paid Rs. 86,251 tax on an income of 28 lakhs. All other professions yielded only 195 assessees who paid Rs. 22,400. The above figures show to what extent the province is dominated by the money-lender. He represents the richest single class. His profits probably exceed those of all the cultivators put together. Beside him, the professional class is inconsiderable; the industrial class is insignificant; even trade and commerce take second place. The Punjab is dominated by the money-lender to an extent unknown in any other province. In the whole of India, excluding this province, the proportion of money-lenders to total population is 1: 367 ; here it is 1: 100. Although the population of the Punjab is only one-eleventh of the whole, one-fourth of all money-lenders found in British India reside and work here. (1)

Before leaving this part of the subject, it may be necessary to make clear that, up till the advent of the British, the " shah " or money-lender was perhaps the only source whence the cultivating class could secure help in time of stress. When a sudden demand was made by one powerful enough to enforce it, it was he who gave credit ; and so great was the obligation felt towards him that *takkavi* was regarded as severing a common bond. But he does not seem to have been able to save the people from the effects of such a calamity as famine, for while these led to starvation, death, migration, ruin and desolation, they do not seem to have led to indebtedness in earlier days. The people sold their cattle and their chattels to the money-lender, and this exhausted their credit, for the land was not sold, being at the time unsaleable. In a period when prices fluctuated to an extent now unknown the money-lender was exposed to great risks of loss. The grain he took might prove valueless if the local market was glutted; for export to more distant places was not easy or always practicable. The sudden fall in prices in 1858 is said to have ruined the shopkeepers, who had taken the produce in return for payment of the revenue into the treasury ; and there were other obvious risks when means for transport and facilities for communications were primitive. Under circumstances such as these, only exorbitant rates of interest could cover losses ; and, perhaps, such rates were not unreasonable.

(1) The actual figures in 1911 were :—Bankers and money-lenders in British India =803,560 ; ditto in Punjab =193,890. Thus in British India outside the Punjab the number is 609,670. These figures include dependents, so should be divided by about 5 to yield the workers.

As to the reasons which induced the cultivator to borrow, the demand for land-revenue by a fixed date would seem to have been one and the need to replace cattle lost by disease was probably another. Mr. Thorburn found that 12 per cent. of the debt was borrowed to pay land-revenue, and 11 per cent. to purchase cattle. In the last Report on Co-operative Societies in the Punjab, it is shown that 12·5 per cent. of the money advanced is for the former object and 17·5 for the latter. The close approximation of the results of two enquiries made 21 years apart is certainly striking.

These two causes were mentioned and discussed at a very early stage in the revenue history of the Punjab. The administration has always boasted of the ease with which the land-revenue has been collected. In the Report for 1870-71 the Financial Commissioner protested against the suggestion that transfers of land were due to the revenue demand; he asserted that, while in "other parts of India" land was sold for Government revenue, "we have never taken such harsh measures in the Punjab". In 1871-72, however, the Lieutenant-Governor was disposed to believe that "in some districts of the Punjab the rigidity of the Government demand may force the people into debt", but in 1875-76 the view taken was that "the revenue system was sufficiently elastic to afford relief to the people where it may be necessary". From 1882 onwards successive steps have been taken to render the system more elastic and more adaptable to the variations in the harvests. The Government of the Punjab has never evaded the difficulties of this problem. It was clearly stated that "the rigid enforcement of the revenue demand, irrespective of calamities of seasons, is no part of its revenue system", but it seems to have borrowed from Agra and Oudh, whence many of its officers were obtainede a rather narrower conception of elasticity than was suitable to the new province and many years elasped before Collectors were given power to suspend the revenue of their own motion. Even now, as the figures from Co-operative Societies show, there is a great deal of borrowing to pay the revenue. The heaviness ot the demand could hardly be a cause for such borrowing, as the province has always been lightly assessed. In 1868-69 the average assessment per cultivated acre was Rc. 1-1-3; ten years later it was only 15 annas 3 pies; in 1888-89 it was 15 annas 7 pies; in 1898-99 it was Re. 1-2-0; and at present it is Re. 1-8-6. During these 50 years the irrigated area has increased 144 per cent., while the unirrigated area was remained practically stationary. The revenue averaged about Re. 1-4-10 per head of population in 1868-69; to-day it is Rs. 2-4-0.

The second cause of indebtedness mentioned is loss of cattle. This is sometimes very heavy indeed. In 1877-78, for instance, there was truly terrible mortality. Some districts lost half, some two-thirds, of their stock. "The loss of cattle during the year", says the Report, "was most disastrous, and has made a serious impression on the wealth and comfort of the people." The loss in one district alone would seem to have been nearly one crore of rupees, which was probably more than one-third the sale value of the whole cultivated land in the district. Obviously such a calamity must have led to extensive borrowing and, once in the clutches of the usurer, the peasant seldom gets free. As it was officially admitted that "the loss of agricultural capital annually caused by preventible deaths of cattle is enormous", this may safely be accepted as one of the main reasons for borrowing.

The indebtedness of the Punjab peasantry may thus be ascribed (1) to the sudden enhancement of credit due to new conditions introduced by the British Government, (2) to the abuse of this credit by clever usurers who encouraged borrowing in order to secure control of the produce, (3) to the famines of 1861, 1869, etc., and heavy mortality amongst cattle which drove the cultivators to borrow and so involved them in the money-lender's clutches, (4) to the rigidity of land-revenue collection accentuated by the tactics of the usurer who seized the whole produce and so compelled the cultivator to borrow afresh for the State demand and (5) to a system of civil law which was unsuitable inasmuch as it favoured the clever money-lender against the ignorant peasant. (1) Of these causes the most important from the cultivator's side is undoubtedly mortality amongst cattle and for this, of course, the responsibility lies with the religious scruples of the people. There are certain diseases of cattle which it does not seem practicable to deal with by ameliorative treatment. When in 1754 cattle plague raged in England an order in Council was issued directing that all infected cattle should be shot and buried four feet deep. The Cattle Disease Act has to a large extent perpetuated this and the Board of Agriculture still insists on the slaughter of animals under certain circumstances though the owners now receive compensation. By these and similar drastic measures, England manages to protect her cattle to an extent which is not possible amongst Hindus and Sikhs and, until those who abhor these measures bring forward equally effective substitutes, it is difficult to see how this heavy loss is to be avoided.

The assumption, frequently made, that debt is due to poverty cannot be entertained Debt is due to credit and credit depends upon prosperity and not poverty. Without someone to lend there can be no borrowers and without the wherewithal to lend there can be no borrowing. There must be men with money to lend before a peasantry can become involved in debt. If it be said that the agriculturists are thriftless and improvident, it may be urged in reply that thriftlessness may be encouraged by excessive facilities for borrowing and that improvident borrowing is only another aspect of improvident lending. (2) It is true that a body of small peasant proprietors must borrow at times as the are too often unable to save enough to meet unforeseen calamities; but hthe history of the co-operative movement in the Punjab shows clearly that tey people need not increase their debt, that they need not borrow from money-lenders and that, under a sound system of credit, they will soon save enough to meet all ordinary needs. Experience further shows that the needs of the cultivators for capital to carry on his industry are ordinarily quite small and certainly much smaller than is often assumed. (3) The evidence from

---

(1) *Cf.* Famine Commission Report, 1880:—" A rigid and elaborate legal system has too often proved only an additional instrument of oppression in the hands of the more wealthy or better instructed litigant and an additional cause of ruin to the impoverished agriculturists.

A critic would add as cause of debt the general insecurity of harvests in a province with a markedly capricious rainfall. This is a milder phase of (3).

(2) It is interesting to find Thorold Rogers writing of England in the middle ages, when the verse in St. Luke, VI, 35, " Lend, oping for nothing again ", was rogarded as prohibiting the taking of interest, that " the denunciation of usury stimulated the prudence and thrift of the husbandmen". In all his volumes there is nothing to suggest that rural debt ever assumed considerable proportions amongst the cultivators of the soil. The passage quoted is from Vol. IV, Chap. II.

(3) The average loan in a dry (*barani*) tract is about Rs. 60 ; in a well irrigated tract Rs. 80 to Rs. 90; in a canal irrigated tract Rs. 120 to Rs. 250. The actual um varies with the price of bullocks.

Egypt is the same : the real needs for credit on the part of the small proprietor who cultivates his own land without outside labour are far less than has been supposed, and such funds as he has been in the habit of borrowing on the security of his land have been too often devoted to unproductive purposes and to maintaining an extravagant standard of living. (1) Poverty and improvidence will not by themselves lead the cultivating class into debt. Enquiries in the Punjab show that the tenant is less in debt than the occupancy tenant, and the occupancy tenant less than the small proprietor and the small proprietor less than a larger one. In short, where the people are too ignorant to make a proper use of borrowed capital, debt follows credit and will increase as credit increases, until reckless lending as well as reckless borrowing are discouraged and the potential borrower becomes learned in the business side of his industry. As this view may not command general acceptance, some references may be given to the opinions of others competent to speak on the question. The old theory that land owned by a large number of small proprietors is almost invariably heavily mortgaged is emphatically contradicted by Mr. Rowntree's enquiries in Belgium, but it is interesting to note that the proportion of mortgaged proprietors was found to rise with more or less steadiness until those with from 37 to 62 acres were reached, where it is 40 per cent., then it dropped again downwards to proprietors with from 247 to 370 acres. (2)

To return to India ; in 1879 increased credit and increased prosperity were regarded as special causes of indebtedness. (3) Mr. Thorburn says that the *zemindar* used not to borrow, or if he borrowed he did so to the extent of his share of the next crop or so only. His self-denial was due not to virtue, but to his want of credit. Now he borrows to the value of his assets ; (4) and further that enquiry showed that alienations were larger in villages with exceptional facilities for borrowing, *e. g.*, near towns or money-lending centres than in villages with fewer temptations to indebtedness in their midst. (5) Again, whatever the security, *sahukars* must lend, having to employ their capital ; villages with evenly certain crops are not less depressed than those with precarious yields, as money-lenders prefer to operate in the former and only invest from necessity in poor land or land yielding exceptionally uncertain outturn. What they want is a good and regular return on their outlay. (6) The Famine Commission of 1901 noted that the unrestricted right of the cultivators to transfer their holdings was an accentuating cause of indebtedness. It invariably happens that, when an ignorant and improvident peasantry can dispose without restriction of valuable rights in land, the cultivators sink deeper into debt and their property begins to pass out of their hands. (7) Similarly Mr. Datta in his monumental Report on the Rise in Prices writes :—(8) With increased wealth in the country there are now more persons with money to lend than before and they compete with one another in offering loans to the cultivators at lower rates of interest. Owing to an increase in prices, land has considerably risen in value throughout India and now forms ample security

---

(1) Report on Finances and Administration of Egypt, 1913.
(2) Land and Labour : Lessons from Belgium, p. 50-51.
(3) Sir T. Hope, quoted by S. C. Ray ; Agricultural Indebtedness, p. 145.
(4) Report on Peasant Indebtedness, 1896, p. 10.
(5) *Ibid*, p. 42.
(6) *Ibid*, pp. 42-44.
(7) *Cf.*, Ray: Agricultural Indebtedness, pp. 33-34.
(8) Pp. 160-2-3.

for a much larger loan in comparison with what it would have secured 25 years ago ; and this increased credit the ryot is far too prone to utilise for foolish and improvident purposes. The temptation is too strong for him to resist borrowing, the dangers of which are unrealised. This applied specially to the case of cultivators with small holdings.

It seems unnecessary to labour the point further, although there would be no difficulty in bringing evidence from European countries, were this necessary, to prove that as credit rises the tendency is for debt to rise too. The great enhancement in the value of land and of the produce obtained from it, and the marked increase of wealth in the province. have already been discussed. The rapid rise in the number of money-lenders, and of the capital employed by them, has also been fully dealt with. If it be remembered that spending follows, and does not precede, borrowing, it will be easy to understand that the improvidence of the cultivators is largely a result of the facilities for borrowing. The fact that they had valuable land that could be sold attracted those possessed of the money wherewith to buy and accordingly sales of land increased rapidly in volume.

As to the extent of the evil, it is difficult to give accurate figures. From 1866 to 1874 sales averaged about 88,000 acres a year. In the following quinquennial periods the acres sold averaged 93,000, 160,000, 310,000 and 338,000 acres a year. Mortgages amounted to 143,000 acres a year in the first period, and to 212,000, 296,000, 590,000 and 554,000 acres a year in the succeeding quinquennial periods. These figures give an exaggerated view inasmuch as they refer to the total area. The cultivated area may be roughly calculated at half the above. On the other hand, they minimise the evil, inasmuch as they omit the following consideration. In 1866 the sale value was about Rs. 10 per cultivated acre ; in 1893 it was Rs. 59 ; and the consideration for a mortgage rose from about Rs. 10 to Rs. 46 in the same period. Thus between 1870 and 1893 the sale money rose from, roughly ine lakhs to one crore, while the consideration for mortgages similarly rose rom nineteen lakhs to 166 lakhs. In 1900-01, 436,000 acres (235,000 cultivated) were sold for 182 lakhs of rupees and 523,000 acres (376,000 cultivated) were mortgaged for nearly 231 lakhs of rupees. These figures are sufficient to show that transfers of agricultural land were increasing at a very rapid rate, and there is ample evidence to show that a large number of these were in favour of the money-lending class. It does not ever seem to have been argued that the new owners would have turned to actual cultivation. There are, of course, instances of these engaging in cultivation, but they are rare. Generally speaking, the old agricultural class was regarded as the source whence should be drawn the actual workers on the soil, and no alternative has been suggested. There was thus no attempt to supplant them. They were to remain, but with their old status of owner replaced by that of tenant.

II.—The Land Alienation Act.

Such being the position, it became necessary to devise a remedy. It was recognised that the evil was largely the result of the system introduced by the British with the best of intentions. They reduced the State's share of the proprietary profits of land in order to bring benefit to the landed classes, but the fruits of Government's sacrifices were being diverted into the pockets of the money-lenders. To a large extent Government was responsible, and Government had to discover a remedy. Inaction, as the Viceroy at the time pointed out, was not an alternative to adopting a remedy, it would be an evasion of responsibility. Palliative or even remedial measures would have been insufficient to meet the gravity of the circumstances ; the evil had to be prevented. It must not be assumed that the decision to impose restrictions on the power of alienation was arrived at without full consideration of all the interests involved. For 25 years, as the Annual Land Revenue Reports amply testify, the subject had received unbroken attention, but it was realised that it would be no light matter to restrict a power which had been deliberately and formally conferred. The old-time cultivator had been recognised as full landed proprietor with all the privileges of a yeoman, and in the desire to prevent him from losing his proprietary status nothing could be contemplated that might be regarded by the people as undermining that status. The remedial measures that suggested themselves were somewhat as follows :—

(*i*) the demand for land-evenue and its collection could be made so elastic as to remove this from the list of causes that led to borrowing; this has since been carried into effect ;

(*ii*) borrowing might be discouraged by limiting the security which the landowner had to offer or by diminishing the facilities for the recovery of debt ;

(*iii*) the system of agricultural loans could be extended ; it was, however, obvious that these could never replace the money-lender ;

(*iv*) the enforcement of inequitable contracts could be refused ;

(*v*) the liability of the land and its produce for unsecured money debts could be restricted ;

(*vi*) the power of sale or mortgage of land could be restricted. Of these Nos. (*iv*), (*v*) and (*vi*) are merely varieties of (*ii*) and, as the remedies referred to in (*i*) and (*iii*) were admittedly insufficient, it became necessary to concentrate on those referred to in (*iv*), (*v*) and (*vi*).

The refusal to enforce inequitable contracts has been dealt with partly by amending the Civil Procedure Code and partly by the recently enacted Usurious Loans Act ; in the Land Alienation Act it appears in the declaration that mortgages with a clause of conditional sale are illegal.

Similarly the liability of the land and its produce for unsecured money debts has been much curtailed by the liberal exemptions from attachment in execution of civil decrees contained in section 60 of the Civil Procedure Code.

There remain the proposals to restrict the power of sale or mortgage which is now embodied in the Act. It is unnecessary to discuss objections raised at the time but now shown by experience to be groundless, such for instance as that the cultivator's credit would be dangerously restricted. It was realised at the time that transfers, even though forbidden, would not be wholly prevented, but it was hoped, and time has justified the hope, that they would be enormously decreased in number.

On the 8th June 1901 the Punjab Alienation of Land Act came into force. It was the result of many years' most careful enquiry and was passed into law amidst gloomy forebodings. The Lieutenant-Governor, Sir Mackworth Young, marshalled the opinions of many eminent revenue officers of the past in support of his own view. He complained that the Act was not due to the initiative of the Punjab Government and indeed went beyond its utmost recommendations and explained that he was refraining from opposition only because "the best experience available" of his own officers was in favour of the measures. All sorts of evil seemed to be impending. The value of land would be depreciated, the provisions of the Act would be disregarded or evaded, the money-lender's trade would become impossible and the borrower would be pinched. In point of fact all these gloomy prognostications proved groundless. The Act was quietly received, apathy was more observable than excitement, no special difficulties were encountered and the new law was soon absorbed into the routine life of the province. Its main provisions are very simple. Sale of agricultural land in execution of a decree is forbidden. Sales of their lands by members of agricultural tribes to others who are not members of these tribes is similarly forbidden; though sanction may be accorded to such sales in special cases. The Bengal form of mortgage, with a conditional sale clause, is rendered illegal and even in the case of old mortgages the conditional sale clause becomes inoperative. All mortgages of land by agriculturists in favour of non-agriculturists are illegal except such as provide for automatic redemption. To obviate evasion, land may not be leased for a period longer than five years.

The Act caused no undue contraction of credit. The average price of land was Rs. 78 per cultivated acre for the five years prior to the passing of the Act; it fell to Rs. 75 for the next five years but rose to Rs. 98 in 1906-07 and has since steadily continued to rise until it is now well over Rs. 200. (1) Confining attention to cultivated acres only, the average area sold in the five years preceding the Act was 162,000; for the next five years (1901-02 to 1905-06) it dropped to 135,000; in the next period (1906-07 to 1910-11) it fell further to 121,000. Since then it has risen and for the period 1911-12 to 1915-16 the average area sold was 140,000 acres. This increase is due to large sales of land by Government in the canal colonies, and does not indicate that there is any

(1) Rs. 275 in 1919-20.

tendency for agriculturists to part more freely with their land. The following figures show that these tribes are now actually regaining land :—

Average area sold in acres.

		By agricultural tribes.	To agricultural tribes.	Gain or loss.
1902-03 to 1905-06	..	150,000	149,000	—1,000
1906-07 to 1910-11	..	170,000	178,000	+8,000
1911-12 to 1915-16	..	188,000	217,000	+39,000
1916-17	..	183,000	203,000	+20,000
1919-20	..	166,000	191,000	+25,000

(The figures relate to the province as at present constituted. The figures given in the text for the five years prior to the passing of the Act also relate to the area now included in the Punjab.)

The figures for mortgages are also very striking. The average area of cultivated land mortgaged annually during the five years preceding the Act (1896-97 to 1900-01) in the area now included in the Punjab was 339,000 acres. The annual average for the three succeeding quinquennial periods was 180,000, 211,000 and 226,000 acres, respectively. But these figures are misleading and the result of the Act is more accurately shown in the following table (the figures of which include both cultivated and uncultivated area) :—

		Area mortgaged by agricultural tribes.	Area redeemed by agricultural tribes.	Area mortgaged to agricultural tribes.
1902-03 to 1905-06	..	190,000	178,000	162,000
1906-07 to 1910-11	..	240,000	296,000	219,000
1911-12 to 1915-16	..	264,000	270,000	238,000
1916-17	..	246,000	199,000	220,000
1919-1920	..	284,500	348,000	267,500

The figures show clearly that agricultural tribes are gaining by redemption and mortgage far more than they are losing by mortgage. The average mortgage money per acre has increased from Rs. 61 per cultivated acre in 1900-01 to Rs. 106 in 1916-17 and Rs. 163 in 1919-20. The actual total cultivated area under usufructuary mortgage is slowly declining from 3,287,000 acres in 1901-02 to 3,200,000 in 1916-17 and 3,117,000 in 1919-20; the area owned by agricultural tribes and mortgaged must have decreased still more. The percentage of the mortgaged cultivated area to total cultivated area has declined from 12·3 to 10·8 in the period named. The district figures show improvement in the most encumbered tracts and retrogression in some of those previously more free. Thus :—

District.	Percentage of total cultivated area mortgaged.		
	1900-01	1916-17.	1919-20.
Gurdaspur	25·5	20·9	21·2
Sialkot	25·1	23·5	23·6
Multan	17·7	10·1	9·7
Amritsar	17·0	16·3	16·5
Gujrat	16·1	12·4	11·5
Kangra	16·2	12·9	11·5
Rohtak	10·0	12·3	11·5
Gujranwala	10·0	7·1	9·3 (1)
Jhelum	9·0	7·7	6·6
Karnal	7·0	8·4	8·4
Hissar	5·6	8·0	5·8
Jhang	4·2	10·4	10·1

The explanation of this curious variation appears to be that in the early days of British rule, as already mentioned, the money-lender was most active in the more prosperous districts; prosperity was the source of temptation. With the passing of the Land Alienation Act this same prosperity has enabled the agricultural tribes to retrieve their former position. In the poorer tracts the land was of little value, crops were precarious and hence the money-lender was less active until the all-round rise of prices gave him security. Rohtak, Hissar and Karnal belonged to the old Delhi Division where the conditional sale mortgage was most common and the rise may be due to the conversion of these into usufructuary mortgages under the Act.

It remains to discuss two objections frequently raised against the Act. The first is that it discriminates unduly against Hindus, and the second that it has failed of its real object inasmuch as it has left the poorer agriculturist at the mercy of the agriculturist money-lender who is rapidly buying him up and reducing him to the status of a tenant. The first objection is easily met. Exactly one-third of the agriculturists protected are Hindus, and these Hindus far outnumber all the non-agricultural Hindus in the province. The objection is, of course, based on the fact that the shop-keeping and money-lending classes, who are also the most thrifty, happen to be, in this province, for the most part Hindus, and it is these who are prevented from acquiring land. But the object of the Act is mainly to prevent

(1) This increase over percentage for 1916-17 is due to the formation of Sheikhupura district, where the percentage is 5·1.

certain classes from parting with their ancestral property, and, thus far, it merely embodies ancient Hindu laws and so can hardly with fairness be described as due to religious discrimination. Further, the Act has its counterpart in other countries, which have the same problem to contend with but which contain no Hindus. The American Homestead Law absolutely reserves from alienation a certain area, usually about 50 acres, which is regarded as necessary for the support of the family. (1) In England, about four or five hundred years ago, changes were taking place somewhat similar to those observable in the Punjab now. The old self-sufficing, agricultural economy was beginning to break up. The capitalist class was increasing; the successful merchant and lawyer were acquiring land and supplanting the country gentry. There was an intense land hunger. Efforts to establish the system of entails were resisted. But circumstances brought a change of view and the system of strict family settlement was devised under which the great bulk of the estates in England are now held. (2) Restrictions on these entailed estates are more absolute than anything by the Alienation of Land Act. In other countries there exist laws embodying the homestead principle.

To return to India; it must be remembered that when the British took over the administration they found cultivators in possession of a right to hold land on payment to the State of a revenue demand which practically amounted to a full rent. If this demand were not paid, the State unhesitatingly evicted the occupant and put in another. The cultivator, in fact, possessed no rights in the land that he could alienate. There was then no question of the right of a trader to purchase land; there was nothing worthy of purchase. If the British Government had maintained the land revenue at the old proportion, it is probable that sales would never have reached a volume to attract attention. Thus the fact that, in this province, those desiring to purchase land are mostly Hindus, while the proprietor of the land may be Hindu, Mohammadan or Sikh, is a pure accident of history. Egypt has now its Five Feddan Law, absolutely exempting this area from sale, but the would-be urchasers in Egypt are not Hindus, but Musalmans and Christians.

The second objection mentioned above is that the Act has failed of its objects inasmuch as the Hindu usurer has been replaced by the agriculturist money-lender, who is free to purchase as much land as he can from members of his own tribe or from tribes in the same group. To a considerable extent this objection is due to misunderstanding. It was never intended that all transfers should be prevented. The power of transfer had grown up to an extent which, though limited by custom, was regarded as dangerous, and it was considered desirable to restrict the power just so much as would be necessary to obviate the dangers that threatened. It was never considered that all transfers were objectionable. When an agriculturist, who has more land than he needs, sells some of it to another who has less, or when a landowner desires to raise money for improvement by disposing of a fraction of his estate, the

(1) In Belgium an owner is prohibited from mortgaging that large proportion of his land, the inheritance of which is prescribed by statute. In Egypt the Five Feddan Law was, it is understood, enacted as a result of the success of the Punjab Act.

(2) Curtler: Short History of English Agriculture, pp. 122-123.

transaction would, in most cases, be beneficial. Similarly objection could hardly be raised to a prosperous agriculturist investing his savings in the manner most suitable to his manner of life, or to an owner of an uneconomic holding, who has gone to Australia or Canada and there saved money, using this money to buy a few fields so as to make his land sufficient for the support of a family. It must be remembered also that, in the Punjab, land is held by village communities, and free unrestricted sale of ancestral property by individuals has never been allowed by custom. The present Law of Pre-emption is only an attempt to put this custom into legal form. If an individual wished to sell land, other members of the community had the first claim; the shopkeeper or trader had no claim at all. This prior claim is too old to be disputed, but it would be quite a new idea to suggest that it only exists where the purchase price is not the result of money-lending. There is still, however, in the second objection this element of justification, that if it were found that a new class of agriculturist money-lenders was springing up and was buying out small owners on a large scale and by this means reducing them to tenants, there would probably be ground for considering the advisability of further legislative interference. But it has yet to be shown that such a process is taking place to any appreciable extent. There does not seem to be any accurate information available showing the extent to which snaller owners are being bought out by others. Assuming, however, that this process were in active operation, it does not follow of necessity that the results would, in the balance, be evil. Already there are far too many people dependent on agriculture; under the existing system of cultivation there is not a full day's work for all. The holding in very many cases seems to be too small to maintain a family in comfort, and good might result if these surplus cultivators could be forced into industries. There would be distress, just as there was distress in England during the period of enclosures, but it is now generally admitted that enclosures resulted in ultimate good to agriculture and to the country at large. This, however, is mere speculation. The point relevant to the argument is this, that in a country where the means of livelihood are divided into hereditary pursuits, there is more economic objection to land passing into the possession of non-agriculturists than there is to its accumulation in the hands of hereditary agriculturists. The experience of the Punjab amply shows that, with a few brilliant exceptions, the new owner, drawn from the professional or trading classes, does not cultivate the land himself; he does not inves tany capital in improving it (1) or devote his undoubted intelligence to the promotion of agriculture, but contents himself with obtaining the best rent he can.

Ireland presents a parallel. After the Napoleonic wars the price of agricultural produce increased greatly. Irish farmers felt the full benefit. The population rose rapidly and with it the pressure on the soil. The people lived largely on potatoes and sold their wheat. About 1846 came the potato blight followed by a terrible famine. The old landlord class suffered with its tenants and many were impoverished; the opportunity to buy land attracted speculators from Dublin who had no interest in agriculture. There thus came

---

(1) Mr. Emerson writes that in Multan the non-agriculturist owner has put more capital in the development of land than the agriculturist owner. The money-lender is generally willing to invest where he sees a good return. He puts more money than the zemindars into improvements. But the sum total of his investments is very small.

into existence a new body of landlords whose only interest in the soil was the rent they could get out of it. The old cultivating class clung to its ancestral fields with a tenacity that will be well understood in this province. The new owners wanted a good return on their investment which the old tenants promised, but could not pay, and to this cause is traceable much of the agrarian trouble of the next forty years.

The case of the agriculturist of the Deccan was clearly described by Sir T. Hope in Council in 1879 (1) :—It may be argued, he said, that it is indispensable that the land should be in the hands of those who by their capital, intelligence and industry are qualified to turn it to the best account. If the land be held by a class who, through ignorance, improvidence and want of energy, has burdened their heritage with debt which can never be repaid, and thus have deprived themselves of all incentive to labour and all interest in its results, then the only remedy is to promote a gradualrestoration of healthier conditions of society by the bankruptcy and eviction of the people. True as such principles are to Europe, considerable caution is necessary in applying them to oriental life. Those into whose hands the land is passing are not yearning for it in order to improve it by their intelligence, enterprise and capital ; most have no wish to invest their capital in comparatively unprofitable agricultural experiments ; they prefer to keep the ryot on his land, and extract all they can from him ; the punctual discharge of their advance is the last thing they desire, the occupier is reduced by pressure of debt to a tenant-at-will holding at a rack-rent from, and sweated by, his Marwari creditor.

A discussion on economics is not perhaps the proper place wherein to introduce a reference to a political grievance ; but it is difficult to leave this subject without mentioning that the Land Alienation Act is so regarded by a small, but important, section. History does not support them. Nor does their own ancient law. Where Hindu law prevails, there could be little reason to enact a measure designed to protect ancestral property from alienation by a single individual member of any generation. When land was cheap in the Punjab, the non-agricultural Hindu did not buy it. Prior to 1901 he had ample opportunity to acquire rights, but he preferred that the rights he acquired should be those of a mortgagee, and not a proprietor. The fact is that the desire to purchase land is quite a new feature. It was gathering strength when the Act imposed restrictions upon alienations. From some discussions of the subject, it would be imagined that similar restrictions were unknown elsewhere ; whereas, if anything, they are the rule rather than the exception. (2) Certainly they existed under Hindu law and in the customary law of the Punjab. Whether such an Act should be retained in the interests of economic develop-

(1) *Cf.*, Ray : Agricultural Indebtedness, p. 139. The effect of the Deccan Agriculturists Relief Act was to make the professional money-lender more cautious in advancing loans and the agriculturists more reluctant to borrow where the security of his land was required. The result was a marked reduction of unnecessary borrowing.

(2) See, for instance, the case of Belgium, where the ownership of land is strictly regulated by the State. Children have an absolute right of inheritance to a certain part of a parent's holding ; an only child must succeed to one-half of the family land ; if there is more than one child, each of them has a right of succession to an equal share. The proportion of land thus reserved for certain heirs may not be mortgaged or otherwise burdened, and the death duties upon land left to strangers in blood are very high.

It may be added that in England the difficulties in transferring land impose a considerable check upon too frequent alienations. In Roumania they serve almost to prohibit them.

ment, must depend largely upon whether the people, now excluded from purchase, devote themselves to agriculture in a more progressive spirit than those who now own the land. At present no such tendency is observable, although the total area owned by them is considerable. In conclusion it may be added that no reasoned argument in favour of the repeal of the Act has come under notice. That there is a feeling amongst the high caste Hindus against the retention of the Act is undeniable ; and this feeling is not confined to the Punjab alone. There was similar opposition to the Bundelkhand Alienation of Land Act (1903) and the Bombay Act of 1901. In Oudh the problem has been dealt with by the Settled Estates Act of 1900.

CHAPTER XI.

The Price of Wheat.

The subject of the price of wheat is an important one for the Punjab as the consumption of this grain has increased in recent years until it has become the staple food of the people. In towns it is now eaten by almost everyone all the year round, and the consumption of the cheaper grains, millets, etc., such as Bajra and Chari, appears to have declined. The religious sentiment against the use of meat and other foods has the effect of throwing the people into a position of dependence upon this single article; and as the Punjab is situated far from any seaport this dependence is confined to the crop produced within the province or in the neighbouring United Privinces. Where the diet of the people is varied, it is always possible to meet a rise in the price of one article by consuming less of that and more of other food-stuffs; but where diet is confined to a few articles the variations in price of those articles becomes possessed of interest to every household. Thus it is that the price of wheat is on everyone's tongue; everyone is talking about it newspapers contain articles about it and politicians use it as an excuse for attacking Government. Everyone wants to know why wheat is so dear, and what can be done to bring the price down and when a fall may be expected. The subject is not an easy one. There are many factors to be considered, and, as may be expected, popular remedies propounded by those who have not given the matter close study are not only useless, but sometimes actually dangerous. As an example of uninstructed criticism, the suggestion that the high price is due to the land-revenue may be mentioned. The average land-revenue in this province is at present Re. 1-9-6 per acre. The average acre of wheat may be taken as yielding not less than ten maunds, so that the land-revenue is 2½ annas a maund. As no one is concerned with so small a matter as 2½ annas a maund it is clear that the land-revenue is not a factor in the present high price of wheat. If anyone doubts this, he might be asked to consider the fact that half the land in the province is cultivated by tenants who do not pay land-revenue, but rent, which is much higher than the revenue. But no one appeares to attribute the high price to high rent. Wheat and rice are the two great sources of human food for many millions. They differ in one important particular; rice is consumed almost entirely in the country where it is produced; very little enters into the world's trade; but wheat is the chief staple food export; a larger proportion of the total produced enters into international trade than of any other grain. Although considerably over half the total world's production is grown in Europe, yet France, Germany, Italy and the United Kingdom are large importers, and it is the demand from these countries that determines the price obtainable by the grower. The countries producing the largest amounts of wheat before the war were Russia, the United States and, a long way behind, Austria-Hungary and India. India was the fifth in order amongst the exporting countries, while the United Kingdom was the largest importer. The result is that the dominating factor in the price of wheat in India is the demand from England. The biggest market for this food is Liverpool, so that the price in Liverpool sets the price for the world, and in other places the price is apt to be the price at Liverpool minus the cost of getting it there. In normal seasons, when there is no restriction in trade, the price of wheat in the Punjab follows the price at Liverpool. If wheat can be bought here and shipped to Liverpool at a profit, it is so bought and shipped. When no profit would result from such a transaction, wheat is not shipped to England (1). It is necessary to lay stress upon this fact that wheat is an important article of international trade because some people prefer to ascribe to local causes results that are due to events outside the Punjab. When there is any restriction on trade, the price of wheat tends to depend upon local causes; similarly, when the price here is so high or the price at Liverpool is so low that no profit can be gained from its export, then again the price depends upon local causes. But, apart from these two occasions, the price is a world price, dependent largely upon the production in the whole world and the demand from the whole world. In discussing the price of wheat, it is thus necessary to take a broad view of world conditions.

The fact that wheat is an important article of international trade is no solely due to its popularity as a food. There are several other foods that are more widely consumed than wheat; there is milk, for instance, which is not an object of international trade at all. Wheat possesses special qualities that make it easy to buy and sell it. It does not deteriorate quickly; it can be eaten many months after it ripens; it can be easily carried from place to place without suffering much harm; it can be stored without loss; and, what is of almost more importance than these, it can be classified and graded into well-known kinds and can then be sold by description. Wheat at Karachi can be sold in Liverpool without moving it from Karachi, and without sending a sample to the buyer. It is this which tends to keep the price all over the world at a figure closely following the price at Liverpool. It is the same quality which facilitates gambling or Satta. If a merchant has a godown full of wheat, he can sell this almost anywhere in India, and the purchaser can resell without either he or the new buyer seeing it. Coming now to closer grips with this subject, it must be remembered that this question of the price of wheat is not a new one. In England, certainly for over eight hundred years, the trade in wheat has been the subject of interference, first by the King and later by Parliament; in that period various devices have been tried to control its price and a vast deal of experience has been gained, with the net result that modern Governments nowadays are very reluctant to touch the subject. Wheat is not the only crop which the farmer can grow, and the farmer will not grow it unless he can make a profit out of it. For nearly four hundred years after William the Conqueror came to England the English Government tried to control the wheat trade so as to favour the consumer; then apparently

---

(1) A rate of Rs. 5-8-0 per maund at Lyallpur is about equivalent to Rs. 6-2-8 free on rail Karachi; from Karachi to England, the freight before the war was about seven annas per maund. This rose threefold during the war, but freights are coming down now. If they stabilise at double the prewar rate wheat at Rs. 5-8-0 per maund at Lyallpur will be exported if the price in England is above Rs. 6-10-0 per maund (with the rupee at one shilling and fourpence). Low freights tend to equalise the price of wheat all over the world. The present higher freights will tend to restrict export from India to an extent greater than before the war, in the same way as an export tax would.

they learned that there was another side to the question, namely, that plenty of wheat was more important than cheap wheat, a lesson which some writers in the papers seem to have forgotten. It is no good having cheap wheat if there is too little of it. After four hundred years' effort to please the consumers, the English Government have spent the rest of the time trying to encourage the farmers to grow more wheat ; they have realised that the producer needs consideration as well. For the last three or four hundred years the efforts of Government have been directed towards keeping the price up sufficiently high to make it worth the farmers' while to produce more of it.

When the interference with the export of wheat had the effect of reducing the price which the cultivator received for it, he took to other products which might pay him better and might be more free from interference from those who thought only of the consumer. The English farmer gave up, to a large extent, the growing of wheat and turned his land to pasture for the grazing of sheep. As it happened, sheep paid better than wheat ; and, later, when more was discovered about the improvement of cattle, the pasture was preserved for the production of milk, butter and other commodities of animal husbandry, until, when the great war led everyone to feel anxious about his food supply, only about 5 to 10 per cent. of the cultivated area in England was bearing wheat, and special measures had to be resorted to in order to induce the farmer to break up his rich and profitable pastures to grow more grain for the people.

These facts are mentioned because at a time like the present, when the price of wheat is a matter of common concern, there is a strong tendency to advocate measures which centuries of trial have shown to be useless, or even dangerous. Those who write in the local newspapers seldom take the trouble to examine the evidence, which past history has collected, for and against the policy they advocate. In Europe, and more especially in England, there still exist the original records of transactions which took place centuries ago, so that it is easy to check the statements of public men by historical documents.

So far, it has been attempted to show that in dealing with wheat, a very wide survey of world conditions is necessary; wheat is so important an element in international trade that its price depends upon world factors, and owing to its qualities it can be sold by description so that the owner of any quantity can ascertain its value by watching the cables giving the rates in the Liverpool market. It has also been mentioned that attempts by Government to regulate the trade in, and the price of, wheat, have been made from earliest times, first in favour of the consumer and later to encourage the producer to maintain his cultivation of this most important grain. As everyone knows, the Corn Laws in England were repealed in the middle of last century, but in France import duties on wheat were imposed as late as 1885, and have been raised several times since, the last occasion before the war being in 1897. There the object was to keep up the cultivation of wheat by ensuring to the cultivator a fairly good price and a fairly good profit.

In the Punjab, hitherto, there has been no need to take any measures to keep up the price of wheat, as the zemindars have been only too ready to put a large proportion of their land under this crop. In order to understand the present circumstances, it may be of advantage to look back to the earlier years when Punjab wheat was not affected by world prices. It has been pointed out that, where there is any restriction on trade, the price tends to depend upon local causes; and, where there are no facilities for the transport of the crop to market, the price may be purely local, varying widely from place to place. Before the construction of railways prices in the Punjab depended upon the local harvest. Taking Dera Ismail Khan as a place unaffected by railways till late, it appears that wheat was 22 seers to the rupee in 1842; in 1850 a good harvest brought the price down to 50 seers; while a bad one in 1869 sent it up to 13 seers. In a good year there was apt to be a glut and the grain would become unsaleable. This happened in Amritsar about 1858, when the dealers or Banias bought from the zemindars at the current rate, and were almost ruined by a heavy fall in prices due to the supply being far in excess of the demand; they could not find a purchaser and the wheat rotted in their godowns. A bumper harvest in the days of defective communications was not always a blessing to the cultivator. About 1875 the zemindar was still getting only about one rupee for 40 or 50 seers in a good year. Generally speaking, it may be assumed that the average price at this time in the towns was 28 to 30 seers. There are some people who wish these prices to return again and consider that Government should take some action that would bring this about. These forget the changes that have taken place since 1870: they also forget that large changes in the price of food are good for nobody except speculators. Before the construction of railways it must have been very difficult to know when to buy wheat and for how long to lay in a store. The price varies widely according to the season. It might be 15 or 16 seers in June and 9 seers in January; these were the prices in Delhi in 1870. In the same year the prices at Sirsa were 11 seers in June and 6 seers in January.

These differences were due to the absence of proper transport facilities; each area consumed its own wheat, and only a large difference in the rate would lead to any movement of grain between one area and another. The price varied from district to district and from month to month. The zemindar might one year have no crop to sell, and the next be unable to sell on account of the market being flooded by a good harvest. At such a time there was no inducement to grow more than the local market would absorb. A cultivator only grows what he can sell; if he cannot sell he will not grow. So that, without some certainty of finding a market for his surplus he had no object in extending his cultivation. This point is very important, for it means that without an export trade there can be no surplus produce from year to year. About 1870 the area under wheat in the Punjab (as it was then constituted) was 5,660,000 acres, or about 31 per cent. of the whole cropped area. The value of the wheat exported was only four lakhs of rupees. At that time there was no railway system; there were few canals; the only ones at work were the Bari Doab and Western Jumna, and the receipts from these did not cover expenditure. The Sirhind Canal was commenced in 1869-70, and it led to some increase in the area under wheat. By 1895-96 the area under wheat had risen to 6,260,000 acres. Of this, over half, or 3·2 million acres, was irrigated, and 3 million unirrigated. This area was about 32 per cent. of the total. Owing to the extension of irrigation, the total yield appears to have risen by about 23 per cent., from approximately 43 to 53 million maunds. Of this, about 8·4 million maunds, or less than one-sixth, was exported.

Since 1896 the province has undergone an extraordinary change. This year will probably be accepted as the turning point in Punjab history, when backwardness and poverty gave way to progress and prosperity. The chief event concerned was the opening of the great Chenab Canal, and the colonisation of Lyallpur. The immediate result was ani mmense increase of trade, and, with it, wealth and a marked rise in the general standard of living. There is no doubt that the consumption of wheat within the province increased; and that of the inferior grains declined, especially in the towns.

The opening of the Chenab Canal was followed by the construction of other great works, and the area under wheat expanded in consequence. For the nine harvests, 1912 to 1920, the average area was over nine million acres, (90 lakhs). The Punjab in these years was the present area, that is, without the Frontier Province or Delhi; so that if the same area be taken it will be seen that the wheat crop has doubled since 1870. The total outturn may be estimated as over 81 million maunds, as compared with 43 million maunds in 1870 and 53 million maunds in 1896. This increase far exceeds the increase in the population. In 1871 this was about 162·5 lakhs, while in this year it is about 200 lakhs. These figures deserve attention because they show that the outturn of wheat in the province is now far more than is needed to feed the people, even if their consumption per head has increased since 1870—more than many critics are prepared to admit. It is this surplus production which forms the basis for the export trade, and so for the import trade and for that great increase in the wealth of the commercial classes which is such a marked feature of recent Punjab history.

In the years 1886 to 1895, that is, before the opening of the Chenab Canal, the average export of wheat was 278,000 tons a year. In the three years before the war it was 1,376,000 tons, or nearly five times as much. The average for the next six years has been 1,050,000 tons. The value of this exported wheat increased in the same period from Rs. 168 lakhs to 880 lakhs. To illustrate the importance of this trade to the province, it may be pointed out that in the last nine years the Punjab has received over Rs. 80 crores for its wheat from foreign consumers. This vast sum has been received partly in manufactured goods, partly in treasure, gold and silver and partly in other commodities. On both export and import trade the commercial classes have been able to make a profit which would not otherwise have accrued to them. These facts are important in the face of those who advocate restrictions on the trade in wheat. The outcry against dear wheat comes mostly from the towns, which are large gainers from theh igher prices. If the export of wheat were permanently restricted, many commercial firms would be ruined, and the prosperity of the towns would suffer.

The point deserves to be emphasised because many people seem to think that high prices for wheat benefit only the zemindars; whereas the higher prices which are received by the cultivators have to be set off against higher prices of bullocks, implements and other things that make up the cost of production. A commission agent, or Arhti, works on a percentage of the price of whatever goods he deals in, so that his commission increases directly with the rise in price. The fact that the trading and commercial classes have grown prosperous in recent years is obvious to everybody, but it seldom receives mention from those who desire to see measures taken to reduce the price of wheat.

The next question to which an answer is required is whether, on the whole, the amount of wheat left in the province after the exporters have taken away their quota is growing more or less. Is the total quantity of wheat actually consumed within the province becoming less in consequence of the export trade ? To this it does not seem possible to give an exact answer in figures because the export statistics include wheat from Native States, whereas the figures for production refer to the Punjab only. Further it is not possible to separate the share of the frontier province from the railway figures. There does not appear to be any evidence to show that the amount consumed is declining, while practically everyone who remembers the conditions twenty years ago can testify to the general increase (1). So far it has been attempted to show that the present prosperity of the province is in large measure due to the expansion of the cultivation of wheat and to the export trade in this article. This in turn is due to the opening up of the province by railways and to the construction of the great canals. The railways have had the effect of making prices more steady ; there is no longer the wide difference in prices at various centres ; and there is less divergence throughout the year. Fluctuations in prices from year to year have also become less marked; so that generally the price of wheat is now more even throughout the province, throughout the year, and from year to year. On the whole the general trend of prices of wheat is steadily upwards. Until there was a good service of railways throughout the province, prices depended upon local conditions, the cultivator could only get what the nearest market would give him ; and when the nearest market did not require all his produce the surplus was left with him to rot. In such circumstances there was little inducement to increase the area under crops. A cultivator will not grow more than he can be certain of disposing of. The effect of the construction of railways was to open the Punjab to the great markets up and down the world, to enable him to get a full, or at least a better, price for his produce, and so to encourage him to place more and more land under cultivation. In consequence, the cultivated area has increased faster than the population, there is more produce per head than before and a higher standard of living has become possible.

It seems desirable here to refer to a misapprehension that sometimes creeps into discussions about this trade in foodstuffs. It seems to be thought that the wheat exported is taken away from the people who might otherwise have consumed it. It is suggested that somehow there is less to eat in the Punjab because so much goes out. It has even been said that the cultivator sells his wheat to the foreign consumer and so inflicts harm on the townsman of the Punjab. Now in point of truth, as everyone knows, the cultivator sells his produce to the Bania or grain dealer in his village, and having received the price he is not concerned with what becomes of it. He does not sell it to the foreign consumer at all. The village Bania usually sells in turn to

---

(1) Sir James Wilson in his paper " The World's Wheat " estimates that the consumption in India increased nearly 5 per cent. during the war period.

the big merchants of the nearest Mandi, and he too is no longer concerned with what becomes of it. The big merchant of the Mandi is a business man, and sells his wheat to the person who offers the highest price. He is indifferent to the ultimate fate of the wheat. It is for sale, and it is sold. Everyone who likes can buy. No distinction is made between the consumers of this province or of neighbouring provinces or of Europe. If anyone complains that wheat is being exported from the Punjab, he is free to stop the export by purchasing the wheat. The trade is free.

At this present moment (1) the price of wheat has risen to a height which is undoubtedly causing serious distress to many, and, as usually happens when there is distress, the people are turning to political remedies for economic ills. They want to know why the price is so high, and what can be done to bring it down to a reasonable level. If what has already been written is borne in mind, it will now be possible to attempt an answer to these problems.

The general rise in the price of wheat was a natural result of the general rise in world prices of all commodities that is the inevitable consequence of the war. If millions of people are engaged for years in destruction, instead of production, the price of things must rise until production once more proves sufficient to meet all needs. Further, any interference with the currency of a country that leads to the substitution of gold or silver by paper, especially if the total currency is very much enlarged, is apt to have the effect of raising prices. During the war the gold currency of nearly all countries disappeared from circulation, so that prices were really quoted in paper money. Here in India there arose a great demand for silver rupees, partly owing to a feeling of insecurity, and partly for the use of the armies in Mesopotamia, Palestine, Egypt, East Africa and elsewhere. Before the war the average coinage of new rupees varied from year to year, but amounted to 74 million per year for the five years ending 1913-14. In the next two years the amount turned out by the mints fell to 18 million in 1914-15, and to 14 million in 1915-16. Those were the days when it was not always easy to get notes cashed, and when Government was being strongly urged to make them inconvertible. In 1916-17 the new rupees coined amounted to 298 millions, in 1917-18 the total was 225 millions, in 1918-19, the huge total of 501 millions was reached. From that date there was no longer any difficulty in getting notes cashed. Apart from rupees, there was an unprecedented issue of currency notes during the war. The effect may be shown by the simple statement that the value of notes in circulation was about 66 crores in 1914 and 153 crores in 1919.

If only we could get back to a gold basis again, it is probable that prices would fall. But some years must still elapse before that can be accomplished (2)

During the war the export of wheat was to some extent controlled, and accordingly the full effect of the rise of world prices was not felt. The control

(1) The autumn of 1921.

(2) The question of the influence of the currency changes on prices is too intricate to be dealt with here. The figures are given to indicate the great changes.

reduced the amount of wheat exported to about 2 per cent. of the total produced, a very small item indeed. Moreover the maximum price for purchase for export was fixed at Rs. 5-8-0 per maund at Lyallpur; so that this export could hardly have caused the present price. Unfortunately the autumn harvest of last year (1920) was a bad one so that the amount of the cheaper grains was below normal, and more people were led to eat wheat. Still more unfortunately the Rabi harvest of this year (1921) was very poor. All over India, where wheat was grown, the outturn was well below the average. The deficit in all India was about 25 per cent.; in the Punjab it is estimated that the wheat crop was 40 per cent. below normal. In this province alone about 4 crores maunds of wheat less than the normal were produced. It is this deficiency of 4 crores of maunds that is the chie cause of the present difficulties. In February last the price at Lyallpur was Rs. 5-8-0 per maund. By June it had risen to Rs. 6-9-0. Then came a sudden rise. For this there was no reason so far as the harvest was concerned, nor so far as exports were concerned. Export was under strict control. The chief cause seems to have been gambling; or Satta. There was a shortage of wheat so that the stocks were certain to be sold soon. The next wheat harvest was still some months distant and imports from abroad were unlikely. The opportunity was too good for the dealers and many indulged in gambling, with the result that prices rose to Rs. 9-12-0 in August and Rs. 9-14-0 in September. Since then there has been a fall.

This large fluctuation in the price has led to much misunderstanding. It seems desirable to say something of the influence of the export trade on internal conditions.

Owing to the extreme caution with which official estimates are prepared, it is not easy to say what proportion of the total produce of the Punjab is actually exported outside the province; at a rough estimate it may be assumed that about one-sixth, or 16 per cent. is consumed outside. The Director of Agriculture estimates that the export of wheat and wheat flour is about 28 per cent. of the total production; but obviously the proportion depends on the gross outturn assumed. Some regard this as a danger and would like to prohibit it being sent outside. These fail to understand the real advantage of a surplus. It is said that if export is prohibited there will be ample for everybody, prices will fall and everyone will be happy. If, however, the remark is applied to, say, the case of cloth in Bombay or Ahmedabad, the fallacy becomes at once apparent. Let it be argued that there are many in Bombay who cannot afford to buy clothes and go about almost naked, while there are lakhs and lakhs worth of cloth being exported, therefore this export should be prohibited. Is there anyone who will believe that the prohibition of the export of cloth from Bombay would result inany reduction of the price? The mills would stop making cloth which they could not sell at a profit, and there would be less cloth than ever. Similarly with the case of wheat, if the export is prohibited, there will be less grown, the zemindar will turn his attention to cotton and other crops with which Government is less likely to interfere. Even now, if the price of wheat were forced down without any corresponding reduction in the price of other articles, or in the costs of production, the zemindars would proceed to grow what gave them more profit.

The fact is that an export trade is the best insurance against famine. It provides a stimulus to grow more wheat than the province requires, so that every year there is a surplus. This surplus has been taken above as between 16 and 28 per cent. If there is a bad harvest, then there will be less for export. If the harvest is within 16 per cent. of the normal, then there will still be sufficient for the food of the people. The surplus in normal years serves as a sort of a buffer against a shortage of food. Let it be assumed that, on the other hand, the province produces only enough for its own consumption, then if a bad harvest comes, even 10 per cent. below normal, there will be great scarcity. The amount available for export is a reserve against bad seasons. In 1921 the deficit was 41 per cent., so that the reserve was insufficient to protect the people from distress.

It has been explained that the price at which it was profitable to purchase wheat for export was about Rs. 5-8-0 per maund, so that the rise above that rate is due to internal causes, the chief amongst which is the failure of the spring harvest. So long as the surplus production can be kept at an amount so much greater than the local consumption that a failure of the harvest will merely reduce this surplus and leave the local demand fully satisfied, there should be no danger of the price rising above that at which export is profitable. Thus an increase of production, obtainable either by improved methods of cultivation or by extension of irrigation from canals, is the best security against the recurrence of the high prices of this year.

A steadily increasing yield per acre does not of itself ensure an increase of the crop harvested. In France, between 1862 and 1910, the constantly increasing yield per acre was accompanied by a steady decline in the area under wheat from 18 million to 16 million acres. In this case the yield per acremore than counterbalanced the decline in area, but it does not follow that an export tax on wheat in the Punjab would be met by an increased yield per acre. The area under wheat might decline faster than the yield increased, and the total coop would then become progressively less. If there were no increase in the yield per acre, the area would almost certainly become less, as a consequence of the decrease in profits.

Until this result can be achieved, the simplest remedy is to form Co-operative Societies, which will save much of the costs of distribution and will enable the members to obtain their food supplies at the lowest rates possible. A society, for instance, which bought its supply of wheat in June 1921, saved its members all the loss due to the high prices which followed in July, August and September.

There are those, however, who will do nothing to help themselves but advocate interference by Government with the normal trade of the country. There is an idea that prohibition of export would alleviate the situation and bring benefit to those who now suffer from high prices. Prohibition of export is a clumsy method which would end in the ruin of the province. When transport facilities were defective or lacking, there was practically no export, and in consequence there was no attempt to cultivate wheat in excess of local requirements. There was not, and could not have been, a recurring surplus from year to year. In 1871-2 the amount exported was valued at only Rs. 4 lakhs; it was not until communications had brought markets into touch with the producers that cultivation could be extended with a reasonable certainty of profit. The construction of the great canals afforded some certainty of a crop every year, so that the old need to lay by a store gradually disappeared; yet this is ignored by those who advocate a great State storage system sufficient to prevent prices soaring high in time of scarcity. It is sometimes urged that one year's consumption should be thus held by the State; the value of this would be about Rs. 30 crores, and the loss of interest alone would be nearly Rs. 180 lakhs a year, for the State would have to borrow the price.

Prohibition of export would force the province back into the old times of famines, poverty and distress. It would remove the stimulus to production of the normal surplus, and would throw back the scale to the consumption of a normal year. As a temporary administrative measure, it may be justified, just as war may be justified; but as an ordinary permanent feature of a policy of lowering prices it could only do harm. Prohibition of export from India would still leave the people of the Punjab subject to high prices, and even scarcity as a result of a large demand from other provinces; while prohibition of export from the Punjab could hardly be advocated at a time when the province is importing grain from its neighbours. Another point that is apt to be ignored by those who advocate interference with trade is that an artificial lowering of price would tend to increase consumption, and as the measure of this increase cannot be estimated the effects of the prohibition cannot with any approach to accuracy be estimated. The history of this province and of other countries suggests that the cultivator would turn his attention to some other crop with which the Government of the day was less likely to interfere as a result of popular clamour.

It must be remembered that, where the produce of a season is insufficient to meet the local demand, the price tends to rise till it reaches a level at which it allows of no profit on export. When export is thus stopped, future variations in price are due to local causes. Long before August of this year the high price of wheat rendered export unprofitable, so that it could not have been the export trade or the world price that caused the rise in August and September. Similarly a good Rabi would serve to bring down the price till it reached a point at which export became profitable, when it would be steady at about the maximum price at which the exporters were prepared to buy. At this present moment it is probable that world prices have no effect on local rates.

A further point that must be mentioned is that a slight shortage tends to raise prices to a larger extent than the actual shortage would seem to justify; similarly a small surplus of supply over demand would bring down the price out of proportion to the amount of the surplus (1). These considerations become very important when a proposal for an export tax is put forward. What the Punjab is suffering from at the present time is a too small surplus of production over local demand. The real cure is to increase the outturn so as to create a larger buffer against shortage. As local demand is already met in a normal year, any increase of production would be added to the quantity

(1) Gregory King's Law.

available for export, which, as has been explained, is the real buffer against famine. The best means to increase the output are to improve the cultivation of the present area, and to extend that area by the construction of more canals. In both directions the people of the Punjab can take an important share by pressing for more money to be spent on the development of the Agricultural Department, and, when the time comes, by subscribing to the loan which will be required to finance the new great canal projects, the Sutlej Valley scheme and the Indus scheme.

As regards the proposal to impose an export tax on all wheat exported, it is not clear whether the advocates of this measure wish to impose the tax on wheat leaving the country or on wheat leaving the province. If there be merely a duty levied on wheat leaving the province, then a bad harvest in another part of India would still send up the price in the Punjab by enhancing the demand for Punjab wheat, just as at this time the United Provinces complain that the price there is high owing to the heavy demand from the Punjab. Thus such an export duty would merely involve the sacrifice of one part of India in the interests of another. It is doubtful whether any considerable number of people would be in favour of such a proposal.

An export duty on wheat exported to foreign countries might appear to be a good remedy for high prices in the eyes of those who prefer not to examine into its effects in the light of experience. It has already been pointed out that such a measure as the control of export was tried in England in old days; it began as a means of keeping down the price in the interests of the consumer and ended as a bounty to encourage cultivation by keeping up the price in the interests of the producer. It has also been mentioned that elsewhere the object of Government is to encourage cultivation, not to discourage it.

The object of such a duty would be to restrict export to an extent necessary to bring down the price to the urban consumer; if it were so small that it could be met by a reduction in the profits of the exporters, it would not achieve its purpose. Further, to be successful, it must be so high as actually to reduce export. Now, as has already been explained, the trade in wheat is free. The wheat is for sale. and anyone can buy it; it is assumed that if the price were reduced more would be consumed by persons who cannot now afford to buy it. But these people might be outside the province, and their demand might be great enough to make it as hard as at present for the poor in Punjab towns to buy this grain. The same argument may be applied about almost every article of food and clothing in every country, or indeed about any of the amenities of civilisation. So that an argument in favour of an export tax on wheat would apply to every foodstuff and most other commodities. Wheat is an important article in the food of the people, but it is not a necessity of life in the sense that people would die who did not get it. Millions do not eat wheat, but rice. Further, although the supply of an adequate quantity of wheat to the people is a matter of great importance, it does not follow that an increase of consumption above the present amount would lead to any economic advantage. People in Europe vary their diet; many cannot afford to eat good wheat; the Italians, for instance, sell their superior wheat which is fit for flour (or *Atta*), and have to put up with inferior wheat fit only for macaroni. The poorer classes in France and Germany cannot afford to consume large quantities of wheat, and eat potatoes and other foodstuffs instead. The argument that the State should interfere to enable the people to eat more wheat is untenable (1).

The price of wheat in the world's markets varies from time to time, so that the tax would also be variable if some export were desired, while it would have to be high if all export were to be prohibited. If all export were prohibited as a permanent measure, the price would fall at the first good harvest but, as this would not necessarily be accompanied by a fall in the costs of production, there would be a danger, amounting to a certainty, that the profits of cultivation would disappear. If there were no profit from cultivation, the cultivators would reduce the area under this crop and grow what was calculated to pay them better. There would just be less wheat, and the poor would stil remain without it.

But it may be that the advocates of this export duty would try to adjust it so as to allow of some export, but still keep the price down. One difficulty would be to determine exactly at what rate to fix the duty, or at what rate to fix the price at which wheat must not be allowed to rise. The duty would have to be adjusted for every district, and even for stations within a district. The main point, however, is that export should be reduced, and that the price should be kept low.

As exports pay for imports, a reduction in the exports of wheat would result not only in the loss of a considerable portion of the nine crores which the province now gains, but also of the corresponding import trade which represents the form in which the nine crores is received. There would thus be a grea. loss of income not only to the cultivators, but also to the commercial classes, The reduction in the price received by the cultivators would reduce their income, and automatically increase the proportion of their produce which they have to sell to pay their land revenue.

In the old days, when the revenue was about fourteen annas per acre this represented 26 sers of wheat; now it is about twenty-five annas representing about ten sers per acre when wheat is six rupees a maund. The export tax would thus raise the revenue against the cultivator, who would thus lose twice over. Having ten maunds an acre of wheat, he would lose twenty rupees an acre from a duty which reduced the price from, say, six rupees a maund to four (or about Rs. 6 per acre, if we assume that he sells one-third); as the outturn for the province is about 800 lakhs maunds, the loss to the cultivator would be several crores a year. The proposal amounts to the advocacy of a particularly unsuitable type of Poor Rate on the rural class in favour of a relatively small number of urban residents, who will not improve their efficiency so as to enable them to increase their earnings. The final result of such a policy would be disastrous to the province. The great problem is how to

(1) *Cf.* Sir James Wilson. "The World's Wheat": "it is to be remembered that, although wheat is the favourite food-grain in the temperate regions, the great majority of mankind prefer to consume other grains, such as rice, maize, rye and millets, even when they are well enough off to buy wheat if they wished. Moreover many wheat eaters, without much sense of hardship, substitute other grains for wheat if it is exceptionally dear. The experience of the war has shown that farmers can, and will, rapidly increase their wheat area whenever it promises to be more profitable to grow wheat than other kinds of produce".

increase the national income, how to help everyone to increase their earnings so as to secure a rise in the general standard of living. The problem is not how to reduce the national income, how to prevent the people from earning more and how to increase poverty. The experience of the war demonstrated that State control over prices of particular products tended to reduce the total national income. Professor Pigou, in his Economics of Welfare (Ch. IX, para. 7) writes :—" It is obvious that any general State policy of cutting down prices in any industry below the competitive level, on occasions when the conditions of demand and supply would enable that industry to obtain exceptional profits, must, in effect, penalise it as compared with stable industries.... If, for instance, the State adopted a general policy of forbidding farmers to charge high prices when they have power to do so on account of a bad world harvest, this would check investment in agriculture because people expect bad world harvests from time to time and look to high prices then to set against low prices in bumper years".

Of the dishonesty of a proposal to penalise a large majority of the population in order to benefit a minority, to rob the cultivators of 16 crores a year merely to give cheap wheat to those who should adapt their food to their means, just as millions in other countries do, it is not necessary to say much ; it seems worth while to point out that the precedent would almost certainly serve to draw attention to the fact that in other countries the policy is one of encouraging the cultivation of wheat by keeping prices up. In a province where the majority of the members of the Legislative Council are themselves producers of wheat, it is more than likely that, having once experienced the effect of State interference, these members would press for measures designed to assist the cultivators, such as a bounty on export when wheat was cheap.

Another remedy suggested is to stop the Satta, or gambling, which was to some extent responsible for the rise in price in July-September 1921 ; the chief difficulty is to discover how to do it. The province is intermixed with the territories of Native States, so that those who wished to evade the law could carry on Satta by a short journey. A proposal to interfere with the dealings of the big merchants may find popularity amongst some, but anything that discouraged these from performing their useful functions without setting up some alternative machinery would be apt to involve serious disadvantages. There must be someone to store wheat, to prevent violent fluctuations and to maintain touch with other sources of grain. The feeling against these dealers is but a recurrence of the old antipathy against the corresponding class in England. At one time, forestalling, as it was termed, was penalised ; everyone, it was held, should be satisfied with a fair profit, and anyone who attempted to buy with a view to selling when prices rose, *i. e.*, who sought to forestall others, was liable to punishment. Satta is not a necessary accompaniment of the big dealers' business, but it is doubtful if it can be entirely eliminated from it by law.

The real and only permanent remedy is to encourage the investment of more and more capital in agriculture and industries. The continuous investment of all available capital within the province in productive enterprises would tend to find employment for all, it would lead to an increase in the national income and would provide an opportunity for more to earn a decent livelihood and so to meet high prices by higher earnings. Capital invested productively in large amount is the best remedy for the trouble arising from the high price of wheat.

APPENDIX.

Statement showing total produce and export by rail and river of wheat (including wheat flour converted into wheat), in tons, in the Punjab, including Native States.

Year.	Total production (in tons).	Total net exports (in tons): exports in following financial year.	Exports to Karachi: practically all of which goes overseas.	Balance exports to places in India, other than Karachi, outside the province.
1	2	3	4	5
1900-01	2,623,094	(24) 625,826	(16) 424,587	(8) 201,239
1901-02	1,834,484	(29) 525,894	(23) 424,373	(6) 101,521
1902-03	2,303,929	(38) 881,942	(35) 804,770	(3) 77,172
1903-04	3,062,030	(39) 1,193,388	(37) 1,136,447	(2) 56,941
1904-05	2,844,270	(28) 783,277	(22) 611,493	(6) 171,784
1905-06	3,498,895	(33) 1,165,299	(24) 826,006	(9) 339,293
1906-07	2,641,285	(44) 1,164,933	(31) 826,101	(13) 338,832
1907-08	2,482,146	(13) 312,866	(7) 171,794	(6) 141,072
1908-09	3,350,887	(26) 884,514	(24) 801,444	(2) 83,070
1909-10	3,607,774	(27) 978,400	(24) 881,300	(3) 97,100
1910-11	3,709,481	(25) 932,393	(23) 845,085	(2) 87,308
1911-12	3,830,453	(31) 1,179,624	(28) 1,056,642	(3) 122,982
1912-13	3,242,375	(29) 948,529	(23) 756,273	(6) 192,256
1913-14	3,188,537	(32) 1,007,889	(23) 720,070	(9) 287,819
1914-15	3,725,000	(19) 701,095	(13) 477,208	(6) 223,887
1915-16	2,481,296	(35) 878,646	(28) 694,880	(7) 183,766
1916-17	2,937,212	(34) 996,660	(29) 860,119	(5) 136,541
1917-18	3,425,500	(19) 648,001	(10) 331,490	(9) 316,511
1918-19	2,893,378	(15) 434,454	(3) 84,113	(12) 350,341
1919-20	3,884,372	(25) 965,775	(11) 439,075	(14) 526,700
1920-21	2,301,388	..	..	..
Average 20 years	3,078,320	(28) 860,470	(21) 658,664	(7) 201,806

N.B.—Figures enclosed in brackets represent percentages on Col. 2.

The above statement was prepared by, and is repeated here by the courtesy of, Mr. C. H. Townsend, I. C. S., Director of Agriculture, Punjab.

CHAPTER XII.

The Prospect for Industries.

In the preceding chapters frequent references have been made to rural conditions in other countries with a view to extracting therefrom lessons of value applicable to local problems. The position taken up has been that agriculture is and must remain the greatest and most important of all industries and the dominating factor in both the wealth and the welfare of the people. But agriculture alone will not suffice to secure for the Punjab all the advantages that would accrue from the fullest development of its natural resources. It has been shown that, in other countries, small holders require the help of subsidiary industries to enable them to earn a decent livelihood; while in the Punjab such village industries as exist are carried on by separate tribes or castes, and not by the agriculturists, in their spare hours. In some quarters there seems to be a desire to see these village industries helped on to a more prosperous footing not in order to afford occupation for the cultivators, but from a patriotic feeling that their regeneration would somehow reflect credit on the province. The position of the economist would seem to be that these ancient industries should be encouraged only in so far as they provide for the workers a better income than they could obtain in any other way, or until some way of earning a better income has been devised. The great defect of all these is that they afford very little opportunity for the employment of capital, and it is only by the employment of more and more capital that man can produce more wealth and increase his income. Moreover individuals, working independently, lack the advantages that accrue from specialization and organizations, and so cannot compete on equal terms with others who enjoy these advantages; in consequence, there is a tendency for the village artisan to be overworked and underpaid.

So long as costs of transport from the factory to the village are high and expenses of distribution heavy, the independent worker may be able to earn some sort of livelihood, but as these charges decline he will be driven from the manufacture of articles to the repair of articles, and his position willthen remain for a long time unassailable.

There is, however, a small body of opinion which considers that, in the pursuit of wealth, agriculture may be practically ignored, and that the energies of the people should be directed to the introduction of factory industries on a large scale with a view to a large export trade in manufactured goods. The means to this end are, however, so obscure that those who advocate its adoption are not prepared to support their opinion with their money without external aid. A larger and more influential body realizes that raw materials come for the most part from the soil, and that accordingly a careful examination of these raw materials should be made and experiments should be carried out to test which of them can be profitably worked up, within the province, to a stage nearer to that in which the consumer requires them. Here too there is hesitation when it comes to a question of bearing the expense of the experiments, and accordingly there has arisen a definite demandf or the adoption of a policy of State participation in industrial development, and even of State assistance to industrial ventures. This demand is, in some measure, a reflection of the impression that commonly prevails as to what has occurred in Japan (1). It is believed that Japan has great industries and is, by their means, becoming a wealthy country; and that it only remains for the Punjab Government to subsidize industries to a similar extent for similar results to follow. The whole problem obviously calls for the most careful examination in all its aspects.

The problems in certain of these aspects have been examined in the Report of the Industrial Commission, and it is unnecessary to repeat what has there been said. This book is primarily concerned with the Punjab, and it is clear that statements that may be true of India as a whole may not be accurate when applied to a province so peculiarly situated. The limitations imposed upon this province by its geographical position have already been dealt with. The great advantages conferred upon England or Japan by their configuration, and the consequent facilities for an extensive coastwise transport system, or the gain to Belgium or Holland from their rivers and canals are insufficiently recognized by some publicists in this country. There is a childlike faith in the power of the State to produce industries by subsidies or other forms of aid, in spite of the evidence available from other countries that if there are to be industries that will last they must be such as exploit some great natural advantage of the locality. Other countries have tried and are trying to encourage their people to embark upon such enterprises, and undoubtedly some measure of success has been secured, but nowhere does there seem to be any result at all comparable to the great industries that have sprung up unaided except by some conspicuous natural advantage. The need for some occupation for the people, alternative to agriculture, is, however, so very important in this province that every measure that promises to help in providing such occupation deserves to be carefully examined and tried out. If what follows seems to be more discouraging than encouraging, it should be remembered that an honest appreciation of difficulties is frequently the best preliminary to ultimate success.

First, as to State aid, the smaller countries of South Europe afford material that should not be ignored. In Serbia "the Government has done its best to foster the country's manufactures. To promoters of new branches of industry it has been specially liberal, giving them building lands, allowing them to import plant and raw materials duty free, and reduced railway rates in favour of their goods . . . Nevertheless, the manufactures of Serbia have hitherto been of little account. Most of the factories which figured in official returns were only small workshops, and very few had an annual production exceeding £ 50,000 in value. The raw material used consisted almost entirely of products of Serbian agriculture" (2).

---

(1) There is some confusion between the industries of a country, and the distribution of those industries throughout a country. America is a great industrial country, but its industries are for the most part concentrated in a relatively small number of towns. New York city, for instance, has a greater net manufacturing output than any State except its own and Pennsylvania. Marshall, p. 151

(2) F. O. Handbook

In Bulgaria primitive manufacture by the old-fashioned methods is still the rule: domestic handicrafts have not yet been displaced by the factory system. "The State has always been alive to the importance of encouraging modern methods, and by a succession of special laws has endeavoured to arrive at the best ways of stimulating industry. But, except in the textile industry, which had long existed as a domestic industry in many parts, progress has been slow . . . . The most important provisions of the law of 1909 'for the encouragement of Native Industries and Trade' are as follows :—

(1) The establishment of an Industrial Council whose duty it is to advise the Minister of Industry and Commerce as to the granting of privileges.

(2) The grant of certain privileges to concerns which—

(*a*) use mechanical power of not less than 10 horse-power ;

(*b*) have invested in machinery not less than 20,000 leva (or about £ 800) ;

(*c*) employ not less than ten workmen for at least six months of the year.

(3) These privileges are—

(*i*) free grant of water-power ;

(*ii*) free import of machinery, if such machinery is not manufactured in the country ;

(*iii*) free import of raw material ;

(*iv*) free grant of land for factory sites ;

(*v*) reduction of 35 per cent. on railway rates ;

(*vi*) preference over foreign goods for the supply of the requirements of public offices and the State, district and municipal authorities.

(4) The exclusive right to carry on certain industries in certain areas is conferred by the National Assembly for certain periods. These enactments have greatly stimulated industrial enterprise, but the number of concerns entitled to benefit was only 389 in 1912, of which 158 were for the production of food-stuffs, beer and alcohol, mostly flour mills. The number of persons employed in these manufacturing industries in the same year was only 15,600. The decline of handicraft and the eclipse of the individual by machinery have made the position of the workpeople difficult" (1).

In Greece and European Turkey there are no considerable industries the lack of coal being a great obstacle. In Italy industries were to a large extent dependent upon German capital and German direction. In this province, however, it is Japan which is regarded as the example to be followed, and as there is much misunderstanding of the economic situation in that remarkable country some details may be given.

In that country there is a cultivated area of 15 million acres to support 55 million people, or 1 acre to feed a little under four people. In the Punjab

(1) F. O. Handbook.

there is a cultivated area of nearly 30 million acres to support about 20 million people, so that four people have 6 acres to draw food from, instead of 1. The result is that the people of this province have ample food for themselves and for export. They can in fact earn a living by producing food, etc., for export, which is not possible for the Japanese.

In the second place taxation in Japan is very high, amounting in all to nearly 15 rupees (1) a head; the national debt is about 50 to 60 rupees a head. It is thus incumbent on the people to work hard.

In the third place it is doubtful if those who desire to see Japanese success repeated in this province would be prepared to accept the amount of State compulsion and State interference that the Government of Japan found necessary. It is quite certain that no British Government would adopt such unfair methods as are to be found in the Japanese record. There, however, circumstances were hard. The people were sunk in poverty, the country was overcrowded, the cultivated area was barely sufficient to feed everyone, there was no outlet for the surplus population, and, what is of great importance, the articles manufactured by hand were such as could, for the most part, be better and more cheaply made by machinery and so were not suitable for export. Once the country was opened out to foreign trade (after 1853), the Japanese set about learning all they could, importing Western machinery and copying Western methods. The marvel about Japan is not that she is a great industrial country (2), but that she has attained her present position in such a very short span. The Japanese Ambassador to the United States told an American audience that in 1913 the city of Philadelphia had an annual industrial output double the total industrial output of the whole State of Japan. Japanese foreign trade is swollen by two important factors. The country consists of a series of comparatively narrow islands facing a large continent, and possessed of sixty harbours open to foreign steamers; such extensive sea communications favour foreign trade. In the second place the new industries cater not for home consumption, but for overseas markets, and hence an unusually large portion of the output is exported. In 1917 the total of exports and imports was 2,638 million yen, or about 48 yen per head of the population. The average for the Punjab for the three years 1916—19 for exports and imports was 8,272 lakhs, or about 41 rupees per head (3). Both figures omit treasure. As the Punjab is completely landlocked and suffers from disabilities of geographical position already described, there is little ground for despondency. In 1913 the average per head of the total foreign trade (exports and imports) was less than Rs. 33 for Japan and about Rs. 25 for the Punjab. That factory industries are not necessary for large foreign trade is exemplified by the fact that the *per*

(1) *i.e.*, 10 yen. A yen used to be equal to about Re. 1-8.

(2) The number employed in factories in 1917 was 1,281,000; of whom 58 to 60 per cent. were females; 10 per cent. were children under 14. The total number of persons employed in factories in India in 1917 was about 1,120,000; the total for the Punjab was 16,000.

(1) A yen at par is worth two shillings; before the war 1½ rupees=two shillings; the new exchange is designed to be one rupee = two shillings. It is important to remember that in the Japanese figures cotton is included twice over; the raw cotton is included in imports and the same material worked up into cloth appears as exports. If Japan is only credited with the value she adds to the raw cotton in manufacturing it into cloth, etc., the resultant foreign trade per head is less than that for the Punjab,

capita exports of agricultural produce alone from Denmark exceed the above figures. The value of the whole of Japan's exports in 1917 was less in proportion to population than the single article of butter exported from Denmark. It should be possible to admire Japan's wonderful progress without losing all sense of proportion, and certainly without decrying the equally wonderful progress of British India.

The following figures show that British India is a far more important factor in Japanese trade and commerce than is Japan in that of British India :—

VALUE OF MERCHANDISE (1).

	Imported into British India from Japan.	*Exported from British India to Japan.*
	Rs.	Rs.
1875-76 (single year)	53,000	61,000
Decennial average 1875-76 to 1884-85 ..	1,06,000	12,00,000
Decennial average 1885-86 to 1894-95 ..	8,80,000	4,75,00,000
Decennial average 1895-96 to 1904-05 ..	73,76,000	5,58,00,000
Decennial average 1905-06 to 1914-15 ..	2,98,00,000	13,31,00,000
1915-16 (single year)	7,56,00,000	18,45,00,000
1916-17 do.	13,34,00,000	28,25,00,000
1917-18 do.	18,33,00,000	34,16,00,000

To such figures as these the objection is put forward that, while India exports raw materials, Japan exports manufactured articles. The real point, however, is not the state of the articles exported or imported, but the advantage accruing from the exchange. From one view it would appear that, if India imports articles ready for use in exchange for articles which require the expenditure of much labour before they can be used, India is the gainer ; but it is urged that, if India exported manufactured goods instead of raw materials, the country would gain the profit accruing from the employment of all the capital, labour, skill and business and commercial experience of her people utilized in transforming the one into the other. This argument assumes that these necessary adjuncts of successful manufacture exist in the country and are being at present used to less advantage than they would be used under the circumstances contemplated (2).

Before proceeding to a brief examination of these assumptions it seems worth while to note that the cry for industries does not take origin from the old hereditary industrial classes. These are regarded usually as Kamins of low social status. They show no marked desire to improve their methods or to increase their exertions with a view to securing better conditions. There is nowhere any large body of this artisan class out of work and seeking new industries as a means of employment. The cry for industries is not due to

(1) Statistics of British India, Volume I, Commercial Statistics. Japanese exports to all countries, except China and America, fell away materially in 1919. "This means that Japan has not realized her opportunity and consolidated her position in the many markets which were thrown open to her manufacturers byEuropean inability to compete during the war. She was obsessed by the desire of obtainingq uick. and exorbitant profits, and paid too little attention to the quality of her output." Report by H.M.'s Commercial Secretary at Yokohama, quoted in *Mysore Economic Journal*, June 1920.

(2) Some advocates of factory industries seem apt to forg,t that raw materials may also be the result of capital, labour and enterprise. Of course more capital, more skill and more enterprise are required to advance the raw materials through the various stages to the manu factured article,

lack of opportunities for exploiting new ideas or new inventions; nor is it due to any surfeit of technical ability. It originated (a fact which modern critics are apt to forget) in the desire of Government to mitigate the dangers due to the almost complete dependence of the people upon the monsoon. The monsoon fluctuated in character and would, in all probability, continue so to fluctuate. In consequence, it seemed inevitable that there must be recurring periods of severe distress, unless, as the Famine Commission of 1880 pointed out, some diversity of occupation could be secured whereby the surplus population could be drawn from agricultural pursuits and led to find the means of subsistence in manufactures or somes imilar employments. In their opinion, this result would only follow upon an increased desire to apply capital to industrial pursuits, and this, in turn, could only arise from a growing conviction that adequate profits would be secured on investments. The Commission considered that there were difficulties in the way of Government guarantee or direct State aid, but urged that "to whatever extent it is possible Government should give assistance to the development of industry". Since 1880 the situation has changed in a truly remarkable manner. At that time poverty was the basis of the demand for industries which were desired by Government in order to diminish the dependence of the people upon agriculture. Since then, however, wealth has increased rapidly—new canals have been constructed, railways have been extended and education has spread—and it would seem that the modern cry for industries is due to the considerable amount of money seeking profitable investment and the number of educated young men, for the most part not agriculturists, seeking profitable employment. The cry for industries is no longer due to poverty, but to surplus wealth and the rise of a class, not traditionally connected with industries, but now desirous of embarking upon industrial enterprise with the laudable hope of increasing wealth. That there has been a great increase of wealth in the Punjab in the last fifty years is obvious to all. The great canals have led to a large increase in the cultivated area, and to a still larger increase in production. Whereas in 1872 the province received only four lakhs of rupees for its surplus grain, in 1913 it received 1,448 lakhs, and in 1918-19 no less than 2,437 lakhs, of rupees. In 30 years exports increased sevenfold in value, and imports increased fourfold. The income-tax returns testify to a large increase in the income of the trading and commercial classes. Bankers and moneylenders increased in number fourfold between 1868 and 1911, and their income subject to tax has more than doubled in the last 20 years. The net import of treasure (gold ands ilver coin and bullion) into India in the last 50 years totals 770 crores: latterly it has been 32 crores a year. In November and December 1917 13 crores of rupees were absorbed. In the year 1917-18 no less than 23 crores of rupees were coined. Between August 1914 and March 1918 over 40 per cent. of the entire estimated world production of silver passed into circulation in India. These figures relate to India as a whole but, in proof of the contention that the Punjabh as been receiving a goodly share of this enormous wealth, the following figures may be quoted :—

Triennial Period.	Gold and silver treasure absorbed in the Punjab in 3 years.
1911-12 to 1912-13	Rs. 1,000 lakhs.
1913-14 to 1915-16	„ 1,617 do.
1916-17 to 1916-19	„ 2,169 do.

To understand the meaning of these figures, it must be remembered that they show net absorption, so that the effect is cumulative.

The Punjab entered upon an unbroken era of prosperity after 1895-96 with the opening of the Lower Chenab Canal. The figures for money orders are suggestive :—

Net balance, for the Punjab, of money orders paid in the province, less money orders issued.

	Inland.	Foreign.
1880-81	—21,33.000	—1,63,000
1885-86	—26,28,000	—1,57,000
1890-91	—33,57,000	—34,000
1895-96	—31,28,000	+33,000
1900-01	+56,56,000	+25,28,000
1905-06	+59,59,000	+14.93,000
1910-11	+92.05,000	+43,57,000
1915-16	+1.18,01,000	+33,14,000
1916-17	+1,65,63.000	+45,37,000
1917-18	+2,35,84,000	+53,69,000

The above figures indicate the net gain to the province and show the effect of Punjabis sending to their homes within the province savings from earnings made outside. They effectively dispose of the old myth of the economic drain. In the last 10 years the total net gain from remittances by monthly orders alone is over 16 crores of rupees.

Deposits in the Post Office Savings Bank have also increased largely, and it is of special interest to note that the average deposit in the Punjab (=Rs. 150) is double the average for the rest of India, excluding the Punjab (=Rs. 75).

The rapidly growing mortgage debt and the high price paid for land afford evidence of surplus wealth seeking investment; and the resentment of certain classes against the Land Alienation Act is a clear indication of their possession of idle money for which they naturally enough desire profitable employment. The second important cause of the cry for industries is the existence of an educated middle class competing for occupation. Apart from agriculture, the only considerable means of livelihood in the province are moneylending and the law. From the income tax returns it appears that 15,035 moneylenders are in receipt of an income above the taxable limit, that the number of all other persons engaged in commerce and trade with similar incomes is 13,039; while there are only 575 persons engaged in manufacture (excluding registered companies) with taxable incomes. Turning to the professions, the reare 1,268 persons with incomes above the taxable limit ,all of whom, except 195, are barristers, attorneys, pleaders, etc. Moneylending and the law are thus the two most profitable callings and, as the latter offers the higher average income of the two, there is a marked tendency for educated young men to take to it. In the province, as at present constituted, there were, in 1868, 40 pleaders, barristers, etc., of whom 25 were in Lahore. By 1896 the number had risen to about 360; whereas it is now over 1,200 (assuming the income-tax returns to be accurate, the average net income is somewhat under Rs. 220 per mensem). One predisposing cause is the rise of an urban middle class which has acquired a taste for a college education. This class has risen so rapidly, and its sons have taken to education so readily, that opportunities for employment are too few for the candidates. It would, perhaps, be more correct to say that the demand for well-paid billets is increasing faster than the supply. At the same time it is worthy of remark that there is a general dearth of trained, competent and well-qualified men in almost every branch of activity (1). This curious state of things is dealt with in the Report of the Calcutta University Commission. It was found that, while the proportion of students in colleges to the total population of Bengal was roughly equal to that in Great Britain, the proportion of these students to the total *literate* population was ten times as great in Bengal, that is to say, a tenfold larger proportion of literate people goes in for a University course in Bengal than in Great Britain, and, of these again a far larger proportion takes the Arts course and a very much smaller proportion goes in for a strictly vocational training. The result is the large number of educated young men searching for employment, but not trained for any particular vocation. With these all can feel the greatest sympathy, even though all do not agree with some of the consequences. In England such young men are left to fight their way in the economic struggle. There an Arts course is regarded as very much of a luxury which a poor country cannot afford (2).

Some attempt may now be made to forecast the lines on which industries can be developed with reasonable prospects of profit. It must be remembered that the difficulty is not to manufacture something that is at present imported. Japan has shown how easy it is to imitate, but to manufacture goods under conditions as to price, quality, etc., which will ensure for them a ready sale. The following classification does not claim to be complete, but it will serve to indicate the possible lines of development :—

A. Old—{ 1. Improvement in existing industries.
2. Development of agricultural industries.

B. New— 3. New industries based on agriculture.
4. New industries not based on agriculture.

C. Unknown—*e. g.*, industries that may take their rise from some new invention or discovery which can be exploited within the province.

1. The existing industries obviously afford great scope for improvement and deserve first consideration. The chief are weaving, dyeing, tanning iron work and wood work, and in these much can be done—

---

(1) There is considerable misunderstanding as to the objects of education. Even in America, says Prof. Marshall, where education has always been taken seriously, it has never been regarded as reaching far, by itself, towards making men efficient in business. It has never given the same prestige as can be obtained by the evidence of keen mother wit, which is afforded by a new contrivance, or a new scheme of organization which is effective for its purpose. Industry and Trade, p. 155.

(2) The history of English industries provides ample illustration of the great influence of economic distress in strengthening resolution, enforcing thrift and savings, stimulating pride in conquering difficulties and driving men to work strenuously to save themselves from lapsing again into the poverty and pain form which by their own efforts they were just emerging.

(a) by educating the workers in their craft so as to improve their technical skill ;

(b) by introducing more capital, in the way of improved machinery, implements and materials, and in the provision of more power ;

(c) by providing the element of intelligent enterprise so as to enable the workers to use the capital employed to the best profit.

In so far as these industries are developed in villages, it is probable that the labour will be supplied by the existing classes of artisans. If the economic position of these people is to be improved, they must produce more wealth, and this end can best be achieved by securing the intelligent control of more capital and more power.

It may be noted that, as India advances in industrial organization, the manufacture in the Punjab of articles from imported iron will tend to decline, as it will be cheaper to import the manufactured articles than the raw material. This tendency may be defeated if the article is of a special type protected by a patent. The Nahan Sugar Mills are manufacturing in Nahan State from iron and coal brought from Bengal by rail and camel transport, and then distributed by camel and rail to the villages of the province. Clearly it would be cheaper to manufacture these nearer to the source of the iron and coal and send them by rail to wherever the demand existed.

2. Development of agricultural industries.

Instances are afforded by oil pressing, flour milling, cotton ginning, rice hulling, sugarcane crushing, wool washing, etc., etc. ; all stages in the preparation of raw produce for consumption. These processes are at present being carried out in a generally inefficient manner. To a considerable extent it is probable that the labour required will be supplied by the agriculturists themselves, as is now largely the case with sugarcane crushing. The most promising lines of development appear to be the introduction of more efficient machinery and power, and the elimination of waste, and the purification and refinement of articles of export so as to raise the value in proportion to the bulk.

3. New industries based on agriculture.

This class appears to promise the most hopeful results, in the first place, because already the scope is very wide and, in the second place, because there is the ever-present possibility that the climate and soil of the province may be found suitable for other crops, not at this time grown, of great industrial value, such, for instance, as some source of sugar other than sugarcane. The industries that seem to deserve early investigation are sericulture and silk (Japan's largest and most important industry after agriculture) ; the manufacture of straw board from wheat stalks (bhusa) ; of paper from rice stalks and hulls ; alcohol, as a source of power, from potatoes or cellulose ; fruit and fruit preserving, canning and drying ; vegetable and vegetable dessication ; bees and honey ; castor oil and castor cake manure ; poultry and poultry products ; and perhaps dairying and dairy products.

All these industries seem to be within the capacity of the agricultural classes, provided they can be supplied with intelligent guidance.

4. New industries not based on agriculture.

One industry bridges the gulf between this class and the last inasmuch as, though the raw material is not derived from agriculture, the manufactured product is used in agriculture, this is the manufacture of improved agricultural implements. Examples of the class are petroleum and its derivatives; cement making; glass making; salt mining (not, of course, new); iron (Kangra); coal (Mianwali); gold washing (Indus) and industries based on the utilization of forest products such as turpentine extraction, paper from wood pulp, etc., medicinal principles, etc.

It will be seen that this group consists of industries for which, to a very large extent, labour will have to be specially trained. None of the existing vocational tribes or castes will hold any monopoly. Very considerable amounts of capital will be required and highly skilled management will be necessary.

Unknown industries may be exemplified by the manufacture of artificial manures, such, for instance, as may be obtained from the fixation of atmospheric nitrogen.

Having set forth the possible lines of industrial development, it remains to discuss the local obstacles that will tend to limit that development.

First amongst these is the geographical position of the province of which an account has already been made. The general effect of this will be to protect the home market against competition from outside, to hamper the export of manufactured goods and to reserve to the province the bulk of the work of repair. The extent to which industries will be effected will largely depend on the development of communications and transport facilities within the province. At present it may actually cost less to transport goods from Lancashire to Amritsar than to distribute these from Amritsar to the villages. The obstacle to an export trade in, say, cotton cloth will tend to prevent the Punjab manufacturer from expanding his business to the scale required to secure the fullest benefits from the law of increasing returns and from the high specialization and organization that are to be found in Lancashire. Owing to its isolated geographical position, the sparsely inhabited tracts that spread for several hundreds of miles on three sides of it, and especially its distance from the sea, it is unlikely that the Punjab will ever develop industries on the scale attained by Japan (1).

The second limit to industrial development is to be found in the amount of capital that is likely to be forthcoming. As has already been shown, there is ample wealth in the province seeking investment and a considerable further sum could be rendered available by ready acceptance of redemption of mortgages, sale of scattered plots of land by non-agricultural owners, and the replacement of the money now employed in moneylending by co-operative credit. It is not exaggerating to say that forty crores could be set free for industries by the expansion of the co-operative movement. But, although there is ample

(1). The fact that over 500 miles of very sparsely inhabited country separates the Punjab from its port of Karachi imposes a severe handicap. Punjab trade has to bear the major portion of the cost of both railway and port facilities. Were Sind a rich and populous province Karachi could serve the Punjab better and more cheaply.

capital for the initial requirements, it is doubtful if it will come forward for investment in industries. Hitherto, the development of the country has been carried on by the use of foreign capital. In all India, in all kinds of joint stock companies, there was in 1917-18 only about 100 crores paid up capital (1) before the recent boom ; whereas nearly 600 crores of rupees, mostly borrowed from Great Britain, have been invested in railways and canals alone. The amount of capital required in big industries is not always clearly realized. Taking the figures for India, it appears that on the average Rs. 612 are required for each person employed in cotton mills, Rs. 1,863 per person employed in woollen mills, Rs. 2,521 per person employed in high grade woollen mills like those at Dhariwal, and Rs. 8,300 per person employed in railways.

In this connection it must be remembered that Indian investors before the war were very shy of lending money to Government and consequently, as has just been remarked, nearly the whole of the 600 crores required for railways and canals has come from England. In the future it seems unlikely that India will be able to borrow freely from Great Britain; the home country spent 9,600 million pounds during the war, and her public debt now amounts to 44 per cent. of her total estimated wealth. There is ample scope near home for the employment of spare capital; investment in India is likely to be regarded as less secure under the new regime, and high exchange will make foreign borrowing less profitable to Government. It therefore seems likely that the money required for public works will have to be raised in India. The demand for money for this purpose in the near future is likely to be considerable. Expansion of railway facilities is sorely needed, and several irrigation projects are becoming ripe for construction. Of these, the Sind Sagar Doab Canal, which will serve two million acres, is estimated to cost 929 lakhs of rupees and to yield, when completed, 10 per cent. on this outlay ; the Bhakra Dam will cost about 1,450 lakhs; it will be 395 feet high ; its capacity will be 120,000 million cubic feet as compared with the 36,000 million cubic feet of the famous Assuan Dam, and it is expected to yield 7 per cent. The Sutlej Valley Canal projects are estimated to cost 1,200 lakhs ; they will serve 2,500,000 acres, and are expected to yield 10 per cent. profit (2).

Thus the development of the province will depend to a large extent upon the readiness of the Indian investor to come forward with his capital for public loans as well as for industrial ventures.

A more serious obstacle to industrial development arises from the scarcity of men trained to perform the duties of supervision and management.

---

(1) Distributed as follows : Banking, etc., 11 crores, Trading 17 crores, Railways 13 crores, Mills and Presses 35 crores, Tea and Planting 6 crores, Mining and Quarrying 1½ crores, Land and Building 3 crores, Sugar Manufacture 1 crore. In the Punjab the total paid up capital of companies engaged in manufacture was in 1920 under 41 lakhs. In Japan the paid up capital of 6,677 industrial companies in 1917 was over 1,071 million yen (=107 crores of rupees when both rupee and yen=2 shillings). Since then, however, thereh as occurred an extraordinary boom in company promoting. According to the Mysore Economic Journal, since 1914 20,000 companies have been formed with an aggregate capital of 4,000 million yen (say 400 crores rupees). The promoters have unloaded their shares on to ignorant country people and, as was to be expected, a widespread collapse of unsound concerns resulted.

(2) The Hon'ble Mr. Woods in the Punjab Legislative Council, reported in the Punjab Gazette of 26th March 1920, Part V, pages 95-96. The area irrigated from the Sutlej Valley project will be largely outside the British Punjab.

It should be unnecessary to point out that far-reaching political changes tend to restrict the free flow of capital into industries, etc,

Upon the efficient performance of these duties in the higher stages hangs the success of industrial enterprise. Skill and capacity are not gained in the course of an ordinary college education; but, where latent, they can be developed and strengthened by such a course. Experience, however, seems to show that the best training for the future manager is to be acquired in the mill and amongst the men he is to manage. The art is picked up in the atmosphere of industry. It is here that difficulties will appear most insuperable. Without established industries it will be next to impossible to train young men to manage them. Japan attempted to meet the difficulty by importing skilled managers from Europe and by sending young men to Europe to learn, and a somewhat similar policy will probably be found necessary here. But industrial leadership is not gained by imitation. It is of little use learning to manufacture things which long-established firms can turn out much more cheaply by mass production. There must first be energy, intelligence, capital and enterprise devoted to the production of those things which the province is naturally best fitted to produce; when full experience has been gained in the use of these factors in combination, there will be less difficulty in the way of developing new lines of activity. In the absence of trained instinct and experience there can be little hope of success without an amount of artificial protection that will inevitably dull enterprise. In modern industries long tradition and the specialized atmosphere of large manufacturing centres mould the mind into lines that make for success. The aptitudes and faculties that are fairly common, say, in Manchestor or Sheffield are almost entirely lacking in the Punjab. There the ambition of young men is stimulated by difficulties which in this province would probably serve but to deter. There is a difference in the attitude adopted towards hardships and obstacles. Most Englishmen believe that these, encountered in gradually increasing measure, develop strength and spontaneity of mind; and the benefits of a public school education are ascribed to the system whereby this training is secured. In India the tendency seems to be to take an exaggerated view of bodily pain and of the inevitable inconveniences of a rough and tumble life. Compulsion is resented; discipline, to the European mind, seems undervalued (1); the submergence of the less fit is regarded with something akin to horror. The fact that life's successes represent merely the few survivors in a struggle where many fail lacks proper appreciation. In Lancashire it is a common saying that only two generations separate master and man; that is to say, that the master of to-day is probably the son or grandson of a mill hand, and his grandson, pampered with luxury, will probably fall back to the position of a wage earner. In America it is said that almost every famous manufacturing concern in the country was founded by a mechanic, a clerk or similar worker from the lower grades. The idea, then, of a separate manufacturing caste which shall provide the capital and the brains that will find employment for lower caste workers is not likely to develop into fact. The great industry of the Punjab is agriculture; when capital, intelligence and enterprise come to be applied to its improvement and to the development of industries subsidiary to it, there will come into being a rough, hard school for the training of minds, and those already endowed

(1) Discipline lies at the root of all organization; it is impossible to create industrial organization unless the sense of discipline is strongly developed.

with natural business genius or originality will push through to the position of industrial leaders. In the beginning only a few such men will be forthcoming, but only a few are required (1). In such imitative industries as are to be found in India the number of conspicuous leaders is very small, and even the proportion engaged in management and supervision is not great.

Taking all factories in India, it appears that of every 100 persons employed, three are employed in direction, supervision and clerical work. Of these the European proportion is ·4 and Indian 2·6. The remaining 97 consist of 26 skilled and 71 unskilled workmen.

In the cotton industry the proportion of persons employed is ·19 European, 4 Indian (in higher posts), 54 skilled and 41·8 unskilled workmen.

In the woollen industry the proportion is ·7 European, 10 Indian (supervision and direction), 2 Indian (clerical work), 57 skilled and 29 unskilled workmen. The difference is due to special conditions, the machinery employed, as already noted, is more expensive, and the wool has to undergo a greater number of processes on its way to the finished article (2). The actual proportions vary with the industry, but in all the number of persons engaged in superior direction and management is very small.

The next difficulty to be considered is the supply of labour. Already the greater part of the unskilled labour employed in the province on earth-work of canals and railways comes from outside. There are very few, if any, surplus labourers ; although there are probably a large number not fully employed all the year round. A more important consideration is that, as is illustrated by the figures given above, industries require more skilled workers than unskilled, and of skilled labour there is already a distinct deficiency. It will thus be necessary to take unskilled labour and train it, and this will prove a long and tedious process. It is this problem which has baffled Japan. There labour is plentiful and cheap ; but the qualities required to turn out a high standard of manufactured article are lacking. The marked desire to force the pace, to expand industries rapidly, and to turn out a large volume of goods led to the employment of workmen who were inadequately trained for the task they were called upon to perform, and the result has been that low quality of goods which has brought Japanese manufactures into disrepute. Over 55 per cent. of the employees in Japanese factories are females (3). Children of not less than 12 years of age are permitted to work, and the law allows 11 or 12 hours' work a day. The labourers are said to be apathetic, they evince no interest in their work, they are unable to concentrate, they take frequent breathing spells, and they require constant supervision to prevent them from becoming slovenly. The one quality that has contributed so much to the astonishing development of industries is imitativenes shown by the

(1) Professor Alfred Marshall's Industry and Trade is a valuable mine of information as to the conditions that have led to the growth of industries in different countries ; needless to say in no case have protection and Government subsidy been dominating factors in permanent success, though their influence may for a time be great.

(2) For details relating to the New Egerton Woollen Mills Company, Dhariwal, I am much indebted to the courtesy of the Manager, Mr. Lilley. Requests for information addressed to some Indian-managed mills met with a refusal.

(3) Women work at the same jobs as the men in the coal mines where the labour is said to be 40 per cent. female.

ability faithfully to copy Western methods. The skill in the use of the fingers which is valuable in other work is of less account where machinery does most of the mechanical work.

The rapid industrial development of Japan has been appreciably facilitated by low wages, long hours, child labour and night work even for girls. The new international restrictions on labour are expected to have a serious effect (reducing the output by as much as one-third), and it is interesting to note that Japanese manufacturers rely on labour troubles in the countries of their rivals to diminish competition and to enable them to retain their markets. In Japan there are no trade unions. Those who seduce or incite others to strike are liable to six months' imprisonment (1).

From the above it will be seen that a slavish imitation of Japan is neither possible nor desirable. Cheap plentiful labour coupled with a desire to get rich quick may lead to serious evils. Labour in the Punjab is neither cheap nor plentiful. Skilled labour is distinctly scarce, and the recent history of Japan clearly shows that without an adequate supply of sufficiently skilled labour it is impossible to build up, with anything approaching rapidity, large indus tries on a sound basis (2).

In these circumstances it would seem that the chief hope lies in training existing labour to be more efficient so that if the existing work can be done by fewer men there will be a surplus available for new industries. In thi country the average holding is small ; if a man secures 50 acres in a new colony he will either employ labour or let out part of the land to a tenant. Now in England it is found that one farmer with his family will look after 50a cres, and employ no outside labour. Thereafter labour employed is as follows :—(3)

Farms	50—100 acres	1·5 employee
	100—150 ,,	4 do.
	150—206 ,,	7·5 do.
Above	300 ,,	16 do.

so that it would seem that it should be possible to train the cultivators to look after more land without any fall in production. An estimate made in Madras showed that the average cultivator only works the equivalent of 120 days a

(1) See Report on Japanese Labour by His Majesty's Vice-Consul at Osaka (Commercial No. 1, 1920), and the Japanese Year Book.

(2) The following extract from a report of His Majesty's Commercial Secretary at Yokohama, taken from the Mysore Economic Journal, June 1920, is interesting in this connection : " The economic situation of Japan is pregnant with possibilities of danger ; much has been said and written about the unprecedented prosperity of this country, but it is not elearly recognized that practically all this prosperity is due to abnormal conditions consequent on Japan's peculiar position during the war. The spirit of the nation has not undergone any radica change which would warrant alarm in competitive countries. It is true that Japan hal attained a greater measure of independence and that her industries have showed considerabls development ; but hitherto unknown evils, suoh as labour unrest and fictitiously high cose of living, have arisen as an offset. Added to this there is a growing mania for speculation and company promoting out of all proportion to the needs of the country . . Shareholders are improvident in the extreme."

(3) *See* International Review of Agricultural Economics, November, December 1919, pp. 661 ff. ; also Report on Wages and Conditions of Employment in Agriculture Cmd. 24-1919; In the Punjab the agricultural system will always require more labour.

year. In England some considerable improvement has been made in the last forty years in the number of animals the average man looks after :—

Number of cattle per man unit.	1871.	1911.
Cattle	3	5·4
Sheep	14·2	17·2
Horses	0·63	0·95

This increase of horse-power by 50 per cent. is one of the chief reasons for the increasing amount of work done per man employed (1).

It would thus at first sight appear that by educating the cultivators on practical lines so as to improve their technical efficiency it should be possible to set free a considerable amount of labour for industries. But there are one or two important factors to be considered. One is that the new canal projects will, if carried through, irrigate large tracts that at present are hardly cultivated at all and so will create a demand for more cultivators.

The second factor is the increasing demand for ghi and milk. If prices go much higher it is probable that dairy farming may become a profitable industry. Any tendency towards a milk and cattle industry becoming profitable will lead to increased employment on land, for this class of work requires fully twice as many men per 100 acres as does ordinary cultivation (2).

In spite of these factors, however, it is clear that a large amount of labour could be spared from the fields if those remaining could be induced to put forth greater exertion, and this can, probably, best be effected by ensuring them a full and adequate return undiminished by the exorbitant demand of the usurer.

One other possible source is the towns. No one wandering through an Indian bazaar can fail to be struck with the great waste of time and labour involved in the large number of small shops. The large multiple store has become a common feature in England and if some enterprising people would start large shops on sound economic lines in the towns it is not improbable that a great amount of potential labour would be set free. Town labour, however, will probably prove unsuitable for work involving physical strength and endurance so that, from whatever aspect the problem is viewed, it is clear that the labour question will prove a big factor in restricting and retarding industrial development.

A further consideration of importance, restraining the rapid development of industries, is the lack of business experience. Technical training will teach how goods should be manufactured, and an ample supply of skilled labour will enable the process of manufacture to be carried through, but much more will be required if the industry is to prove profitable. For this there will be needed men gifted with commercial aptitude and hard business sense, and, owing largely to lack of opportunities for gathering experience, it will be difficult to select the right men. Modern industry is intensely specialized, and a long apprenticeship is required to instil the proper appreciation of

(1) International Review of Agricultural Economics, November, December 1919.

(2) *Ibid.* In England the number of persons employed per 1,000 acres is: cattle and sheep rearing and milking 115 to 129, milking and cattle rearing 16, predominantly arable 46.

the multitude of sometimes conflicting factors that make for success. Neither in England, nor in the Punjab, nor anywhere else is it the case that the man with capital is necessarily possessed of business ability or of the capacity to manage a large industry. The English lawyers and merchants, like those of this province, put their money into land until the middle of the last century. The sons of wealthy manufacturers have frequently found themselves forced to give over control to men of less education, but possessed of character, adaptability and hard business sense. The British Universities have played a very small part in the industrial history of the country. For the successful establishment of manufactures there is required a quality for which there seems to be no test except that of experience. Japan is now gaining this experience at heavy cost, but it is yet too early to say whether she will ever produce the business ability and other qualities required to enable her to compete on equal terms with the highly organized industries of Western countries. The great importance of slowly acquired skill and experience is illustrated by the big shipping companies of Great Britain.

These have carried specialization to such a degree that they are practically beyond the reach of the competition of other countries, a fact tacitly admitted in the unfair discrimination, subsidies and other measures resorted to by America, Germany and Japan. The policy of free trade adopted in the United Kingdom embodies the consciousness of ability to beat rivals on equal terms; the demand for protection arises from a consciousness of weakness and inability to compete with rivals. Protection may facilitate the establishment of new industries; it will not dispense with the need for high skill, business sense and the other faculties required for successful industry.

One of the most important components of business sense or experience is marketing ability. It is unnecessary to insist upon the obvious fact that, until goods are marketed, their production is seldom of much avail, but there seems to be a tendency to overlook the importance of marketing as an essential concomitant of industrial production. In a large manufacturing centre like Lancashire, where there are a number of mills all approximately similarly situated as regards equipment, labour, management, source of raw material and facilities for export, the success or failure of this mill or of that depends to a considerable extent on the ability of the manager to secure a good market for his goods. It is of little use locking up material, labour and capital in the manufacture of cloth for which there is no sufficient demand; few companies can afford to risk manufacturing for a speculative market, and accordingly the market dominates production. In discussions as to the technical possibility of establishing industries in theP unjab this important feature is apt to be overlooked; it seems fairly easy, for instance, to erect spinning mills that will convert raw cotton into yarn, but the outside world at present demands from the Punjab not yarn, but raw cotton. The cotton spinners, and not the weaving mills, form the market for the produce. The proposal to spin Punjab cotton into yarn within the province involves the discovery of an entirely new market.

If the proposal be advanced to the stage of manufacturing the yarn into cloth, then the competition from Bombay and Japan will have to be faced, and no one is likely to stand forth as an advocate for the protection of the Punjab against Bombay. Marketing ability of a constructive order can only be highly developed where there is abundance of free capital; and control over a large capital gives to the person possessing it great advantages over one with only a small capital at his command. Thus the new industry with a comparatively small capital will be heavily handicapped in competition with an established organized centre like Bombay, even though in other respects it is not behind its rivals (1).

It seems probable that the industrial expansion of the province will be limited in some directions by the diet of the people. It is not always fully realized that diet is very much an accident of circumstance or of locality. Unfortunately for India, the question has become involved with religion and so does not lend itself freely to discussion on economic lines. The fact that residents in Australia and New Zealand are the biggest meat-eaters in the world is not due to any unusual appetite on their part or to the greater need of such food in those countries; but to the fact that mutton is a cheap by-product of their main industry of growing wool. A live sheep is worth more than one that has died of disease or starvation and, as the number of live sheep that can find grazing on a given area is limited, systematic slaughter is practically a necessary adjunct of successful wool growing (2). Mutton thus becomes a cheap and very plentiful form of food and so is freely consumed. In early England, before the discovery of roots (turnips, etc.) and other crops that now supply winter food, it was not possible to keep all the cattle alive throughout the colder months. The rich crops of artificial grasses, now so common, were then unknown. Native grasses were collected, dried and stacked as hay, and this, together with such straw as was available, had to meet the winter demand for food. Accordingly the farmers or the agents of the big owners every year, after calculating for what live stock this food would suffice, had to kill as many sheep, oxen and calves as exceeded the number that would be kept alive. The meat was salted and spiced to preserve it, and was consumed during the winter. Even then live stock was always starved in winter (3).

At the same time the pasture of England was relatively rich owing to the damp and temperate climate and bore more stock than a similar area in other countries. The result has been that from the first the English have eaten considerable quantities of animal food, and this comparatively rich diet in ordinary time is regarded as the main cause of their immunity from the worst effects of famine and pestilence (4). This accident of climate had another

(1) For an able and interesting account of the many aspects of the problem see Marshall's Industry and Trade, especially Book II, Chapters VI and VII.

(2) The sheep yields the best wool at 2 years old, and in England it is usual to kill it for meat after the second shearing. A sheep might normally live for 5 or 7 years, but, if there were no slaughter, there would be a smaller proportion of sheep of the best wool yielding age. If there were a successful agitation against the slaughter of sheep this great industry would disappear.

(3) Thorold Rogers: History of Agriculture and Prices, Vol. I, pp. 16 and 53. It was the demand for spices for this purpose that led to the opening up of trade between Europe and India. This dependence upon natural grass for food has from very early times caused pasture land to be more valuable than land under plough. In some rural communities in the United States of America it is still the practice to butcher in the winter time the meat supply of the year. Vogt, p. 160.

(4) Marshall: Industry and Trade, pp. 700, 701.

advantage. Although a vegetarian population can exist on the produce of one-eighth as much land as would be required by purely meat-eaters, it is also true that meat, when produced in small quantities as a by-product of agriculture, is one of the most economical articles of diet which a country can yield (1). This distinction between the production of meat as the sole object to which land is devoted and its production as a by-product of other agricultural activities are apt to be overlooked. In England it serves to give the people an article of diet at once cheap and sustaining. It is generally agreed, at any rate in countries outside India, that for sustained energy and efficiency some more concentrated food is necessary than is afforded by a purely vegetarian diet. It has been found that French labourers cannot perform as much heavy work as English unless they are fed on an equally good diet, and the meagre food of her working classes kept France back industrially for a long time. In Japan it is found that sustained heavy work on the English scale cannot be accomplished on the existing low diet (2). Since the revolution, the eating of meat has been steadily spreading, as religious prejudice has weakened, but it has not yet become available for the labouring classes.

Fortunately for the Punjab, its people are already accustomed to a stronger diet than is usual in the rest of the India. It is the only province in which wheat is regarded as an indispensable article of food, and the more or less occasional inclusion of meat in the diet is usual amongst the majority. The Mohammedans in this respect will possess a great advantage in industries involving heavy manual labour (3).

The question as to how far the low diet is responsible for the lethargy of the people is outside the scope of these studies. A man cannot gave out in work more energy than he takes in as food; the latteri mposes a maximum limit to the labour he can expend; but it does not necessarily follow that a richer diet will result in the accomplishment of more work, and accordingly a higher standard of living is not necessarily an economic advantage. In so far as such a higher standard directly leads to the exertion of greater energy in productive work, and so to an increase in wealth produced, it is to be desired and aimed at, but a higher standard of diet that is not accompanied or followed by such a result is to be deprecated as wasteful. The Mohammedans are not more industrious cultivators than the Hindus, and it is doubtful if the Sikh Jats, who also eat meat and consume food in the highly concentrated form of alcohol, are harder workers than the Ahirs, who are vegetarian and teetotal, though they are physically stronger. It would seem that the present diet of the people is ample for the energy actually expended under present conditions, but will need to be improved if they are to engage in that intense labour which will be a necessary preliminary to any considerable increase in prosperity.

This discussion of the prospects of industries in the Punjab cannot be closed without a reference to the question of power. Hitherto, the great

(1) Sir A.D. Hall: Agriculture after the War, p. 89. Carver: Principles of Rural Economics, p. 163. Goats in the Western Punjab afford a clear example.

(2) Marshall: Industry and Trade, pp. 115, 161.

(3) Many Bengalis eat a considerable amount of meat and are capable in consequence of developing great physical strength.

manufacturing industries of the world have centred round deposits of coal and iron. Until the discovery of the steam engine, mining could not be carried on to any great depth as there was no known method of keeping the underground works clear of water ; with the advent of the steam pump, this difficulty was surmounted, but previously factories were constructed on the banks of streams and depended on water-power. As soon as this narrow dependence on natural water-power was removed bythe discovery of the steam engine and the advent of a plentiful supply of coal, factories congregated in the areas where coal and iron were to be found, and the fact that in England these were in no case far from the sea gave to British industries a great advantage. In France the main coal fields are confined to the north, while the chief source of iron is in Lorraine ; the result has been a concentration of French factory industries in the north-east of the country, or near ports or towns connected with the sea by navigable rivers. Omitting these narrow areas, nearly the whole of France is singularly devoid of great factory industries.

Germany remained poor and backward relatively to England and France until after 1850. In 1870 she seized from France the provinces of Alsace-Lorraine, with their rich iron fields, and was then enabled to use her coal mines in conjunction with the newly acquired iron to build up large industries. The German Empire, it has been well said, has been built more truly on coal and iron than on blood and iron. The skilled exploitation of the great coal fields alone made possible the development of the steel, chemical and electrical industries which established her as the first industrial nation of continental Europe (1). Under the Peace Treaty the iron mines of Alsace-Lorraine revert to France, and special provisions have been inserted to ensure to the latter a large supply of German coal. Italy has no coal and is dependent on supply by sea and so new industries lie at the mercy of the coal-owning nations. She is now turning her attention to the utilization of her vast water-power. Japan has considerable quantities of iron ores, and in addition has more coal than she requires and exports her surplus ; she also has considerable water-power. The Punjab has no iron mines, although there is iron ore in the country ; there is coal, but not apparently of very good quality, and most of the coal consumed in the province is imported (2). Such coal as there is, is in the west of the province, the ironis in the north ; the great central plain yields neither of these. There is vast untouched water-power in the Himalayas, but this is far from any present centre of industry. The Attock oil fields may soon alter the situation, while the hydro-electric scheme in connection with the Bhakra dam promises to develop very considerable power that will be available over the north-east of the province. So far then it would seem that, while at present there is neither the coal nor the iron to support considerable power-using industries, there is some prospect of power at least being available in the near future.

From the foregoing discussion it must not be concluded that the prospects for industries in the Punjab are very dark indeed. The various consider-

---

(1) J. M. Keynes : The Economic Consequences of the Peace, ch. IV.

(2) It may be again necessary to remind the reader that the Punjab is unable to import coal by sea or river, a crushing handicap which needs to be constantly borne in mind in discussing industrial possibilities.

ations discussed indicate the improbability of the establishment of large factory industriesi n the immediate future ; theys uggest that more is required than capital and educated young men. Government can start factories, but it cannot build up an industrial organization ; this must inevitably be of slow growth. Nothing that Government can do will dispense with the need for capitalist enterprise. It can show the way by means of pioneer factories, but it cannot instil the peculiar faculties and aptitudes that distinguish the successful businessman. The general discussion of industries is apt to be confined too much to questions of technical possibilities, and accordingly stress has been laid on those factors that are essential to success in a world of fierce competition. It must be remembered that the war has imposed on nearly all peoples the necessity of greatly increased production if the enormous financial burdens are to be borne ; this increase can only be attained by the more efficient use of the human material available, and there will accordingly be so much the less opportunity for those not so fully efficient to extract a living out of industries affected by international competition. It will take years for the people of the Punjab to accumulate the experience acquire the skill and develop the faculties necessary for large factory industries. But there is ample scope for the employment of capital, skill and enterprise in activities for which the province possesses special facilities. The preparation of hides, for instance, offers great scope, and there are other industries requiring relatively little coal and little skilled manual labour (1). Most of these are subsidiary to agriculture and it will probably be found that the devotion of the resources of the province in men, intelligence, capital and enterprise to these industries will provide ample training ground for the faculties required in other pursuits. If the Punjab is to have a great industrial future, the beginnings must be small, the foundations carefully laid and construction must not outpace the capacity of the people. Little but failure and disappointment will result from any attempt to compress six hundred years of the industrial history of Europe into a short period of State subsidized activity.

One other important consideration deserves to be discussed at some length. For great industrial enterprise, and in less measure for most manufactures, there must be association of capitals. It so happens that, in England, the foundations of her prospertiy were founded by single men or partnerships, and the limited liability company did not appear until the efficient exploitation of her mineral resources became impossible without the utilization of more capital than one man or a partnership cared to risk or, perhaps, had at command. The joint stock principle in commerce and manufacture took its origin in the claim of the Crown to grant monopolies of trade. In the seventeenth century this led to the institution of the Chartered Company, of which the East India Company is a well-known example. For some time this charter was confined to associations dealing on a scale, or in an enterprise, which was deemed to be beyond the scope of private action. The claim of the King was later transferred to Parliament, which thereafter alone could grant monopolies of trade. The Bank of Eng-

(1) Tanning is a good example of an industry that requires little coal. There may be others based on chemistry for which the province is not placed at a disadvantage. The discovery of oil in Attock may revolutionize the whole future of the Punjab if it leads to the supply of a cheap and plentiful source of power.

land is an example of such a grant. The Chartered Company was composed of members whose liability was unlimited, and it was only gradually that the idea of a limited liability partnership was able to secure parliamentary approval. Acts of the first half of the nineteenth century permitted the principle in special cases only; and even the general Limited Liability Act of 1856 excluded banks and insurance companies from its scope. This was altered in 1859. Thus for 250 years the system of charter with unlimited liability prevailed, and this period did not prove sufficient to train the people up in those rules of association which are acknowledged to be essential to successful combination. In this province the few years that have elapsed since settled law and order provided the opportunity for industrial and commercial enterprise on a large scalec an hardly be regarded as ample for the same purpose, and accordingly there is to be found considerable misunderstanding on the objects and necessity of company law. The Indian Companies Act is designed to facilitate, not to hinder, the formation of companies on the joint stock principle with limited liability. But it regards the interests of all parties, and not only those of the company. It seeks to provide a constitution that will protect the shareholders against their directors, and the directors against charges from the shareholders; it seeks to build up confidence amongst creditors and others by insisting on proper accounts, audit and publicity. It surmounts the difficulty of joining a large number of persons in litigation by creating a legal corporation, that can sue and be sued and hold property. Further, it apportions liability and responsibility for acts done and duties to be performed. The actual restrictions are the conclusions of prolonged experience not only in England, but throughout the world, and so may be regarded as representing the necessary minimum. Unfortunately, however, there is lacking full recognition of this view. The promoters of companies incline to resent the conditions which are intended to assist their enterprise to lasting success. They seek to omit this safeguard or that, especially those intended to protect others against themselves. The result is that the joint stock system enjoys little favour; confidence grows but slowly; industrial concerns are very few in number and failures are distressingly frequent. The remedy, of course, is to insist on more strict compliance with the conditions which the accumulated experience of the world has found to be necessary. By no other means can confidence be built up. The joint stock company must become a popular means to the development of the resources of the province, for the simple reason that there are not enough private capitalists with sufficient wealth to carry on the work. But this popularity must be won from a doubting and hesitating public by honest work and well-earned success. At present, the investigating public seem unable to differentiate between the sound company and the most obvious fraud, and neglect almost completely to take advantage of the facilities afforded them by the law to acquire the information needed for prudent transactions. Actual interest in the affairs of a company in which they hold shares seldom reaches to the extent of attendance at a general meeting; very few seem able to understand a balance-sheet. The attitude of the public toward joint stock enterprise must undergo a marked change before great industries can arise.

Of 79 companies in the province, 14 are under British management with a paid-up capital of 247 lakhs of rupees ; 65 are under Indian management with a paid-up capital of 78 lakhs. Only 20 are engaged in manufactures with a paid-up capital of 40 lakhs. The following table indicates the slow growth of confidence :—

Year.			*No. of Companies.*	*Paid-up Capital.*
				Rs.
1889-90	..	..	22	39,60,000
1894-95	..	..	20	47,80,000
1899-00	...	..	52	74,10,000
1904-05	...	..	59	1,01,80,000
1909-10	...	...	136	1,72,06,000
1914-15	...	...	99	1,49,70,000
1919-20	...	..	79	3,25,14,000

The highest number of companies was reached in 1911-12, when there were 194 in existence. Of the paid-up capital in 1919-20 no less than 88 lakhs are contributed by the Alliance Bank of Simla. The paid-up share capital of all co-operative societies in the same year was 66 lakhs.

In the foregoing pages the discussion has shown that no immediate relief from the present economic position can be expected from the development of industries. There are many factors necessary to success, and no amount of State aid or State protection can produce everything as with a magician's wand. It is not denied that the State could, by heavy expenditure, bring about a rapid change, but the advantage would not be lasting, and the subsequent collapse would be inevitable. The example of Japan shows the great danger of the artificial stimulus of industry where all the necessary factors are not present in the proportion required. During the great war Japanese manufacturers had opportunities for expansion which are without parallel in industrial history, but failed to make the most of them. Complaints arose on all sides that, although the first shipments ordered were fairly up to the samples shown, succeeding shipments were below this quality. Indian importers complained that they had endless trouble owing to failure to answer business letters and general unbusinesslike methods. As a result, Japanese traders and their wares earned a rather unenviable reputation in Indian markets (1). Japanese statistics showed an immediate decline in the export of goods for which the war created such a demand ; this was in part due to the rise in prices in Japan, but still more to the resumption of peace conditions amongst the warring nations. The expansion in industries in Japan was abnormal and unhealthy. In 1919, for example, there were erected 2,700 factories involving a capital of 522,000,000 yen, but depression set in and a great slump in business followed, and many failures ensued. The unbridled speculation and wild company promotion led inevitably to severe reaction. In the single month of June 1920 no less than 134 joint stock companies went into liquidation (2). It is important to secure a proper understanding of the industrial position in Japan as there are exaggerated ideas abroad as to what this is. Some writers speak of Japanese and British industries in the

1) *Cf.* Report on the Conditions and Prospects of British Trade in India, 1919.

article in the *Pioneer* for August 27th, 1920.

same sentence as if they were at all comparable ; and they urge the Indian Government to follow the example of Japan as if the advantage gained were beyond dispute. Japan has made marvellous progress, but she is no more exempt from making mistakes than other countries ; and she is as much exempt from the operation of economic laws. The Punjab has its special natural advantages, and it is to the proper development of these that it should look for that wave of prosperity which everyone desires to see. No magician's wand will do what persistent, unceasing, well-directed effort will accomplish. But that effort must aim at making the best possible use of the potentialities of the province, and not at a slavish imitation of industries for which it may not be well situated.

CHAPTER XIII.

AGRICULTURE *versus* (?) INDUSTRIES.

Whether there ever was in India a time when great industries existed and flourished, is not relevent to the present discussion, which is more concerned with the future than with the past. Some writers delight to dilate upon a description of former prosperity concerning which there is practically no evidence of value. Prof. Kale, for instance, seems to subscribe to the popular view that India was once a great manufacturing country, and writes of " the history of Indian shipping and ship building", and adopts the view that " to reduce India to the condition of a nation of cultivators would be to retard the progress of the people in all directions". The truth seems to be that before the West made its great leap forward in the seventeenth and eighteenth centuries, its industries were not in advance of those found at the time in India ; and it seems probable that Indian handicraftsmen were ahead of their European fellows in many directions. Using the term " industry " in the sense a man of the time of Akbar or Elizabeth would use it, there were great industries in India. But that there were ever industries in the sense a modern inhabitant of Lancashire or Staffordshire would use the word is so highly improbable that the idea may be safely rejected. All that the India of old ever exported in a year could be easily carried in a single ship that now crosses the Atlantic ; just as the whole annual industrial output of Japan before the war, was less than that of a single town in England or America. Japan is not an industrial country in the sense that England is, or even as Belgium is. The industries of India astonished the English travellers of the seventeenth century, but nothing like so much as would those of a town like Belfast or Glasgow now. The discussion is barren, inasmuch it leads to no conclusions of value to the present purpose (1), which is the discovery of the right lines for future prosperity. The great advance of the West was largely due to new discoveries and inventions, which brought to an end the stagnation of centuries, and precipitated, Europe, or rather North-West Europe, into a race for wealth which is still the dominant feature of its activities. These discoveries and inventions came to India late ; they were adapted to conditions quite different from those prevailing here ; and the people, until recently, had dominant interests which were not those of accumulating wealth. In this province indigenous inventive talent has not yet shown much achievement ; the conditions that develop it have been lacking ; the stimulus of competition has been absent, and the still greater stimulus of incessant fear of starvation has been less in evidence. What about this controversy is of considerable importance is the point of view adopted by those who cast their looks backward instead of forward. And most conspicuous is the idea that the manufacturing industries call for more intellectual and moral qualities than does agriculture and that the former are a sign of progress to

(1) The break being too complete. The Punjah could have had no extensive industries, such, for instance, as Bombay possesses for several centuries past. There is no inherited aptitude for massive organisation, no highly developed spirit of enterprise, nothing which could be set before the young mind as an example of a real captain of industry.

an extent that is unattainable with the latter (1). In short, compared with industries, agriculture is hardly a subject of legitimate pride. Now, in the discussion of industrial development, the fact is apt to be overlooked, that, the world over, agriculture is and is likely to remain the greatest and most important industry. It is said to be the largest single industry in England, though it is small when compared with the total for all industries. It is certainly the predominant occupation in Japan, over 60 per cent. of the people being engaged in it. It is the leading activity in most countries, in most States of America, and in several counties in the British Isles. It may well be a source of wonder, then, that the educated and more wealthy people of this province call for Government aid to industries and evince little interest in the provision of Government aid for agriculture. Some of the reasons for this have been discussed in an earlier portion of this book. A further cause is that the cry is not so much for industries as for a profitable means of investing their surplus wealth at a high profit. All over the world this is at bottom the bedrock motive. It is this which makes Englishmen take such interest in other countries, as South America, Russia, China, etc. The opportunities for investment at six per cent. are ample, but not satisfying, and the eye wanders over the globe for something above this. If the educated people in India were convinced that agriculture would pay better than industries, they would seek in that field the investment they desire. But they assume that this is not the case. Upon what grounds exactly this assumption is made is not clear. It is true that large fortunes are seldom made from agriculture but it is equally true that agriculture affords a decent livelihood to a far greater number of men than does industry. Industries offer, both to speculators and to men of original genius, opportunities which are unknown in agriculture. The lucky few may rapidly acquire fortunes which impress the public mind out of all proportion to their number and importance. As Professor Marshall points out :—

"The giant fortunes that are made both in production and trade, by some men of exceptional genius, impress the imagination ; but yet when such fortunes are added together, they are a very small percentage on the total capitals that have been invested in their several branches of business. The returns on large parts of those capitals have been but moderate, while other large parts have disappeared through losses ; but those who fail are lost to sight" (2). Taking the Punjab, there is the example of the great canal system as an agricultural improvement on a large scale ; this, in 1918-19, yielded a net profit of 13·5 per cent. on a capital outlay of Rs. 2,245 lakhs; the Lower Chenab Canal yielded a net profit of 40 per cent. and the Lower Jhelum of over 20 per cent. These are far higher returns than those earned by the North-Western Railway, which are about 8 per cent. ; particular portions of the line, of course, give far higher returns. These examples are both the result of State action ; and it surely will not be argued that the State can beat private enterprise in the profitable improvement of land or in the introduction of transport facilities ; unless this be urged, it is fair to assume that there are awaiting

---

(1) Prof. Kale, Indian Economics, 3rd Edition, p. 148.
So far is this view from representing conditions in, say, Denmark and England, that the reverse would be nearer. Modern agriculture on scientific lines requires a higher standard of education amongst a greater proportion of those engaged in it than do large-scale industries.

(2) Industry and Trade, p. 293-4.

exploitation still more profitable methods of improvement. The average earnings of capital in industries are not large, unless some patent or invention is being exploited, or the business is a risky one. If a factory is doing well in a line than can be imitated, it will be imitated and competition will reduce profits. The profits are thus more or less automatically adjusted to a percentage that does not invite too much competition (1). If an enterprising man finds that he can, at the prices of the day, construct and work a rival factory that will yield a higher profit, he proceeds to do so. The fear of this influences the original factory owners, who must depreciate their position in order to be able to meet such competition by the acquisition of new plant or the introduction of new methods. It is obvious that, in a world of highly organised competitive industries, were returns from industry markedly higher, compatible with safety, than returns from agriculture, the capital now invested in the latter would be withdrawn and invested in the former.

An actual comparison between the earnings of a worker in both callings is not easy to arrive at. For the industry may be highly organised and the agriculture unorganised. Where both are unorganised, as in the Punjab, it would seem that the average income from agriculture is the greater ; and where both are highly organised, as the industries of England and the agriculture of Denmark, it is probable again that agriculture yields a higher average income. But this is not the case if comparison is made between the highly organised industry of England and its comparatively unorganized agriculture (2). The highly organized industries are able to employ the best ability available, they are well supplied with capital and have, through a banking system developed to meet their special needs, a command over great additional resources (3). Outside Denmark, the effects of thorough education and the intensive business organization of agriculture have not been fully tried out, but it is significant that that country is said by some to possess greater wealth per head of population than any other.

It is not possible to assist in the solution of the question by giving definite figures for average production per person employed. In England, before the war, it was estimated that the average annual production was £90 per person engaged in agriculture and £ 104 per person engaged in other industries (4). In a moderately-well organized industry, represented by the Bombay Cotton Mills, the average production per person employed is Rs. 1,115. In all India the average is Rs. 912 ; but these figures include the value of the raw material. In Indian coal mines the average production seems to be as low as Rs. 415 per person emplyed ; in woollen weaving, owing to the high cost of wool, the average production is Rs. 2,300. The average gross earnings per person employed in Indian railways is Rs. 1,180. It is impossible to give any accurate figures

(1) It is doubtful if there are many factories engaged in work capable of easy imitation that yield more than 8 per cent. on capital. It is certainly difficult to conceive of industries in this province that will yield a higher return than money-lending does to the same amount of intelligence.

(2) *Cf. Economic of Progress* (*p.* 143). In this country (England) agricultural production is in general not more but less profitable than manufacturing ; a given amount of capital and labour will secure a larger return in value than the same amounts, with existing methods and implements, in agriculture.

(3) *Cf.* State Help for Agriculture, p. 16.

(4) Ashby : Position of the Rural Worker in Industry, p. 77.

for cultivators, but the average annual production in the Punjab may be taken as somewhere between Rs. 350 and Rs. 650. If it were possible from the information available to calculate the additional wealth produced by the labour of the person employed in agriculture and in industries, it is probable that the balance would be in favour of agriculture. If the agriculture of the province were organized and placed under as skilled direction as is the cotton weaving industry of Bombay, any doubt as to which side the balance lay would disappear. It must be assumed that the average worker in the Bombay mills is producing as much as he can under the conditions that exist, that no unnecessary surplus labour is employed, and that he is employing as much power and capital as he can with profit. These conditions do not exist in Punjab agriculture. There is, as has been seen, an excessive amount of labour for the work to be done, the power used seems to be below what is required and very little capital is employed. Were even the methods of cultivation of all raised to the level of the best to be found in the province, there would be a great enhancement of the yield (1). But even the best methods now in use fall far short of the most profitable methods known. In discussing the relative advantages of developing industries and developing agriculture, it is important to remember that, in discussing industries, probabilities only are being dealt with ; while in agriculture the stage of practical certainties is being rapidly approached. By this it is not meant to imply that the raw cotton, for instance, produced in the Punjab cannot be spun and woven within the province. That is a simple problem, a matter only of imitating what is being regularly done elsewhere. But it is easier to repeat the processes of manufacture than it is to repeat the conditions of successful manufacture, a difference which is not always borne in mind. The former is a simple question of technical ability, the latter is a difficult question of economic profit. No one would assert that the existing industries of the province such as hand-loom weaving, tanning, iron work, bring much profit to anyone. The attempts to introduce weaving under factory conditions have not proved unvaryingly successful. The mere imitation of a well organized industry is easy and what is easy is seldom very profitable. The Railway workshops owe their success largely to an assured market ; the Jallo Resin Factory has a practical monopoly of raw material ; this or that other factory is successful because it can supply fully the local demand and hence there is no room for a rival. But the Dhariwal Woollen Mills live on the merits of their goods and supply an instance of what can be done under highly skilled management that suggests that success is not impossible in other directions. But considerable progress in agriculture seems to be attainable with less risk. Already Mr. Milne's variety of American 4 F cotton is estimated

---

(1) This is certainly true of the Punjab. It is also asserted of England, *cf.* State Help for Agriculture, p. 28 :—The value of the produce of one farm would often be double that of another in the same district–due solely to superior management and the employment of amplee capital. The Dewan of Mysore addressing the State Economic Conference in June 1920 said :—the value of the crop produced on one acre of dry land in the State is about Rs. 15 and of wet land Rs. 30—comparing even within the State, the average yield of crops on the same class of land under the best methods of cultivation prevailing in the State is three to six times as great as under ordinary methods. The profits from agriculture alone could be easily doubled almost immediately even though the people follow their old established methods but pursue their occupations with greater intelligence and have more facilities to obtain capital.

In cases where a tenant is able to lea se a fairly large area of land, as in Mianwali, his annual produce may be worth Rs. 1,000 to Rs. 1,200. A trained agriculturist with capital could produce more.

to yield in one year 90 lakhs of rupees more than the same area (1) would have yielded under *desi* cotton ; and this annual gain increases as the popularity of the crop grows. Still better results are promised by another variety now under trial.

The new types of wheat are estimated to yield Rs. 15 per acre more than the mixtures in use and the advantage derivable from sowing only the pure type will probably prove to be very great (2). From the progress already made by the Agricultural Department it seems clear that the gross value of the produce of the existing area could be very largely increased by the use of pure seed of improved types, of better implements and by resort to better methods of cultivation. The new canal projects, already mentioned, will, if carried through, irrigate over two million acres and so still further enhance the total produce. Tube-wells and other improvements will add their quota. With the knowledge at present acquired and with the labour at present available, it is probable that a hundred crores could be added to the value of the gross produce of the province (3). Much capital will be necessary ; a great effort will be required to spread technical agricultural education throughout the land, and the co-operative movement must be developed until the mass of the cultivators are thoroughly organized on business lines. Could all this be accomplished there would result a great expansion of trade and commerce and a great impetus would be given to industries subsidiary to agriculture. In trying to envisage the future of agriculture it would be a mistake to confine consideration to what has already been achieved. Research in Indian agriculture is as yet in its infancy ; progress is hampered by seasonal limitations and local conditions ; the caprice of the weather is such a large factor in this province that experiments have to be carried on through long series of years before definite advice can be given with confidence. The workers are few ; reliable records of past experience are scanty ; the scientific side of the university is not yet sufficiently developed to accord that aid in pure science which is invaluable to the technical investigator. What has been gained in the past seems to be as nothiug compared with the promise held forth by the future. It is such considerations as these which suggest that the prosperity of the province will in all probability be better sought in the development of agriculture and of the many industries attending on its needs or drawing their material from its produce, than in any attempt to follow slavishly the example of Japan and set up large factories on the European model.

No one could desire to see repeated in the Punjab the miseries that attended the introduction of factory organization in England, nor the doss houses of Japan or even the chawls of Bombay (4). The many problems of sociology, and hygiene created by factory conditions have not yet been solved even in England. Injury to health, weak physique and crabbed outlook may not be inevitable but they are almost universal accompaniments. The glamour of

(1) The area in 1919-20 is estimated at 525,000 acres.

(2) In 1919-20, the remarkable yield of 43 maunds (=57 bushels) per acre was obtained at Lyallpur from Punjab 8 A. The area under Punjab 11 was 377, 500 acres.

(3) This 100 crores produce would be available to raise the standard of living. The value of all exports from the province in 1919-20 was 44 crores. Thus the trade of the province could be trebled by a proper and extensive use of knowledge already acquired.

(4) See Prof. Kale's Indian Economics, 3rd Edition, para. 60, etc., for an interesting view of Indian opinion.

factory industries arises from the fortunes made by a few capitalists. The average earnings are not very high even in England where the workmen are probably the most skilled in the world. If, as Professor Marshall says in another connection, we were to divide all profits earned in factory industry by all the capital invested in such industries (including, those that failed involving loss of capital) the average return would be very small.

Moreover factories are not essential to prosperity or to the accumulation of wealth; Denmark is the classic instance and another is furnished by a large part of France. She affords, says Professor Marshall, the most important instance of a great industrial country, whose people are not inclined to the methods of massive production... The great economic solidarity of the French family fosters a disinclination to the steady and unyielding routine of the factory... The wealth of France has been due to the individuality, artistic tastes and skill in fine work of her people, whereas England has derived hers from her leadership in the arts and resources of routine mechanical manufacture (1).

If it be assumed that the popular vote has gone against the argument here set forth, and that continuous sustained efforts are initiated to encourage industries, there will still remain the need for a corresponding development of agriculture, for as the urban factory population increases the demand for food will increase too. For the industrial population food will have to be grown in greater quantity than at present, and as the new industries bring new wealth to the people, their requirements will grow. Situated as the Punjab is, it is unlikely that her population could be fed upon imported foodstuffs. It must be remembered that the definite acceptance of the policy of State participation in industrial development and of State aid thereto is not confined to this province, but is to be the feature of future activities in other provinces too; so that there is little likelihood of surplus foodstuffs being available from neighbouring tracts to meet any future deficit here. The distance of the Punjab from the seaboard would serve to prohibit import from overseas for many years to come. Thus whatever may be the result of the new movement toward industrial development, there must be a great improvement in agricultural methods and production. In other words, the development of industries on a large scale is dependent on such a development of agriculture as will at least suffice to feed the increasing urban population. The apparent antagonism between the two great occupations is thus unreal. It would be a shortsighted policy to concentrate attention on the one to the neglect of the other.

Of the many fallacies contained in the dissenting note to the Report of the Indian Industrial Commission, one of the most remarkable is that, owing to political action by one nation, there has resulted a great decline in Indian industries which has, in turn, led to frequent famine. With a given population, the greater the proportion engaged in agriculture the greater would be the amount of food produced; and the greater the proportion engaged in industries the amount of food produced would be so much less. There can never be a large industrial population unless the agriculturists are producing a large excess

---

(1) **Industry and Trade, Book 1, Chapter VI.**

of foodstuffs above their own requirement or unless food can be imported. It is not in evidence that India was ever a large importer of foodstuffs; and accordingly the country must have been dependent on its own resources. Thus the existence of a large industrial population would have accentuated the evils of a failure of the monsoon, not have mitigated them. For the same reason those who argue that in a normal year India does not produce enough food for the full requirements of her own population must advocate not industries, but agriculture. The development of industries will tend to an increase of population and to feed this increased number of mouths there must be more food produced.

But there is much more than the mere question of food for workers. If industries are to spring up they will require raw material. The carriage of this over long distance by rail will be prohibitive; so that it may be accepted that the industries of the future will be engaged with the raw material which the province produces. That is to say the soil of the province will be the source whence its industries take origin. There do not seem to be many alternatives. Thus whatever antagonism may have appeared to exist between agriculture and industries now disappears. If industries are to spring up and flourish in this province, they must be based upon what the soil can produce; and there must be a prolonged, indeed probably unending, investigation into the capacity of the soil to produce material of industrial value. It is not a question of agriculture *versus* industries, but of the too great occupations expanding side by side, with agriculture always necessarily taking the lead.

If reference be now made to what was said in an earlier chapter on the effects of the geographical position, it will be seen that the line of future investigation must be toward the discovering of those articles for the production of which the province is best suited or possesses some advantage over possible rivals. Sentiment, in such a matter, will have to give place to Nature. If other people adhere to science and economic laws, while the Punjabis allow sentiment to rule, there can only be one end to the competition. It is now clear that a close study of rural economics is as essential to the firm foundation of an industrial era as to agricultural prosperity. The cultivator must be educated to appreciate all the possibilities of his calling, for amongst those possibilities is the inception of great industries. The intelligentsia of the province must look to rapid progress in agriculture for the material for those factories they hope to direct. The potentialities, the problems, the special features of the Punjab must be closely studied. Its history, in so far as it explains the present position, must be carefully elucidated, and the correct lessons drawn for future guidance. The ground must be thoroughly prepared if the present policy of State encouragement of industries is to bear lasting fruit. Without these, there can only be further failures, losses and disappointments. The hope of the people is that great and rapid strides will be made, so that the time lost in the centuries of invasions and internal disturbances shall be recovered. To achieve this at all successfully, accurate knowledge and disciplined reasoning will be essential. In the following chapters, it is proposed to suggest some indications of the factors that must be considered.

CHAPTER XIV.

THE PLACE OF CO-OPERATION IN A MODERN STATE.

It is, perhaps, unfortunate for India that, England being essentially an industrial country, the British officials brought with them the idea of co-operation prevalent in the manufacturing centres, namely, the co-operative store for distribution of household requirements. Of co-operation as a panacea for rural ills little seems to have been known in England until towards the close of the last century. It is true that much of the preliminary work of trial, failure and success was carried out by British workers, and that the idea which has since been adopted throughout the civilised world was first evolved there ; but of co-operation for farmers as a method of organisation few writers, except Mr. Wolff, showed much knowledge. The system of land tenure in the British isles, of large benevolent landlords engaged with the administration of the land and of tenants on a yearly lease exploiting their skill to the full in the confidence that they would not thereby be risking the penalty of increasing rents was not calculated to show the need for co-operative effort. Where the landlord provided all the fixed capital required for buildings and improvements, and the tenant was able to reserve his slender resources for stock, manures, etc., there was less need for credit than in countries of small proprietors. Moreover, an English farm is a large concern of 100 to 500 or more acres ; the farmers are for the most part men of substance with credit at the bank, and the banks were the old country type that regarded their interests as bound up with the prosperity of the farmers of the locality, and prided themselves on supplying deserving clients with every suitable accommodation that could prudently be given on business lines. Where there was hesitation is asking credit from the local bank, the dealer in implements or manures would grant it. On the Western continent, where peasant proprietorship may almost be said to prevail, conditions were widely different. The small holder had no landlord behind him to share the brunt of bad seasons or low prices ; the period of agricultural depression that came over Europe in the middle and second half of the last century found him without reserve to meet the crisis ; tied to the land, he was left to face poverty and distress in the sole company of the moneylender. The great slump in real property that followed on the advent of cheap American wheat curtailed what little credit he had, and there ensued the black period from which agriculture was finally rescued by the development of co-operation and the discoveries of Liebig and his followers.

The second half of the last century witnessed a revolution in methods, and indeed in the whole economy of agriculture. Among the changes perhaps none was so pregnant for good as the introduction of the co-operative principle into agricultural organisation. From 1870 till the end of the century the new movement spread in many districts, but there was little notice taken in England until Sir Horace Plunkett's campaign in Ireland began to attract attention. The next stimulus came from America, where President Roosevelt started his Country Life Movement ; one step taken in this was to send a commission, composed of representatives of all the chief States and certain non-official members, to tour Europe and study co-operation on the spot. With this commission Canada sent representatives of her own. As a preliminary measure, all Embassies of the United States in Europe were directed to collect material descriptive of the movement in the various countries, and this material was collated by Mr. Herrick, the distinguished Ambassador to France. The commission recorded evidence in Europe and gathered other evidence on rural conditions in America through small committees appointed in each State. The result was an examination of European co-operation by impartial Americans, who brought to their study fresh minds unaffected by the numerous local controversies; some of the conclusions are to be found in the official reports, others of great value are recorded in books written by several members of the joint commission. The analysis of European systems thus carried out has been of the utmost value to agriculture. It established the principle of co-operation as the one essential method of organisation necessary to make small holdings a success, and as most likely to enable large holdings to continue profitable. It raised the village credit society to its proper position in rural finance; it put almost beyond the range of discussion the generalisation that co-operative sale was the only really satisfactory method of disposing of produce.

Such was the position in 1913. In ordinary times it is probable that these conclusions would have struggled for acceptance for several generations, but the course of the war brought into a prominence that could not be ignored the fact that every country must in the long run depend upon itself for its food supplies. Agriculture bounded to the forefront as the one essential industry for war, as well as for peace. As Mr. Lloyd George expressed it:—" The interest of the State is paramount, and the interest of the State is increased production " (1). In every country there was almost feverish activity in introducing measures designed to promote the formation of all kinds of agricultural co-operative societies, and since the signing of the armistice these societies have been entrusted with the reconstruction of agriculture and of rural industries in the regions most seriously affected by the operations of war. The continent of Europe has looked to co-operation as the best means of encouraging the revival of an industry which had been eclipsed by the amazing development of manufactures in the previous fifty years (2).

The American Commission soon realised that the question that confronted them was at once larger and more intricate than the problem of procuring cheap money for farmers. At an early stage in their investigations the conviction was borne in upon them that they were concerned in a question no less fundamental than the entire problem of rural life. The application of the co-operative principle, they found, to agricultural production has contributed not only to the economic improvement of the farms and the conservation of agricultural resources, but also to the educational development of the individual and the progress and integration of rural society. Agriculture, the first industry to be learned, was the last to be developed (3).

---

(1) Exeter Hall, October, 1919.

(2) In 1920 Mr. M. L. Darling, I.C.S., and Mr. C. F. Strickland, I.C.S., both of whom had served as Deputy Registrars in the Punjab, spent some months on deputation in European countries studying the movement. Their reports show the present position of co-operation after the war.

(3) The quotation is from the Saskatchewan Report, p. 13.

Another American verdict is even more emphatic : We are just beginning to learn the Kindergarten principles of co-operation, and failures are due to this lack of knowledge of what true co-operation is. Co-operation does this : We are not stating a to-be-proven hypothesis ; we are stating a fact, emphatically and without equivocation. Practicallyevery country in Europe has demonstrated it beyond argument or denial. Co-operation cheapens and vastly betters supplies, increases returns and ensures a certain market, strengthens human power and ability for productive labour. Its indirect effects are diffusion of practical knowledge, remarkable educational capacity, stimulation of thought. It means making farming profitable and easier, the creation of a high, prosperous, contented rural civilisation, the vital need of our time. What benefits the farmers of necessity benefits the State (1).

The great benefits to be derived from co-operation are admitted by all who have made a close study of the subject, but appreciation of an achievement is easier to secure than the achievement itself. For the latter, there are required leaders with a knowledge of what is necessary to be done, and with the unselfishness and the capacity to devote themselves to successful constructive work. Now the cultivator seldom thinks for himself. As a class he is little apt to lead, and has seldom produced the pioneer of a new movement affecting even his own interests. It is a remarkable fact that the leader of a successful co-operative movement has practically never sprung from amongst the cultivating class (2). The original organiser in each country has usually been some one man, or set of men, not engaged in agriculture (3).

The intelligent youths from the country are led, by the circumstances of their education, to seek their careers in the towns, and it is from the towns that there must emerge the leaders with the intelligence to grasp the essential needs of the rural community and the determination to construct the organisation required to satisfy them. Thus, whethert he type of co-operation under consideration be urban or rural, the stimulus must come from the town. The townsman must be educated to take an active interest in the problems of the country (4).

The first successful co-operators combined elementary business ability with great faith in the social benefits to be derived from their business. They were working men, possessed of little education, but endowed with sound intuition. They realised that the most wasteful and ill-managed business of the country was that of marketing goods to the working classes ; that, if they could devise a means whereby these classes could secure better food at cheaper

---

(1) American Evidence, Tennessee Committee, p. 64.

(2) *Cf* Smith Gordon. Co-operation for Farmers, p. 57.

(3) *Cf.* Herrick p. 456. Denmark is an exception : The co-operative movement in Danish agriculture was not started by a circle of philanthropists, or even by the landlords, for the purpose of benefiting the practical farmers. It has grown up locally and gradually among the peasants in the villages, and takes its root in the feeling of solidarity and a sense of the benefits of mutual help among the peasants which can be traced back to remote centuries. The date of the foundation of the agricultural co-operative movement in Denmark cannot therefore be given as it can in some countries where it owes its inception to the action of a single man or of a committee. Faber : Co-operation in Danish Agriculture p. IX. The attempt in 1866 by philanthropists to introduce the Rochdale type of Co-operative Store into the towns was not a success.

(4) *Cf.* Rural Life Problems of the United States of America, p. 151.

rates, they would be making a great stride towards the amelioration of the conditions under which they lived. On to a comparatively simple business proposition they grafted a great social ideal, the supplanting of soulless competition by more humane co-operation. Of the progress of this movement this is not the place to write ; it will suffice to record that the original society of Rochdale Equitable Pioneers, founded in 1844, has now 22,257 members and a share capital of more than £300,000, that the total membership in the United Kingdom is over 3,770,000, that the annual sales exceed 143 million pounds and that the members have, in the last five years, received back over sixty million pounds as dividend on their purchases. The great wholesale and retail distributive societies have over 18 million pounds invested in buildings and over 30 million pounds in mortgage and other securities (1).

But, although co-operation has rendered, and is rendering, noble service to the British people, the original ideal of a co-operative commonwealth, wherein every one would work for the common good and receive the full returns on his labour, and all would be peace and harmony, is, perhaps, as far from realisation as ever. Competitors have woke up to the great advantages of the multiple store, strict cash sales and small profits with a large turn over. Success in business nowadays depends on highly developed qualities of mind, originality of ideas and an intensely trained sense of what will pay. The committee system of control that is essential in co-operation is not well adapted to these modern requirements. Many decisions in the course of business require prompt action, based in large part on intuition associated with reason : the time and strain involved in proving to other members of a committee that the best course is not that which appears best at first sight are very great ; and only a man who possesses the rare combination of fine and sensitive insight, with a strong, and even rugged, character, is likely to persist and succeed in his efforts to bring a committee composed of ordinary men round to his point of view. Further, every successive step in the marvellous progress of the co-operative movement has tended to weaken the relative strength in its counsels of those in whose breasts the original co-operative faith is cherished.

It is becoming more and more a huge business, managed by men few of whom have had extensive business training. Its problems are approaching to those of ordinary trade in their general character, and alert competitors are quick to pick up the features that have made for success (2).

Professor Marshall's conclusion may be accepted that co-operative undertakings, that is, those which are entirely in the hands of the manual labour classes and other people of small means, are seldom able to engage successfully in industries other than those of marketing staple goods for general consumption, especially by the working classes ; and in the production of some kinds of these goods. The organisation of industries on purely business lines is the task of the able business promoter and skilled organiser. Many small industries run on co-operative lines by small capitalists remain undeveloped largely because his help is not forthcoming, and they have not leaders of their own ready for the work.

---

(1) Annual Report of the Chief Registrar.

(2) For a broad view from which I have freely quoted see Prof. Alfred Marshall's Industry and Trade, Book II, Chapter VII.

So far then as co-operative distribution is concerned, there appears to be a fairly well-defined limit to its expansion ; this limit is fixed by the extreme specialisation of modern business and the difficulty of finding leaders of the requisite qualifications willing to accept duties in a co-operative organisation. From this it must not be concluded that town co-operation has been a failure ; it has achieved vast results, both moral and economic, in ameliorating the conditions under which the working classes live, and there is a field in India that will provide scope for all the unselfishness and enthusiasm that this or the next generation is likely to see. It will probably remain as the only protection of the poor against the less scrupulous middleman and profiteer and continue to offer the best prospects of escape from economic servitude.

Apart from distribution, urban co-operation has achieved much in providing sound credit to small tradesmen and craftsmen in Italy and elsewhere through the medium of People's Banks, but their cumulative effect is overshadowed by the truly marvellous results gained in the sphere of agriculture.

Organisation is the keystone of commercial success. So long as the farmer sought to supply only his own needs, he felt but little the need of any form of combination, but, with the improvement of communications and the consequent opening up of markets, he became subject to the attentions of traders who sought to take as much and give as little as possible. When all around are organising to secure greater profits for themselves, the farmer must organise or go under. The organisation may be imposed upon him from without, as by some middleman such as the village shopkeeper who seeks only his own immediate gain, or it may arise from within, that is to say, from amongst the farmers themselves (1). It would appear that the earlier forms of organisation invariably came from without and that the greed of the middleman has ever been a powerful stimulus to induce the farmers to agree to form an organisation of their own (2). As the largest and most important industry, as well as the source of nearly all commerce, agriculture must be organised. But the peculiar conditions attendant upon its pursuit make this unusually difficult. The industry is carried on by a very large number of comparatively very small capitalists, who in the aggregate control a vast amount of capital. The farmer has to be both capitalist and labourer, as well as a technical expert, and few are able to specialise in all three. As soon as he begins to grow things for sale he must learn how to market them to the best advantage or he will inevitably come off a poor second in the competition that he will find at the place of sale.

He cannot adopt the ordinary forms of organisation suitable for other manufacturing industries ; his is an industry of small units ; his land is not capable of being moved or concentrated ; there can therefore be no association of the greater part of the capital used, there can be only an association of the persons carrying on the industry. For reasons such as the above, agriculture has everywhere been the last to be organised. But, apart from these,

---

(1) *Cf.* Todd, pp. 1--3.

(2) *Cf.* Bubnoff, Co-operation in Russia, p. 37. The elimination of the middleman who pockets a large profit to which he has no right provides the ideal which inspires the co-operative movement, whose cry is : "Down with the middleman !" The agricultural societies are, perhaps, an exception in this respect, but in all the other co-operative societies the desire to get rid of the middleman is the basis of the movement. This is rather an extreme view.

other causes also have been at work that deserve mention. For several generations past it has been possible to gain wealth more rapidly from industries and commerce than from the soil. The enterprising, ignoring the many failures, have concentrated their energies upon the rapid accumulation of wealth possible in the cities and have passed agriculture by. Now it is true that there are probably few fortunes made in agriculture ; it is not a business that lends itself readily to the amassing of large profits through speculative undertakings. It provides a better living for a greater number of persons than any other occupation but, as at present managed, it possesses little attraction for men of high spirit and enterprise ; there is a tendency in almost every country for the less vigorous, the less capable and the less enterprising youths to be left on the farms ; there is a sort of idea that any fool can be a farmer ; most people seem to have the belief that they could make a success of farming if they had the opportunity, and few realise that to be a thoroughly equipped scientific farmer probably requires a higher education, certainly a more complete scientific education, than any of the learned professions, with the possible exception of medicine (1). Under these circumstances it is small wonder that agriculture has been neglected ; the farmer has been the forgotten man and, until comparatively recent times, he has attracted little or no interest from Government or the rest of the people (2).

Agriculture is still an unorganised industry. It is still distracted by the need of producing the necessaries of the cultivator, instead of concentrating on those crops that will bring the best return in the market, a return that will enable him to secure these necessaries by purchase (3). If every manufacturing concern were to waste time turning out goods of the quality and quantity required for the labourers engaged, before producing for sale, a severe handicap would be imposed on its prospects of success, and yet, amongst farmers, this is the almost invariable custom. It is only recently that recognition has been found for the principle that it was little use improving the technical efficiency of farmers if they could not market to the best advantage. They have to produce independently from the very nature of their calling, but there is no necessity to handicap themselves further by buying and selling independently. The old-type farmer always bought in the dearest market and sold in the cheapest ; hence, perhaps, the prevalent idea that there are greater profits to be made from other industries than from farming. Now, however, the application of the co-operative principle to the business side of agriculture has changed all that. Whereas twenty years ago co-operation met with either indifference or actual opposition by State agencies, at the present time it is being fostered by all progressive Governments in the Western world (4).

Agriculture has become a business, and the farmer must become a business-man. More and more, as he tends to produce only those crops for which his land is best suited, he ceases to live directly upon the products of his farm and

(1) *Cf.* Principles of Rural Economics, Carver, p. 200. State Help for Agriculture, p. 49. Rural Reconstruction in Ireland, p. 261.

(2) *Cf.* Smith Gordon, Co-operation for Farmers, p. 231.

(3) *Cf* Orwin, Place of Agriculture in Industry.

(4) *Cf.* Vogt, p. 232. Herrick (p. 456) : Co-operative Credit is now being agitated for agriculture throughout the civilised world.

begins to live on the profits of farming; he becomes more and more dependent upon markets and market conditions; he must study the most approved means of handling and marketing, as well as of raising, his goods (1).

Independently he cannot do this with any hope of success; he must adopt the prevailing measures by which alone any large industry can withstand the strain of competition. He must organise; as he cannot combine his capital; with that of his neighbours, he must combine himself with them, and this is what is meant by agricultural co-operation. For agriculture to be successful co-operation is essential. Throughout the world this truth has been recognised by thinking men, and is being pressed upon the attention of all concerned. Cultivators can no longer ask themselves "Shall we co-operate?" but "When shall we begin to co-operate?" For India this truth is of urgent importance. As Sir John Strachey said so long ago as 1873: "The whole present and future prosperity of this country, and the future financial position of our Empire in India, depended on the development of the vast, and practically unlimited, though too often neglected, resources of the country. If advantage were taken of the means which science and wealth had placed at our disposal for the improvement of the land, and if we abstained from putting into operation theories which ignored the only really great and progressive source of wealth which India possessed, it might be safely predicted that the increase of agricultural prosperity in India would be rapid and immense".

It has to be remembered to the credit of the British Government of the nineteenth century in India that it recognised the principle that it was the duty of the State to make use of its resources in encouraging and developing agricultural improvement. It accepted many of the duties of a good landlord for the improvement of land and advancement of agriculture (2), and it has now definitely accepted the principle that for the permanent amelioration of the conditions of the mass of the rural population the spirit of co-operation must be developed, the principles of co-operation must be explained and the organisation of agriculture on co-operative lines must be spread throughout the length and breadth of the land (3).

From the above it will, it is hoped, be clear that if a country, dependent on agriculture, is to aim at increasing prosperity, it must be organised on co-operative lines. It certainly seems to be true that all attempts of farmers to combine on other principles have invariably ended in failure. But it is sometimes urged that the spread of the co-operative organisation will throw out of employment many people who now perform some of the functions which it is the object of co-operative societies to perform, and that the increased wealth of the cultivators will be obtained at the expense of increased poverty for others. The

---

(1) Rural Wealth and Welfare, p. 18. Carver, p. 16. See also Nourse, p. 10: Agriculture aims not at bigger corn and fatter hogs as such, but at larger financial net returns......the hope of both the farmer and his friends has come to be placed more and more upon a broader and deeper understanding of the price relationships involved in the carrying on of our commercialised business of farming.

(2) *Cf.* Report of the Famine Commission, 1901. Ray, pp. 42—44.

(3) *Cf.* Nourse, p. 11: Co-operation is urged as a panacea for all rural ills, not as one particular form of economic organisation, whose effectiveness in operation is determined and limited by the appropriateness of that special type to the given situation.

It is claimed that it is due to the thoroughness of the organisation of agricultural co-operation that Denmark has more wealth per head than any other country in Europe.

argument deserves passing notice. It must be remembered that the assumption is made that the increasing prosperity of the province is desired, that the improvement of the economic condition of the people is to be aimed at and that an increase of material welfare is admitted to be a necessary prelude to the fuller development of social and moral welfare. It is necessary to bear these basic assumptions in mind because it would sometimes appear that the object to be aimed at is the complete economic subjugation of the producing class under the heel of a small moneyed minority. The population of a country may be roughly divided into producers and non-producers. Of the latter, some perform no very useful functions and do not concern the argument. Their disappearance would probably be an economic, though not always an æsthetic, gain. Others, however, do perform useful functions, and these may again be roughly divided into those who receive a fair remuneration for the services they render, and those who receive a remuneration that must be regarded as excessive in view of their value to the economic fabric. The former have nothing to fear from co-operation. The latter constitute the incubus which co-operation seeks to remove. They are a source of weakness, and it is largely in proportion to their number and influence that a country is poor. Even of England it is recorded that its agriculture supports a disproportionate fringe of dealers and middlemen (1) ; and of India it has been said that, had the agriculture of the district to support only its own producers, it would be sufficient to maintain them at their present number, and larger returns might be obtained from the land by improved cultivation to meet still further increase. But agriculture pays a heavy tax to the sowcar, much of which neither represents expenditure on account of the land nor ever returns to the land (2). In the Punjab a careful estimate suggests that, for every rupee a cultivator pays in land-revenue to Government, another rupee is lost in litigation and two, at least, are paid in interest to the moneylender. If any doubt the serious effect of this drain, let him calculate the good that might result were all this money devoted to land improvement (3). Anyone who contributes to this loss contributes to the prevailing poverty. In so far as the services rendered are necessary to the community, they will continue to be required. In so far as they gain for the performer excessive rewards, they must be subjected to an organisation that aims at the economic uplift of the people. It is not the performers of necessary services that will be thrown out of work ; it is the excessive remuneration that will suffer diminution. The useful middleman will remain, though not, perhaps, with the same power for harm (4).

---

(1) Hall : Agriculture after the War, p. 14.

(2) Report of the Deccan Riots Commissions, 1875, see Ray, p. 10.

(3) *Ibid*—Ray pp. 7—8. That their present state of indebtedness prevents the ryots from making efforts to improve the outturn of their land there can be no doubt. They find that the land broken up and the wells dug with borrowed capital yield a profit only to the sowcar. The ryot toils that another may rest, and sows that another may reap.

(4) *Cf.* Marshall, p. 812. A stratum of middleman, which appears at first sight superfluous, often does work which would need about an equal number of men if the stratum were eliminated.

It is probable that the decline of the small village industry in India is largely due to the excessive exactions of the middleman : the weaver can earn enough to keep himself, he cannot also keep in comparative idleness the middleman who makes a big profit out of his yarn and another big profit out of his cloth.

Of one thing there seems to be little room for reasonable doubt, and thet is that, if agriculture is to attract the brain and intelligence and capital that it must attract, if it is to attain its maximum prosperity, it must yield to those who pursue it the full profits of their labour. In questions of improving land or methods of cultivation or popularising crops the importance of securing to the cultivator the higher profits of his enterprise is paramount. When it is objected that the spread of co-operation will lead to unemployment amongst any class of middlemen, the reply must be made that the real test is whether the person threatened is performing functions necessary to the community or not ; if he is, he need not fear the loss of his livelihood, though his gains may be reduced to something nearer to the economic value of the services he performs. In so far as he performs no functions that can be regarded as necessary, he is a source of weakness to the State, and his disappearance will advance that prosperity which it is assumed everyone desires to see.

There is little reason to fear that absolute unemployment, due to a lack of demand for labour, will become a serious practical problem. The increased prosperity of the main industry will lead to the development of subsidiary industries ; the increased income will lead to increased expenditure on a higher standard of living, or to the greater practice of thrift that will provide capital for yet further enterprises. Under circumstances such as these, trade must improve, transport and distribution must occupy more and more workers, the rising standard of living must create new demands. Wherever more wealth is being produced, there is little likelihood of any serious unemployment.

It is one of the beliefs of those who have made a study of economics that, if there be an economic ill, there must be economic causes, and there will probably be economic remedies. Unfortunately, in India, there is a strong tendency to adopt a view of present conditions that seems to be unduly pessimistic. Writers give expression to views that suggest either that the poverty of the people is a result of misgovernment, or that it is beyond the reach of remedy. It is frequently noticed that statements are made about India that most certainly are not true of the Punjab. Conditions in this province, when compared with those in other countries in Europe, apart from the few more advanced, do not support anything savouring of pessimism. There is much to be done. There is much leeway to be made good. But it should be possible for workers in this province to profit from the experience of success and failure in other countries, and to make progress at a greater speed along a road thus marked out, than has been possible in the case of those with less experience to draw upon. It is, for instance, clear that, where agriculture is progressive and prosperous, the State is devoting energy and money to its development, and also to the spread of co-operation. Where agriculture is stagnant, there it will be found that the State leaves innovations to private sloth and neglects the supreme importance of organising the peasantry on co-operative lines. It is not possible to substantiate a broad generalisation like this without entering into an examination of rural conditions in many countries ; but, if there be anyone with the temerity to deny the truth of it, it may fairly be required of him to name any country wherein the conditions do not support it. The evidence is now overwhelming that agriculture requires stimulation from without; and that, if it is at all to compete with town industries for the intelligence of the nation and for the returns on capital and labour, it must be organised on co-operative lines. In a rural State co-operation must become the framework which holds the whole community together. Applying this to the Punjab, it becomes clear that, if the province has, in the past, contained a large number of people unable to enjoy a fair standard of comfort, this is to a large extent due to the fact that it has not been organised on lines conducive to the steady increase of wealth. In a few years some 8 per cent. of the cultivators have accumulated over one crore of rupees in their little village banks. If all the cultivators could be persuaded to organise themselves to practise thrift even on the limited scale that is at present usual in societies and to set themselves to obtain whatever advantages co-operation can place within their reach, there would, in the course of one generation, be a revolution in the economic conditions of the peasantry. Co-operation may yet work a miracle in the Punjab comparable to that accomplished in Denmark.

CHAPTER XV.

The Economic Causes of Punjab Poverty.

On few subjects is there more misapprehension than that of poverty in this country. For some abstruse reason, it is deemed necessary to write always in a tone of pessimism for which it would be very difficult to bring forward adequate justification (1). There is ample material available to controvert many of the current views ; but it needs to be handled by persons skilled in economics, and determined to bring to the task minds free from bias, both political and religious. There are so many fallacious statements uttered that it is not easy to trace the origin of the misunderstandings. Some are palpably absurd. Such, for instance, is one that this is the only country where land-revenue is collected (2). Any book of reference would have provided a correction. Similarly, to argue that the rise of prices of agricultural produce has not brought benefit to the rent receivers (3) indicates an omission to note that about half the land in the province is cultivated by tenants paying rent in kind, so that the rent receivers secure full advantage of any rise in the price of the produce in which their rent is paid. Most of these fallacies when examined seem to owe their origin to a marked disinclination to admit the responsibility of the people for their present state. It is everybody's fault except their own.

In extenuation of the prevailing misapprehensions, it may be at once admitted that there does not appear to be any publication containing a summary of the facts of rural problems in various countries. A patriotic Punjabi, desirous of placing before his fellow-countrymen an accurate comparison of conditions in other rural countries with those prevailing here, would find his task beset with difficulties. The library facilities are inadequate ; there is no reference book for the province setting forth in convenient from the salient facts contained in the many official reports, so that, as non-officials seldom read these, they retain views that are easily open to refutation ; the form in which official statistics are maintained is apt to vary in a manner which is puzzling ; it is not easy to ascertain the total land-revenue of the province ; it is impossible to learn with any approach to accuracy what exactly is the cultivated area which represents the Punjab holding ; the outturn of crops, which a serious economist may reasonably assume is not available in any publication, for all official estimates are designedly based upon the most cautious figures, so as to relieve the administration of the charg of error in the direction inimical to the interests of the owners. Perhaps, the most

(1) *Cf.* Sir M. Visvesvaraya, Reconstructing India, p. 237—8 : "The general outlook upon life in India, as things are now, is too gloomy to permit sound individual or social development. Far too common is the belief that life is merely a transitory stage in the passage of the soul to another world. That notion chills enthusiasm, kills joy and promotes fatalism......In some cases the joint family system tends to produce drones ; some Indians actually take pride in the number of persons they maintain in idleness......While Indians feel that life is a burden, people in the West are full of hope and intensely active."

(2) A member in the Punjab Legislative Council.

(3) A Professor of Economics.

inaccurate views currently held relate to the incidence of the land-revenue. There is ample material in the multitude of assessment reports to indicate what a very cautious attitude is adopted by Government in framing new demands from the landowners; yet, in spite of this, there are spread abroad suggestions that can only be described as grotesque. In another part of this book it has been shown that the actual demand of the State amounts to about 5 per cent. of the gross produce. In Japan the demand is about 17 per cent.; in Turkey it used to be 12½ per cent., but this was raised in the course of the war to 25, 37½, and even to 50, per cent. This demand was based upon the estimate of officials for the year, so that it was a not infrequent occurrence for the official, from private motives that need not detain this discussion, to frame an estimate that would bring out the share of the State equal, or even more than equal, to the whole produce. In England taxation on land is usually based upon the annual value, and on the whole is very heavy. It is, however, assessed in ways that render a comparison with the Punjab difficult. In Holland the land is valued, the sum arrived at is regarded as capital and on this capital 4 per cent. is assumed as income; this income is then taxed, the tax being divided between the owner and occupier. In Spain there is a land tax, but its assessment is so defective that many owners escape, while others are made to pay far more than their share. In one province alone it was estimated that over a million acres of land had not been declared for the tax. Belgium has a property tax and a succession duty. Greece levies a direct tax on income from land. Bulgaria taxes the land, as also does Rumania. In short, a land or property tax is an important source of public revenue in practically every country, but it would be difficult to name one wherein the assessment of this tax was levied with greater care or more caution than in this province.

Another common misapprehension that constantly recurs whenever the question of poverty is discussed is that India is poor, while Europe is rich. In the note to the Report of the Industrial Commission distinction is drawn between India and Europe, and much argument is advanced to defend the Indian from the charge of being less capable than the European in the matter of industries. Europe, in the opinion of the writer, is industria while India is agricultural, and this is the main reason of Europe's welth and India's poverty. Now, so far from Europe being mainly industaal, the industrial tracts are strictly confined to definite areas, usually possesring some special advantage facilitating the prosecution of some particular siidustry. North-Western Europe may be described as predominantly indusral; but there are large divisions of England, and still larger of Scotland and Ireland, where there are no manufacturing industries, and yet whereahere is a high average standard of prosperity, and where a charge of being bckward would be resented. Southern Europe and European Russia are mainly agricultural; lack of power in the form of coal being an important cause of the absence of manufactures. It is difficult to make a comparison that will be accurate and useful; but it may be noted that of Spain it is said that "Agriculture has suffered from systems of land tenure which have militated against good cultivation. The cultivation of the land is left to men who are too poor, as well as too ignorant, to do it justice.... The agriculture of Spain is inevitably bad...it is given up to antiquated routine.... Where little is produced by hard labour with poor instruments, the poverty must needs be great. . . . The labourers are huddled in squalid outhouses, are paid very ill and are fed on inferior bread mixed in salads with vinegar, a little oil and vegetables. . . ." In Greece " in many parts the methods and implements of agriculture are very primitive. There is little use of manure or scientific rotation of crops. In Thessaly the wooden ploughs used differ little from those of more than 2,000 years ago". In old Serbia the methods of cultivation have varied from place to place. " In the less fertile parts they have always been very crude, the primitive wooden plough, which does little more than scratch the ground, being in general use." In other tracts the efforts of Government to improve agriculture are bearing fruit. In the new territories, however, " owing to the exactions of corrupt officials and the ravages of brigands, the peasant never enjoyed security of life or property. . . . The methods of cultivation were still more primitive than those employed in the old kingdom. Agricultural implements were crude, manure was seldom used, and there was general ignorance about the rotation of crops. . . ." Of European Turkey it is said that " Agricultural methods are in general most primitive. Ploughing is commonly done with the one-handed plough used in Biblical times. The ground is not deeply ploughed or dug, and manure is used only in some of the villages inhabited by immigrants from the lost provinces of Europe. Sowing and reaping are done by hand. The grain is threshed on floors in the open air. The wind is used for winnowing. The grain is very seldom screened, even when intended for sowing, the effect on succeeding crops being lamentable " (1). In Bulgaria the primitive wooden plough is still in use ; little is known about the rotation of crops, and artificial manures are seldom used. In short, in South Europe, agriculture is as little advanced in comparison with its condition in ancient times as it is in the Punjab. Everywhere, if there is improvement to record, this is due to the action of Government stimulating study, encouraging the formation of co-operative societies and establishing colleges, experimental farms, etc., etc. So far then from this province being behind Europe, it, now at least, is as progressive as South Europe and more advanced than large portions of that continent. Those who like to ascribe poverty to the political circumstances of this country should remember that all the most poverty-stricken States are self-governing.

In the countries briefly mentioned the majority of the population is dependent upon agriculture, and the general standard of wealth is low. Turning to North-Western Europe, although industries are comparatively more important, there is still appalling poverty. Generally speaking, wealth s more evenly divided in an agricultural country than in one wherein industries play a greater part. The return from agriculture, over a period of years, is more certain than that from industries. In the latter, failures are frequent, and the losers in the race sink to the slums or constitute that crowd of unemployed or unemployable which presents to the statesman the most difficult of problems. It may be true that the average income is higher in an industrial country than in one predominantly agricultural, or amongst workers in factories than amongst workers on the land ; but this of itself means little. Generally speaking, industries are more highly organised, there is more capital

(1) The quotations are from the various Foreign Office handbooks.

employed per worker, higher skill and intelligence is found in the direction and financial facilities are better developed (1). The nearest approach which agriculture can present to these factors is afforded by Denmark, and the most patriotic may well be satisfied if this province attains to the standard of comfort that is found there. In a country like England or the United States the greater portion of the wealth is accumulated in the hands of forty or fifty thousand persons or corporations (2). Agriculture does not tend to such vast accumulation of wealth, so that in a country predominantly agricultural there are seldom many very rich persons. From the above, it may be considered that the present demand for the encouragement of industries is to be deprecated, but this is far from being correct. Industries provide for local agriculture an assured market which renders possible the cultivation of products which yield a higher profit than those now grown, or enable the cultivator to secure a higher price for the same things. If the Punjab cultivator could get for his wheat the price which the English factory workers pay for it, he would be so much the better off; and he may reasonably hope that the development of industries in this country will bring him some such advantage.

Successful industries will tend to send up the standard of living, including the more general consumption of articles of food now regarded as luxuries. The cultivator will find himself able to use more intelligence and more capital with greater profit than he can in growing wheat. In such a commodity as milk, for instance, he will have a monopoly of supply, and may be expected to reap the advantage open to all monopolists: in other articles of which the transport over long distances presents difficulties he will possess a partial monopoly, or at least a protection from competition that will enable him to demand and secure high prices.

Connected with this argument, there is another common misapprehension that must be discussed; that is, that industries will prevent famines, and that famines are the result of the absence of industries (3). A famine in the old days meant an absolute shortage of food in the area affected, due to some natural calamity such as a failure of the monsoon; nowadays it means the inability of the people, or a section of them, to purchase the food that is for

---

(1) See Orwin: Agriculture in Oxfordshire, p. 87.—"The view of some is that agriculture as a basis of investment cannot offer any satisfactory prospect comparable with other industries. There are, however, a sufficient number of estates and farms on which the management gives results that do not support the theory...... While comparisons have frequently been drawn between agriculture and other industries with reference to their capabilities as producers of dividends, little has been done in the way of examining the different methods under which they are organised."

(2) In England only 59,000 enjoy incomes over £ 2,500 a year. In the U. S. A. it is estimated that 9 per cent. of the population own 70 per cent. of the total wealth, 21 per cent. own 5 per cent. and 70 per cent. share the rest, with an average of £ 43.

(3) The writer of the dissenting note to the Report of the Industrial Commission went so far as to suggest that it was the British, or at least the English, who throttled Indian industries and so were guilty of causing frequent famines. An educated man penetrated for the first time into a tract, where hitherto no one able to read or write had ever gone. He found snakes. Previous to this visit, the presence of snakes there had never been recorded. Therefore, previous to his visit, there were no snakes in that tract. Therefore the educated man brought the snakes into the tract.

Ancient Hindu writings mention severe famines; the Shanti Parva of the Mahabharata, I understand, describes one of twelve years' duration, in which the renowned Rishi, Vasishtha, had to eat dog's flesh to escape death from starvation.

sale. When communications were defective and means of transport primitive, it was possible for one tract to suffer the rigours of acute scarcity, while another might have a surplus over its immediate requirements. Where there was no free commerce in foodstuffs, there would seldom be any attempt to produce more than was required for local consumption. A slight surplus would lead to a glut which would render it unsaleable. In such circumstances a large industrial population would merely serve to accentuate the gravity of the situation ; so much is this the case that, on this ground alone it would be safe to assume that there could never have been any considerable industries before the improvement of communications and means of transport rendered the free movement of foodstuffs easy. Far from the seaboard, or the banks of navigable rivers, large industrial centres would have been impossible.

In a country like England, where every part is within easy reach of the sea, and therefore of imported foodstuffs, the development of industries has enabled the people to earn enough to purchase food from abroad. And, so long as food can be so imported, industries serve to prevent famine (1). But when, as occurred during the late war, the import of foodstuffs is impeded, then great industrial populations increase the gravity of the situation. The movement towards the cultivation of small allotments as a means to increase the amount of food, which was a feature of England in 1917-18, indicates the fallacy of the argument that industries prevent famines. When food was scarce and could not be imported, more food producers had to be found. It was the deliberate policy of Germany to starve England, a policy in which, in spite of the great industries, she was nearly successful.

Turning again to the Punjab, it will be obvious that for the growth of great industrial centres there must first be a surplus of food produced within the province which can be drawn upon to feed the factory hands. Those who object to the export of foodstuffs when many are ill-fed overlook the fact that an annual surplus for export provides a reservoir which can be drawn upon in time of scarcity. If, for instance, it be assumed that in a normal year the Punjab exports six hundred thousand tons of wheat, then, before there can be any danger of an actual shortage of food within the province, the production must fall below the normal by an amount equal to this quantity usually exported. Any shortage will fall first upon the export trade (2). Thus a large export trade, which reflects a large surplus production of food, is the surest preventitive against actual famine. On the other hand, where food is available, but the income of the people is apt to sink suddenly owing to calamity of seasons, then industries will serve to eanble them to earn the wherewithal to buy. In this province a large industrial population will always constitute a menace when a failure of the rains leads to a marked decrease in production, so that a large normal annual surplus available for export

(1) Assuming, that is to say, that population is going to increase, then industries provide an alternative source of livelihood, and enable the people to earn what will enable them to purchase food. A local shortage of home-grown food will not lead to starvation. But it is not correct to say that industries relieve the pressure on the soil for the supply of food when food cannot be imported. If a country is dependent on its home-grown food, industries will not relieve the pressure, but will tend to increase it, and so increase the distress resulting from a failure of crops.

(2) There could not, of course, be a normal surplus unless there were an export trade ; a simple fact sometimes overlooked.

must be encouraged as essential to the growth of manufactures. As has already been pointed out, the geographical position will serve to place difficulties in the way of importing food on a large scale. It is not easy to imagine conditions under which imported foodstuffs will normally form a large portion of the diet of the people, and, if a sudden emergency ever renders the people of the Punjab dependent on food thus brought in from distant places, it may be assumed that a considerable proportion of them will be unable to pay for it. Thus progressive agriculture is a necessary preliminary to progressive industry.

If the above argument seems far-fetched, it may be recalled that it was not until the discovery of the great American prairie lands as wheat producers, of steamships and of railways that any really rapid industrial development took place in Europe. So long as a nation was dependent upon home-grown produce for its food supply, and importation was beset with difficulties, there could not occur that rapid increase of population which was so marked a feature of the industrial revolution (1). There is a limit to the number of human beings that can be supported on a given area ; what that limit is and whether it has been reached is immaterial ; if foodstuffs can be imported from abroad, then the growth of industries will enable a country to support a population far in excess of what agriculture alone would render possible. But, when a country becomes dependent upon imported food, it becomes dependent upon those countries from which this food is imported and upon all countries which have the power to stop that import. If ever the Punjab becomes dependent upon outside sources for the food of its people, its position will indeed be precarious.

Thus far, the discussion has been concerned with refuting some of the more common fallacies that clog the proper understanding of the problems of Punjab poverty. It has been shown that this province is not more poor than many parts of Europe ; if its agriculture is less advanced than that in the North-Western portions of that continent, it is certainly not so in greater degree than in South Europe. Also it enjoys internal and external peace, and is less heavily taxed than the countries bordering upon the Mediterranean ; it has probably a better railway service ; and if its roads are inadequate to its needs they are less so than in many tracts in the countries referred to. It is difficult to make an accurate comparison, but there is reason to believe that the majority of the peasants in this province are better clad, and better fed, than their fellows in these countries.

Poverty is a relative term. It generally means inability to secure more than the bare necessities of existence. It is a negative phase, of which wealth is the positive. Wealth results from the combination of intelligent direction, capital and labour or power. Poverty results from the absence of one or more of these factors, or from their inefficient combination. The broad fact is that the ordinary human being, unaided by these factors, can only gain the

(1) Agricultural improvements preceded the industrial revolution Thorold Rogers wrote : "The improvements effected in English husbandry during the course of the seventeenth century more than doubled the population" (Vol. V, p. 64). In the nineteenth century the sudden influx of cheap food led to a large increase of population that could hardly have occurred without this supply.

bare necessaries of life, and nothing more. This applies to all races and to all countries. It is the basic cause of poverty in India. The common phrase that the average income is low is misleading. It is the average earnings that are low. And this is because the average production is low. And average production is always and everywhere low when man struggles without the intelligence, the capital and the power necessary to enable him to extract more wealth from his surroundings (1). There are, of course, more causes of poverty, but in one form or another they come under the above heads. The reasons for the existence of these causes are to be found in the history of the province. Centuries of disturbed conditions have served to prevent the growth of those characteristics which in other countries have rendered the accumulation of wealth possible. Foremost amongst these is the spirit of thrift. There is hardly any understanding of the place occupied by thrift in North-Western Europe. In England hard times, famines and bad seasons rendered the practice of thrift a necessity if a farmer were to survive; and, as Thorold Rogers has pointed out, the practice, through long enforcement, became a habit. When, later, the industrial revolution brought in its train fortune and distress, success and failure, the sufferings of the people once again compelled thrift as the one means of escape from starvation. It is frequently deplored that the factory workers of the British Isles are not as thrifty as their earnest friends would wish; but hardly anywhere is there to be found such a network of organisations with thrift in one form or another as their object. In France the thrift of the people is the basis of the country's prosperity; in Germany the lesson has been well learnt, and many thousands of credit societies systematically encourage the deposit of small savings, with results that are truly astonishing (2). In Great Britain the co-operative societies possess nearly one hundred million pounds share and loan capital, and in a single year their surplus on transactions amounts to twenty million pounds, most of which is returned to the members. Over 18 million pounds are invested in buildings and 30 million pounds in mortgages and other securities. The vast majority of the members, estimated at 95 per cent., earn incomes that are below the income tax limit. That it to say, they are drawn mostly from the working classess. It is not surplus money that has built up this enormous edifice, but half a century of well organised thrift practised by the poor. It is hardly correct to say that, as a condition of saving, "the income of individuals and communities must be sufficient to enable them to lay by wealth for future use" (3). Almost every individual and every community wastes sufficient money every year to found future prosperity. The twenty million pounds surplus, referred to above, is the result of systematic organisation to save waste. It represents not savings from income, but savings from expenditure, *i. e.*, what was formerly wasted. Until the Postal Savings Bank was introduced into the province there was no organised institution to which small savings could be entrusted. These banks were originally intended for Government servants, clerks and other wage-earners in the towns. They have never

---

(1) Compare the poverty in the western counties of Ireland, or in the Scotch Hebrides, with that of the Punjab.

(2) It was only by systematic thrift, resulting in large accumulations of capital, that Germany was able to embark upon that policy of economic penetration which gave her such influence in the world. For instance, prior to 1914 Germany had acquired almost complete economic control over Rumania and extensive influence in Italy.

(3) Professor Kale: 3rd Edition, p. 106.

appealed to the agricultural class ; about 97 per cent. of the depositors are not agriculturists, and the total number of these latter using the banks does not exceed 3,000 in the Punjab.

Sufficient has been said to show that the first cause of poverty has been the absence of thrift ; only by thrift could there be accumulated the capital required to improve the land and make it more productive. This absence of thrift is largely due to prolonged continuance of unsettled conditions, but, to some extent, it may be attributed to the fertility of the soil, to the small amount of labour required to make it produce a crop, to the fact that two crops could be grown in a year, thus reducing the period of waiting (1), and to the Hindu family system which does not permit of the lazy and incompetent being thrown on to their own resources. There is also to be borne in mind the fact that the accumulation of wealth was not only dangerous, but was outside the philosophy of the people (2).

The cultivators of the province do not seem to have any folklore indicating the use of any implements more efficient than those now in common use ; and it would appear that agriculture has never reached a stage that would be regarded as advanced. The land yields so easily to the simplest kind of tillage that the need for something more productive does not seem to have been felt. Thus there has been wanting the stimulus that might have led to the employment of more labour per acre or of extra power. The holder of four acres still grows wheat as if he held forty acres ; the application of the extra labour needed to grow vegetables or small fruits is regarded as derogatory. It is obvious that the employment of less labour or power than the land will yield a profit to must in the long run prevent the increase of wealth.

But more than anything else, the lack of skilled direction is responsible for the poverty of the country. The mass of the people have not known how to increase their outturn. For centuries the agriculture of England remained stagnant ; for yet more centuries the agriculture of Southern Europe has remained stagnant. The Punjab has not yet felt the stimulus of those discoveries which led to the great advance achieved in North Europe, just as their influence is still barren in Spain, Italy, Greece and other countries of the Mediterranean (3).

There is one generalisation that can usefully be made because it will assist in the discussion of a programme of construction, and that is that the Punjab is poor because it is not organised on the lines that lead to wealth. Such organisation as has existed has been more or less military, designed to preserve in power the dynasty of the day, or religious. Social organis-

---

(1) The long, trying English winter, when the soil produces so little, must have played an important part in developing the idea of saving. In this province the normal period between crops is so much less that it is not so necessary to look as far ahead. The English winter has had much to do with thrift amongst the working classes.

(2) *Cf.* Professor Kale: Indian Economics, 3rd Edition, pp. 41—43, especially p. 41, footnote 2. India differs from England in that in the latter country "the past has been devoted to the accumulation of wealth". The people of the Punjab could easily pay for the canals and railways, and so save interest from being paid in England.

(3) It is worthy of note that the self-sufficing type of agriculture common over the greater part of the province is antagonistic to changes designed to produce bigger profits. Until the cultivator regards his fields as a source of profit he will never progress far.

ation is almost entirely on religious lines, and unfortunately the religious leaders have not made economics their study. The greatest organisation for the promotion of the prosperity of the people in countries like Belgium or Italy is the Catholic Church. The priests have taken practical interest in the material welfare of their flocks and have led the movement to establish co-operative societies. There is no parallel to this in the Punjab. The religious influence has, if anything, exalted the spiritual and ignored the material. If the denial of the world, the withdrawal from the search after material gain and the resignation of all wealth are regarded as virtues, there must be a powerful influence working against the steady accumulation of capital and goods from generation to generation which cannot escape responsibility for much that is deplored to-day. The economic effects of religious beliefs can no more be neglected in India than they can be in Europe (1). The distribution of sects and of wealth throughout the European continent are not accidents. Nor are they entirely independent of each other.

If the arguments advanced above are accepted, then the methods by which wealth can be increased should not be difficult to find. The province can never be prosperous until it is thoroughly organised on economic lines. In some respects it will apparently be impossible to take full advantage of its potentialities ; the Mohammedan view of interest has not, as in England, served to stimulate thrift, for the reason that, while refusing to accept, they have not hesitated to pay, interest. Were it otherwise, were the Mohammedans of the province as sturdy in their refusal to pay, as they are in their refusal to take, interest, then they would be forced into thrift as the sole means of insurance against recurring bad seasons. On the other hand, the Hindu veneration for the cow imposes an insuperable barrier to its exploitation as the most valuable animal known to man, and prevents the growth of a profitable animal husbandry. The loss to the province and is, must remain, incalculable. It is beyond doubt one of the most potent influences retarding the advent of prosperity (2). In other directions the religious feelings of the people encourage waste and prevent the economic use of potential wealth. Pigs, bones, hides and eggs are articles of great importance in poor countries, but cannot be exploited to the full here (3).

In the above discussion, so far as it has gone, stress has been laid on the negative causes that account for poverty. Of positive causes, the greatest is undoubtedly waste. The East has not yet learned to convert waste into wealth. Other things being equal, the wealth of a country will vary with the proportion of its population engaged in production, so that a large number of persons who derive a livelihood from pursuits that add nothing to the general dividend are a source of weakness. The waste of human material in this province is very great. There is waste due to the high death-rate, which removes from productive employment many who are of the best ages,

(1) *Cf.* Thorold Rogers. Vol. V p. 11, *et seq*

(2) The modern agriculture of North-West Europe is founded upon animal husbandry what is best worth teaching is thus not acceptable here, and hitherto local talent has not provided an adequate substitute.

(3) At a time when much land in England was owned by monasteries the monks were amongst the most skilful cultivators in the land, and set an example to all around them.

or who have gathered skill or experience. There is waste due to preventible illness, and the inefficiency that results from frequent suffering; what this amounts to is beyond computation, but the advanced stage reached by medicine in Europe is a powerful factor in industrial efficiency. The number of days' labour lost through malaria alone must be a serious item in prolonging poverty. There is waste in the defective agricultural system that results in men doing little or no work for a considerable portion of the year. It is probable that the work done by the average cultivator does not represent more than 150 days' full labour in twelve months. But, even in the days when men are occupied, their idea of what constitutes a full day's task is well below that prevalent in Northern Europe. A complete change of the generally accepted notion in this respect must occur before the province can advance far along the road to prosperity.

There is waste in the number of unnecessary middlemen engaged in distribution. Probably 80 per cent. of the shopkeepers in the ordinary bazar could be spared for more useful employment, but the big multiple store has yet to appear. There is waste in the diversion of the best educated brains from productive into non-productive channels, such as the law. It is estimated that about three or four crores of rupees are wasted every year in connection with litigation (1). Meanwhile the province is starved of men with efficient knowledge on banking, industry and commerce, while the soil, the source of all new wealth, is in the hands of illiterate people who send their educated sons to the towns. There is waste in the relation between landlord and tenant, whereby the former provides no skilled guidance to the latter, supplies practically no capital to his enterprise and himself remains ignorant of what is best for the soil he owns. There is waste in the miserable system of rural credit, whereby a large number of usurers entangle the unwary peasant into a net from which there is only one escape. The drain of interest each year is not less than from eight to twelve crores, a sum which, devoted to improvement, would yield results of incalculable benefit. It is curious that with the baneful results before them there are still people, people too who claim to be educated, who

---

(1) Excessive litigation is due in large measure to prosperity. See Thorold Rogers, Vol. IV, Chap. II:—"The opulence of the fifteenth century encouraged litigation, and the growth of the spirit of litigation was a concern to the legislature and the moralist. At the beginning of Henry IV's reign complaint is made in Parliament of the number of attorneys........So dissatisfied was the Parliament in the beginning of the fifteenth century with the increase of the legal profession, that the whole profession were declared ineligible for the representation of the counties. There was little chance of their being chosen by the boroughs."

In the Punjab there are, in an average year, 520,000 civil, criminal and revenue cases instituted; appeals, civil executions and miscellaneous applications total 250,000. The number of persons involved must be about 1,200,000 in original cases and about 300,000 more must appear in other proceedings. The number of witnesses is over one million. Thus about 2,500,000 persons attend the courts every year either as parties or witnesses. If each person attends on the average twice, and if each attendance involves the loss of two days, both estimate being on the safe side, then the total loss amounts to ten million days a year. These persons are for the most part neither women or children, but men of the working ages, and there are not more than six million of these. Assuming a loss of one rupee per day, the total is one crore of rupees. But the litigants purchase stamps to the value of nearly forty lakhs; they pay about five lakhs for the issue of two million processes, and there are other incidental expenses for pleaders, etc. The capitalised value of the annual expenditure on litigation would suffice to redeem the whole mortgage debt of the province. The sum devoted to rural education would effect a revolution; devoted to medical relief, it would bring skilled aid within the reach of every village. Indeed, if the time, energy, intelligence and skill devoted to litigation could be diverted to medical relief, one of the biggest problems of the province would be solved, and incalculable good would follow.

fail to see the difference between a system of rural credit that has involved the majority of the owners in debt, amounting in the aggregate to 50 or 60 crores of rupees, for which they can show practically nothing in return, and a system which, wherever tried, has led the people out of debt into comfort, has converted them from borrowers into depositors and has left prosperous communities where before were usury-ridden disheartened families. The evil of usury is not confined to India or the Punjab; it so happens that this province has afforded a more profitable field for its practice than any other in India, but it does not appear that it is more debt-ridden than were several parts of Europe before co-operation came to the rescue. There and here the system of co-operative credit applied to agriculture is showing the way from debt to savings, and there is some prospect that in a few years this most damaging source of waste will diminish until it ceases to possess any importance.

There is a vast waste of female labour, due primarily to custom and prejudice. In most other countries the proportion of female labour to the whole is high; while its efficiency is equal to the tasks performed; the contribution to the national dividend resulting from this forms an appreciable part of the whole. If there were in Western countries a movement aiming at the exclusion of female labour from all except purely domestic tasks, that movement would endanger the whole economic fabric, and, if successful, would involve those countries in ruin. The Punjab discards what in England and elsewhere is an absolutely necessary element in the maintenance of their civilisation. The fact that there are tribes, such as Brahmins and Rajputs, which do not allow their womenfolk even to work in the fields is alone sufficient to explain their poverty. The work of women as clerks, shopkeepers, post and telegraph operators, factory hands, etc., and in connection with the fish industry, market garden, pit-tops, etc., has no counterpart here. In the course of generations the loss from this waste alone must have made material progress almost impossible. No European country could maintain its present standard of living without the assistance derived from female labour (1).

There is vast waste from the depredations of insects and other animals; this waste is the greater where religious sentiment forbids the killing of these for food. The pigeons at a railway station where much grain is dealt with are sources of loss when they cannot be eaten. But this is a small matter compared to the loss suffered from insects that attack crops, or rats that consume in the course of a year appreciable quantities of wheat. The religious objection to the destruction of such vermin is a contributory cause of poverty, and will continue to be one until ideas undergo a change.

There is great waste in the use of infertile seed; what might form good food is thrown into the ground to rot, in the hope that some at least will ger-

(1) There is a striking passage in "Reconstructing India" by Sir M. Visvesvaraya, p. 246:—If early marriages were stopped, there would be fewer widows in the land; and the superstition which prevents the remarriage of widows would be less keenly felt. Both common justice and prudence require that the evils of enforced widowhood and its attendant inhumanities and barbarous practices be removed. And he proceeds to deplore the appalling price the country has to pay in the shape of loss of work and intelligent effort from half the population of the country.

minate. Yet, although, amongst many intelligent men, the truth of this must be obvious, there is no attempt to induce shopkeepers and others to sell only pure seed.

There is waste of manure. For centuries past the farmers of England were bound by the terms of their leases to return to the fields the straw, litter, etc., and were not allowed to sell it off the farm (1).

There is waste from the weak sense of discipline, the real economic importance of which is not realised. In England centuries of hardship impressed the truth upon all classess; in Japan the Government has appreciated its value, and practically orders farmers and industrialists to do what is deemed most advisable. It is as if the statesmen had decided that the country was too poor to permit of every man doing what he chose, and that poverty could only be fought by skilled direction from the rulers. In Germany the extent of State regulation has long been a matter for comment, but it must be assumed that the rulers knew their people and considered that it was necessary to guide their actions in directions regarded as desirable for their own benefit. In England the legal restrictions upon the individual are so readily obeyed that they seem to be a part of the character of the people, and to be the result of habit; far less stringent restriction of individual caprice is regarded here as interference with liberty. If ever industries spring up in the province, strict discipline will be needed amongst all concerned; but it is doubtful whether the lesson will easily be learnt.

The real waste of fragmentation is seldom understood; where fields are open and scattered throughout the area of the village, it is customary to turn the cattle on to the stubble as soon as the crop is cut; there being no field boundaries to keep them on to the land of their owners, they wander over the whole ground and use it as if it were common. So long as everyone grows the same crops ripening at the same time, little harm results; but such a practice becomes quite unsuitable if any variation in cropping is sought to be introduced. Any cultivator, more intelligent than his fellows, who desired to work on an improved rotation involving the abolition of fallows, would find his neighbours' cattle straying all over his lands; while they in turn would object to his cattle grazing on their stubble unless their own were in turn allowed to graze on his. A simple example would be a cultivator devoting his land to fodder crops which were still on the ground when the cattle were let loose by his neighbours. The open field system thus serves to prevent the introduction of new methods, and even of new crops, unless these are cut at the same time as those of others. Under present conditions the labourers of the village (the *kamins*) and others possess by custom a right to send their cattle to graze upon the stubble; a system abolishing fallows would have to meet the objections of this class. The fact is that the open scattered fields do not give the cultivator complete freedom over his cropping; he cannot devote his land to what he considers best and most profitable. There is incalculable waste in the devotion of land to crops not because they are the most profitable, but because, in times when communications were bad and

(1) In Japan it is said that there is no need of sanitary arrangements as every morning the cultivators from the surrounding fields come in to remove the night soil, and even the urine, and carry it off to their fields.

means of transport defective, it was necessary to grow food for the home on the home fields. This concentration of effort on the production of food for his own family, rather than on the needs of the market, tends to retard change towards more profitable agriculture. It prevents the land being put to that use which will yield the highest profit.

The hills in the submontane tracts are probably capable of producing fine crops of fruit, etc., but are devoted to the cheapest form of millets, because millets were the customary things to grow before the great canal colonies ensured a regular supply of wheat, and railways were constructed to distribute it. It would appear, from present knowledge, that this utilisation of land for crops other than those which would prove most profitable is costing the province a greater annual loss than any other single cause.

There is waste in the uses to which various products are put. Cotton seed is fed to cattle in a crude form which is beyond the power of the animals to digest. From the seed there should be extracted the short fibres which could be used to make felt for hats, etc.; the husk should then be decorticated to form a fuel; the kernel should next be crushed to separate the oil which is of value as a cooking material, or as a basis for soap, etc.; the resultant cake is a food which cattle can digest, or which will serve as an excellent manure. This is only one example of the immense waste of the products of the province. Many others could be enumerated. The waste of vegetable matter that could be utilised as a source of power is only recently attracting attention, but in every activity there is waste, and in every waste there is loss and a further cause of poverty.

There is waste in the vast areas left to Nature to wreak her capricious will on; perhaps, in no other single item of the catalogue does the essential difference in outlook between North Europe and India appear more clearly. The peoples of the North-Western portion of Europe adopt as their cardinal economic creed that: "God helps those who help themselves", and accordingly they measure progress in terms of man's increasing knowledge of the powers of Nature and increasing ability to divert them to his own ends. In South Europe and in this continent there is an almost fatalistic lack of faith in man's power to influence his destiny and an equally fatalistic readiness to accept whatever Nature unassisted may give forth. The idea that an acre of uncultivated waste may produce more fodder than an acre of cultivated land irrigated by canal constantly appears as a sort of background in discussions relating to ghi and milk. The Legislative Council and Assembly are asked to endorse the argument; Government is appealed to to frame its policy on the false premise. Put in the language of vulgar plain truth, the argument is grotesque; clothed in a fervent appeal to religious prejudice, it commands the votes of those whose knowledge of rural economics is as yet elementary.

There does not seem to be anything in the province which destines it to everlasting poverty. There are definite causes which should prove amenable to suitable remedies. What these remedies are is matter for investigation, and some suggestions for the reconstruction will be given in another chapter. The main reason for the present low standard of living is writ large in the history of the last five centuries. There is nothing to be gained from the attempt to place responsibility on other shoulders than those indicated by a survey of this period. If the English of the present generation enjoy comforts and luxuries and all the amenities of life which wealth can procure, it is because for centuries their ancestors practised thrift and saving, strove hard against unfavourable natural conditions and sacrificed themselves freely to gain and to hold what they considered of value. The present generation enjoys a vast heritage: harbours, canals, roads, bridges, buildings of every description, investments in foreign countries and other forms of material wealth; but, perhaps, more valuable than these, it has also inherited that great experience and knowledge of the world which their forefathers gained through much toil and suffering. In special measure, the history of England is contained in original documents, so that it is possible to trace movements in greater detail than in most other, if indeed not in all other, countries. The result is that there are lessons that can be driven home to Englishmen which, though based upon facts within easy reach, appear to others as merely obstinate beliefs. But these lessons guide the actions of all in greater or less degree, and serve to maintain a high standard of sanity in affairs of importance. In the Punjab trustworthy records of any value or age are rare; there is little material for the historian; in consequence, there is not that balance which is secured when refutation of a false argument is certain and quick. It is some such reason as this which accounts for the persistence of common misapprehensions. Ignorance lies at the root of poverty; knowledge gives power to rise. In 1848 the Sikh Kingdom (1) did not possess any metalled roads, or big bridges or any other considerable public work of value. There were inundation canals and the remains of an old one of better type, but generally the great potential wealth of the rivers was running to waste. The present generation of Punjabis inherit very little, beyond wells, from their predecessors. Big productive works were unknown, there were no accumulations of capital yielding annual profits to their owners. Such buildings as existed were mostly for religious or military purposes. In 1848 the Punjab was practically devoid of any form of economic organisation, beyond the hereditary caste system. There were no books of merit on agriculture or other industries; there was nothing to guide the people except the wisdom handed down from mouth to mouth. Such leaders as were recognised were either military or religious; the former were almost exclusively officials of the Sikh regime, and were in no sense qualified to prescribe a programme of economic development; the latter do not seem ever to have used their undoubted influence to persuade their followers to adopt measures designed to promote their material welfare.

Of the precise economic effect of the curious system of occupational tribes or castes, it is difficult to write; but it may be presumed that where a natural aptitude for any work has to be suppressed because that work is the task of another caste there must be a great obstacle to progress. In one respect, it is probable that the system serves to maintain the stagnation of agriculture. Extensive cultivation as practised by the agricultural tribes provides little opportunity for the study of plant life in detail. While the culti-

(1) The high rate of interest would prevent any large expenditure on productive works out of borrowed money. It is not sufficiently understood to what extent a high rate retards progress. Many projects would be profitable with money at 6 per cent., but not at 12 per cent.

vation of vegetables and other crops under an intensive system which these require gives to the grower ample education in plant life, in the variations which human care and intelligence can produce, and in the needs of the individual plant. The grower of fine produce, vegetables or root crops imbibes more knowledge of the details of plant life than one who grows wheat on canal irrigated land. Unfortunately the cultivation of such vegetables and special crops is relegated to a class whom the great tribes affect to despise; the majority of the peasants prefer ignorance of such things; thus they lose the valuable experience and knowledge which might be of such great value in the development of their own art. In England it has been the garden which has shown what could be done in the field; under the Punjab system the field has despised and rejected what the garden could teach.

There is another matter which appears to be the result of the occupational caste system and which deserves to be mentioned, although the view put forward will not escape controversy. The higher castes are not themselves handworkers; they do not, or up till recently did not, take part in the labour of agriculture or of manufactures. As a consequence of this they are apt to misunderstand the position due to these activities, or regarded as due, by Western thinkers. Prof. Kale, for instance, refers to agriculture as a noble industry, but adds: "to reduce India to the condition of a nation of cultivators would be to retard the progress of the people in all directions. The existence of diverse industries, particularly those that call for the exercise of high intellectual and moral qualities, is essential for the healthy development of the people" (1). The words quoted seem to contain the suggestion that there is something in other industries which is not to be found in agriculture, and which calls for higher intellectual and moral qualities, and moreover that for progress and healthy development something more than agriculture is necessary. There is, of course, much truth in this, but the implication against the soil should not be allowed to pass without comment. In another work another Professor of Indian Economics writes: "the lesson that history teaches is, that so long as a country has remained a predominantly agricultural country, it has remained poor and in a lower stage of civilisation as compared with manufacturing countries. To what does England owe her prosperity? Would the United States have become the wealthiest country in the world if they had not learned to manufacture? What is the cause of the progress and prosperity of Japan during the last half century? Industrialism alone can save India" (2). Here again there is the same implication detrimental to agriculture. England achieved Empire and greatness before the agricultural revolution, and laid the foundation of her future industrial supremacy by generations of thrift, sacrifice and unending struggles with the forces of Nature. The United States earned wealth by the exploitation of vast natural resources; to this day many of the States are predo-

(1) Indian Economics, 3rd Edition, p. 148. A curious neglect of the teaching of history. The great moral and religious leaders of the world arose in countries devoid of factory industries.. No religion owes its origin to an industrial atmosphere. The wonderful genius of the Elizabethan age was not associated with any industries in the sense in which that word is now used. Poetry and industry, philosphy and industry, are usually regarded as antipathetic.

(2) Essays in Indian Economic Problems, by Professor Brij Narain, p. 39. A sane book with some interesting views.

minantly agricultural; the industries are for the most part confined to small well-defined areas. Japan is still predominantly agricultural; her industries are still in the infant stage and can hardly yet be called well established; her wonderful progress has been largely due to the determination to cast away all trammels of caste or prejudice that hamper development, to the willing sacrifice of her people and their ready submission to a firm discipline wielded by a strong bureaucracy. Japan has at last reacted against a poverty that was crushing her, but which was mainly due to her previous policy of aloofness and contempt for the West. Japan has not yet solved all her problems.

To regard agriculture as something rather derogatory to a progressive country is to take away a source of wealth. Exalt agriculture, appreciate all that it is capable of becoming in the hands of highly educated men with sufficient capital and enterprise to extract the utmost profit, and there is the seed of a public opinion that may lead to the realisation of the dream. Decry it, and there is another force making for stagnation and poverty. The suggestion is offered that it is this attitude towards the soil adopted by the ancestral leaders of the people that is partly responsible for much of the poverty that now exists. It was certainly the reverse attitude adopted by the ancestral leaders of the English people that set that country on the road to her present high position (1). In the above the discussion has strayed into conjecture, and the argument may be brought to more solid earth by pointing out the waste that results from a diet that is prescribed by custom, religion or prejudice, rather than by strict economic considerations. In the West poverty has fixed the diet of the people, with the result that the general scale is far lower than is commonly supposed in this province. For many generations the pig was the staple food of the English labourer not because he liked pig, but because pig was the cheapest food and the easiest to raise. Amongst edible flesh, the pig is distinguished as the most prolific, and therefore the most economical. Actually the animal is a by-product of dairying, as it eats the skimmed or separated milk, and the wheat husks, which are otherwise useless. Similarly another staple article of food is the potato, which is amongst the most prolific yielders, and therefore the most economical. It is obvious that, given a definite area, a diet that can be grown on the smaller share will set free a larger one for crops that can be exchanged for other commodities; wheat will give ten or twelve maunds on an area that will yield one hundred maunds, of potatoes; so that the replacement of wheat by potatoes will set free much land for money crops. Between 1870 and 1914 Germany almost entirely replaced wheat with potatoes, and so was able to feed her population through the war. In South Europe the diet of the ordinary people would astonish

(1) The importance of leadership in the development of agriculture has already been emphasised. In the absence of a genius as leader, farmers are encouraged to form associations in almost every country; the object of these associations is to stimulate them to adopt improved methods, and to afford facilities to them in doing so.

These associations, under various names, have done great good. Their absence in any country must tend to withhold this advantage, and here again the past history of the province discloses a negative cause of poverty. In the industrial sphere the conditions of competition render such associations unnecessary. A manufacturer with a new idea can exploit it. A farmer with a new idea must persuade his neighbours to adopt it in order that he may find a good market. The special produce of a single farm will not be sufficient to create a good market. The farmer, being an individual producer, cannot go in for mass production.

those who regard that of the Punjab peasant as something unusually poor In England the mass of the population cannot afford butter at all and eat margarine, made from the Cocoa Nut obtained from South India; their portion of meat is small, and it is comparatively recently that pure wheat flour has become general. In Australia and New Zealand a large quantity of mutton has to be eaten because sheep rearing is not a paying industry unless there can be found a use for the flesh of the older animals. The Italian peasant sells his superior wheat because he cannot afford to eat it, and consumes inferior wheat in the form of macaroni (1). The German eats cabbage and the American maize not because they have a natural taste for these things, but because these things have been forced upon them by economic conditions, and ingenuity has enabled them to serve these articles up in a palatable form.

The dependence of the Irish upon potatoes was, similarly, not a matter of choice, but of poverty. Olive oil in South Europe takes the place of ghi in the Punjab for cooking; in all probability the people would much prefer ghi, but they cannot afford it. A broad survey of the diet of the mass of the people in any country indicates that it involves the use of less area per head that is needed in this province. Poverty has dictated the food to a greater extent than appears to be the case here, where the people seem to have responded to hard times by reducing the quantity consumed, rather than by altering the articles consumed. In the last twenty years, there would appear to have been a marked increase in the consumption of wheat and a decrease in the consumption of the cheaper millets; and one of the causes of the scarcity of ghi is the greater demandf rom persons who formerly could not afford to consume it. Mr. Emerson is of opinion that the tenants who formerly sold their ghi now keep it for themselves, and this seems to be correct. There is an idea abroad that an improvement in the diet of the mass of the people is a good which should be aimed at for itself. From the economic point of view this is not correct. A more expensive diet is an economic loss unless it results in the production of a greater amount of wealth than is lost in the extra consumption. Peasants in Denmark and Holland will sell their better class butter and their fresh eggs to the big industrial centres of England and Germany, and will consume less valuable butter and eggs from Siberia. By this means they save a considerable sum without any perceptible diminution of efficiency. If the diet of the Punjab peasant or townsman were made richer and more expensive, without the extra energy of the food appearing in extra work or more efficient labour, then there would be a serious loss, although there might, and probably for a short time would, be more pleasure and enjoyment. In point of fact, it is probable that a richer diet will be necessary if the greater exertion needed for economic progress is to be forthcoming; but this is more likely to take the form of meat, vegetables and potatoes than of more milk and ghi. The latter are very valuable articles, but the idea that they are necessaries is refuted by the example of Japan where they are beyond the reach of the mass of the people. Those who say

(1) Also rye, barley and maize; his consumption of wheat flour is estimated at one-third of a ser a day. His total consumption of cereals is much below that of a prisoner in a Punjab jail. His consumption of olive oil (six sers a year) is exactly the same as the scale of mustard oil in the jails here.

that these commodities are necessities under the conditions of India are stating not a physiological, but a religious, doctrine. Many Indians scoff at the idea of the potato becoming a common article of diet; they are 150 years behind the times. In Europe there was the same prejudice; this article was at first thought to be suitable for the poor, but the peasants disliked growing it and the poor could not be induced to eat it; Arthur Young found that in France the people would not touch it; yet now it is almost impossible to realise that until almost the end of the eighteenth century the food problem of Europe had to be faced without this valuable tuber (1).

In Germany the potato had been making headway long before 1800. . . . it had made more progress in Germany than in France before 1815. Prejudice against it is said to have died out so early as 1770 in consequence of a period of dearth (2).

The fact is clear that the diet of Europe has been dictated by poverty to a far larger extent than in this province, and that no country in Europe could afford to live on the scale which is here advocated as necessary. Take away the potato from the West and starvation appears as night follows the day. Let the potato become a common and every day article of consumption in the Punjab and there will be food for all and a vast saving of land for other purposes. The European has become so used to this particular article of food that deprivation is now a hardship; the present prejudice will give way before familiarity as it yielded in England, France and Germany to poverty. The world being constituted as it is, it is worse than useless to fight against the adoption of the most important vegetable article of food known to man.

There is waste in the heavy mortality amongst cattle; much of this is preventible, but here again religious feelings interfere in the application of scientific knowledge. Amidst the wild talk of the loss from export and slaughter, there is silence concerning the immeasurably greater loss imposed upon the people by religious sentiment and their own ignorance. Although the census returns show an increase in the number of cows and bullocks, including young stock, from about seven millions in 1872-73 to over twelve millions at the present time, there are still to be found those who assert that export and slaughter, both completely negligible items, are responsible for a *decrease*. Economic progress can only result from a resolute facing of facts, and nothing but disaster can follow misrepresentation of this type.

There is waste from the fragmentation of holdings; the custom of partition leads to each heir receiving a portion of each field, or at least of fields situated in different portions of the village area. The result is that a single owner may possess his tiny property in ten or twelve places, and may have to waste time, labour and energy in the cultivation of these scattered plots. The evil is serious in Japan, and in many countries of Europe, such as France, Switzerland, Belgium, etc., and this province can learn much from the experience of those who have tried to combat it.

To sum up the argument, it may be stated that the main causes of the poverty of the Punjab are to be found in the history of the province. It should be

(1) Economic Development of France and Germany. 1815-1914; by J. H. Clapham, p. 22.

(2) *Ibid*, p. 51.

sufficiently obvious that, if the mass of the people in any country are poor, it must be because they are not doing what is necessary to make them rich; they are not using the factors of wealth in sufficient degree. From this it follows that what they are doing must be economically defective; and so any inquirer must, if he is honest, catalogue a series of faults, omissions and defects.

There has been no systematic thrift resulting in the accumulation of vast wealth, such as is now found in the North-West of Europe. Such leaders as have arisen have been concerned with dynastic or religious matters, rather than with problems of increasing production. The general sentiments of the people have not run in favour of the steady accumulation of wealth; on the other hand, they have been directed to the condemning of mere material welfare and the exaltation of things spiritual. Even now a mendicant excites more respect than an efficient artisan; and thousands will listen to a policy of destruction who would remain unmoved by the advocacy of harder work and more efficient labour and skill as a panacea for common ills. The attitude of the people is still not towards material things. Further, and connected with this, there is too much reliance upon a Higher Power and too little reliance upon individual effort in struggling along the lines fined by that Higher Power. Government or God is expected to make good all the deficiencies of the people. Until it is absolutely burnt into the minds of ever one that his economic position is mainly his own fault, there can be little improvement. The spirit of self-help must be nursed into a position of dominance.

There being no savings inherited from generations gone by, there is no capital earning incomes for the present. In the absence of capital there is wanting the development of the ingenuity to use it to the best purposes. Intelligent direction of large sums has had no chance to grow.

The agriculture of the world stood still for centuries, until the great landlords of England turned their attention to its improvement. In some ways the peasants of Holland (1) led the advance, but many new ideas were due to a few Englishmen, even if the original stimulus came from knowledge of what was being done across the narrow sea. Later the discovery of the close connection between chemistry and agriculture led to a revolution in the use of manures and other changes of great importance. Animal husbandry has for centuries been the object of study, and with the advance of knowledge of the science of breeding the British Isles became the great source of pure bred stock. In this line countries, such as Denmark and Holland, seem to have made more rapid progress recently; but the more Southern portions of Europe seem less well adapted for high-grade stock-breeding. The States bordering on the Mediterranean and apparently all Asia and Africa were left untouched by the great strides being made in their main industry; there does not seem to be any trace of a knowledge of the principles of stock-breeding

(1) In the seventeenth century "the Flemings and Hollanders were the teachers of the new agriculture. They adopted the artificial grasses, and cultivated winter roots in the fields long before their neighbours adopted either of these capital discoveries........Not only were they the pioneers of progress in agriculture, but in finance, in commerce and in banking." Thorold Rogers, Vol. V., pp. 64—5.

in the Punjab ; while the sentiments of the people are opposed to their practical application.

For reasons chiefly political, the province has lacked capital, intelligence and skill ; it has lacked the factors essential to the increase of wealth.

The small holding is not of itself a cause of poverty, the holding is not put to the most profitable use. The stimulus to make the most of the soil has not been present. A cultivator will not grow more than he can sell or use ; he will not sow more than he can reap, and, having reaped, find some use for. Situated as it is, there could be no market for the surplus of the Punjab except in the uncommon case of a shortage in a neighbouring area ; without an assured market, there would be no object in expanding cultivation. Centuries of this experience have left habits which half a century of other conditions has not yet sufficed to change.

Everywhere man, unaided by capital, power or special knowledge, can produce little more than he consumes. Until production exceeds consumption, there can be no increase of wealth. There is no stimulus to increase wealth until there are amenities to be obtained and enjoyed from its expenditure. Until the province was opened up by railways and roads, and until security of life and property was maintained, there was little on which surplus earnings could be expended. The people, as a whole, have not made the search after wealth their aim in life. The prevailing religious beliefs have prevented the attainment of the atmosphere in which the economic sense grows up ; in some respects they are responsible for the poverty of the people ; and to a serious extent they threaten to prevent full advantage being derived from modern scientific knowledge on such subjects as the improvement of cattle. The occupational caste system seems to have operated to prevent the growth of those subsidiary cottage industries which are found almost everywhere else. The German and Russian peasants make toys and wooden articles in their spare time ; the English produce honey, poultry, fruit, baskets, etc. ; and similar activities are found in almost every country. The Indian peasant appears to be the only instance of a small holder trying to live upon the plant products of his holding, and efforts to induce him to imitate his fellows have not yet achieved any measurable success. It is probable that the traditional place allotted to the cultivators in the Hindu hierarchy has tended to retard the growth of a more progressive agriculture. A rough survey of rural conditions suggests that there are few problems here that have not their counterpart in other countries ; and the common reasons for local ills are generally easily refuted by the existence of the same ills where the reasons alleged do not exist.

For all this, the essential remedy is a close study of Rural Economics ; the collected and tested experience of the world must be drawn upon to aid Government in its task of stimulating the more rapid development of the resources of the province. Public opinion needs to be guided towards a more intelligent realisation of the potentialities of modern agriculture, and to a better idea of its position and influence in regard to the possibilities of establishing industries.

The attempt to foretell the future is seldom profitable ; but it may be hazarded that ignorance of these matters will retard progress and may lead to disaster and waste.

In the foregoing pages stress has been laid upon waste as the main cause of poverty; it is not necessary now to repeat the tale of the loss suffered by the destructive forces of competing dynasties or of the anarchy and confusion which from time to time have spread throughout the province. The geographical position of the Punjab has exposed it in special degree to the ravages of invaders and the spoliation of retreating hordes. Prior to 1848, there did not exist the conditions under which orderly progress towards a higher standard of life could alone be found. These, however, are matters of history; they explain the present; they must not be overlooked in any examination of the causes of poverty, but they need not be overemphasised when the time comes to discuss the prospects for the future.

The influence of caste in retarding industrial development is a subject too delicate for detailed investigation in this book. Leading Indians have expressed quite clearly all that needs to be borne in mind. Current history shows clearly that industrial progress is only possible with a loosening of the ties which bind a man to an ancestral occupation, or group of occupations. If the province is ever to see great industries achieving prosperity its people will have to accept the principle that natural aptitudes must be allowed to find their natural bent, irrespective of ancient bonds.

The agricultural produce of an average year has been estimated at Rs. 80 crores; at present prices, Rs. 100 crores, would, perhaps, be nearer. Of this sum, it has been pointed out that between 8 and 12 crores goes to the moneylender; part of this is not profit at all, but compensation for bad debts resulting from a radically faulty system of credit; to this extent there is dead loss to the province. Some four crores may be taken to represent the economic loss due to litigation. Between three and four crores may be assumed as the loss resulting from cattle mortality that is preventible, and which could be saved by a greater willingness to adopt modern scientific methods of prevention and cure. Besides the 40,000 moneylenders with which the province is burdened, there are nearly one million people supported by petty trading. The number of small shops is excessive, with the result that there is not a decent living for all engaged. There are some 200,000 workers in the small *nun, tel* shops of the villages. The waste of human labour here is great, and yet there is little tendency towards the multiple store. The figure suggests the amount of intelligence wasted which should be diverted to industrial pursuits where skill is required. The number engaged in selling cloth nearly doubled in ten years. Apart from these, there are over 158,000 persons supported by gold and silversmiths' work. Amongst these, if it is be assumed that 32,000 are adult males earning somewhere about one rupee a day, then the cost to the province is over a crore a year. It is through the agency of these that the hoarding of the precious metals takes place, and the net loss resulting from their activities must be very great indeed. The Sunars are skilled artisans, whose energies might well find more productive scope in industries of a more valuable type; as it is, they are instruments of waste. It is unnecessary to continue the catalogue further; everywhere there is waste—waste of intelligence, of skill, of human labour, of capital and of energy. If the education, the intelligence, the skill, the labour, the capital and the great resources of the province could be utilised to the full in the production of wealth, there would be no longer occasion to deplore the poverty of the Punjab.

CHAPTER XVI.

PROTECTION OR FREE TRADE.

In a previous chapter it has been remarked that the demand for industrial development is largely due to the presence of men with capital for which they desire profitable employment and to the presence of youths with education who also desire profitable employment. These desires are both natural and commendable, and they form a strong argument in favour of the encouragement of industries. The policy of State aid in technical education, scientific research, supply of information, etc., has been definitely accepted; but there are many who would go further and would impose upon India a protective tariff designed to preserve the Indian market for Indian manufactures. This proposal must now be examined in the light of the special circumstances of the Punjab.

The peculiar geographical position of the province has already been described, and its effects upon the economic potentialities have been discussed. It dominates, and must continue to dominate, all attempts to improve the material condition of the people. The outstanding tendency of European and American industries is to move towards the sea-coast or a navigable river. In a world of competition, whether open or restricted, those factories will survive which possess some distinct advantage over their rivals. Such advantage may take the form of proximity to coal or other cheap source of power; but where the factory is engaged in international trade the facilities for cheap transport, such as the sea provides, exert a more powerful influence than any other single factor. In England, as has already been pointed out, no part is distant more than about 40 miles from the sea; the industries of Japan are to be found on the coast. In Germany and France they are collected around the coal-fields and navigable rivers. It may be accepted that no imitative factory industry established in the Punjab will be able to engage in international trade in rivalry with other factories more favourably situated.

This argument does not apply to manufactures engaged in the production of some article for which the province possesses something approaching to a monopoly of raw material; or which works up bulky raw material, usually exported, into a commodity far less bulky in proportion to its value. The oil-seeds at present exported as such may be submitted to a process here, which will prepare the oil for export and leave the residue for cattle food or manure; and the bones, raw leather and similar articles of the export trade may be put through one or more of the processes on the stage towards consumption before being sent overseas. But any attempt to install a replica of the Bombay cloth mills will lack the advantages which Bombay enjoys from its position around a great port.

The idea of protection is to enable a local factory to compete with imported goods in securing the local demand. It is protection against import; it does not apply to the export trade, and therefore will not directly affect those industries just mentioned which are, or may be, established to work up the raw material before export. In an agricultural country it is such industries which offer the greatest scope and, in so far as these are concerned, protection will afford no assistance to the most promising fields for industrial activity in the Punjab. Another important consideration is that, in a world of competition, there is little chance of the survival of a single industry in a place where other industries have not yet made headway. The modern factory requires so many things, and is in constant need of so many services, that experience teaches the promoters to locate their works where these things and these services are freely available. A new cloth weaving company would select Bombay in preference to Rohtak or Lyallpur for the simple reason that its requirements in everything except the raw material will more easily be met there than in towns where the absence of similar mills has prevented the establishment of the many subsidiary industries which are necessary for its recurrent needs. The tendency of localities to become the site of highly specialised manufactures is not the result of chance. Where there are many factories of the same type, repairs, skilled advice and guidance, experienced managership, technical knowledge and all the subsidiary needs of the particular industry tend also to aggregate. A lonely pioneer factory will not have any of these advantages, and the attempt to build up in this province an imitative industry in competition with the big centres in other provinces will surely fail. It is for this reason that the argument has been advanced that, in so far as the Punjab is concerned, new industries will require protection against the older established factories of other provinces as much as against factories overseas ; and, as such inter-provincial tariffs are outside the scope of practical politics, it behoves the patriotic Punjabi to be careful as to how he votes on the general subject of protection.

Assuming that there are at any moment both capital and intelligence not yet utilised to the full, then the problem is how to put these to the most productive use ; before deciding to invest both these factors of wealth in this or that industry, it should first be made clear that this employment will produce greater net advantage than any alternative, such as the construction of new canals. The popular cry for industries is not based upon exact knowledge of the potentialities of the province ; much of it is due to sentiment, the feeling that, unless the Punjab can develop manufactures on a large scale, it will remain backward ; but this sentiment, laudable though it may be, will not avail against superior equipment in the essentials to success possessed by other provinces. It is yet far from certain as to which industries can be established with profit in the Punjab. The effect of protection for India in general cannot with any assurance be foretold ; the subject bristles with difficulties ; the fact that there is so much difference of opinion in countries which have adopted protection, as to the advantages they have gained from it, and further the fact that there are strong parties in free trade countries opposed to the policy in vogue, afford sufficient indication as to the complexities that beset the problem. In such circumstances it may well be argued that, before embarking upon a vague policy, there should be some detailed inquiry as to what it is intended to protect and what result it is desired to produce by protection. It is a common mistake to assume that, with protection adopted, industries will spring up like mushrooms in the night. There are many industries in India that have been found profitable without protection; there are many that have not yet sprung up in spite of the high measure of protection afforded by geographical position, etc. From time immemorial ploughs have been in common use in this country; of import from overseas there is practically nothing; the local manufacturer has had the monopoly of supply; yet there is still lacking the large factory turning out ploughs for the multitude. Protection will not produce industries without the many other essentials of those industries. Unless those essentials are assured, it is useless trying to protect an industry that will never be established. In an agricultural country the demand is usually for a measure of protection of home-grown wheat, etc., against the foreign producer, so that the cultivators will be encouraged to grow enough for the towns by a certainty of a market with high prices; such a measure would not be popular with the Punjab townsman, and, were the alternative to rest between free trade and protection of everything, including foodstuffs, it is not improbable that general opinion would regard the dearness of food as too high a price to pay for the encouragement of factory industries.

Another point that is not always clearly understood is that the artificial encouragement of factory industries would tend to ruin the indigenous hand industries. It is difficult to see how these could survive against mills within the province. It may be that, with more modern factories established, the disappearance of these ancient cottage occupations would be viewed with equanimity. From the purely economic point of view, what is desired is that every worker should be given the opportunity to devote his labour to that use which will yield him the best return; and, as the more capital a man employs the more wealth he tends to create, it will generally be found that a weaver, for instance, will earn more when using machinery worth several thousands of rupees than when depending upon an ancient loom worth but a few rupees. The replacement of existing handlooms by machinery will not cause regret amongst economists, but experience indicates that, if the latter be owned by non-Indians, nationalist sentiment would feel aggrieved. The point need not be stressed, but it is worthy of mention.

Another argument against protection as a policy is that the province is too poor to be able to afford the consequential rise in the cost of living. There is evidencethat, in other countries, protection has encouraged the development of industries and, as this policy is persisted in, it may be assumed that many people believe that, on the whole, the balance of loss and gain is in favour of protection; it may be accepted that such a policy will likewise lead in India to the encouragement of industries; but it does not follow that the balance of gain over loss will be so widespread as to compensate every province, including the Punjab. The chief gainers will be those maritime provinces which already possess considerable experience and organisation, and their gain will be derived largely from those portions of the country which are unable to compete in manufactures, while compelled by high duties to confine their consumption to the products of the mills of Bombay, Calcultta and Madras. It will be poor solace for the higher cost of living in the Punjab to know that this is the price paid for Indian industries in the cities just mentioned. In most other countries there is protection against imported agricultural products as well, so that the cultivator receives some benefit as a set-off against the higher prices of the things he buys, but here the cultivator will have to wait long before the expansion of towns and cities provides him with a market wherein he will be able to get higher prices for his produce than he at present receives from foreign consumers. What advantage the residents of Punjab towns can derive from the encouragement of mills in Bombay is not clear.

The question of the relative advantages of rival tariff policies is so confused with other issues that a dispassionate discussion is seldom heard. Naturally enough, manufacturers welcome the opportunities afforded by protection to sell their articles at higher prices and so gain higher profits; the chance of eliminating competition by State action, rather than by some superiority of their own, appeals to them. So much is this the case that they will contribute to the funds of the political party which promises to secure this benefit for them; these parties control newspapers and other organs of publicity which find nothing but good in the policy advocated, and the man in the street is apt to be convinced that protection must be good because both press and politicians say it is good. But, what one manufacturer wants to sell dear, another wants to buy cheap. The yarn manufacturer wishes to get the highest price for the yarn he makes, while the cloth manufacturer desires to obtain it in the cheapest market. The question of protection against foreign-made yarn affects them in different ways, so that, unless some arrangement acceptable to both can be devised, they will take opposite sides in the controversy. It is this necessity of coming to some arrangement which brings in its train that corruption of politics which accompanies protection; no country seems to be exempt from it. The agitation against the Corn Laws in England seems to have been as much due to resentment against selfish manipulation, dishonesty in administration and meddlesome interference with commerce as to any proper appreciation of the benefits of free trade. It is this corruption which prevents the withdrawal of protection when the former infant industries have become well established; and it is the same cause which makes it so difficult to gauge the results of this policy where it has been tried. While most countries are protectionist, those most advanced in education and civilisation are free trade.

England, Holland, Belgium and, in most respects, Denmark maintain a general policy of non-interference; Germany resorted to protection because the Imperial Government wanted funds which the component States refused to contribute; as the Central Government had no power to impose direct taxation, Bismarck was forced to enhance the tariff, and to popularise his measure he gave it a protective bias. The position of America is peculiar inasmuch as that country attracted the attention of capitalists, manufacturers and skilled artisans from Europe, and more especially from the United Kingdom, who naturally enough desired to capture the local market undisturbed by competition from England. American manufactures were originally to a large extent the result of English enterprise, or, perhaps, it would be more correct to say the result of the enterprise of people of English birth. At one time the leading artisans were drawn from English industrial centres, while, until the late war, much of the capital invested came from Great Britain. The United States were thus enabled to borrow capital, skill and enterprise from across the Atlantic, and with the aid of these to build up some great factories. The Japanese have not lost the lesson, and they too borrowed machinery, management, capital and skilled control from Europe. It is open to question as to how far the Punjab is in a position to follow the above examples. The great heat of summer militates against prolonged effort within the walls of a factory; and there appears to be sentimental objection to the adoption of the policy described.

Were it satisfactorily proved that there are industries which cannot be introduced or developed within this province owing solely to foreign competition, and that by a measure of protection they could be put upon an independent basis, and, further, that their establishment would bring to the province a balance of advantage, then there would be a strong argument in favour of that measure of protection being accorded to those industries. But this does not yet appear to be the case. Unsuccessful manufacturers are inclined to ascribe to foreign competition the failure due to their own incompetence or lack of experience, foresight or skill, and their own evidence should therefore be received with caution. There does not appear to be any industry which is in any sense a special subject of controversy. In fact, there is as yet no agreement as to which industries it is desired to protect. To quote an Indian economist: "The industries of the country, says every journalist and every public man, are young, and, managed as they are by men, necessarily as yet of lower business experience and ability than those of the West, need a definite support from the Indian Government by means of import duties and bounties. . . . . . It is, however, a striking limitation of the new industrial spirit which has been awakened in India that there is no clear public opinion with regard to the nature of the industries which ought to be started in the country and protected by Government"(1). It was this doubt as to the immediate objects of protection, and the fear that it would be used to encourage what many Indians would not desire, that led the late Mr. Gokhale to say that "it is my deliberate conviction that, in our present circumstances, a policy of free trade, reasonably applied, is after all the safest policy for us".

The Punjab is at present an importer of manufactured articles and an exporter of food and raw materials. It will take time for new industries to develop to the extent required to satisfy the local demand for articles at present imported, and during that time protection will involve economic loss. The people will still need those articles, and until local manufacturers can supply, they will have to be imported from abroad. During this period the people of the province will be paying more for what they import, and the proceeds will go to the Imperial Treasury. It is not yet definitely certain that these articles now imported can be manufactured within the province. The idea that protection will lead to industries growing up conflicts with experience. There is no foreign competition in the supply of milk or the manufacture of ghi; there is a demand, but there appears to be a shortage of supply; yet there does not appear to be any tendency for capital to be invested in the production of these articles. In other countries their production has assumed the proportions of a large industry, with capital, trained intelligence and enterprise all playing a prominent part; but here all three fight shy of this important source of wealth. Glass is heavily protected by the high costs of transport from Belgium and Austria, and during the war these sources of supply were

(1) Professor Radhakamal Mukerji, pp. 342—3.

cut off. Yet the glass industry shows no sign of assured prosperity. On the other hand, there are large numbers of men working at the production of cloth, leather, jewels and other articles who have survived the present system of free trade ; if they have been able to earn a livelihood in the past, there should be more prospect of improving their callings by scientific training, technical assistance and modern machinery, than there is of introducing new manufactures into the province.

From what has been said above, it should be clear that, apart from the general question of Free Trade *versus* Protection, there are for the people of the Punjab some special matters upon which information is required before they commit themselves to one side or the other of the controversy. The general question is itself confused by the introduction of selfish interests to such an extent that it is difficult to arrive at any definite conclusion as to where the balance of advantage lies ; in this country the element of sentiment adds further complexities ; the educated Indians want industries, but they do not appear to have decided as to what industries they want, or where they want them or whether they are prepared to pay the price necessary for them. Are the people of the Punjab prepared to pay higher prices for the articles they consume in order that Indian industries may flourish in the maritime provinces? If so, are they prepared to pay 30 per cent. more, or 50 per cent. more or 100 per cent. more, according as the manufacturer says this is necessary for his business to survive ? Are they prepared to pay this extra cost on all articles or only upon some ? If so, upon which ? All sorts of unsuitable industries can be started and run at a profit to somebody if the protection be complete enough. Unless the Punjab shares in the industrial development of India, her standard of living will be forced downwards by the higher prices of the protected article. She cannot share in that movement unless she possesses some natural advantages over possible rivals in the manufacture of some article or another sufficient to compensate her for the absence of a seaboard, of good coal and other essentials of success. It cannot be assumed that industries will inevitably spring up ; it is not yet clear what industries should or will spring up. The Punjab people desire to see manufactures within their province from which they will be enabled to derive advantage. The continued progress of agriculture demands the establishment of such factories ; and there seems to be a poor future for the middle class unless this hope is consummated. But it is far from being clear that protection will achieve this result.

On the other hand, there is no room for doubt as to what will be the immediate effect of a change of policy. The object of protection is to remove from the market an article manufactured abroad and sold at a price below that at which the same article manufactured locally can be sold. It is designed to enhance the price of imported articles. Unless it does that, it fails of its purpose. It protects the market for the locally produced article. This article is assumed to be dearer that its counterpart imported from abroad. Higher prices, then, are inevitable under a protective tariff. Whether this leads to the development of indigenous industries or not, the higher cost of living is a certainty. Whether this higher cost is compensated for by increased earnings, is less certian. The harm is assured from the date the new tariff comes into force and effect ; the benefit must be long in coming ; it may never accrue to the Punjab at all ; it may be secured by methods more scientific, less clumsy and less open to abuse than heavy duties. Should the people of this province be asked to pay the price and trust to the future for the return ?

INDEX.

A.

B.

C.

D.

E.

F.

G.

H

I.

I—*concluded.*

P—*concluded.*

W.